LIBRARY MANUALS

Volume 1

THE BRITISH MUSEUM LIBRARY

THE BRITISH MUSEUM LIBRARY
A Short History and Survey

ARUNDELL ESDAILE

LONDON AND NEW YORK

This edition first published in 2022
by Routledge
2 Park Square, Milton Park, Abingdon, Oxon OX14 4RN

and by Routledge
605 Third Avenue, New York, NY 10158

Routledge is an imprint of the Taylor & Francis Group, an informa business

First published in 1946 by George Allen & Unwin Ltd

All rights reserved. No part of this book may be reprinted or reproduced or utilised in any form or by any electronic, mechanical, or other means, now known or hereafter invented, including photocopying and recording, or in any information storage or retrieval system, without permission in writing from the publishers.

Trademark notice: Product or corporate names may be trademarks or registered trademarks, and are used only for identification and explanation without intent to infringe.

British Library Cataloguing in Publication Data
A catalogue record for this book is available from the British Library

ISBN: 978-1-03-213109-2 (Set)
ISBN: 978-1-00-322771-7 (Set) (ebk)
ISBN: 978-1-03-213301-0 (Volume 1) (hbk)
ISBN: 978-1-03-213305-8 (Volume 1) (pbk)
ISBN: 978-1-00-322858-5 (Volume 1) (ebk)

DOI: 10.4324/9781003228585

Publisher's Note
The publisher has gone to great lengths to ensure the quality of this reprint but points out that some imperfections in the original copies may be apparent.

Disclaimer
The publisher has made every effort to trace copyright holders and would welcome correspondence from those they have been unable to trace.

THE BRITISH MUSEUM LIBRARY

a short history and survey

by

ARUNDELL ESDAILE
M.A., LITT.D., F.L.A.

*Formerly an Assistant Keeper in the
Department of Printed Books and
Secretary to the Trustees*

With an Introduction by
SIR FREDERIC G. KENYON
G.B.E., K.C.B., ETC.

London
GEORGE ALLEN & UNWIN LTD.

First published in 1946

THE PAPER AND BINDING OF THIS
BOOK CONFORM TO THE BINDING
ECONOMY STANDARD

All rights reserved

PRINTED IN GREAT BRITAIN
in 11-Point Old Face Type
BY UNWIN BROTHERS LIMITED
WOKING

INTRODUCTION

By Sir FREDERIC G. KENYON, g.b.e., k.c.b., etc.
Late Director and Principal Librarian of the British Museum

THE British Museum is, next to the British Navy, the national institution which is held in most universal respect abroad. A visit to it is almost obligatory on travellers to this country; and foreign scholars regard it with a reverence which they sometimes extend to the temporary custodians of its treasures. Yet no adequate history of it exists. Its foundation and early years have been described by Edward Edwards and others; but of its growth in the nineteenth and twentieth centuries there is no record except a few popular works and the official guidebooks. My immediate predecessor, Sir E. Maunde Thompson, after his retirement, set about a history of the Museum, but could not carry it beyond the end of the eighteenth century. The fact is that an active administrator has not the time for the necessary research; and a retired officer, unless he lives near at hand, cannot have the constant access to archives in which the research has to be made.

There is, however, a further difficulty. The Museum is now so large, and its collection so multifarious, that no one person can adequately deal with the whole of it; what is needed is not a single history of the Museum, but a series of histories of its several Departments. The Departments of classical antiquities, of Egypt and Assyria, of Oriental art and archaeology, of ethnography, of prints and drawings, need separate histories by their own specialists. Some slight beginning has been made with such specialized records. An account of the growth of the buildings of the Museum was drawn up at the time of the opening of the King Edward the Seventh Galleries in 1914; and in 1929 Mr. G. F. Barwick published a history of the Reading Room. Now a more comprehensive attempt has been made by Mr. Esdaile to do for the Library Departments (that is, the Departments of Printed Books and of Manuscripts) what it is hoped may be done for the other portions of the great Museum.

THE LIBRARY OF THE BRITISH MUSEUM

It is only within the last century that the Library has attained the commanding position which it now holds. For this it is indebted above all to Panizzi in respect of the Printed Books, and to Bond and Thompson in respect of the Manuscripts. They, more than anyone else, established the traditions of comprehensiveness on the one hand, and of conscientious discharge of duty on the other, which have been maintained by their successors. The story is told in the pages that follow; and Mr. Esdaile, as a sometime officer in the Printed Books Department and subsequently engaged as Secretary in the general administration of the Museum, is well qualified to tell it. His work needs no commendation from me; but as I have been asked to wish it Godspeed, I gladly do so, on the day that is at once my own eightieth birthday and the one hundred and eighty-fourth of the Museum.

January 15, 1943

NOTE

THE design on the cover of this book represents one of the bronze lions, designed for the British Museum by Alfred Stevens, which originally surmounted a low railing in Great Russell Street, and were later placed inside the Museum.

To keep the publick stock of Learning, which is in Books and Manuscripts, to increas it, and to propose it to others in the waie which may be most helpful unto all.

JOHN DURIE, *Royal Librarian*, 1650.

Man without learning, and the remembrance of thinges past, falls into a beastlye sottishness.

ANON., 1653.

I want a poor student to have the same means of indulging his learned curiosity, of following his rational pursuits, of consulting the same authorities, of fathoming the most intricate enquiry, as the richest man in the kingdom.

ANTONIO PANIZZI, 1836.

IN PIAM MEMORIAM
COSMO GORDON, ARCHBISHOP, LORD LANG OF LAMBETH
FOR SEVENTEEN YEARS CHAIRMAN OF THE TRUSTEES
OF THE BRITISH MUSEUM,
D.D.D.

PREFACE

An adequate history and description of the British Museum would require a very large volume. What has been attempted here is something less ambitious. My aim is to provide in small compass what can only be found scattered through a large number of books and periodicals, a summary account, historical and descriptive, which shall be full enough to be useful for reference and information, and at the same time to bring out the true significance of the collections and of the tale of their gathering—in a word, to be readable.

I have confined myself to the Library, that is to the three Departments, of Printed Books, of Manuscripts, and of Oriental Printed Books and Manuscripts. I have left untouched that of Prints and Drawings, once, like that of Coins and Medals, an integral part of the Library, as was usual, and often still so reckoned, regarding it as more closely allied to the Art side of the Departments of Antiquities. To complete the work thus left incomplete there would be required two more volumes, dealing respectively with the Antiquities and with the Natural History collections, the latter now constituting the sister Institution, the British Museum (Natural History) at South Kensington, commonly called the Natural History Museum. Some part of the account of the foundation of the Bloomsbury buildings and of the administration would be common ground to the three parts; and in hope that the remaining two may be produced before long I have borne the fact in mind in writing the pages which follow.

I would thank the Trustees for their kind permission granted to me to make use of their archives, a permission of which I would have made fuller use had the papers not been evacuated in 1939. I have also to thank Messrs. Grafton & Co. for allowing me to use the collection of books, pamphlets and cuttings relating to the Museum formed by the late George R. Potter. A larger collection of cuttings, for the earlier period only, of which I have made use, is that, bound in four stout volumes, to the making of which Sir Frederic Madden, with his first and second wife in succession, as his diaries tell, devoted so many evenings. It is in the Printed Books (4 vols., C. 55. i. 1.). Someone ought to do this work in each generation; and I regret that it is too late for me to begin it now.

Anyone writing on the first century and a quarter of the Museum's history must be indebted to the industry, while somewhat regretting the verbosity, of Edward Edwards, and also to the kindly and chatty Cowtan, as well as to the encyclopaedic appendices to the Reports of the Committee of 1835–36 and of the Royal Commission of 1847–49; while for the later period he must be grateful for the reminiscences of Richard Garnett, Sir Frederic Kenyon and Dr. A. W. Pollard. But even with the aid of these and of a cloud of lesser witnesses no member of the Museum staff could of his own knowledge describe the whole even of his own Department. This is one of the first lessons every Museum man learns on entering the service. Much less therefore can he describe his own and two others, one of them remote from his education. As Scott so justly observed of the Ettrick Shepherd's labours towards his book of Jacobite songs, "it is an awkward thing to read in order that one may write"; but that has inevitably been my lot, and while I have to thank many colleagues, Dr. H. Idris Bell in particular, for generous help, I have also to bless the practice, followed (not quite unfailingly) by the compilers of the catalogues, of prefixing an account of the collection described and of the acquisitions by which it had been built up. I have made large use of these prefaces, and in the absence of references they may be taken to be my sources. I may remark that the notes of the catalogues appended to the sections in Part II are intended to provide a complete list. I have made no attempt at providing a bibliography, which would by itself fill a considerable volume; but many of the chief sources will be found adequately referred to in the notes. Adequately I hope; at least the classic reference, "*see* Smith," will not be found there. The notes, I would add, are by no means all given to the dull duty of reference; though aware that those who do not read notes do not read prefaces either, I would urge here that most of those in this volume are designed to be read.

ARUNDELL ESDAILE

June, 1943

CONTENTS

PART I

HISTORICAL

	PAGE
CHAPTER I. THE FOUNDATION:	17

1. The Act of 1753 and the Opening.—2. Origins of the Foundation Collections.—3. The Suppression of the Monasteries: Archbishop Parker and the Antiquaries.—4. Robert Cotton, the Harleys and the Old Royal Library.—5. The Royal Society and the Scientists: Arundel.—6. The Movement towards a Public Library.—7. The Establishment of the Museum.

CHAPTER II. MONTAGU HOUSE AND THE FIRST FIFTY YEARS: 38

1. Bloomsbury.—2. Montagu House.—3. The Departments and Officers.—4. Publications and Acquisitions.—5. Finances.—6. The Reading Room.

CHAPTER III. NEW WINE AND AN OLD BOTTLE: 56

1. Changes after 1799.—2. Increase: Gifts and Purchases.—3. Copyright.—4. Increased Parliamentary Grants.—5. Three great benefactions lost in twelve years.—6. Reorganization.—7. The Prints and Drawings.—8. Publications.—9. New Men, 1824-35.—10. The Reading Room, 1803-38.—11. The King's Library and the New Buildings, 1815-52.

CHAPTER IV. TWO PUBLIC ENQUIRIES: GROWTH AND
DISSENSION (1835–50): 90

1. The Parliamentary Enquiry, 1835-36.—2. Changes and Appointments.—3. Watts and the Removal: the Survey and the Purchase Grant: Acquisitions.—4. The Grenville Library.—5. The Copyright Act of 1842: Collection of Copyright Books.—6. The Manuscripts: Acquisitions made and Acquisitions missed.—7. The Nitrian Syriac Manuscripts.—8. The Printed Books: The Catalogue.—9. The Royal Commission, 1847-49.—10. Action on the Royal Commission's Report.

CHAPTER V. THE READING ROOM AND IRON LIBRARY:
PANIZZI, PRINCIPAL LIBRARIAN (1851–66): 117

1. The Reading Room and Iron Library.—2. Panizzi, Principal Librarian.

THE LIBRARY OF THE BRITISH MUSEUM

PAGE

CHAPTER VI. INTERLUDE: WINTER JONES, PRINCIPAL LIBRARIAN (1866–79):   125

1. Winter Jones, Watts and the Printed Books.—2. The Manuscripts: Bond follows Madden.—3. The Maps and the Oriental Manuscripts.

CHAPTER VII. BOND, PRINCIPAL LIBRARIAN: PRINTING THE GENERAL CATALOGUE (1879–88):   132

1. The General Catalogue.—2. The Subject Index.—3. Buildings: the Sliding Presses: the White Wing.—4. The Manuscripts.

CHAPTER VIII. MAUNDE THOMPSON, DIRECTOR AND PRINCIPAL LIBRARIAN (1888–1911):   141

1. Staff Reorganization: Copyright: Building.—2. The Oriental Library.—3. The Printed Books and the Reading Room: Garnett and Others.—4. The Manuscripts: Warner and Others.—5. Maunde Thompson.

CHAPTER IX. THE LAST THIRTY YEARS: 157

1. Sir Frederic Kenyon, Director and Principal Librarian: the King Edward VII Building.—2. The Copyright Acts, 1911 and 1915.—3. The Four-Years' War.—4. Between Two Wars.

PART II

THE COLLECTIONS AND THEIR CATALOGUES

CHAPTER I. THE PRINTED BOOKS: 175

1. The Sloane Library
2. Major Edwards's Library
3. The Old Royal Library
4. The Thomason Tracts
5. The Cracherode Library
6. The Croker French Revolution Tracts
7. The Banks Library
8. The Burney Library
9. The King's Library
10. The Grenville Library
11. The Huth Bequest
12. The Ashley Library
13. Incunabula
14. Early English Books
15. Early French, Spanish, Portuguese and Icelandic Books
16. Americana

CONTENTS

	PAGE
CHAPTER I. THE PRINTED BOOKS—*continued*	175

    17. Newspapers
    18. Music
        A. The General Music Library
        B. The King's Music Library
    19. Maps
    20. English Book-Sale Catalogues
    21. Bindings
    22. State Papers
    23. Postage Stamps
    24. Exhibitions and Guides

CHAPTER II. THE MANUSCRIPTS	226

    1. The Cotton Manuscripts
    2. The Harleian Manuscripts
    3. The Sloane Manuscripts
    4. The Old Royal Library
    5. The Birch Manuscripts
    6. The Lansdowne Manuscripts
    7. The Hargrave Manuscripts
    8. The Burney Manuscripts
    9. The King's Manuscripts
    10. The Egerton Manuscripts
    11. The Arundel Manuscripts
    12. The Stowe Manuscripts
    13. The Ashley Manuscripts
    14. The Yates Thompson Manuscripts
    15. The Additional Manuscripts
    16. Charters and Rolls
    17. Seals
    18. Maps, Charts, Plans and Topographical Drawings
    19. Music
    20. Papyri
    21. Biblical and other Ancient Greek and Latin Manuscripts, other than Papyri
    22. Medieval and Modern Languages
    23. Illuminated Manuscripts
    24. English History
    25. English Literature
    26. The Class Catalogue
    27. Exhibitions and Guides

CHAPTER III. THE ORIENTAL PRINTED BOOKS AND MANUSCRIPTS	294

    A. THE NEAR AND MIDDLE EAST:
        1. Syriac, Karshuni, etc.
        2. Hebrew and Samaritan
        3. Coptic
        4. Ethiopic
        5. Arabic
        6. Persian
        7. Turkish
        8. Armenian and Georgian
        9. Near Eastern Bindings

    B. INDIA, WITH CEYLON AND BURMA:
        1. Sanskrit and Pali
        2. Hindi, Panjabi, Hindustani, Sindhi, Pushtu
        3. Marathi, Gujarati, Bengali, Oriya, Assamese
        4. Kannada, Badaga, Kurg
        5. Burmese
        6. Tamil
        7. Telugu
        8. Sinhalese

    C. CENTRAL AND EASTERN ASIA:
        1. Chinese
        2. Japanese
        3. Tibetan, etc.
        4. Southern Asia

THE LIBRARY OF THE BRITISH MUSEUM

	PAGE
APPENDICES:	323

1. The Elected Trustees
2. The Keepers and Deputy Keepers
3. The first Reading Room Regulations
4. Alienation, Lending and Removal
5. Binding
6. Classification of Printed Books
7. Photography
8. The Natural History Museum Library
9. The Staff: a Note
10. The Report and Quarterly

NOTES   349

INDEX   376

PART I
HISTORICAL

I

THE FOUNDATION

1. THE ACT OF 1753 AND THE OPENING

THE story of the foundation of the British Museum has been too often told and is too well known to be related again at length, but it must be told here in outline before its significance is discussed. The outline can be followed in the Act of Parliament (36 Geo. II, c. 22) of 1753[1] which founded the Trust. The preamble of that Act tells how "Sir Hans Sloane of Chelsea, in the County of Middlesex Baronet, having, through the Course of many Years, with great Labour and Expence, gathered together whatever could be procured either in our own or foreign Countries, that was rare and curious," by a codicil dated 1749 to his Will desired that his collection in all its branches, as described in forty-six volumes of catalogue, should be kept together, and that his trustees should offer them to the Crown for the sum of £20,000.

It proceeds to recite previous Acts, of 1700 (12 & 13 William III, c. 7) "for settling and preserving the Library kept in the House at Westminster, called Cotton House, in the name and family of the Cottons, for the benefit of the Publick," and of 1706 (6 Anne, c. 30) "for the better securing Her Majesty's purchase of Cotton House" and the building of a room to be called the Cottonian Library, to contain the manuscripts and other collections of Sir Robert Cotton, very little having been done in pursuance of the former Act. It is then recorded that the Act of Queen Anne had had no better result, but that in 1731 the Cotton Library had suffered by a fire. That Arthur Edwards, Esq., by his Will of 1738, had bequeathed his books and (subject to the life interest of Mistress Elizabeth Milles) £7,000 to erect a house in which to preserve the Cottonian Library, or should such a house have meantime been provided, to purchase manuscripts, books of antiquities, ancient coins, medals and other curiosities to be added to the Library. And, further, that the Countess of Oxford, the

THE LIBRARY OF THE BRITISH MUSEUM

widow, and the Duchess of Portland, the only daughter, of Edward Harley, Earl of Oxford, were prepared to sell the valuable manuscripts collected by the late Earl and his father Robert Harley, the first Earl, for the sum of £10,000, to be kept as an addition to the Cottonian Library, and to be called the Harleian Collection of Manuscripts.

The Act then established a body of Trustees, headed by the Archbishop of Canterbury, the Lord Chancellor or Lord Keeper, and the Speaker of the House of Commons, as Principals, and consisting beside them of the other great Officers of State, and of two trustee representatives each of the families of Sloane, Cotton and the Harleys, and also, elected by all these, fifteen others.[2] These Trustees are to find a "repository" within the Cities of London or Westminster or the suburbs thereof; the collections named and any additions to them, "received into the said General Repository, shall remain and be preserved therein for publick use, to all Posterity," and free access to them is to be given to "all studious and curious Persons." The three Principal Trustees are to recommend two candidates to the Sovereign, who will appoint one of them (and by inference, be it observed, nobody else) to be Principal Librarian, the only statutory officer, who with the other officers and servants (again, be it observed) is specifically forbidden the common and corrupt practice of the period, of employing a deputy to do the work of his office.[3]

Then follow twenty-four sections providing in minute detail for the conduct by the Archbishop and other Trustees of a lottery for raising the necessary money to pay the £20,000 for the Sloane collection and the £10,000 for the Harleian manuscripts, to purchase or erect and furnish the "repository," and to set up an endowment of £30,000 for current income, the balance if any on the profits of the lottery to be reserved for the future disposition of Parliament.

The conduct of the lottery, despite its dignified auspices, was not free from scandal;[4] but the Trustees were able to pay the £20,000 required for the collections, invest the £30,000, buy for another £10,250 Montagu House, in Great Russell Street, in the Parish of Saint George, Bloomsbury (28 Geo. II, Sess. 2, Private Acts, c. iii), and at a cost of £12,873 to repair and fit it and put the garden in

THE FOUNDATION

order. This high cost is due to the fact that the house had stood empty for some years.5 The Trustees had rejected in favour of it Buckingham House, which was offered them by Sir Charles Sheffield for £30,000; it had previously been decided by Sloane's trustees to remove his collection from Chelsea. While the new Trust was engaged in settling into its home, the House of Lords deposited Thomas Rymer's collection of documents not printed in his *Foedera* and also sixty-four volumes of Rolls of Parliament; and, more important, in 1757 George II transferred to it the Library of the Kings and Queens of England, now called the Old Royal Library. In 1758 the first Statutes were drawn up, and on 15th January, 1759, the British Museum was opened.

2. Origins of the Foundation Collections

Let us now look backwards.

Behind these events, thus for the most part recorded in the dry language of Parliamentary draftsmen, lay a long and far from dry history of two at least of the great intellectual movements of Western Europe of the previous two centuries. For the new Museum was of twofold inspiration, historical and scientific. It brought together, for preservation in the first place, and as it proved later for vast development, the accumulated results, so far as they had gone, on the one hand of the studies in national records of the Elizabethan and Jacobean antiquaries, and on the other of the researches into nature and natural law of the enquiring minds of the preceding hundred years, originating before the foundation of the Royal Society at the Restoration, and marked by an increasing foundation abroad of academies with a wide scientific outlook.6

The essence of the whole was the gathering together of the libraries. In the list of the classes of Sloane's collections set out in the Act of 1753 his library of books stands first, and curiously enough, except for crystals and mathematical instruments, nothing that we should now call science is mentioned, though the chief value of his collections was and is in natural history. It was not too late to be encyclopaedic, and, broadly considered, the books and the "curiosities" illustrated each other. But it is with the books, manuscripts and written documents alone that we are here concerned.

The latter half of the fifteenth and the sixteenth century saw the foundation and the refoundation or development of libraries throughout the more advanced parts of Western Europe, in answer, as it were, to the ferment of new knowledge and new criticisms of the old which took triple form as the Renaissance, the Reformation and the Counter-Reformation. After the return from Avignon Popes Nicholas V (enriched by the alms of the Jubilee year, 1450), Sixtus IV, Leo X and Sixtus V, gathered a new and splendid Papal Library in the Vatican; Francis I of France, a great patron of the new scholarship, issued in 1527 the first decree (the Ordonnance de Montpellier) ordering a copy of every book published in France to be sent to his Library at Blois, and appointed Guillaume Budé, the greatest classic of the time, as his Librarian; the Medici family, and notably Lorenzo the Magnificent and Pope Leo X, regarded the Biblioteca Mediceo-Laurenziana as one of the most precious possessions of their house, and finally opened it to the public in 1571; Albert V of Bavaria, with the help of the wealth and culture of the merchant prince of Augsburg, Johann Jakob Fugger, founded the Court, now the State, Library of Bavaria at Munich in 1561; the Emperor Maximilian I and still more Ferdinand I (1503–64) created that of Vienna; Philip II of Spain that of the Escorial in 1576; Julius Duke of Brunswick and Lüneburg the Wolfenbüttel Library (1572); while the libraries of universities were either, like that of the Jagiellonska at Cracow, vastly developed by the acquisition of manuscripts, or were refounded, as was Oxford's by Sir Thomas Bodley in 1603.

In Italy and the neighbouring countries the chief quarry of the Renaissance collectors was the classical literature of Greece and Rome, of which manuscripts were being discovered in monasteries and elsewhere, and which more and more men were able and eager to read. Some of these, mostly Latin, came from Northern monasteries such as Fulda and Corvey, where they were found by a tribe of hunters, headed by Poggio Bracciolini; but few remained, and few went, north of the Alps, except to Paris and Munich; most of the classical Greek texts (being in fact the most ancient known) pos-

THE FOUNDATION

sessed today by the more northerly libraries, such as the Paris Alcman, and the British Museum's Bacchylides and Aristotle, 'Αθηναίων πολιτεία, have come from the comparatively recent discoveries of papyri in the rubbish-heaps of ancient Egyptian towns. It is significant that "the best MSS. of Homer are now in Venice; of Hesiod and Herodotus, in Florence; of Pindar, in Rome, Florence, Milan and Paris; of Aeschylus, Sophocles and Apollonius Rhodius, in Florence; of Euripides, in Venice, Florence and Rome; of Aristophanes, in Venice and Ravenna; of Thucydides, in Florence, Rome, Munich and London; of Demosthenes and Plato, in Paris; and of Aristotle, in Venice, Rome and Paris."[7] Much the same is true of classical Latin literature. And Oriental literatures were collected for the Vatican, the Escorial, Munich and the Royal Library of Paris long before (with the exception of Laud's gift to the Bodleian) they reached English Libraries, at least in any quantity.

In the North, and in England especially, the dominating study was controversial theology. Thomas James, Bodley's first librarian (and perhaps also, in less degree, Bodley himself), conceived the function of the University Library to be to certify the text of the Christian Fathers against the supposed falsifications of Romanist divines.[8] Wolfenbüttel also was intended to be an armoury of Reformist theology with which to meet the Roman Counter-Reformation. And the Counter-Reformation in its turn was soon (in 1609) to be crystallized in a library foundation, Frederic Borromeo's Ambrosiana at Milan.

3. The Suppression of the Monasteries: Archbishop Parker and the Antiquaries

A third interest may be observed coming into play at just this time: that in the national history and antiquities. In the late fifteenth and early sixteenth century the ancient shadow of the Holy Roman Empire was fading from men's veneration, and in France and England at least the Crown consolidated its power, and reduced the independence of provinces and nobles; Louis XI and Henry VII by this common policy of theirs did much to create national patriotism, an inevitable fruit of which is an interest in national history. That the period saw a crop of chronicles in this country is therefore no independent phenomenon.9

The first and chief step which led to the foundation of the British Museum Library has now to be mentioned. That step was the suppression of the monasteries by Henry VIII. It is true that cause and effect were divided by over two centuries; the connection between them is not the less certain and vital. The monastic libraries were the chief repositories of the chronicles and other vernacular literature of the country, and still more of the church-books, dating from the days of Theodore and Bede, and almost of Augustine himself, which were the chief documents proving the pedigree of the Christian Church in this Island. Neither Henry (though he had had a theological training) nor Cromwell cared for these things. It has been well pointed out by Edward Edwards[10] that in all the eighty-six detailed Visitation Articles of the Royal Commissioners of 1536 there is no mention whatever of books or of the ability to read, let alone of libraries or learning. Except for such altar-books as had bindings of precious metals or jewels, the monastic libraries, which were often rich, were scattered unregarded. To save what books survived from them, and provide for their preservation, was the problem of the next two generations of English scholars.

The sins of omission of the Commissioners of Henry VIII in 1536 were followed in 1550 and 1551 by the sins of commission of those of Edward VI, or rather of the Protector and Council, who purged the Oxford libraries of popery by indiscriminate destruction of quantities, though fortunately not all, of their books;[11] amongst the rest went Duke Humfrey's books and "d'Aungerville's Library," i.e. Richard de Bury's, given by him to his foundation of Durham College. Similar purges were made at Cambridge[12] and elsewhere by the fanatics of the new ideas and the new order, in the hope of exterminating the old. It is a proceeding natural to such men at such times; we have seen in recent years some, and those probably by no means the last, examples.

There were a few who saw the loss and did what they could to stop it. The suppression was visibly coming before it came; indeed it

THE FOUNDATION

had begun long before in a small and irreproachable way under orthodox Church authority, and the foundations of colleges at Oxford and Cambridge by Bishops Fox and Fisher between 1505 and 1515 had foreshadowed the coming change clearly enough. John Leland, who had been Keeper of the King's Library from some time before 1520 and in 1533 was appointed King's Antiquary, made his celebrated "laboryous journey and serche for Englands antiquities" between the latter date and 1543, noting important books in the libraries he visited, as well as ancient buildings, coins, and the like. On 16th July, 1536, the year of the final and great suppression, he wrote to Cromwell, entreating him to extend the duties of the Commissioners of Enquiry to cover the monasteries' books, so that the best of them could be taken for the King's Library; but the Articles of Enquiry, as noted above, bear no trace of this, and though Leland did secure some volumes, they were few. Of the Royal Library we shall have more to say in a later section.

Leland's mind gave way soon after this; his collection and notes were published in 1549 by John Bale, an ardent convert to the Reformation, who, though endowed with a taste and talent for vituperation which is unhappily too common among the advocates of change, was nevertheless a real lover of learning. In his well-known preface to this work Bale lamented that the opportunity of the Suppression had been lost and that among the Commissioners "men of learnyng and perfyght love to their nacyon were not then appoynted to the serche of theyr lybraryes, for the conservacion of those most noble Antiquitees" (i.e. the English Chronicles and other ancient MSS.), and "in every shyre of Englande but one solempne library" founded to preserve "our noble monumentes."[13] The works of orthodox theologians, schoolmen and canonists on the other hand were in Bale's eyes best burned. "If the byshop of Rome's lawes, decrees, decretals, extravagates, clementines, and other such dregges of the devyll, yea if Heytesburyes sophisms, Porphyryes universals, Aristotles olde logyckes and Dunses dyvinite, wyth such other lowsy legerdemaynes and frutes of the bottomlesse pytte, had leaped out of our libraries . . . we might wele have ben therwith contented." Bale's enduring work is based on Leland's; it is the first bibliography of English writers.[14] He also collected books himself and helped to find them for Archbishop Parker.

Matthew Parker, born in 1504, elected Master of Corpus Christi College, Cambridge, in 1544, and consecrated Archbishop of Canterbury in 1559, had spent the best of his years in the time of violent change and iconoclasm; a moderate Reformer, he more than anyone made the Elizabethan Church settlement. In his mind what needed insisting on most was the continuity of the Church of England with that of Augustine, a continuity fiercely denied by extremists from both sides. For the establishment of Parker's position the surviving pre-Conquest manuscript books, documents and inscriptions were obviously of the first importance. He set about collecting them from many sources and especially of course from the dispersal of the libraries of Christ Church (the Cathedral) and St. Augustine's at Canterbury, books from which were to be found scattered in private hands in Kent and elsewhere.[15] And he edited, or caused to be edited, the works of Gildas, Asser, Aelfric, Matthew Paris and other early chroniclers, and employed John Day, the best English printer of his time, to cut the first Anglo-Saxon type and to print for him. He was not, it must be admitted, either an editor with modern standards of integrity or a palaeographer with modern standards of dating manuscripts. Thus he hopefully attributed a group of MSS. to the ownership of the seventh-century Archbishop Theodore of Canterbury, who was a notable Greek scholar. This provenance he based on the appearance of the name $\Theta\epsilon\delta\omega\rho\text{os}$ on one of them, a Homer which he had bought of a baker at Canterbury. But only one of the group was as old as the twelfth century, and the rest were much later still.[16] The Homer was in fact still modern, and was probably new when it was brought back by Prior Sellyng from one of his tours to Italy at the end of the fifteenth century. But this detracts little from the debt we owe to Parker. Helped by his high position and influence, he gathered a noble collection of four hundred and thirty-three volumes, many of them very early monuments of the writings of the Church in England, and secured their permanent preservation in his College after his death in 1575.[17]

Archbishop Parker's opportunities were, naturally, exceptional;

THE FOUNDATION

but he was not alone in his historical studies. Laurence Nowell, Dean of Lichfield, was an ardent student of Anglo-Saxon. John Stow, "Citizen and Taylor," who brought himself by his enthusiasm from prosperity to an impoverished old age, is best known by his *Survey of London*, but was also an editor of old chronicles and author of two, his *Summarie of Englyshe Chronicles*, and *Annales of England*. And in the same generation appeared the first of a distinguished succession of legal antiquaries, such as in the next generation were Sir Henry Spelman and John Selden; this was William Lambarde, the first historian of Kent, or indeed of any English county. Lawyers in every period (until the Law of Property Act was passed) have had occasion to be familiar with old deeds and documents.[18]

But a greater antiquary and historian even than these, and one whose collections, unlike most of theirs, have come into the Museum,[19] was William Camden. Like Stow and Speed, Camden was neither an ecclesiastic nor a lawyer; but whereas they were London citizens,[20] raised to scholarship by their passion for history, he was a professed scholar. Having missed a fellowship at All Souls, he spent four years in archaeological tours, in the manner and very likely in conscious imitation of Leland, after which, in 1575, he was appointed Undermaster of Westminster School; in 1593 he became Headmaster, and held the office till 1597, when he was appointed Clarenceux King-of-Arms. At Westminster he was able to continue his tours in vacation, and he also became librarian of the Chapter Library, which gave him access to valuable materials. The Dean for the long period 1561–1601 was Gabriel Goodman, whose patronage of Camden is believed to have begun when the latter left Oxford, and who certainly shared his tastes, contributing historical material to his great work, the *Britannia* (1586). Camden's studies were not purely antiquarian or heraldic, eminent as he was in both fields; his widely known *Annales* of Elizabeth's reign up to 1599, published in 1615, showed an interest in recent and contemporary political history also; both interests appear strongly in a Westminster pupil of Camden's, and may well have been inspired by him.

THE LIBRARY OF THE BRITISH MUSEUM

4. ROBERT COTTON, THE HARLEYS AND THE OLD ROYAL LIBRARY

That pupil was Sir Robert Cotton,[21] who may be regarded as one of the two posthumous founders of the Museum. Filled with the spirit of learning which Camden gave him, he had also what Camden had not, plentiful leisure and money, being an early and salient example of a class that has done great things for this country, the private gentleman with public spirit and an enthusiasm. Immediately after taking his degree in 1585 at Jesus College, Cambridge, he settled at Cotton House in Westminster, the best centre for his lifework, to which he now set himself. This was not merely to collect, but both himself to study and to enable others to study as many ancient manuscripts, and above all historically important documents, not necessarily ancient, as he could come by. Some contemporaries more than hinted that he did not always come by them very honestly. But the fact is that enormous quantities of books, parchments and papers were then to be picked up by the keen hunter. Of the wreckage of the monastic libraries only a small part was yet in safe hands; not only the religious books and chronicles, but cartularies, or lists of charters to lands, and the charters themselves, had gone astray, and constituted a solid foundation-stone of history. Moreover then and long afterwards statesmen treated as their private property papers which would now be preserved as state property in the Public Record Office; to this practice is due the existence of great national archives still owned and cared for by the descendants of statesmen, such as Cecil's at Hatfield. Quantities of such papers were to be gathered by a collector of political as well as antiquarian interests like Cotton. And he had, it was said, some official sanction.

With his old master and dear friend Camden he worked in close contact, sharing at least one of his antiquarian tours, lending him manuscripts, and inheriting his papers. He became the recognized leader of the little band of English antiquaries; the first Society of Antiquaries, founded by Archbishop Parker with the help of the young Camden and others in 1572, met regularly at Cotton House till its extinction in 1604 under suspicion of opposition to the Crown.[22] Younger students, like Selden and Sir Symonds D'Ewes, owed much

THE FOUNDATION

to his help and encouragement; and his fame spread wider still, among scholars of the new school of medieval and modern history which was arising on the Continent as well as in England. He lent his most treasured volumes with great freedom, and in 1601 gave some to Bodley for his new library at Oxford. In fact he regarded his collection as a public institution; and so it was, though not in name until nearly seventy years after his death in 1631, when, still famous, indeed a legend, but little used, it was secured under trustees from Sir Robert's grandson, Sir John, by the Cotton Library Act of 1700.

Neither the life of Cotton nor the astonishing wealth of his collection can be dwelt on here (for the latter see below, pp. 226–31); our immediate point is purely to show how there culminated in him, and eventually contributed to the founding of the Museum Library, the tradition of the historical and antiquarian scholarship of this country in the sixteenth and seventeenth centuries. To the work of Cotton that of the Harleys, father and son, may be regarded as an appendix.

Robert and Edward Harley, first and second Earls of Oxford (of the second creation), were the third and fourth in a continuous succession of four generations of high officers of State, and it was natural that English history should be, at least equally with Biblical study, the main object of their collecting. Their vast and noble collection, since known as the Harleian MSS., consisting of nearly 8,000 volumes, rich not only in these fields but also in many others and especially in the schools, foreign as well as English, of illumination, in classics and in Church history, was largely assembled by a librarian of genius, Humphrey Wanley, the best palaeographer of his day (see below, pp. 231–9). It joined Cotton's and Sloane's at the foundation of the Museum. The printed part of the library had previously been dispersed.

Here we may perhaps best mention the Old Royal Library, though not one of the foundation libraries, strictly so-called, as were the Sloane, Cotton and Harleian. Four years after the creation of the Museum Trust and two before the opening of the Museum in Montagu House, George II presented the library collected by his predecessors from Edward IV downwards, both printed and manuscript. The latter were the more important, and especially famous for including the Codex Alexandrinus, then and for long after believed to be the oldest surviving text of the Greek Bible, which had been presented to Charles I in 1629 by the Patriarch of Constantinople. Of the sovereigns up to James I only Edward IV had been a collector, though miscellaneous valuable volumes had accrued at different times, notably by such gifts as that of Queen Mary's Psalter. But Henry Prince of Wales was a born student, and his father, himself a scholar, bought for him Lord Lumley's library, originally Archbishop Cranmer's, and other collections. The Civil War, Restoration and Augustan period were all unpropitious, except for some miscellaneous buying (and fine binding) under Charles II, and for Bentley's Keepership under Queen Mary II, who took an interest in the Library; but some books were received under the Licensing Acts of 1662, etc., and the Copyright Act of 1709.

Apart from these chief acquisitions, the printed portion of the Royal Library was a somewhat fortuitous assemblage, but with valuable sections of Spanish and Italian history and poetry. (See below, pp. 177–80, 240–8.)

5. The Royal Society and the Scientists: Arundel

The second intellectual current which, joining with that of historical enquiry, went to create the Museum and its library, was that of scientific discovery. The sixteenth and still more the seventeenth century had seen a wonderful series of brilliant advances in the knowledge of nature. Those in mathematics, physics and astronomy are no doubt the most celebrated. The work of Copernicus in the early Renaissance had led, through Galileo in the first half of the seventeenth century, to Leibnitz and Newton; in 1638, Descartes' *Discours sur la Méthode* had revolutionized geometry; and in 1600 Gilbert had published his classical treatise *De Magnete*, the earliest work on physics produced in England. In medicine and surgery experiment and observation had succeeded to tradition and the authority of Galen and Avicenna; autopsy, from being frowned on, became

THE FOUNDATION

the regular practice, and in the French wars of religion (a rich opportunity for getting experience) the art of surgery was immensely improved by Ambroise Paré, whose work was speedily absorbed and translated in other countries, including our own; in 1628 Harvey published his revolutionary *Exercitatio*, based on lectures given at the College of Physicians, and by it established the true facts of the circulation of the blood. The experimental method, indeed, erected by Bacon into a philosophy, had conquered in every field of enquiry. Its triumph may be seen even in such semi-scientific writing as Browne's *Vulgar Errors*, though backwaters still existed, and Nicholas Culpeper could in 1652 put forth his astrological herbal, *The English Physician*, and even later the *London Pharmacopœia* included fantastic as well as revolting remedies. The last execution for witchcraft in England took place in 1685.[23]

Geographical knowledge had made even greater strides; the discovery of the West was itself based on the revival of the sound if imperfect cosmogony of Ptolemy, editions of whose *Geographia* were published before the end of the first quarter of a century of printing. Ptolemy, like other ancient cosmographers, knew that the earth was round. He miscalculated its circumference, bringing the Eastern coasts of Asia into mid-Atlantic. Hence the explorers, and above all Columbus, seeking to reach the land of pepper and spices by a route which was not barred by the Moslem Empire, reached America. And the successors of Columbus found their task enormously helped by a school of scientific mathematicians and map-makers, of whom Mercator stands at the head.

The early voyages of discovery were scientific in one of their results if not at all in their motive. The plantations which resulted abounded in hitherto unknown birds, beasts and plants. The first settlers had naturally no leisure for such studies; but in the following generation a great stimulus was given to zoological and botanical knowledge. The younger Tradescant, whose father (like himself) had been both a travelling botanist and gardener to the King, visited Virginia in 1637 and brought back plants for his collection at Lambeth. The "Museum Tradescantianum" was the first scientific museum known to have been formed in this country;[24] in 1683 it was presented by Elias Ashmole to the University of Oxford, where it still exists. The elder Tradescant had made a systematic collection of plants during a visit to Archangel; but European botany was for the first time systematically surveyed and classified by John Ray. In 1662 Ray conceived, and with his friend Francis Willughby undertook, a complete record of organic nature, Ray concentrating on botany and Willughby on zoology; but after the latter's death Ray (in addition to educating his orphan children) edited and carried forward his part of the work. Ray is much the most important predecessor of the great Swede Linnaeus. For our present purpose it is significant that the collections made by Sloane during his years (1687–89) as physician to the Governor of Jamaica were communicated by him to Ray, who published them a year before his death in vol. 3 of his *Historia Plantarum*, 1704.[25]

At the time of the Restoration in England the sciences had reached that stage at which organized co-operation and record are needed if the work of scattered pioneers, however brilliant, is to be fertilized. In spite of the political troubles of the time a small group of "philosophers" had begun to meet weekly at least as early as 1645, and were presently centred in Gresham College, and in about 1648 a similar group formed itself at Oxford, close touch being kept between the two. At the Restoration Charles II patronized the London meetings, and, after being (of course at his own request) entered simply as a member, conferred on it in 1662 a Royal Charter. Thus was founded the Royal Society, which gathered together men of scientific attainments and curiosity, and in its *Philosophical Transactions* issued the first regular scientific periodical.

Nearly a century was yet to elapse before the foundation of the British Museum; but the work of the Royal Society, as much as that of the second Society of Antiquaries, founded in 1717, and granted its Royal Charter in 1751, led straight to it. Of its first Trustees a large proportion were members of one or the other body.[26] Nor were their spheres so sharply delimited as they are today. Knowledge had not yet so accumulated as to be perforce split into a number of specialisms, unconscious of each other. It was still possible for a man of wide intellectual curiosity to be, if not a *doctor*, at least an *indagator*

THE FOUNDATION

universalis. Sloane, in turn Secretary and President of the Royal Society, collected in very wide fields of knowledge. (For his large library, see below, pp. 177, 239–40.)

The same width of interest is well shown by another episode in the very early history of the Royal Society which was in time to affect the Museum. Henry Howard of Norfolk, who entertained the Society's meetings at Arundel House after the destruction of Gresham College by the Fire of London, gave it in 1666 part of the splendid collection of manuscripts and printed books formed by his father, the second Earl of Arundel (the collector of the Arundel marbles), though they were only to a very small extent concerned with the natural sciences.[27] The later growth of specialism rendered this noble possession of little use to the Society, and first the manuscripts and then the printed books were alienated, the manuscripts being acquired by the British Museum in 1830 (see below, pp. 254–6). In 1707 there was a proposal to unite the Royal Society's Library with the Royal (then called the Queen's) and the Cotton, the second Act securing which had just been passed.[28] This came to nothing; but it is another expression of the faith in which the Museum was founded, that all sciences illustrate each other.[29]

6. THE MOVEMENT TOWARDS A PUBLIC LIBRARY

For a great capital London was thus very late in acquiring a general public library, far behind Paris, for example, where the Mazarine had been opened in 1643, and where the Royal Library had been in practice open for some time and was in 1753 formally opened under the enlightened rule of the Abbé Jérome Bignon. The English Royal Library, on the contrary, was useless for anything but the collation of particular manuscripts, which Bentley, *pro solita humanitate sua*, had begun to make easy; the main collection of books appears to have lacked arrangement, let alone facilities for access; nor was it methodically formed. The other libraries of London belonged to the professions of the Church and the Law, and a scholar belonging to neither of these professions, like Johnson, when he came to London in 1737, had little access to books. The Inns of

THE LIBRARY OF THE BRITISH MUSEUM

Court, the nearest approach to a university, though that of only one faculty, Lambeth, and (except through clerical friends) Sion College, were not open to him. There was the small library founded in St. Martin's Fields by Archbishop Tenison in 1684, which is known to have contained valuable manuscripts and standard books,[30] but that was all that was his of right. Probably he borrowed from the stock of Cave, Osborne and other booksellers, as we know Benjamin Franklin did when he came to London. If he made the right friends he might also no doubt draw on private collections of books, such as those of Sunderland, Dr. Mead, Harley, Sloane. But then and for long after the University towns, and especially Oxford, were the only real places for easy access to books of scholarship.[31]

The want had been increasingly felt as civil life in London became more secure and culture broadened. In the sixteen-eighties John Evelyn had wished to see a public library founded at St. Paul's.[32] Access to the Cotton Library was generously given by the founder's descendants; Anthony à Wood, Burnet, and most of all Dugdale are known to have used it largely, though when the family were out of town admission was not easily arranged. And the Cotton was not a general library but a special collection. Signs of the times were the publication of the catalogue of the Cotton Library by Smith in 1697, the passing of the Act securing the Library in 1700, the appointment in 1703 of a Committee of the House of Lords to report on the state of the public records preserved in the Tower, and the publication about the same time of two important general catalogues of manuscripts, Edward Bernard's *Catalogi librorum manuscriptorum Angliae et Hiberniae*, 1697, and the list of known Anglo-Saxon manuscripts drawn up by Humphrey Wanley, afterwards Harley's librarian, and published as an appendix to Hickes's *Thesaurus* in 1706. The creation of a public library in London was in the air and was often canvassed in the first half of the eighteenth century. For example, a proposal put forward in 1743 by Thomas Carte, the historian, would have placed it, with the Harleian Library, in the Mansion House, then newly built; this would, nearly a century earlier than the refoundation of Guildhall Library, have restored the City's loss of that founded by Sir Richard Whittington and destroyed by the Protector Somerset.[33]

THE FOUNDATION

John Anstis, Garter King-of-Arms, had before this suggested that the Cotton and Royal Libraries (Robert Harley was still living) should be removed to "the noble room in St. Paul's opposite to the present library" of the Cathedral, i.e. to the room in the South-West corner.[34] And in 1750 two of the Cotton Trustees petitioned for the foundation of a national library and museum.

7. THE ESTABLISHMENT OF THE MUSEUM

This happy result was not achieved without difficulty. Sloane's collections were spoken of slightingly by some, notably Pope and Edward Young, who called him "the foremost toyman of his time." Horace Walpole, who was one of his Trustees, and no doubt really interested in the matter, but who feared ridicule worse than death, accordingly found it necessary to affect a tone of aloofness, as we see in his often-quoted letter to Sir Horace Mann of February 14th, 1753. It is from this letter that we learn that the King, to whom the collection was first offered, "excused himself, saying he did not believe that there were twenty thousand pounds in the Treasury." When the Sloane Trustees' petition came before Parliament, a Committee was appointed under the chairmanship of Philip Yorke, afterwards 2nd Earl of Hardwicke; it reported on 19th June on lines which were followed in the resulting Act. The Lord Chancellor, Henry Pelham (*d.* 1764), is said to have been not unfriendly to the scheme, but to have been averse from the lottery. Lotteries were in some disfavour, which this particular one was about to justify. But the Speaker, the celebrated Arthur Onslow, a man of high public spirit and cultivation as well as integrity, who as ex-officio Trustee of the Cotton Library had played an active part after the fire at Ashburnham House in 1731, was a strong influence in favour of the proposal, and was probably responsible for adding the Cotton manuscripts to the terms of reference of the Committee, which recommended their inclusion, and added the purchase of the Harleian manuscripts also. Alas, it was too late to add the Harleian printed books as well. They had been sold a dozen years before to Thomas Osborne the bookseller, and though Osborne got rid of them but

THE LIBRARY OF THE BRITISH MUSEUM

slowly, selling the great collection of English historical pamphlets by auction in 1747–48, the printed library in its glory no longer existed.

The ex-officio Trustees were from the first:

- The Archbishop of Canterbury
- The Lord Chancellor or Lord Keeper
- The Speaker of the House of Commons
    (These three are the Principal Trustees)
- The First Lord of the Treasury ("The Lord Treasurer")
- The Lord President of the Council
- The Lord Privy Seal
- The First Lord of the Admiralty ("The Lord High Admiral")
- The Lord Steward
- The Lord Chamberlain
- The Bishop of London
- The Principal Secretaries of State
- The Chancellor of the Exchequer
- The Lord Chief Justice of England
- The Master of the Rolls
- The Chief Justice of the Court of Common Pleas
    (This Office lapsed in 1873, the Court being merged in the King's Bench Division)
- The Attorney General
- The Solicitor General
- The President of the Royal Society
- The President of the Royal College of Physicians

To these were added 1824 (by 5 Geo. IV, c. 39):

- The President of the Society of Antiquaries
- The President of the Royal Academy

Nominated Trustees were:

- Sloane family, two
- Cotton family, two
- Harley family, two

to whom were added later in consequence of three great additions of antiquities, representatives of the

- Towneley family (1806)
- Elgin family (1816)
- Knight (Richard Payne Knight) family (1824).

THE FOUNDATION

And since 1832 (by 2 Guil. IV, c. 46, in recognition of the gift of the King's Library made in 1823) the Sovereign appoints a representative.

The Trustees elected by these are fifteen in number. The list of them represents so remarkable a body of distinguished men over a period of nearly two centuries, especially when we remember those who have been Trustees by right of office, that it seems worth while to print it from the Statutes (see App. 1). Very soon the body came to be looked upon as an Academy, the English counterpart of the French Forty. The honour is one which many have desired. Dr. John Taylor coveted it, and called it "the blue ribband of a scholar."[35] Richard Gough (*d.* 1809) hoped for it, but stated with some bitterness that it "was now become an object of successful canvass," and, perhaps partly because he was not successful, altered his will and left all his collections to the Bodleian. But the fact is that mere eminence as a specialist has rarely been regarded as a claim to election. The work of specialists can be done by the Staff; that of policy, relations with Government and the like, cannot; the latter is the function of the Trustees. The Trustees are therefore, and always have been, a mixture of public men with wide intellectual interests, and men of intellectual eminence with capacity for affairs, which includes (as capacity for affairs always must) the ability to work with others. The history of the Trust reveals in the early period a want of large views, which were rare anywhere in relation to the Museum; and in the eighteen-thirties and forties it can only be said that there was incompetence; no competent body would have insisted for years on the performance of an impossibility in the face of full and clear advice from their expert, or have allowed itself to be hoodwinked by its Secretary. But those days are far past, and the most distinguished men have long been among those who have taken their Trusteeship the most seriously. It is a notable fact that as Prince of Wales both King Edward VII and King George V, neither, one would say, a man with strong academic leanings, were Trustees and were over a period of thirty years (1881–1911) most regular and interested members of the Standing Committee.

The conduct of the Museum's affairs is in the hands of this Standing Committee of twenty, on which sit the three Principal Trustees and (since 1881) the Sovereign's nominee, and which reports to the General Board twice a year the Minutes of its Monthly Meetings. The same Standing Committee meets also monthly at the Natural History Museum.36

Of the Principal Trustees at the foundation the Archbishop was Thomas Herring (d. 1757), a Whig ecclesiastic of amiable character but no great force; and the Lord Chancellor was Philip Yorke, 1st Earl of Hardwicke, who retired from office in 1754. Neither of these had time to do much for the infant institution. But, as we have seen, the Speaker was very different. Onslow was rightly elected to the first vacancy (the Duke of Argyll's) for an Elected Trustee on his retirement from the Speakership in 1768.37 The President of the Royal Society was the Earl of Macclesfield, the astronomer, who had been Chairman of Sloane's Trustees in 1753.

The first election, held in that year, set the tradition. The fifteen elected included statesmen who were patrons of letters, such as the Duke of Argyll, whose portrait at Glasgow shows him with an open folio; the Duke of Northumberland; "the good" Lord Lyttelton, himself an author, high-minded and absent-minded alike, for, though he had been Chancellor of the Exchequer, "he could never comprehend the commonest rules of arithmetic"; Philip Yorke, afterwards 2nd Earl of Hardwicke, who had been Chairman of the Committee of the House for the Sloane-Cotton-Harley business;38 Sir John Evelyn, F.R.S., builder of the library at Wotton, whose famous grandfather would surely have rejoiced to know of this activity of his grandson; two members of Sloane's family (beyond the nominated representatives), William Sloane and Colonel William Sotheby; and several of the leading spirits of the Royal and Antiquaries' Societies, such as Dr. Thomas Birch, a friend of the Yorkes, who was the most active of the Trustees; according to Johnson "Tom Birch" was "as brisk as a bee in conversation," while Horace Walpole described him as "a worthy good-natured soul, full of industry and activity, and running about like a young setting-dog, in quest of anything new or old, and with no parts, taste or judgement"; he was one of the Museum's first considerable benefactors as well as Secretary and first centenary historian of the Royal Society; James West, the great collector, afterwards (in 1768) as P.R.S. an ex-officio Trustee; and

THE FOUNDATION

Dr. (afterwards Sir) William Watson, the naturalist, who stocked the large garden of Montagu House with plants, and was, curiously, the only practising man of science of the whole fifteen.

In 1757 the Trustees, as empowered by the Act, drew up their first *Statutes and Rules to be observed in the management and use of the British Museum*. Principles were laid down in these which have been constantly adhered to in the Museum's later history. Thus the preamble states that "altho it was chiefly designed for the use of learned and studious men, both natives and foreigners, in their researches into the several parts of knowledge; yet being founded at the expence of the public, it may be judged reasonable, that the advantages accruing from it should be rendered as general as may be consistent with the several considerations above mentioned."

The Statutes proceed to set out the days and hours of opening; the deplorable method of admission by ticket of the "studious and curious persons" mentioned in the Act to view the exhibited collections, with an absolute prohibition, very necessary then, of the taking of fees; rules of admission for study;[39] to order the provision of catalogues and labelling, and to forbid lending "unless upon some extraordinary occasion." This last exception is more rigidly defined in the revised edition of the following year as "such books, charters, deeds or other manuscripts as may be wanted to be made use of in evidence," the only exception (other than Governmental war emergency) allowed today; and even then a member of the staff was (as he still is) to take and bring back the volume, and to remain in attendance on it all the while.[40]

Thus was the British Museum born. Of its services to learning in the near two centuries of its life some slight idea may be conveyed by the chapters that follow. Of these none have been more striking than those it has rendered to the study and understanding of the Middle Ages, nor could any have been more grateful to the shades of Cotton, Arundel, the Harleys and Wanley. Medieval learning, which had been active in the seventeenth century, had burned very low in the first half of the eighteenth, even in the lifetime of the later of these men, and still more after their deaths. The beginnings of the new medieval school, the Gothic revival in its best sense, owed much to the foundation.[41]

II

MONTAGU HOUSE AND THE FIRST FIFTY YEARS

1. BLOOMSBURY

THE Bloomsbury of today, though much changed and become the Latin Quarter of London (and in the tourist-season its American Quarter as well), still contains houses which stood there when Montagu House became the Museum. Great Russell Street had existed for nearly a century, having been built about 1670, but it was still the end of the town in that direction. The parish of St. George, Bloomsbury, was cut out of the squalid parish of St. Giles-in-the-Fields, which lay to the South;[1] but to the North were only open fields, across which the hills of Hampstead and Highgate were seen in the distance. So empty indeed were the fields to the North that they were a favourite duelling-ground.[2]

Montagu House was the chief glory of Bloomsbury; it was one of the four houses in London which Pierre Jean Grosley thought comparable to the hotels of the nobility in Paris, and the only one he described.[3] Further West was the house (No. 99) later inhabited by Topham Beauclerk, who, according to Horace Walpole, "built a library which reaches half-way to Highgate. Everybody," adds Walpole, "goes to see it. It has put the Museum's nose quite out of joint." To the East, apparently on the site of the ancient Hall of the Lords of the Manor, the de Blemonds, stood another great town house, though not so splendid as Montagu House. This was Southampton House, afterwards, by way of the marriage of an heiress, to become Bedford House, which occupied till 1800, when it was destroyed and its land built over, the North side of Bloomsbury Square. The Square, one of the first of its kind, was built about the same time as Great Russell Street by the Earl of Southampton.[4] It speedily became not only fashionable but, it would seem, a kind of precursor of Harley Street, for the three most famous and prosperous physicians of the next half-century lived in it: Dr. Richard

MONTAGU HOUSE AND THE FIRST FIFTY YEARS

Mead (till he moved a couple of hundred yards East to the site where the Children's Hospital now stands in Great Ormond Street), Dr. John Radcliffe, and Sir Hans Sloane himself. It is curious that all three are names venerated in libraries; Mead, it is true, made no foundation, his library being dispersed after his death in 1754; but, as befitted one who "more than any man lived in the broad sunshine of life," he was a great and a generous book-lover, and his sale was one of the chief book-collectors' events of the century; while in the Radcliffe Library and Camera at Oxford and in the British Museum are the memorials of the other two. Sloane's collections, which he had taken with him to his country house (as it was then) at Chelsea, thus returned to a spot very near their earlier home.

2. MONTAGU HOUSE

The original Montagu (or Montague) House was designed by Robert Hooke in 1674 and completed four years later for Ralph, afterwards the first Duke of Montagu.[5] It was in the French style, with a large "court of honour," flanked by lower pavilion wings and screened from the street by a colonnaded wing and cupola-crowned gate.[6] This house had but a short existence, for it was destroyed by fire in the night of January 18th, 1686. Evelyn in his Diary for the next day says that it was "burnt to the ground." According to Dallaway,[7] this was during the residence of the French Ambassador, with whom Montagu, then English Ambassador at Versailles, had temporarily changed houses, and after the fire it was agreed that the Court of France should bear half the cost of rebuilding, upon condition that the architect and painters employed should be French. Dallaway adds that "the object avowed was, to teach the English how a perfect palace should be constructed and embellished"; but this avowal, if expressed, was merely diplomatic, since the new house, erected (it is doubtfully stated) by Pierre Puget, was an almost exact copy of Hooke's, and was no doubt erected on the old foundations and existing walls. Houses are rarely burnt to the ground, and outlying buildings almost never; it is certain that Hooke's gate and screen

39

THE LIBRARY OF THE BRITISH MUSEUM

were unaltered.[8] This second house became the Museum and stood till 1845.

Externally the main block, 216 feet long and 57 high, lay back from but parallel to the street, and was joined to the colonnaded curtain-wall and cupola-crowned *porte-cochère* on the street by lower pavilion wings, which were used for official residences—a plan followed in the present building. A very fine courtyard was thus formed. Before the main door there was, again as in the later building, a dignified flight of steps. The North face, broken by a similar flight of steps, looked over a low garden-wall across the large seven-acre lawn, covering the whole site now occupied by Smirke's buildings and the additions to it;[9] to the West was a grove of limes. An excellent view is to be seen in Paul Sandby's aquatint of the encampment in the garden during the Gordon riots of 1780;[10] at ordinary times it presented no doubt a much more decorous appearance, for admission was obtained only by ticket, and that only by persons "of condition." The staff, moreover, was, as we shall see, not only very small, but exclusively composed of grave physicians and clergymen of ripe years. Nor were they free at all times to walk there; there is a well-known tradition that one day, soon after the opening, Dr. Peter Templeman, the Keeper of the Reading Room, finding his charge dreary (and possibly empty of readers) walked out to take the air, only to be driven in by a Trustee with the words "Go back, Sir!"

Templeman's truancy was not surprising, for the Reading Room (of which more in its proper place) was in the lower ground floor, occupying the room in the South-West angle of that floor, and was dark. The two main or state-room floors of the interior were much better lit by high French windows, and were reached by a beautiful main staircase, decorated by Lafosse and Charles Rousseau, and much admired by Grosley and indeed by all.

Roughly the arrangement of the library was, printed books on the lower and manuscripts on the upper floor. On the lower floor Sloane's printed books filled the whole range of rooms on the North front except that that at the West end held the printed part of the Royal Library, the rest of which occupied a small room adjoining the former and a room on the South front to the East of the vestibule.

MONTAGU HOUSE AND THE FIRST FIFTY YEARS

To the East of this last again was Major Edwards's Library,[11] and in the small room at the East end corresponding to the small Royal Library room at the West were placed gifts made and books deposited by the Stationers' Company in the reign of George II (a space which must have been very small and in fact a measure of the Trustees' ideas of growth), and here the Trustees held their meetings. On the upper floor were the MSS.: from the West, Room I held the Royal and Cotton, II the Harleian Biblical MSS. and English medals, III other Harleian MSS., IV Harleian Charters, etc., V Sloane medals, and VI Sloane MSS. A room at the West end of the lower ground floor or "base story" was appropriated to those who came to the Museum for reading or closer examination of objects, and was the earliest ancestor of all the Reading and Students' Rooms of today. The rest of the lower ground floor was used for storage of duplicates and objects of minor importance, and one must have been used for binding, since the Act was always taken to forbid sending anything out of the precincts.[12]

3. The Departments and Officers

The five years which elapsed between the acquisition of Montagu House and the opening of the Museum to the public were no doubt fully occupied in the tasks, first of repairing and furnishing the house and then of arranging the collections. These were divided into three Departments, of Printed Books, of Manuscripts, and of "Natural and Artificial Productions." "Artificial Productions," the nucleus of the later vast accumulation of objects of antiquity and art, were an insignificant appendage to Sloane's collection of natural history. Coins and medals were not included with them; traditionally and correctly they were regarded as inscribed documents and therefore a proper part of a library,[13] and were incorporated with the manuscripts. Most of them had in fact been Cotton's.

During this period admittance was given to one or two enquirers and from time to time to well-introduced visitors. Thus in August, 1756, Miss Catherine Talbot wrote to Bishop Berkeley's widow describing an evening spent there. So far only two or three rooms of

MSS. had been arranged. "In a reverie," she says, "I looked upon the books in a different view, and consider'd them (some persons in whose hands I saw them suggested the thought) as a storehouse of arms, open to any rebel hand, a shelf of sweetmeats mixed with poison, set in the reach of tall overgrown children. A number of learned and deserving persons," she continues, "are made happy by the places bestowed on them to preserve and show this fine Collection. These have comfortable apartments in the wings, and a philosophic grove and physick garden open to the view of a delightful country, where at leisure hours they may improve their health and their studies together."[14]

These learned and deserving persons, the Museum's first officers, were appointed in this year 1756. They numbered seven. The salaries were very small, though free apartments were given in addition, and hours were short, but even so the Trustees' small income was strained; the Principal Librarian received per annum £160 and further £40 as Receiver, later called Expenditor.

The first royal nominee to the Principal Librarian's, the only statutory, post, was Gowin Knight, M.D. (1713–72). Knight, who had some reputation for his writings and experiments in magnetism and the compass, had in 1753 unsuccessfully competed against one of his future masters, Birch, for the Secretaryship of the Royal Society. Possibly tempted by the smallness of his official salary, he engaged in invention and speculation, taking out in 1760 a successful patent for a dwarf venetian blind. Inevitably he fell into money difficulties, and in 1772 he died in debt, fortunately without scandal. The portrait of him by Benjamin Wilson suggests an amiable man of inferior mental calibre; but that the Museum knew no great development under him was hardly his fault.

The men under him in the Library were: Printed Books: Keeper, Matthew Maty, M.D.; Assistant Keeper: the Rev. Samuel Harper; Manuscripts: Keeper, Charles Morton, M.D.; Assistant Keeper: the Rev. Andrew Gifford (succeeded in 1785 by the Rev. Richard Southgate); Keeper of the Reading Room: Peter Templeman, M.D. (appointed 1758 and succeeded in 1760 by the Rev. Richard Penneck). The Natural History and Antiquities were under

MONTAGU HOUSE AND THE FIRST FIFTY YEARS

James Empson (*d.* 1765), formerly Sloane's curator, who also acted as Secretary to the Trustees. The first regular Secretary was a successor in the same Department, Edward Whitaker Gray, M.D., appointed in 1787.

Of the group the best known today is Maty (1718–76). His father, a Provencal Huguenot, took refuge in the Low Countries, and thence the son came to England in 1741, with a medical degree from Leyden, and practised in London. He was elected F.R.S. in 1758. He made many friends, amongst others his future colleague Dr. Templeman, and his future Trustee, Birch, whose executor he was and whom he succeeded in 1765 as Secretary of the Royal Society, having been its Foreign Secretary since 1762. His public reputation was made by his *Journal Britannique*, a critical review of English books for foreign readers, which he founded and produced from 1750 onwards. What is most easily remembered about Maty, however, is neither his friendships nor his writings, but his one recorded enmity, or rather that borne him by Johnson, who (excepting him from his general affection for the medical profession) called him a "little black dog" and was prepared to throw him into the Thames. There appear to have been at least two reasons for this. Maty was a friend of Gibbon, to whom he was of considerable assistance in publishing his first work, the *Essai sur l'Etude de la Littérature*. Moreover he was a protégé of Chesterfield, whom he attended professionally and successfully for the gout, and of whose works he undertook, but did not live to complete, the posthumous edition, contributing a life, and in the *Journal Britannique* he took Chesterfield's part over the affair of Chesterfield's omission to patronize Johnson's *Dictionary*—an affair of which, it may be said, posterity has been led to form its opinion less by the merits of the case than by the merits of Johnson's prose, and indeed by the merits of Johnson himself.

Maty was transferred to the Department of Natural and Artificial Productions on Empson's death in 1765, and on Gowin Knight's death in 1772 was appointed Principal Librarian; he lived to hold the office for four years.

Of Harper, Maty's assistant and successor in the Printed Books, not much is known, though he continued there till 1803, when he died, the last survivor of the first under-librarians. He was of Trinity College, Cambridge (B.A., 1754 and M.A., 1757), was elected F.R.S. in 1766 and became Chaplain to the neighbouring Foundling Hospital about the same year. If Venn identifies him rightly (*Alumni Cant.*, vol. ii), he was a pluralist, holding a curacy at Gamston, Notts, and from 1775 the Vicarage of Rothwell, Leeds. He edited the first Catalogue of the Printed Books.

Harper was followed as Assistant Keeper in the Printed Books successively by the Rev. Andrew Planta (transferred from the Natural History), 1765–73, his son Joseph Planta, 1773–76, afterwards Principal Librarian, Matthew Maty's son, the Rev. P. H. Maty,[15] 1776–82, the Rev. C. G. Woide, 1782–90, and then by one who left more mark on the place than all these except the younger Planta, the Rev. Samuel Ayscough (1787–1804). Born in 1745, the grandson of Nottingham's first printer, Ayscough had been left as a boy, owing to his father's speculations, to help his ruined family by labouring at a mill. Entering Rivington's he found, like Johnson, what education a good bookshop can give, and developed a passion for cataloguing and indexing; he indexed Bridges' *Northamptonshire*, Manning's *Surrey* and the *Gentleman's Magazine*, and published a Concordance of Shakespeare. Before he joined the regular staff he had produced in 1782 the catalogue of the Sloane, Birch and Additional MSS., arranged according to a classification of his own, and the first catalogue of Rolls and Charters, and had begun on that of the Printed Books, of which, when it appeared in 1787, about one-third was his work. He was ordained about 1780, and served under his colleague Southgate as Assistant Curate of St. Giles-in-the-Fields.[16]

Like Maty, who was two years his junior, Morton took his degree at Leyden, the dominant Medical School of the time. His must have been the more important position of the two, for not only were the collections in his charge of far greater value than those in Maty's, but he was set to finish the catalogue of the Harleian MSS., which Wanley and his successors had nearly completed. Morton finished the work in a manner no more exacting than that of Wanley's successors, and it was published in two handsome folio volumes in 1759; he added an introduction in 1762.

MONTAGU HOUSE AND THE FIRST FIFTY YEARS

Morton was F.R.S. (1762) and F.S.A., for his writings combined physiology and philology; in the latter field, and most closely allied to his work in the Museum, is his edition of *Bernard's Engraved Tablet of Alphabets*, 1759.[17] He succeeded Maty as Principal Librarian in 1776, and died in 1799 at the age of 83.

Gifford (1700–84) was the Museum's first numismatist, and also (to the credit of its earliest Archbishop Trustee) a Baptist minister, as his grandfather and father had been before him at Bristol. He took his D.D. at Aberdeen in 1754, and was an F.S.A. He was also the first, and not the last, member of the Museum staff to be a collector of antiquities (coins, books, MSS., pictures and "curiosities") and nevertheless not to leave his collection to the Museum. He was able to collect, for he married a wife of considerable substance, who predeceased him, and he died *sine prole*, except for his large collection, and that he bequeathed to the Baptist College of Bristol. It was hardly felt in his time that the Museum should be made representative by filling its gaps; the collections were rich indeed, but a fortuitous concourse. The conception of methodically illustrating all branches of a science by collecting had hardly dawned. Is it fanciful to think that it was developed by the classifying spirit of Linnaeus, whose best pupil, Daniel Solander, entered the Museum as Assistant in Natural History in 1765? By 1771, however, that intelligent person Mr. Matthew Bramble expressed the wish that the series of medals might be connected, and the whole of the animal, vegetable and mineral kingdoms completed by adding to each at the public expense articles that were wanting, and also all books of a character not found there, which might be classed in centuries and catalogues printed of them—a remarkable prevision, which he declared was idle speculation, never to be reduced to practice;[18] a beginning of such a series of catalogues was made a little more than a century later.

Gifford's collection, however, included at least one possession that he should have known better than to let go elsewhere. This was a group of the fragments of the famous Cotton Genesis—surely Trustees' property; they have luckily returned in late years (see below, p. 230).

Gifford seems to have been an extremely genial and popular person.

45

His only publication of consequence was his edition for the Society of Antiquaries of Folke's *Tables of English Silver and Gold Coins*, 2 vols., 1763.

When Gifford died, a numismatist was found in the Rev. Richard Southgate (1749–94 or 1795). Southgate had been for twenty years before his appointment in 1785, and continued till his death to be, Curate of St. Giles-in-the-Fields, and left there a fragrant memory for his extraordinary goodness to the very poor and wretched with whom that sordid parish abounded. He was expert in Old English coins.

In the Reading Room from 1758 to 1760, when he went to be Secretary of the newly founded Society of Arts, presided another Leyden M.D., Peter Templeman (1711–69). He also had a Cambridge degree (Trinity), and there acquired a reputation as a scholar. His modern languages were unusually good, and we have seen that he was a friend of Maty's early days in London.

Templeman was succeeded in 1760 by another Trinity man, the Rev. Richard Penneck, who held the office till his death in the same year as Harper's, 1803, and four years later than Morton's, these three being the last survivors of the Museum's earliest years. Penneck was a Cornishman; he obtained his post at the Museum, and also about the same time the incumbencies of St. John's, Horsley Down, and Abinger, Surrey, by the patronage of Lord Godolphin, to whom his father was steward. His scholarship is described as solid and unostentatious. His character is rather a puzzle. At the Museum and elsewhere he had a reputation for amiability, never quarrelling with readers or (like the rest) with colleagues. He had many friends outside the Museum, among them Goldsmith and Cumberland. The writer of his obituary insists not merely on his charitable disposition but upon his diffidence and delicacy.[19] He was a frequent visitor at the Burneys',[20] and is described as "purring after Charlotte like a huge black tomcat," and in 1778 as "breaking his heart because Fanny did not make her fortune by *Evelina*." Yet he could produce a very different impression. When he was first introduced into that friendly household by his colleague the younger Maty, Fanny found "the famous Mr. Penneck perfectly sombre," and again "dark and design-

MONTAGU HOUSE AND THE FIRST FIFTY YEARS

ing and perfectly ill-favoured," and "half a madman," and she tells the tale of his having, in jealousy over Miss Miller, the actress, knocked down Colman the actor who, according to her, was half his height.[21] More justifiably he had repressed one Adair, who in a quarrel with him (also at a theatre) had handed him his card with words "my name is Adair, Sir," with the reply "I hear it and am not terrified."[22] This side of Penneck's character may perhaps be partly accounted for by hereditary gout, which for months of every year "disabled him from active exertion" and may well have hastened the Trustees' provision in 1778 of reliefs in the Reading Room from the Departmental Under-Librarians, though active physical exertion, other than much standing, is hardly even today required of the Superintendent.[23]

4. PUBLICATIONS AND ACQUISITIONS

Between the foundation of the Museum and the death of Morton at the end of the century there was little feverish activity, and it must be stated that some of the Under-Librarians soon ceased to be, in Miss Talbot's phrase, "made happy by their places," and found leisure for not very seemly disputes over their quarters in the wings.[24] The officers were only bound to attend for two six-hour days in the week, and even that seemed to the Trustees to require an apologetic justification. In a Minute of 21st June, 1759, the Standing Committee informed them: "The Committee think proper to add that the requiring the attendance of the officers during the whole of the six hours that the Museum is open is not a wanton or useless piece of severity, as the two vacant hours [i.e. vacant from the conducting of visitors] (if it is not thought too great a burden upon the officers) might very usefully be employed by them in better ranging the several collections especially in the Department of Manuscripts [where, one would suppose, they least needed it], and preparing catalogues for publication, which last the Committee think so necessary a work that till it is performed the several collections can be but imperfectly useful to the public." Two years after this pathetic appeal the Trustees were apparently converted by their Officers, for they then reduced the required attendance to two hours a day on two and three days in alternate weeks, extra work being paid extra.

The only publications of this first period, thus desiderated by the Trustees, were the three catalogues (of which more in their places) (1) of the Harleian MSS., 1759–[62], much the larger part of which (as we have noted) had been prepared before 1753; (2) of the Sloane, Birch and the few Additional MSS. to date, 1782, by Ayscough, before his appointment, and (3) of the Printed Books, 1787, which was undertaken by the Trustees' order as early as 1771, and commenced printing in 1780. Ayscough also indexed all the Charters and Rolls, but this was not published. And Thomas Astle, a Trustee, compiled a catalogue of the Cotton MSS., which was published independently of the Trustees by Samuel Hooper in 1777.

The cataloguing of the collections was very summary, however, in the case of the Printed Books by the Trustees' special order. At the same time, soon after 1784, the staff of the Printed Books had another large task, the rearrangement in a single "synthetical arrangement," drawn up by Ayscough, of all the books except the King's Pamphlets, the Musgrave collection, and, when it came in 1799, the Cracherode. This work was only finished about 1805.

Few considerable additions were made during this period, after the Royal Library came in 1757. Da Costa gave his Hebrew books in 1759 and George III the Thomason Traçts in 1762. Birch bequeathed his biographical MSS. in 1765, and with them a sum in the funds to provide a small annual addition to the salaries of the three Under-Librarians, still received by their successors. Garrick bequeathed his wonderful collection of English playbooks in 1779, and they were received the next year.[25] Playbooks, rejected by Sir Thomas Bodley from the Bodleian as "baggage books" which would discredit a serious library, were even in Garrick's day not much collected, though the King had begun to gather the fine series which was to come to the Museum half a century later. Many playbooks, some said to be unique, had perished in the famous conflagration lighted by John Warburton's maid Betsey. In 1780 the Museum was almost as empty of them as the Bodleian of 1603 had been.

Smaller but valuable gifts or bequests, such as Speaker Onslow's

Bibles, 1768, William Cole's Cambridgeshire and Sir William Burrell's Sussex MSS. (1785 and 1796), the former bequeathed under the condition that they were not to be opened for twenty years after the testator's death (a period which had elapsed by 1802), Sir William Musgrave's books and MSS. (like Birch's, in British biography), Tyrwhitt's classical books, Sir Joseph Banks's first gifts, those of his Icelandic books, manuscript and printed, 1773 and 1783, and the Methuen Italian and Portuguese books, 1792, even taken with the larger acquisitions mentioned and with the cataloguing, were hardly enough to create any continuous stir in Montagu House. Some ripples must have been caused, however, by the gifts of "paper-sparing" Pope's original draft of his Homer, largely written on the backs of letters received by him, and of the Articles of Magna Carta, presented respectively by Mrs. Lucy Mallet in 1766 and Earl Stanhope in 1769, and by the acquisition about the former date of Swift's Journal to Stella. There was no great addition till Cracherode's library, prints and gems were bequeathed in 1799.

There was as yet no idea of methodically enforcing on the Museum's behalf the right of copyright deposit previously claimed by the Crown for the Royal Library, and such purchasing as funds could be found for was confined to the necessary current literature of learning. It seems, however, not to be true that no books at all were deposited by the Stationers' Company.

5. FINANCES

Funds were the Trustees' great difficulty. The foundation reserve of £30,000 yielded an income far too small for any real activity, too small even for decent quiescence.[26] To commence publication of the two handsome folio volumes of the Harleian Catalogue in the first year of full existence was a bold act (see below, p. 51). In a well-known letter to Mason (23rd July, 1759), Gray says of the Trustees, "I find that they printed one thousand copies of the Harleian Catalogue, and have sold four score; that they have £900 a year income and spend £1,300 and that they are building apartments for the under keepers, so I expect in winter to see the collection advertised, and set to auction."

Gray was not far out, but he was indulging in agreeable exaggeration. The income from the reserve was £900; but to that was to be added, after the death or other "avoidance" of the holder, Claudius Amyand, which took place in 1774, £249, the net value of the Royal Librarian's appointment (gross £300, fees being deducted) which had been given with the library, and there was the hope, also not realized for a number of years, of the reversion of Major Edwards's £7,000.[27] In 1762 the Trustees made their first petition to Parliament for assistance, which is now an annual form; from that year till 1772 they were given a grant of £2,000 every other year, in 1775 and 1777 £3,000, in 1780 £3,500, and in 1782 £3,000 again; from these sums also fees were deducted.[28] In 1777 Wilkes found leisure of mind from his motion to expunge the resolution expelling him from the House, which he moved next day, to defend the Museum's Vote with vigour; and Burke bettered him by proposing (without success, except over those who wished to reduce it) an amendment raising the vote to £5,000.[29]

The Trustees' Annual Income and Expense Account was first presented at the Bar of the House (by Empson) in 1762, but the first published accounts appeared in 1777, covering the previous decade. The total income was made up of the dividends from the original £30,000, i.e. £900 and net salary of the King's Librarian, £249, to £1,149; but expenses never fell below £1,876, and in 1773, owing to large repairs, rose to £2,661.

To meet this regular deficiency the Parliamentary grant, producing about £900 net a year at first, and later about £1,200, was hardly enough. The accounts for 1783 show how £2,185 was spent;[30] £937 went in salaries and wages, £217 in rent[31] and taxes, and £208 in binding. Purchases had the special Edwards fund, limited to that purpose, which, invested in Old South Sea Annuities, brought in £300 a year, after Mrs. Milles's life-interest expired in 1769. In 1770, accordingly, we find an item, absent in 1767, of £227 for purchases of foreign books, whereas in the first fourteen years the total outgoing on purchases had been only £69, as against £23,215 spent in the same period on the establishment.[32] English books were deliberately not bought at all for many decades. To this income for purchases (which, be it remembered, included natural history and antiquities also) there was added a new occasional source in the form of the sale of duplicate books and coins. The practice was authorized by Parliament in 1767 (6 Geo. III, c. 18) in the anticipation that "great additions will hereafter be made" to the Museum's collections. The Trustees were there authorized to "exchange, sell or dispose of" duplicates; it was laid down that the proceeds must be spent on purchases for the collections. The first sale was held two years later, and realized £564 4s.; the second, in 1788, brought £529 14s. 9d. gross. On binding the Trustees had spent £1,388 by 1767, probably on the Royal Library, which had received its copyright copies from Stationers' Hall in sheets. The garden cost them apparently about £100 a year. Printing, except for small amounts, probably accounted for by the Statutes, tickets and the like, is curiously absent. That the Harleian Catalogue was really published by the booksellers whose names appear on its title-pages might be surmised; but the Trustees held the stock. The Sloane and Cotton Catalogues were not official, but that of Printed Books was.

6. The Reading Room

Before the Reading Room was opened occasional scholars were given access; we know that Robertson the historian was introduced by Birch. The first room, used till 1774 for the purpose, was "a large vaulted apartment,"[33] but had only two windows. It was uncarpeted and the windows ill-framed, and it was damp. It was opened on the same day as the Exhibition Rooms, tickets having been issued three days before to eight scholars, nearly all Fellows of the Royal Society or of the Society of Antiquaries or of both. One of these was the second Earl of Hardwicke's (then Lord Royston's) secretary, Edward Langton,[34] another Royston's old friend and collaborator with him and his brother Charles Yorke in *The Athenian Letters* (1741), Daniel Wray, afterwards a Trustee:[35] three were learned divines, Dr.

THE LIBRARY OF THE BRITISH MUSEUM

Robert Lowth, Prebendary of Durham, afterwards Bishop of London, Dr. John Taylor, Canon of St. Paul's, and Dr. Samuel Chandler, a Nonconformist; two, Samuel Musgrave, a physician, and Taylor White, who had special "permission to send for Books containing specimens of Cinnamon and Cassia," kept up the scientific side of the founders' intentions; while Classical antiquities and the fine arts were represented by "Athenian" Stuart.

To these were added a few more each year, and they included the most learned men of the time. Most notable was Gray, the poet, who came in 1759, and in his letters wrote satirical accounts not only of the Trustees' finances (as quoted above), but also of the Reading Room.[36] Blackstone, Alban Butler, Heberden ("ultimus Romanorum, the last of the learned physicians"), Dr. John Burton of York (the Dr. Slop of *Tristram Shandy*, but in fact another learned physician, then working on his *Monasticon Eboracense*) and Stukeley the antiquary, who was Rector of the neighbouring parish of St. George's, Queen's Square, came in the same year. On the following 8th May, Johnson was admitted on Morton's recommendation. It has been rather rashly assumed that Johnson never went to the Museum; little as he liked Maty, that was hardly reason enough. His prayer, "On entering Novum Musaeum," refers not to the Museum but to his own library. He certainly knew Penneck, as he wrote canvassing him in Thrale's interest before the Borough election of 1768; but he may have met him at the Burneys'. But Johnson was at no time an industrious user of libraries, even at Oxford, preferring conversation with librarians, and at this period, according to Murphy, he was "living in poverty, total idleness, and the pride of literature." His Dictionary was behind him and his Shakespeare a good way off before him; in 1760 Boswell tells us (ed. Hill-Powell, i, 354) that Johnson "had a floating intention of writing a history of the recent and wonderful successes of the British Arms in all quarters of the globe," and quotes from his *Prayers and Meditations* the resolution on 18th September, 1760, to "send for books for Hist. of war." Readers of the early years included in 1769 the learned but eccentric Scotch law lord, Monboddo, whom Johnson loved to deride, but also to meet, in 1771 Burke and Hargrave, whose law library later came to the Museum, in 1781 Francis

MONTAGU HOUSE AND THE FIRST FIFTY YEARS

Douce, and in 1783 a public friend, like Burke, of the Museum Library, Wilkes.

Tyrwhitt worked there on texts of Chaucer: the Museum was already becoming a rival to the Bodleian as a place of pilgrimage and resort for the small but important world of historical and literary research, which included some amateurs such as Horace Walpole and Topham Beauclerk. Women made their appearance very early, but if not in single spies in pairs,37 and their modern battalions would have been one of the greatest surprises to the eighteenth-century readers, could they have foreseen them. In 1762 two, Lady Mary Carr and Lady Ann Monson, and a year later Catherine Macaulay, were admitted; the last became a regular reader. Foreigners were from the beginning, as they have never ceased to be, welcome readers. Gray mentions two Prussians. Grosley says that when he was there, about 1770, the Cotton MSS. were being examined by M. de Bréquigny of the Académie Royale des Belles Lettres; and after the French Revolution émigrés were frequent, as they are today. Gray's first sight of the Room was a favourable one; it was often nearly empty, and sometimes it was completely deserted; Templeman was so far from "congratulating himself on the sight of good company" that on one occasion, as we have seen, he walked in the garden, and on at least one other, "the Room being cold and the weather likely to rain," he retired about one o'clock (closing time being at three) to his lodgings in the courtyard—at least one hopes no further. On the other hand Gray observes that "the stillness and solitude of the reading room is uninterrupted by anything but Dr. Stukeley the antiquary, who comes there to talk nonsense and coffee house news." Dr. Stukeley's practice unfortunately did not die with him; nonsense and the modern counterpart of "coffee house news" have been known to annoy the Room more recently. In 1778 the number of readers had little increased, if at all; Rymsdyk comments on the matter: "I have wondered many times at the small number of gentlemen I used to see in the Reading Room, which certainly must be owing to the want of knowing how to apply for leave."38 Access to the Room had in fact been somewhat facilitated by the Trustees in the summer of 1760 by remitting the power of granting admission to the Principal Librarian when there was no quorum at the Trustees' monthly meetings, and in particular cases between meetings. Their views were more liberal than the small use made of the Room then and later would suggest, and their resolution on the subject deserves to be quoted:39

"As the admission into the Reading Room is by all the regulations hitherto made, entirely left to the Committee, they think it necessary to observe that the liberty of studying in the Museum is the part of this Institution from which the Publick is like to reap the greater benefit; and that, therefore, admission into the Reading Room should be made as convenient as possible: that as the number of persons applying for the liberty of the Reading Room, or at least of those making use of it when granted, has not hitherto caused any inconvenience; the only case necessary at present, is to prevent improper persons from being admitted: though the case may possibly be very different hereafter, when the number of applications may make it necessary to levy some restraints, as to the number of persons to whom such leave shall be granted: that the Meetings of the Committee may not be sufficient to answer the convenience of the Publick. ... It is therefore submitted to the General Meeting whether there is not a necessity of vesting in the Principal Librarian a power of granting admission into the Reading Room when there is not a sufficient number present to form a Committee on their days of meeting; and in particular cases during the interval of the stated meetings of the Committee."

But Isaac D'Israeli, describing (in *The Illustrator Illustrated*) the Reading Room as he knew it in 1786, reveals no improvement. "It had been difficult," he says, "to have made up a jury of all the Spirits of study which haunted the reading room. There we were, little attended to, musing in silence and oblivion; for sometimes we had to wait a day or two, till the volumes so eagerly demanded slowly appeared."

When the first room was abandoned in 1774 on Penneck's representations as to its dampness and darkness, and bad effect on his health, the N.W. corner room on the main ground floor was adapted for the purpose. This room was a great improvement. It was dry and light, and its walls were clothed with bookcases and hung with portraits. The six hours' day attendance ordered by the Trustees in 1764 and again in 1768 and 1769 could no longer reasonably be a grievance. It was, however, made into one, perhaps because of the short hours worked by the Under-Librarians and Assistants since 1761. In 1787 the Trustees reduced the Superintendent's hours to two-thirds, and ordered that the remaining third should be performed by the three Assistants in rotation; they were to have £40 a year extra between them for the duty.

III

NEW WINE AND AN OLD BOTTLE

1. Changes after 1799

THE year 1799 was marked by two noteworthy acquisitions, one was Clayton Mordaunt Cracherode's bequest of his choice and beautiful printed books, raising the reputation of the Museum for the possession of the earliest editions of the classics and of specimens of the first presses, which were then attracting private collectors, but had little attracted the creators of the Museum's foundation libraries. The books were placed in a special room (see below, pp. 183–5). Cracherode had been elected a Trustee in 1784 at the same time as his friend Thomas Tyrwhitt, also a benefactor.[1] Then another Trustee, Sir William Musgrave, who died in the same year as Cracherode, added to a gift of 1790 the whole of his collections, printed and manuscript, in British biography. The printed books numbered some 2,000 and included many rare fugitive pieces. They are dispersed in the Old Library, except so far as their subject keeps them together; but many are recognizable by his bold signature.

In this year and the next four the little band of officers underwent sweeping changes. In 1799 Morton died, full and overfull of years, and was succeeded by Joseph Planta, Keeper of MSS., in which office he was followed by Robert Nares (1753–1829), the philologist and author of the Glossary to Shakespeare. In 1803 Harper died and was succeeded by William Beloe, and he by Henry Ellis in 1806; in the next year Nares and Ellis were succeeded by Francis Douce and Henry Hervey Baber; the latter held his office for a longer and much more important period than Nares or Beloe. When Baber became head of the Printed Books, he was followed as Assistant by H. W. Bedford, who had been engaged as an Extra Assistant in 1805, after Ayscough's death and Ellis's promotion to a regular Under-Librarianship.[2]

Joseph Planta's father Andrew had been Under-Librarian in the

NEW WINE AND AN OLD BOTTLE

Natural History Department till his death in 1773; he was minister of the Reformed German Church in London and a reader to Queen Charlotte. By this last means Joseph, after studying abroad, had been employed as Secretary to the British Minister at Brussels. At the age of twenty-nine, on his father's death, he was appointed Under-Librarian in the Printed Books, being at the same time appointed Secretary of the Royal Society in succession to Maty; and three years later, on Morton's accession to the Principal Librarianship, he was promoted to the charge of the Manuscripts, which he held till 1793.

He was almost the only Museum officer of the eighteenth century who was neither a cleric nor a physician, and he seems to have been more a man of the world than the rest, and also an unusually good linguist. Edwards[3] speaks of his "eminent courtesy of manners," and Nares of his "unaffected urbanity"[4]; these qualities had apparently also marked his father. His diplomatic and court experience and connexions were no doubt of assistance to the Museum.[5] Diplomatic experience is evident in the reply which he made in 1814 to the Czar, whom he was conducting round the Museum during the visit of the Allied sovereigns to London, and who commented on the small size of the national library: "Mais, sire, tout est payé ici"; a keen thrust, seeing that the great Zaluski Library had been forcibly removed from Warsaw to St. Petersburg just twenty years before. Planta was more than urbane; he was also liberal-minded, and promoted easier access to the exhibitions and Reading Room. Not forgetful of his Swiss origin, he published a *History of the Helvetic Confederacy*, 2 vols., 1800, and a supplementary *View of the Restoration of the Helvetic Confederacy*, 1807. It was very probably to obtain materials for this that he sought leave of the Principal Trustees in 1788 to go abroad, but was prevented by the Lord Chancellor's refusal.[6]

The careers of most of the young men who entered the Museum in the early years of Planta's reign will occupy us later; a few biographical details may be given here.

Henry Ellis (1777–1869), later to be Sir Henry and Planta's successor, had enjoyed a remarkable reputation even as an undergraduate; Samuel Denne wrote of him in 1797 to Nichols (*Ill. Lit. Hist.* vi. 689) as "the juvenile antiquary of St. John's College,

Oxon," and employed him to search the muniments of the Colleges for the early use of Arabic numerals. He began as an Assistant in the Bodleian in 1798, and two years later took a temporary post in the Printed Books at the Museum. He was appointed to a regular Under-Librarianship in 1805, after Ayscough's death, and on the dismissal of William Beloe in the next year succeeded to the Keepership. Transferred to the Manuscripts in 1812, he nevertheless continued to work on the Catalogue of Printed Books which began to appear in the following year. In 1814 he assisted the Principal Librarian as Secretary, and in 1827 was his obvious successor.[7] Holding office through the storms of the next quarter of a century, he did not retire till 1856.[8]

Ellis seems to have been as devoid as a man well can be of the combative spirit. Thrust into the background, as we shall see, by the active Forshall, he was, as Richard Garnett, who knew him, tells us, "seemingly unconscious of any change in his position"; and he bore no malice against the equally forceful Panizzi, who, in exasperation at the condition of things, attacked his work on the Printed Books Catalogue with quite needless acrimony.

As industrious as cheerful and talkative (a rare combination of qualities in any post, and in a librarian's as rare as anywhere), Ellis did a great deal of work both in and out of the Museum. In 1814 he became Secretary to the Antiquaries, and he did an immense amount of work for the Society in *Archaeologia* and otherwise. His historical writings retain their importance. Best known are the charming *Original Letters illustrative of English History* (three series, 1824, 1827, and 1846), based on originals among the Museum's MSS.; but most important perhaps is his edition of the *Additamenta* to Domesday Book, 1816, especially the introduction, written in 1813 and published separately in 1833. He was also one of the editors of Dugdale's *Monasticon*, 1817–30.

The Rev. Henry Hervey Baber (1775–1869) was, being two years the senior, already an Assistant in the Bodleian when Ellis entered it. When Ellis became Keeper of Printed Books at the Museum Baber took his place as Assistant Librarian, and followed him as Keeper when he went over to the Manuscripts. The work of the pair on the octavo catalogue of 1813–19 was therefore not a new collaboration for them. The fact that Baber was on excellent terms not only with the amiable Ellis and the approachable Principal Librarian, but also with Panizzi, to whom competence meant everything and seniority nothing, speaks highly for him; and in fact the troubles of his later years in the Library were due to the Trustees' neglect of his recommendations. The vagueness of the line drawn in that period betwen Departments and their specialisms is seen in Baber's having edited the facsimile Old Testament from the Codex Alexandrinus in 1816–28 (the New Testament portion having been edited nearly forty years before by an Assistant in the same Department, C. G. Woide), just as Ellis, and before him Ayscough, worked on the catalogue of printed books while on the staff of the Department of Manuscripts.

Having since 1827 held the Rectory of Stretham, Cambridgeshire, Baber resigned his Museum post in 1837, partly because the Parliamentary Committee of the preceding year had recommended that salaries should be improved and the simultaneous holding of other paid posts disallowed. Cowtan suggests yet another motive, that Baber felt it late in his career to throw himself into the active developments of the Museum resulting from the Committee's Report, and it is probable that the high-handed behaviour of Forshall, the new whole-time Secretary, was not without its influence.[9] Though elderly, Baber was far from spent, and lived as a country Rector for another thirty-two years.

The Rev. William Beloe's Museum career was brief and unfortunate, lasting only from 1803 till 1806.[10] Francis Douce's career in the Museum was also short. Born in 1757, he was an older man than most of his fellow Librarians in the years of his Keepership of Manuscripts, which, following Nares in 1807, he held for only five years. He was already a great collector and student, and in the year of his appointment published his valuable *Illustrations of Shakespeare*. Douce's premature retirement was due, it is said, to a quarrel with a Trustee, but no details are known. He was, except to his intimates, of a rough and strange manner, and the episode may perhaps not be discreditable to the Museum, but discreditable or not it was unlucky, as Douce, who was greatly enriched in 1823 by a legacy from the

59

miserly and wealthy Nollekens, collected on a large scale till his death in 1834 and bequeathed his splendid collection of books, MSS. and works of art to the Bodleian, which published a catalogue of them in 1840. To the Museum he left a box to be opened in 1900; it contained proofs, letters and notes, some of which are of value for tracing the provenance of his possessions. Whether this bequest was intended to be a testator's revenge remains uncertain. The attitude now adopted towards such losses as that of Douce's library is very philosophical; it matters little in which of two great libraries less than a hundred miles apart a collection is preserved.[11]

When Nares became head of the Manuscripts in 1799 he was followed as Assistant by the Rev. Thomas Maurice.[12] Maurice was then a man of forty-five, and a well-known Orientalist, his two large works, *Indian Antiquities* and *History of Hindostan*, being in progress of publication, while his *Sanscreet Fragments* had appeared in the previous year. Before the establishment of a separate Oriental Department of the Library, and especially while the staff was so small, the books and MSS., though not numerous outside Hebrew and Arabic, presented an obvious problem. The Museum's chief Orientalist, Woide, had died in 1790, and his speciality was Sahidic. The Museum had never had, and for long was not to have again, an Indian scholar. When Maurice died in 1824, his successor was Forshall, a Near Eastern Orientalist as well as a good classic.

2. Increase: Gifts and Purchases

Planta's Principal Librarianship was a time of stirring of the quiet waters of the Museum, firstly by acquisitions of great fame and also bulk, which made it necessary to destroy Montagu House and rebuild on a larger scale, and secondly, and especially in the years after Waterloo, by the spread of popular education and with it of interest in the Museum which soon swelled into discontent with the poor service it rendered to the larger intellectual public.

The Cracherode Library had required a separate room in 1799. Three years later the Crown deposited in the charge of the Trustees

NEW WINE AND AN OLD BOTTLE

the splendid and colossal "Alexandrian marbles," as they were called, in other words the Egyptian sculptures collected by the savants whom Napoleon had employed during his occupation of Egypt, and which had fallen to British arms by the surrender of the French army in 1801. They were housed in unsatisfactory sheds. Application was made to Parliament, and a separate building was begun near the North-West corner of the house, designed by George Saunders.[13] The Townley collection of Greek and Roman sculptures was purchased (Parliament's first large purchase for the Museum) in 1805; and additional money was granted for the new building in 1806 and 1808. And in 1815, the Government bought the Phigalian and in the next year the Elgin Marbles and deposited them in the Museum.

Of less bulk and fame than these, but in all ways considerable, were several additions to the Library made in the same period. In 1805, simultaneously with the Townley marbles, there came into the market, on the death of Lord Lansdowne, better known as Lord Shelburne, the very important collection of papers he had formed over a period of fifty years, many of them spent in public life. The Museum was already rich in English historical documents, chiefly derived from Cotton and Harley. They had thrown their nets wider; but Shelburne had practically confined himself to this field. (See below, pp. 248–50). Parliament, approached by the Trustees, voted in 1807 £4,925 for the whole, this only two years after they had voted £20,000 for the Townley marbles as well as £16,000 for building, having before that made only one special grant (£8,410 in 1772 for the Hamilton Antiquities) since the Museum's foundation half a century earlier, which had cost the nation nothing.

In 1813 the widow of the distinguished Parliamentary lawyer, Francis Hargrave, whose mind had failed, petitioned Parliament to buy his library of legal MSS. and printed books. And this the House did for £8,000, and deposited them in the Museum (see below, p. 250). Five years later another similar application, again not by the Trustees, but by the collector's family, was made to Parliament. Charles Burney, D.D., son of the celebrated historian of music and brother of Fanny, was a learned classical, and especially Greek, scholar and textual critic, and in his later life had systematically accumulated a large library of

THE LIBRARY OF THE BRITISH MUSEUM

the best texts of classical authors, MSS. and printed editions, and with them a body of materials for the history of the English stage, and (in our eyes today perhaps most valuable of all) a collection of English seventeenth- and eighteenth-century newspapers. Parliament this time also made the purchase, though reducing the price from £14,000 to £13,500. The printed books numbered from 13,000 to 14,000, the MSS. 525 (see below, pp. 188, 208–9, 251). Three years earlier the Museum had purchased from Burney, by special Parliamentary authority, the collection of books on music formed by his father.

The Natural History Department also attracted acquisitions of bulk as well as importance in these years. In 1815–16 the herbarium and other collections of Baron von Moll, of Munich, were purchased for £4,768. They included a library of over 15,000 volumes. For this purchase the remainder of Major Edwards's bequest was used, the fund being thus extinguished. And in 1820 died Sir Joseph Banks, the great traveller and promoter of scientific exploration and research, and one of the Museum's most active Trustees, as well as the doyen of the Board, having been President of the Royal Society since 1778. Banks bequeathed to the Museum all his collections, including an important library, of which Dryander's catalogue, representing it as it was in 1798–1800, had filled five volumes, and which had increased in the following twenty years. Banks's books did not reach the Museum till the new building was sufficiently advanced (see below, pp. 186–7).

Banks's wife predeceased him by two years and left to the Museum the collections formed by her sister-in-law, Miss (in the form of the time often called Mrs.) Sarah Sophia Banks; these included, with antiquities, a number of books on chivalry.

In 1804 the Printed Books had acquired for £150 the Bibles collected by Dr. Charles Combe; in 1807 there were bought from Richard Cumberland his grandfather, Richard Bentley's books with his annotations; and in 1813 £1,000 was spent on the purchase of a library of modern foreign literature, a class in which the Museum was very weak indeed, though the Old Royal Library had included a fair proportion of Spanish and Italian poets and historians, and the Methuen gift of 1792 had added some Italian and Portuguese books; in spite of

NEW WINE AND AN OLD BOTTLE

later routine purchases, made under Panizzi's influence, it was not strong till the King's and Grenville Library came and the larger grants after 1846 had taken effect. The collection now added was formed for the preparation of his massive *Histoire Littéraire d'Italie* (8 vols, 1811–19) by Pierre Louis Ginguené. It consisted of over 4,300 works, and though its Italian section was specially important, the French was very rich.

Waterloo and the end alike of the Napoleonic war and of the Revolution in France brought to light and into the market a quantity of the fugitive literature of that period, which like the English Civil War and Commonwealth had abounded in pamphlets, fly-sheets and periodicals. At the instigation of John Wilson Croker, the greatest authority in this country on the subject, the Museum bought a large collection of these pieces. It may be noted here that Croker himself commenced to collect French Revolution Tracts, and that two collections of his formation were afterwards bought by the Museum, in 1831 and 1856 (see below, pp. 185–6).

The final stroke, which precipitated building, was when in 1823 King George IV offered to the Government the great library, both antiquarian and general, which his father had begun to collect almost as soon as, coming to the throne, he found himself without a Royal library, that of his ancestors having been presented three years before by his grandfather to the new Museum. Expenditure on the library had been steadily kept up, at the rate of £2,000 a year, by the Regent during George III's years of madness, and it now amounted to 65,000 books and 19,900 unbound pamphlets (see below, pp. 188–93 and 251–2).

The King's Library was followed by some important, if much smaller, collections which enhanced the Museum's importance and helped towards the more truly national position which the Library was now beginning to attain, both in fact and in the public estimation. Three of these, the Hoare, Rich and Hull, came in in 1825.

Sir Richard Colt Hoare, of Stourhead, who had spent some years in Italy, gave nearly two thousand works in Italian local history—the form which before the unification of the Kingdom much later most Italian historical writing naturally took—and he added to this gift in several following years. As their subject-matter ordains, Hoare's books are kept together, but without a special press-mark.

Evidence of the Trustees' want of comprehension of the Museum's functions may be found in their acceptance in 1816 (the year in which they lost the Fitzwilliam collections, see p. 71) of the bequest by the absurd writing master Charles Tomkins of his masterpiece, a copy of Macklin's Bible, pompously decorated with calligraphic ornament, and of Chantrey's head of himself; the head was found in the basement of the Museum over a century later, and for some time defied identification. Tomkins's vanity is derided by Hazlitt in *Table Talk* and by D'Israeli in *The Curiosities of Literature*, but it is to be feared that in this matter of the bequest to the Museum he was not alone in deserving derision.

The Oriental side of the Library, still incorporated in the two Departments of Printed Books and Manuscripts, had had very few additions made to it so far, the Hebrew printed books presented by Solomon da Costa in 1759 being the only substantial earlier acquisition of the sort. The Museum possessed indeed, as Ellis now stated, very few Oriental and no Syriac MSS., while they had of late risen much in value; the chief collections in this country being the Bodleian's, which it owed to Laud and Pococke. Now the Trustees were offered the splendid collection of Near Eastern MSS., Coins and Antiquities, with a few printed books, collected during his short career in the East by the brilliant but short-lived Claudius James Rich. The sixty-eight Syriac MSS. were rich in ancient Peshitto and Nestorian texts of the Scriptures, and in Arabic, Persian and Turkish as well as Syriac the collection was important. The Trustees petitioned the House of Commons, which on the report of the Committee, fortified by the evidence of leading Oriental scholars, bought the whole for £7,500, £2,000 of this being paid for the coins and antiquities[13] (see below, pp. 294–5, 305–6).

The third acquisition of 1825 was the bequest by John Fowler Hull of a small but valuable collection of Chinese and other Eastern printed books.

Five years later the Oriental collections were again enlarged by the purchase from the heirs of Nathan Brassey Halhed of the collec-

NEW WINE AND AN OLD BOTTLE

tion of Sanskrit and other Indian MSS. which he had formed while in India in the service of the East India Company.

In 1827 the Museum's county topographical collections, already rich, were increased by Adam Wolley's bequest of his charters and other Derbyshire MSS., and in the next year by that of Thomas Kerrich's of architectural drawings, including many by James Essex.

In 1831 the Library received two of its most important benefactions of manuscripts, the Egerton and the Arundel. The former was, and has unfortunately remained, with one exception, unique in including, in addition to the manuscripts received at the time, an endowment from which further purchases might be made in perpetuity. This was the Egerton bequest. Francis Henry Egerton, the last Earl of Bridgewater, who died in 1829, was a wealthy and eccentric but benevolent non-practising cleric who lived mainly in Paris, devoted to and surrounded by dogs, but who caused his memory to be honoured by founding the Bridgewater Treatises with the aim of harmonizing religion and science, in which new discoveries were beginning to disturb men's minds, and by his bequest to the Royal Society, and still more by that to the Museum of his collection of manuscripts, with land and residuary estate, ultimately (the land being sold) amounting to £5,000, for augmentation of the collection, as well as £7,000 for the salary of the officer placed in charge of them.[14] Egerton's own manuscripts included a considerable quantity of original and valuable correspondence and papers illustrating French and Italian history, literature and science (see below, pp. 252–4).

The solitary imitator of Egerton, mentioned above, was Charles Long, Lord Farnborough, who in 1838 bequeathed £2,872 to augment the Bridgewater Fund established by Egerton.[15]

The Arundel MSS., 550 in number, were that part of the collection formed by Thomas Howard Earl of Arundel (1592–1646). They were given by Henry Howard in 1666 to the newly founded Royal Society, the other half being given at the same time to the College of Arms, as fell to be recorded in our first chapter. They are rich in materials for medieval English history and French literature, but the larger part are a typical Renaissance collection of classical, Biblical and Church texts, with correspondence of humanists, formed by Bilibaldus

THE LIBRARY OF THE BRITISH MUSEUM

Pirckheimer in the first half of the sixteenth century and bought by the Earl at Nuremberg, in 1636 (see below, pp. 254-6).

Not only could the Trustees now command from the Bridgewater and Farnborough Funds a moderate but steady income to take the place of occasional votes of Parliament for exceptionally important purchases of MSS.; from 1834 they began to receive a regular annual purchase grant, not limited to any Department or class of acquisition. In the following year the printed collection of Spanish history was much strengthened by a purchase from an agent named Rich, and the Museum became a good customer of the leading booksellers, notably Thorpe and Rodd. At the Heber sales, which continued from 1834 to 1837, and were not to be equalled, at least for English books, till the Huth and Britwell libraries were sold nearly a century later, if they were then, the Museum bought many good lots of early English poetry, though William Henry Miller, the founder of Britwell, took most of the best; and advantage was taken of the Hanrott and other London auctions in following years. It is a pity that the nation did not buy the whole vast Heber collection and divide it between the Museum, Oxford and Cambridge; it would have cost about £15,000 apiece for the three, and the books from it bought at the Britwell sales by Mr. Henry E. Huntington (and now well housed in the great library in California which bears his name) fetched enormously higher prices, even if nearly a century's interest be calculated in, for after the "paper-money" crash in 1825—that which ruined Scott and his publishers—books were going cheap. Richard Heber's books were for early printed English literature much what the Harleys' had been for English history.

Two other sources of intake in these years showed increased public interest in the Museum, added to its importance, and strained its capacity.

3. COPYRIGHT

British books had never been bought, unless indeed in the case of occasional books of reference. It is supposed that faith was placed in the theory that the Museum, being the inheritor of the Old Royal

NEW WINE AND AN OLD BOTTLE

Library's rights, was receiving English books from the Stationers' Company. To English provincial, to Scottish and to Irish books even this theoretical right had no relevance at all, and it is a severe condemnation of the eighteenth-century Trustees and of their Principal Librarians and Keepers of Printed Books that for half a century they took no steps in the matter. They were well aware of the situation. As we have seen, part of a small room was set aside at the first arrangement of the Library for books to be deposited by the Company. But the law applied only to books which their publishers registered at Stationers' Hall; and in order to evade deposit the publishers registered only such books as the Deposit Libraries, which had not yet conceived the duty to history of preserving minor literature, would not claim. Planta went so far as to class the copyright books which had reached the Museum among classes of matter which could be turned out, evidence of the poor quality of what had been deposited. But it is not true to say, as has been said, that none were deposited, though we have no exact record of the copyright books received in the early period.[16] The *Synopsis*, first published in 1808, tells us that the Royal Library "has been continued and is still annually increasing by the privilege annexed to it of being supplied with a copy of every publication entered at Stationers' Hall," but adds that "this privilege has of late become very unproductive, partly owing to the frauds of many of the publishers, and still more to the unfavourable construction of the laws respecting literary property."[17]

After the decision of the Supreme Court in 1774 in the case of Donaldson *v.* Becket, by which perpetual copyright was destroyed, there was some agitation to improve deposit. The Universities secured an Act in 1775 (15 Geo. III, c. 53), withholding legal protection from works of which copies had not been deposited in all the nine libraries privileged by the Copyright Act of 1709, i.e. the Royal Library, the Bodleian, Cambridge University, Sion College, the Advocates' and the four Scottish Universities—the influence of the Act of Union of two years earlier being apparent. In 1792–94 Sion College took the matter up, and proposed a joint application by the libraries to Parliament, but nothing came of the proposal. In 1798 the Court of King's Bench decided in Beckford *v.* Hook that, contrary to the common belief, copyright did attach to unregistered books. In 1805 Edward Christian of Cambridge[18] commenced an agitation which lasted several years, and was carried into Parliament by John Charles Villiers, who introduced a Bill in 1808. Christian's agitation, which was concerned only with the other Copyright Libraries, moved the Trustees of the Museum. On 28th February, 1806, they sought Counsel's opinion from the Master of the Rolls, Sir William Grant, and Sir William Scott, afterwards Lord Stowell, on the point whether the right had been transferred to them with the gift in 1757 of the Royal Library. They gave it as their opinion that it had been—a conclusion which must have been welcome both to Grant as an Official Trustee, and to Scott, not only as a Trustee (elected two years before) but also as himself a scholar and a friend of such men of letters as Johnson and his own namesake Sir Walter.

Villiers's ill health, absence and retirement from the House caused this Bill to be dropped, but Christian was not deterred. The University of Cambridge prosecuted a bookseller for non-delivery of a book and won its case, the Court of King's Bench deciding that eleven copies of the best and largest copies (Trinity College, and King's Inns, Dublin, having been added to the list at the Union with Ireland by an otherwise unimportant Act of 1801 (41 Geo. III, c. 107) must be deposited at Stationers' Hall for the libraries, whether the work were registered or not.

On this the controversy between the Universities and the booksellers flared up hotter than before, and the latter petitioned Parliament. In 1813 a Select Committee of the Commons was appointed, and in the following year, after two Bills had been introduced and withdrawn, the third was passed, on 29th July (54 Geo. III, c. 156). By this Act the obligation was extended to cover everything published; the Museum was to receive, but, as with the other libraries, only on demand,[19] a copy on the best paper, though (in the days of aquatint an important and reasonable limitation) the Trustees could not claim hand-coloured copies. The publishers were partly soothed by a valuable concession; the period of copyright was extended from fourteen to twenty-eight years. But the controversy was renewed, and raged for some years; indeed echoes of it can be heard today. After

NEW WINE AND AN OLD BOTTLE

1814, however, the right of the Museum was rarely, and never powerfully, challenged. It was merely evaded where possible. But evasion did not prevent the Museum from adding substantially to its annual intake by tapping this new source. The number of books entered at Stationers' Hall was swiftly multiplied by ten, leaping to over 500 after the passing of the Act.[20]

4. Increased Parliamentary Grants

But Copyright Acts could only provide for the future; over half a century of neglect had somehow to be made up. Two years before the passing of the Act of 1814, and no doubt in anticipation of it, the Trustees made application to Parliament for assistance in purchasing British books, and in that and the three succeeding years were given special grants of £1,000 a year for the purpose.

Meanwhile there was a substantial and continuing increase in the annual Parliamentary grants to the Museum for general expenses, apart from special ear-marked grants for purchases or buildings. The grant had stood fairly steadily at a biennial £3,000 from 1774–75 till 1800; but it was repeated annually from 1801 till 1805; in 1806 it went up to £3,400, in 1807 to £3,872, and in 1808 (the year of the opening of the Townley Building) to £6,790. For the next five years it ranged between £7,000 and £8,000, in 1814 it went over £8,000, it dropped in 1815, but in 1816 (when the Elgin Marbles came in and were not so much housed as stabled) it went over £10,000. After this the grant fluctuated between £8,000 and £10,000 for seven years; in 1824 it dropped to under £5,000, but that was made up by £15,000 in 1825, and after that there was a fluctuating advance till 1835, when the Museum's income reached its highest point till that date, £17,796. Forshall gave the Committee of 1836 some striking figures of the Additional Manuscripts; up to 1782, he said, purchased MSS. had numbered no more than fifty; in the next thirty years a hundred and fifty, in the next sixteen three hundred and fifty, and in the eight years ending in 1836 three thousand five hundred.

Of this increased prosperity, however, the Printed Books had but a small share. Of special grants made up to 1832, the Department had only the £4,000 for British books, the £1,000 for Ginguené's books, and its share of the Hargrave and Burney grants. The Manuscripts had had a share of the Hargrave and Burney grants, as well as the £4,925 for the Lansdowne, and in 1825 £5,300 for the Rich Oriental MSS.

But in the same period the Antiquities received £70,000 in Parliamentary grants, and the Natural History Department, though not so favoured, received the bulk of the Moll collection at the cost of extinguishing Major Edwards's fund, which had been bequeathed to house the Cottonian Library, and on which the Manuscripts surely had the first claim. The Printed Books, Panizzi showed in his report of 1845 on the Department, received in 1801-32 less than £20,000 of public money, i.e. an average of £600 a year or less (at one time, according to Baber, no more than £200 a year),[21] excluding the Hargrave and Burney purchases, but including the £4,000 for British books. And towards this, or rather towards the general purchase funds, were devoted several thousands derived from sales of Library duplicates. Even allowing that large opportunities do not present themselves regularly, it must be admitted that the Trustees showed in this period very little zeal for building up the national library. They were not ignorant. Beloe had reported in 1805 on the Library's desiderata.

At that time it was the practice for the Keeper of Printed Books, like those of the other two Departments, to submit all accessions offered for purchase to the Trustees, not merely in a list, but bodily. This clumsy practice died about 1830, when the Keeper was given power to purchase ordinary books outright. A very active Trustee, Henry Bankes, who was one of the Museum's chief mouthpieces in Parliament, by his energy and constant attendance at Committee meetings caused all books of any substantial money value to be rejected, and this crippling restriction was laid on the Library for many years.[22]

5. Three Great Benefactions Lost in Twelve Years

With all this parsimony, however, the bulk of the Library grew, though not so fast as the Antiquities. And the crisis of house-room

NEW WINE AND AN OLD BOTTLE

would have been precipitated some years before it came, had not three large and splendid collections, now among the glories of Oxford and Cambridge, been lost to the Museum in the dozen years between 1804 and 1816.

In 1799 Richard Gough the antiquary approached Harper with a proposal that the Museum should take charge of the copper plates of his *Sepulchral Monuments of Great Britain*. This request, submitted to the Trustees by Harper, was declined by them, in which they showed more rigidity than worldly sense, though that they "said they would not be his warehousemen," as Gough stated later, was not true; perhaps some individual Trustee used the phrase, as Gough pestered on the subject any of them he could get access to. Three years later he renewed his request, adding the offer to give his whole collection, with the two conditions, one reasonable, the other unreasonable, that it should be kept together and that it should only be consulted either in its own or in the Principal Librarian's room. This proposal was accepted, but whether the Trustees had after-qualms about the second condition or whether mere indolence were to blame, in spite of more than one application Gough never obtained a formal letter of acceptance. So at least he told the Rev. Rogers Ruding in 1808. His library went to the Bodleian.[23]

The second lost collection was Douce's, already mentioned. Though his retirement from the Museum took place in 1812, it was not till after 1830 that he made his bequest to the Bodleian. In that year he visited Oxford, and Bulkeley Bandinel, Bodley's Librarian, received him with such affability as in the event to secure perhaps the most valuable single collection of all which the Bodleian boasts.

The third is a matter of hearsay. But according to common report, confirmed by Ellis before the Committee of 1835–36, Lord Fitzwilliam had intended to bequeath his splendid collection of art and literature to the Museum, but was deterred by the knowledge that the Trustees made a practice of selling presented duplicates[24] (see below, pp. 332–3). His collection was bequeathed in 1816 to the University of Cambridge.

THE LIBRARY OF THE BRITISH MUSEUM

6. Reorganization

Pressed perhaps in part by the earliest of the great new acquisitions of this period, but probably as much by an active-minded Principal Librarian, the Trustees set up Committees in 1805 and 1806 to survey the Departments and consider improvements. The recommendations of the former, so far as the two Library Departments were concerned, dealt chiefly with the catalogues. Materials for a complete catalogue of the Printed Books, i.e. accession-titles, were in readiness, and the whole should be incorporated into one alphabet and printed, though 200 copies of the 1787 Catalogue were still in stock. Shelf-inventories (not for their natural use, but for the Trustees' visitations) should be prepared. Ayscough's classification of 1793, already revised by Ellis, should be printed, as it was in the *Synopsis* of 1808. The cases should be labelled, and in the remaining seven of the twelve rooms should be fitted with wire fronts. In the Manuscripts printed and hand-catalogues and an "analytical prospectus" of the contents of the Department were needed, and Nares's revision of the Harleian Catalogue should be printed. Ayscough's Catalogue of the Sloane and Birch MSS. should be completed by cataloguing the Additional MSS., then numbering about 1,000, and his Catalogue of Rolls and Charters, still in MS., should be revised. A catalogue of the Oriental MSS. should be taken in hand; Nares had reported that a man for this work was the chief need of his Department, no doubt because Maurice, whom he did not mention, was too much an Indian specialist. And a general classed catalogue of the MSS. was needed.

This Committee also summarized the history of the staff arrangements, and found that though the Trustees had, as we have seen, very early called on their officers to set to work at arranging and cataloguing the collections, no specific instructions to that effect had been given, and that the officers had never considered themselves bound by any such specific duty. (They might have excepted the Printed Books, in which direct orders had produced a General Catalogue and a classified shelf-arrangement.) The Trustees had in effect been paying £2,000 a year for having the House shown to visitors and the Reading Room supervised. The Committee feared lest, if this came to the notice of Parliament, its munificence might be withdrawn from the Institution.

Reporting in 1806, the Sub-Committee devoted itself to the Printed Books catalogues. The alphabetical catalogue, it now considered, should be abridged and serve an interim function till a Classed catalogue could be produced. To this latter much detailed attention was paid, and various existing models indicated for the various sections, as recommended by Beloe, who reported on schemes of classification.

A further report of 14th February, 1807,[25] goes into details of Departments, staff and duties. The Prints should be joined to the MSS. (This was fortunately not done.) The Antiquities should be separated from the Natural History and joined to the Coins and Medals—which had been independent for the last four years and anomalously under an Assistant who had no Under-Librarian over him. Annual Reports, which had been first ordered in 1801, were neglected: to date only one had been sent in, by Gray, and that only when specially called for. For the future reports of progress should be made not merely annually, but also monthly; an order to which effect is obeyed to the present day; if at times the reports are tedious routine to compile, they are a most valuable record and check on the work of the staff. The working time of the staff was not recommended to be altered, except that each officer on appointment and on promotion should be expected to give the whole time of the first year. Catalogues, so far as done in extra time, were to be paid for, as hitherto, *quantum meruit*. In making appointments the foreign languages of which knowledge was required should be considered; and finally the Principal Librarian's salary, in view of the increase in the buildings and collections, should be placed on a more adequate footing.[26]

"Additional Statutes and Rules," passed 28th February, 1807, and printed in 1808, lay down the essentials of these recommendations, except that reports were to be made annually and quarterly, not monthly. Antiquities, Coins and Medals, and Drawings and Engravings appear as Departments. On vacancies the Secretary was to report the particular loss in expert knowledge of modern tongues sustained and to be supplied.[27]

7. THE PRINTS AND DRAWINGS

In 1806 there had occurred a most unhappy episode, which had its effect on the Trustees' policy.

Drawings had formed part of the Manuscripts and Prints of the Printed Books, and the collection of the latter had been greatly enhanced in size and still more in value by the Cracherode bequest. The well-known etcher and dealer in prints, Robert Dighton, ingratiated himself with the Keeper of the Department, the Rev. William Beloe, a scholarly but extremely silly divine,[28] who had been brought into the Museum on Harper's death from outside, a bad precedent probably due to Ayscough's advanced age. Dighton took advantage of the facilities so obtained to abstract a number of prints from guard-volumes into which they were lightly tipped. Most of them were subsequently recovered, but it was the end of Beloe's official career; he was dismissed in 1806. Dighton was not prosecuted.[29]

After this the Prints and Drawings were converted into a subsection of the Department of Antiquities. They were placed under the charge of William Alexander the artist, who also acted as draughtsman to all the Departments; he was succeeded on his death in 1816 by J. T. Smith, the author of *A Book for a Rainy Day* and biographer of his old master Nollekens. The Coins and Medals had been similarly transferred from the Manuscripts to the Antiquities in 1803; there had not been a numismatist on the staff since Southgate's death in 1795.

8. PUBLICATIONS

The small staffs of the Library Departments could not without enlargement have dealt with really large accessions. Their time for at least part of the period was occupied in cataloguing. Immediately on Planta's accession there was inaugurated a succession of important publications, for which the Principal Librarian's influence had much of the responsibility.[30] The first catalogues published under Planta, the new Cotton Catalogue, 1802, and the revision of the Harleian, 1808, were initiated and published not by the Trustees, but by the

NEW WINE AND AN OLD BOTTLE

Committee on the Public Records, to whom these two collections, so rich in English historical sources, were naturally of primary concern. The Lansdowne MSS. were catalogued, the catalogue being published in 1819, twelve years after their arrival; and the Hargrave, a small piece of work, in 1818. The Lansdowne Catalogue, by Douce and Ellis, represented a great advance in competence upon the Cotton and Harleian Catalogues of so few years before. But that was because the material was not medieval but of the sixteenth and seventeenth centuries, in which the scholarship of that day had much more experience: medieval scholarship is the fruit of the following century. In the two years 1814 and 1815 Parliament voted a total of £4,000 for printing in facsimile type the O.T. section of the Codex Alexandrinus. The N.T. had been edited in facsimile by Woide in 1786, and he had been assisted in the collations by Harper. Now again the happy absence of Departmentalism was to be shown, for the O.T. was edited by Baber. The work was only completed in 1828, and it was revealed in 1835 to the surprised Committee of Enquiry that the Trustees had constantly borrowed on the printing grant for other purposes. And in the Department of Antiquities the Trustees began in 1810 to publish the handsome series of *Descriptions*, for which William Alexander, the first Keeper of Prints and Drawings, and an Assistant Keeper in the Antiquities, made the drawings till his early death in 1816.

The 1787 folio catalogue of the Printed Books was by 1805 out of date, and hard to use by reason of the accessions, which were added in MS. in the official copies; and a new printed catalogue was then undertaken. It was made by Baber, Ellis and the Assistants, obviously at high speed, and published in seven octavo volumes between 1813 and 1819.[31] Moreover a handy general *Synopsis* of the whole Museum, including the Library,[32] was issued in 1808, and reprinted almost annually for a number of years.

9. NEW MEN, 1824–35

In 1824 the Trustees seriously took in hand what might have been an important publication in its day, a General Classed Catalogue

THE LIBRARY OF THE BRITISH MUSEUM

of the Printed Books, which had been recommended by the Sub-Committee of 1806 and directed by the Trustees in the next year to be carried out as a pendant to the Author Catalogue. The work was entrusted to the Rev. Thomas Hartwell Horne,[33] an industrious bibliographer, Biblical critic and compiler, who had in 1812 made the classed and alphabetical indexes to the Harleian Catalogue of 1808, and after some years on the staff of the Record Office at Westminster had been employed to make a classified catalogue of the library of Queens' College, Cambridge, published in 1827. He drew up a set of *Outlines of Classification for a Library*, which was privately printed for the Trustees in 1825. With Horne, Frederic Madden classified the historical books till 1828, when he was transferred to begin his great career in the Manuscripts; H. F. Cary the poetry; John Tidd Pratt (apparently in the intervals of his practice at the Bar and not continuously) the Law; Lee, the Librarian of the Royal Society (also as a part-time occupation), the Science; and a younger Cary (a son of H.F.?) other sections. The Class Catalogue was ill-fated, ceasing entirely in 1834, when two-thirds finished. Horne was absorbed into the regular staff, on which he remained till 1860, dying two years later.

The King's Library staff accompanied their charge, being added to the staff of the Printed Books. The Librarian was Sir Frederick Augusta Barnard, George III's natural half-brother, who had been in charge of it for sixty years. The Senior Assistant was Nicholas Carlisle, who had eleven years' service. Under them were an old Assistant, W. Armstrong, with forty years' service, a young one, J. H. Glover, with eleven, and two extras. These men were not confined to the King's Library: Carlisle, for example, catalogued a large collection of Mazarinades, and Glover (who was also Librarian-in-Ordinary to King William IV and later to Queen Victoria) had charge of Copyright receipt, Cowtan *père* being Collector of those not entered at Stationers' Hall.

There were also three minor Assistants or Clerks, and twelve Attendants. Besides these, photography being yet unborn, there was frequently employed a facsimilist, John Harris, junior, who has left behind him a not quite credible legend of his skill. Most of his work was in copying pictures or text for facsimiles in publications; he worked in this way not only for the Museum but for T. F. Dibdin and many others. But he also worked for libraries, including the Museum, for collectors and for booksellers in supplying facsimiles of leaves missing from imperfect volumes. Cowtan (pp. 333–38) tells how he could sometimes not at once recognize his own work, and how, a doubt having arisen as to a leaf, Winter Jones and Watts had to call him in to identify it as his, and Jones then ordered that in future each facsimile leaf must be signed. Some account of Harris was published by the late William Roberts in *The Times Literary Supplement* of 23rd January, 1919.

The Department of Printed Books must have been a much busier as well as more populous place than it had been only a few years earlier.

In 1826 the Department acquired a more distinguished regular Assistant than any since Ellis left it in 1812. This was the Rev. Henry Francis Cary (mentioned above), already a man of fifty-three, with an established reputation due to the praise bestowed on him by Coleridge. Cary was an excellent Italian scholar, whose translation of the *Divina Commedia* still takes a high place, as well as being a most attractive man, who was the friend of many men of letters, and notably of Lamb. His resignation in 1837 will be recorded later.

The Department's other recruits, and indeed any that the Museum has ever had, were surpassed in power and importance by Antonio Panizzi, the greatest librarian who has yet appeared. Following chapters will deal at such length as is here possible with his character and career. After his escape from Modena, where he was under sentence of death, and short periods of teaching in London (where, as we shall see, he was introduced to the Reading Room by Cary) and at Liverpool, he was recommended by Roscoe to Brougham and was appointed an Extra Assistant in the Printed Books in 1831, being there set down at first to catalogue the French Revolution Tracts acquired fourteen years before.

The Department of Manuscripts in the same period had less stir and enlargement. When Ellis became Principal Librarian in 1827 he was followed by the Rev. Josiah Forshall, a man whose career in the

THE LIBRARY OF THE BRITISH MUSEUM

Museum was to show him the exact opposite of his predecessor and chief, forcible where Ellis was weak.[34] Forshall, as we have seen, had been appointed Assistant when Maurice died, being an excellent scholar and especially Orientalist, for which latter Maurice's death had made a gap. His accession to the Keepership made a vacancy for an Assistant, and this was filled by the transfer from the Classed Catalogue Staff of the Printed Books of Frederic Madden, already a skilled palaeographer, who like Forshall played an important part in the Museum's history for the next quarter of a century. In ability and difficult temper there was little to choose between the pair. Each, in succession, apart from work on catalogues, attacked with energy the problem, hitherto neglected, of the damaged Cotton MSS., sorting, identifying and restoring the fragments.

Four Assistants who came into the Manuscripts about this time should be mentioned:—(1) John Holmes, appointed temporary Assistant in January 1830, had been trained as a bookseller, and had done first-rate work for the well-known antiquarian dealer, John Cochrane, who gave evidence before the Committee of 1835–36. Holmes became regular Assistant in 1837 and Assistant Keeper in 1850; he died too young in 1854. The Arundel, Burney, MS. Maps and other catalogues of the Department produced in that period were his work. Holmes was not only a very able man, but a very amiable character in a period of quarrels, and was much used diplomatically by his stormy superiors. One of his sons, Sir Richard Rivington Holmes, an Assistant in the Manuscripts and later Royal Librarian at Windsor Castle, may perhaps still be remembered by some.—(2) Joseph Stevenson, who was to be a celebrated archivist, spent in the Museum only three years (1831–34) of a very long life, leaving owing to the low pay (as Holmes stated in 1835) and also no doubt to his recent marriage, for a Sub-Commissionership of the Records Commission. He was later archivist to Durham Cathedral, and, having taken priest's Orders in the Roman Church, examined the Vatican Archives for the British Government.—(3) Stevenson was succeeded by Henry Octavius Coxe, whose high qualities had been perceived, and had earned him an invitation, though he was still an undergraduate. But after five years the Museum lost him to the Bodleian, where an

NEW WINE AND AN OLD BOTTLE

Under-Librarianship led on to his distinguished term of office as Bodley's Librarian.—(4) In the same year came William Upton Richards, a man of less repute, but a good worker. He took Holy Orders, and devoted much interest to the Tractarian movement. In 1849 he resigned to take up parish work.

10. THE READING ROOM, 1803-38

Recent acquisitions and publications naturally aroused public interest, not only in the world of scholars and antiquaries, whose chief organ was *The Gentleman's Magazine*, but reaching down to the lower stratum which we have in a very similar period just a century later learned to call the *intelligentzia*, and which at its best in either period consists of self-educating men and women, eager of any way of approach to knowledge. Even the noise of such enthralling news as the enquiry into the conduct of the Duke of York and Mrs. Clarke did not entirely drown the voices in the press of a new type of interest in the national institution which was praised by so many and used by so few.[35]

The Reading Room in consequence experienced the same congestion as the shelving. The annual attendances of readers had risen by 1810 to nearly 2,000; in each of the next two lustra they more than doubled; in 1825 they were about 22,800, in 1830 about 31,200, and in the next five years this figure was nearly trebled. For every reader in 1799 there were nearly a hundred in 1835. Accordingly the Room underwent several moves and expansions, none of which sufficed to hold the rising tide.

In 1803, when the old Superintendent, Dr. Penneck, died, the Room established in 1774 was abandoned, and a new one, No. XIV, next to it and in the North-West corner which contained the Newspapers (i.e. presumably Sloane's), Gazettes and Parliamentary Records, was fitted up. This room had three windows on the North as well as one in the West wall. The Superintendent's table faced the fire-place, which was in the South wall; and two long tables extended North to South one on each side of the room. Two volumes at a time were allowed. Readers wishing for books pulled a bell-rope. Hours, as before, were 10–4 on Monday to Friday; the Room was not opened on Saturday till 1831. A Libri Desiderati book lay on the Superintendent's table, but can have been of but little use.[36]

The Regulations of 1803 ask readers to allow a reasonable time for search "in so extensive a library," especially for printed books, but anticipate that shortly there will be greater speed in delivering books, whereas two days had been a not uncommon delay, if we are to believe Isaac D'Israeli, a regular reader. The greater expedition was expected from the approaching completion of Ayscough's classified arrangement of the printed books, as shown in the *Synopsis* of five years later. And in 1805 the Trustees declared in a Minute that "the proper management of the Reading Room is essentially important to the utility and credit of the Museum." They had, it is true, not greatly contributed to this ideal by suppressing the post of Superintendent on Penneck's death and distributing the duty between the Assistant-Librarians of all the Departments (to which rota they added the Under-Librarians in 1806). The Officers were at the same time relieved of the work of conducting visitors round the exhibitions by the appointment of three attendants for the purpose. This work must have been very tedious to the men in the Printed Books, whose own Department was not exhibited; since, as the author of the *Synopsis* (differing from Dr. Johnson) observed, "the mere sight of the outside of books cannot convey either instruction or amusement." The Library Departments had no Exhibitions till 1858. Later, Thomas Maurice, Assistant in the Manuscripts, was the Chief Superintendent; at his death in 1824, John Cater[37] was appointed Clerk of the Reading Room, a new title, and he was responsible directly to the Principal Librarian—as indeed his eighteenth-century predecessors were, and as his successors are to the present day, in spite of the disappearance of the original justification for this arrangement, the fact that the Room was shared by all the Departments.

The 1803 Reading Room was outgrown in six years, when a move was made; two rooms, Nos. II and III, were adapted and to these two more adjacent rooms were added in 1817 and 1823.[38] By 1829 the new buildings had reached a stage at which some move could be made into them; and the two rooms farthest to the South

NEW WINE AND AN OLD BOTTLE

of the King's Library (opened at the same time), now the Middle and South Rooms of the Department of Manuscripts, were opened; they held seats for 120 readers. But even this was not enough. Two years later the Secretary (Forshall, at that time also Keeper of Manuscripts) laid before the Standing Committee a statement of the increase of readers since 1825—an increase in that short time of about 50 per cent; the report was referred to the General Board but nothing was done for another seven years. Then the Department of Manuscripts was enabled to occupy the rooms, which properly belonged to it, the two Eastern rooms of the North Wing being by this time ready to serve as Reading Rooms, which they did till the opening of the present Reading Room in the quadrangle in 1857. They held 168 readers, and were approached by readers, not through the King's Library, the cases in which were not yet glazed, but by a lane between recently built houses on the South side of Montagu Place, and by the stairway and door which bring one out in the opening between the two rooms, later the Catalogue and Music Rooms, and now shorn of half their height by the insertion of a mezzanine floor.

The service of books was effected from the West end, an Attendant sitting in charge of the wicket, while the Superintendent's table was close by. The new Superintendent, or rather Clerk, Cater, won the highest regard of readers and superiors alike, though it had to be admitted (to the Committees of 1835–36) that he was not a scholar, and in so far was inadequate. Cowtan, who was himself not qualified to perceive this particular deficiency, speaks however of Cater's good memory for books as well as of his good manners, and adds that he had an athletic form, having been one of the best boxers of his day, and a noble head, and describes him as looking "very much like an old English clergyman." Clearly Cater went most of the way, though not a scholar nor of gentle birth, to realize Fortescue's definition of the ideal Superintendent as "a combination of a scholar, a gentleman, a police-constable and a boatswain's mate." He died in 1855 and was succeeded for the two years which elapsed before the new Room was opened by his deputy, John Grabham. The appearance of the Rooms when full of readers is made familiar by several newspaper wood engravings.

THE LIBRARY OF THE BRITISH MUSEUM

Barwick points out[38] that since after the Copyright Act of 1814 the Museum received a certain quantity of contemporary English books there was a natural tendency to procure foreign books to match; and it may be added that the £4,000 spent at that time from special grants on British books must have contributed much to the more modern and less purely antiquarian utility of the Library. The great increase in the number of readers can certainly be traced, at least in part, to this shifting of the emphasis in the Library. Admission was made easier by the Trustees at the beginning of the century; Planta advised a more liberal policy, and he was strongly supported in all forward movements for the Museum by one of the best Trustees it has ever had, and certainly the best in a period when the Trustees "saw small," Charles Abbot, a Principal Trustee as Speaker from 1802 to 1816, and afterwards, as the first Lord Colchester, an elected Trustee.[39] Recommendations of readers, which had been confined to those by Trustees, were now accepted under the Regulations of 1803, not only from any officer of the House, but also from any two or more outside persons of known and approved character. But this was a period of unrest and disorder;[40] and the Trustees, having in 1805, 1806 and 1807 called for returns of readers, repeated their order in 1812 and this time retracted their more liberal policy of admission and confined recommendation to Trustees or officers. Before the Parliamentary Committee in 1836 (No. 5162), the Rev. G. Stonestreet stated that in 1819 the Trustees alone gave admission; but it has been seen that the increase in numbers of readers exceeded the power of the Museum to seat them, and there does not seem to have been any real grievance, except the very dubious statement that (in the absence of any lesser but useful public libraries in London, other than Dr. Williams's and Archbishop Tenison's) the Room was much used by schoolboys reading elementary text-books or with Virgils in their hands, and also by novel-readers; the latter were supplied, as they had not been in earlier generations, by the products of the recent Copyright Act, and also, it was complained, by a special catalogue.[41] Popular opinion was of course for this indiscriminate admission, whatever the result. It was exactly, if rhetorically, expressed by the writer of a letter in *The Times*[42] of 14th October, 1814, who asked, "Is the library to be for the use of those who keep the keys, or of those who pay for the books?" But the soberer view was well put by Mr. R. Hannay.43 "The Parliament and the Trustees of the Museum," he said, "have two duties to perform; the one to preserve its treasures, the other to offer them to the public so far as safety will admit. But let it never be forgotten that upon their safety depends their use."

Two years before the move to the new Reading Rooms the hours of opening were extended; in consequence of a petition signed by a large body of London college teachers and schoolmasters the Rooms were opened at nine instead of ten in the morning, and were kept open through the four summer months till seven in the evening. Complaints were made that the Rooms were ill-lit and overcrowded. Seating for 120 was at times made to hold as many as 200 readers.

In the same year press-marks were added to the titles in the copy of the Catalogue used in the Room, and readers, to the violent indignation of some of them, were required to add them to their requisition slips, and to enter each book on a separate slip, whereas before this they had merely handed in titles on casual scraps of paper and the books had had to be traced by the Staff. It is easy to imagine what some of these titles were like.44

Rare printed books, as well as MSS., were sent into the Room without discrimination. The Principal Librarian endeavoured in 1837 to impose some restrictions; but Panizzi, who had now succeeded Baber as Keeper of Printed Books, opposed him; the matter was referred to the Trustees, who decided that they were "unwilling to sanction any measures which will have the effect of imposing additional restrictions on the access now enjoyed by the Public to the Museum Library, unless it can be shown that such measures are absolutely necessary to the due preservation of the books." Which condition Ellis (and with him Forshall) evidently believed, while Panizzi did not, to be the case. In the event arrangements were made for the consultation of specially rare books and valuable MSS. in the work-rooms of the Departments.

In the last days of Dr. Penneck there joined the small band of readers a handful of men of the highest attainments, Porson collating the Harleian MS. of the Odyssey, Walter Scott collecting for

THE LIBRARY OF THE BRITISH MUSEUM

The Minstrelsy of the Scottish Border, Southey translating Spanish romances and Sydney Smith launching *The Edinburgh Review*. Their conversation must have been a pleasant change from the "nonsense and coffee house news" which had annoyed readers in the early days, and no doubt did so still.

After the move was made to the new Room in 1803 there were added to these Henry Brougham and Charles Lamb, who worked at intervals from 1804 to 1807 in the Garrick collection for what he could not find in Dodsley, extracting his *Specimens of the English Dramatic Poets*; he was recommended for his ticket by William Godwin, who had for some years been a reader, writing his absurd *Life of Chaucer*, 1803. There came also Henry Hallam, the historian, and Scott returned to London for a time in 1806–7, when his edition and life of Dryden needed books not to be found in the Advocates' Library.[45] Another example of the library antiquary, but one of less unblemished repute, and who was to be a centre of trouble later, John Payne Collier, came as a young man about 1808. In the eighteen-twenties and early thirties the company, as we have seen, had become much larger and more heterogeneous. The old type of topographical antiquary was still represented by Surtees, the historian of County Durham, and the common type of literary compiler by Isaac D'Israeli, and poetical studies by the preposterous but lovable George Dyer, who once exclaimed to Lamb, "What! an epic in twenty-four books and I never heard of it!" and whom Leigh Hunt called "an angel of the dusty heaven of bookstalls and the British Museum." But a sprightlier antiquary who frequented the Room was Richard Harris Barham, just come to London from Kent, whose studies in the *Legenda Aurea* were to bear fruit in the *Ingoldsby Legends*, while young historical students of a wider and more modern school appeared in Grote, in Carlyle, then working on the French Revolution, who was to be the Library's leading critic, and in Macaulay, first admitted in 1828–29, who was to be, after his return from India in 1838, not only one of the greatest users of the Library but also later one of the Museum's most active Trustees; and a great bibliographer as well as mathematician, who was one of the Library's ablest defenders twenty years later, arrived in 1828 in the person of

NEW WINE AND AN OLD BOTTLE

Augustus de Morgan. Moreover journalists like Dilke and Lockhart, and imaginative writers like Harrison Ainsworth, Lever, Browning and Thackeray, began to find the place useful. Thackeray's grateful Roundabout Paper on the room is well known. Among the young people whom the seniors thought out of place were Edward Fitz-Gerald, just down from Cambridge, and Dickens, training himself for Parliamentary reporting. An official of East India House, Peacock, who put in his spare time there, no doubt reading the obscurer Greek authors, would encounter a retired clerk from his Office, in fact Charles Lamb, who, feeling the need of regular work and armed with a recommendation from his friend Cary for a new ticket, had gone back, after an interval of over twenty years, to the Garrick Plays, from which he sent extracts to Hone for his *Table Book*, and who in writing to Hone at the end of 1826 or the beginning of 1827, gave the well-known description of himself in "the princely apartments of poor condemned Montagu House, culling at will the flowers of some thousand dramas. It is like," he added, "having the range of a nobleman's library, with the librarian to your friend. Nothing can exceed the courteousness and attentions of the gentleman [Cater] who has the chief direction of the Reading rooms here; and you have scarce to ask for a volume before it is laid before you."[46] Lamb was not merely a good-tempered man; the books he needed he knew were there; they all stood together and were easily found; especially as he was reading straight through them for "after-gleanings" to his *Dramatic Specimens*, as he told Barton. A reader who wanted single and perhaps obscure books, especially foreign, would either not find them or have much more delay and difficulty.

The French émigrés of thirty years before had either returned to France or settled here; a new group of émigrés who figured in the Room were the exiled Italian Liberals—Gabriele Rossetti, who in the intervals of teaching Italian was writing on Dante as an anti-papal champion and must have had many discussions with Cary, was there, and so, before joining the staff, was Panizzi, admitted in 1830 on Cary's recommendation, and experiencing the inadequacy of the Library to which he was destined to give an entirely new scope and life.

THE LIBRARY OF THE BRITISH MUSEUM

11. The King's Library and the New Buildings, 1815–52

Motion by the Trustees for a new and larger building, to meet the congestion both of the collections and of their public use by readers and visitors, began before Parliament decided in 1823 that the Museum was the right place to house George III's library, which George IV had placed in the Prime Minister's hands for the nation. Two years earlier, little knowing that what was already urgent would so soon be made imperative, but concerned not only at the Museum's rapid growth but also at the dilapidated condition of the house[47] and the fire-risks presented by it, they employed Robert, afterwards Sir Robert, Smirke, whom they had appointed their architect in 1815,[48] to prepare plans for a wing to extend northwards from the Eastern end of the house. The Duke of Bedford, to whose property the existence of the Museum's garden was, as we have seen, of substantial benefit, applied in the next year to Chancery for an injunction restraining the Trustees from building North of the inner garden wall, which had been forbidden by the agreement for the building of the original Montagu House.

Smirke was a young man, but already a brilliant member of the group of architects, working mainly in the Greek style, who effected as great a transformation in the appearance of London in the first third of the nineteenth century as has been effected a century later by their descendants working in the style based on steel and concrete. He had rebuilt Covent Garden Theatre after the fire in 1809 (the fire which produced *Rejected Addresses*), and as architect to the Board of Trade had built the chief portion of the Royal Mint. He was in fact the appropriate man to plan a building which was to house the most famous of Greek sculptures.

The accession of the King's Library, which perforce remained for the time at Buckingham House, at once convinced Parliament of the Museum's need of a larger and safer building. A vote of £40,000 was passed in 1823 (Act of Geo. IV, c. 100), followed by votes of £25,000, £12,000, and £43,000 in 1826–27. Smirke at once drew full plans for a new East wing, including the three rooms of the Manuscript Department (the Saloon and the Middle and South Rooms) at the

NEW WINE AND AN OLD BOTTLE

South end, and two Reading Rooms at the North, together with skeleton plans of the remaining three wings of a perfect square enclosing a quadrangle—the nucleus of the building as it stands today; and they were approved by the Treasury, to which Parliament had referred the matter.

The first part to be erected was, in accordance with the Trustees' original intention, the wing running North from beyond the East end of the old house. The foundations were laid in the autumn, which showed expedition on the part of all, seeing that the King's letter to Lord Liverpool making the gift was dated in February. This wing was completed about the end of 1826; the Manuscripts were transferred from the old house to the Saloon in 1827; and the King's books were brought to Bloomsbury in 1828, and placed in its ground floor gallery, where they now stand, and the two rooms forming the southern end of the wing (now the Middle and South Rooms of the Department of Manuscripts) were, as noticed above, opened as Reading Rooms in 1829.[49] The completion of Smirke's original building may be sketched here. The quadrangle was not finished till 1852; but "poor, condemned Montagu House" was demolished in 1845. The approximate total cost to that date was approximately three quarters of a million pounds, of which perhaps half can be regarded as devoted to the Library.

The remaining stages of this long process were as follows: In December 1831 the Trustees approached the Treasury for funds to enable them to make an immediate start with the North or Library Wing, including the Reading Rooms, the East Wing being then complete in all its material parts, without waiting for the completion of the West Wing, which was already under construction; and they urged the want of space for books and readers so far provided, and also the danger of fire to the old house, which was still standing. But the Treasury refused to undertake the cost of two wings at once, and it was only two years later that sanction was given for the North Wing, at a cost of £24,000. This wing, as originally planned, was completed in 1836, and the whole mass of the Printed Books was moved into its new quarters (mainly by Thomas Watts, see below, pp. 101–2), without, so it was afterwards claimed, putting any part of it out of use for

THE LIBRARY OF THE BRITISH MUSEUM

the service of the Reading Room: a considerable feat, if the library did only consist of under a quarter of a million volumes. In 1838 the two easternmost ground-floor rooms of the suite were fitted and opened, as we have seen, as Reading Rooms;[50] and three years later an extension of the line to the West, outside the boundaries of the quadrangle, was made in the shape of the Arch Room. The Library occupied only the ground floor of the wing. Before the central "Large Room" was converted in 1914 into the "North Library" and the passage surrounding it under its galleries was constructed, there was a very impressive vista through the four tall double doorways along the whole length of the wing.

But accessions in an increasing stream had to be provided for; and Baber made Ellis's mistake (see n. 48), though less grossly, in underestimating them. Smirke's plan provided for 240,000 volumes in the North Wing. But that was soon perceived to be inadequate. So a further addition was made, as well as the Arch Room. This was the "slip," or low line of light structure abutting on to the East Wall of the King's Library, which was commenced from the North End and by 1848 had reached half-way. The northern half of this structure now houses the Printed Books' Keeper's Room and Ante-Room or offices, and the southern half the Keeper's Room and some storage, with a room that was till recently the Students' Room, of the Oriental Printed Books and MSS. It was an absurd fault in Smirke's planning, pointed out by Panizzi in 1836,[51] that there was so little provision of private rooms; these two had to be added to the building, and most of the Assistants have always lived and moved in passage rooms, with the maximum of disturbance and temptation to converse.

The advances made by library building have marked stages in the perpetual contest between the wits of librarians and their architects on the one side and the rising tide of books on the other. A new advance was presently to be made here, and will come to be recorded later. The rooms designed in the eighteen-twenties and thirties took no adequate account of the problem beginning already to be presented by the new use of steam-power in making paper and in printing books. Smirke simply followed the tradition set by Wren in the Library of Trinity College, Cambridge. Wren there fused the medieval English

NEW WINE AND AN OLD BOTTLE

College library plan with the continental. In the former the practice of chaining books to the desks, combined with the poor average daylight of the English climate, had produced the system of a book-press standing out from the wall between each pair of windows, thus bringing book, window and reader together. In the latter, especially in Italian examples, daylight was a thing to shelter from, and windows were small and high-set. Wren kept the projecting presses and intervening bays, but continued them along the wall between, and enlarged the continental window above them. Smirke added a railed gallery above the ground presses, and filled the walls between the windows with an upper range. In the King's Library, whether with a view to exhibition cases or merely for appearance, there were no projecting presses or bays. This splendid gallery, just 100 yards long (it has been raced by young Assistants after hours), 40 feet wide (except the centre, where the width is 55 feet) and 36 feet high, with fine coffered ceiling and four remarkable columns of polished Aberdeen granite at the corners of the central space, was designed to take exactly the books from Buckingham House.

The Arch Room represents a development of Wren's plan. The projecting book-cases are set against short walls, which run up the whole height of the room and meet in arches across it; whence the name. The capacity of the space is thus enlarged by the addition of bays (broken by windows) at the gallery levels; there are two galleries as against one in the other rooms.

In 1839 nine houses in Great Russell Street, adjoining the Museum on the East, which had been built since the destruction of Bedford House about 1800, were bought under authority of Act 1 & 2 Victoria, c. 10, and the front extended. On the ground so provided was then erected (with a linking corridor) a wing of Keepers' residences and on the West of the Front a corresponding corridor (since enlarged into a room occupied by Directors and Secretaries) and wing of residences. To the Department of Manuscripts were also added, as the South Wing advanced, the rooms linking it with the Hall, i.e. the Egerton and Map Rooms on the South, lit by windows under the portico, and on the North of these the room which was presently to house the Grenville Library and to bear that name.[52]

IV

TWO PUBLIC ENQUIRIES: GROWTH AND DISSENSION[1] (1835-50)

1. THE PARLIAMENTARY ENQUIRY, 1835-36

IN the first third of the nineteenth century, then, the Museum and its Library had become a matter of much more public interest than in the previous forty years. It had grown, and it was attempting to give more service to the world of students. Its acquisitions of Egyptian, Greek and Roman marbles in these years had stirred a vague pride in the hitherto rather neglected Library, to match that now taken in the sensational acquisitions of antiquities.

But the service to the student public, though improved, was as yet very inadequate to the actual, and still more to the potential, demand, far behind that given, for example, by the Bibliothèque Royale of Paris. Political agitation, which triumphed with the Reform Bill, had, as always, its social and intellectual aspects and aims. In the industrial towns of the North Mechanics' Institutes were multiplying, and in the capital, though there were few or none of these, the same forces and desires were at work, and there were concentrated there, more than in the provinces, the philosophical radicals.

The Museum could not escape the attentions of those whom a *Quarterly* reviewer in 1850 was to look back on and describe too indiscriminately as "nuisance-abaters and notoriety-hunters." If some such were vocal, there were better men and better reasons for action to improve the Museum in 1835.

The first blast of the trumpet of reform was not very impressive. That able and industrious, but sharp-tongued antiquary, Sir Nicholas Harris Nicolas, had already endeavoured to reform the Society of Antiquaries, and in 1830 he published his *Observations on the State of Historical Literature*, constituting (with side-flings at the Society of Antiquaries and the Royal Society) an attack on the administration of the public records by the Record Commission and in particular on

TWO PUBLIC ENQUIRIES: GROWTH AND DISSENSION

the conditions of public access to them. Nicolas contrasted the Museum with the Record Office in the Tower much to the advantage of the former in this aspect.

"There he (the student) has only to ask for the manuscripts he requires. He uses them as copiously, and changes them as often as he would the books in his own library; he incurs no obligation in gaining admittance; he studies when and for as long a time as he pleases; his mind is undisturbed by fearing to encroach on the politeness of others, he meets with no obstacles; the attendants are courteous and obliging, because they know that their places depend on their behaviour. Anything more delightful in this respect than that establishment cannot be imagined."[2]

But in another aspect his opinion of the Museum was far less favourable. The Trustees, he vehemently complained, obviously not without some political animus and with some plausibility to the unthinking, were nearly all men of rank and not professional scholars.

"It is true that among the trustees of the British Museum there are three presidents of societies who are trustees *ex officio* who do not possess that rank (Right Honourable or M.P.), as well as three of the family trustees who are undignified by titles; yet among those trustees who are *elected* by the others, and who, it might be supposed, would be chosen in consequence of their reputation, there is *not one person* who is distinguished for his attainments in science, in art, or in literature as manifested in his works; but they consist of one duke, three marquesses, five earls, four barons, and two members of parliament!" "This," he concluded, "affords another to the many proofs which might be adduced, of the contemptuous neglect with which genius is treated by the British government."

But it was not Nicolas's apparently reasonable, and anyhow at least not trivial, complaint that brought the public dissatisfaction with the Museum to a head. That required something much more futile. One John Millard had for some years been employed as an Extra Assistant to make a general index of the Manuscripts, but had been found neither competent nor very industrious, and after much charitable delay had been dismissed. Millard found a Member of Parliament who was new to the House and more energetic and eloquent than cautious. This tribune of the plebs was Benjamin (afterwards Sir Benjamin) Hawes, Member for the new constituency of Lambeth, who was later to live down his early follies and acquire much respect. Hawes seems to have been taken in by Millard or by Millard's friends, and brought the administration of the Museum to the notice of the House, moving in 1833 for a return of papers. The House was enough impressed to appoint a Select Committee of Enquiry, under the Chairmanship of one of the Burgesses for the University of Oxford, T. G. Bucknall Estcourt, of Estcourt. Of the rest of the Committee (of which Hawes was one) the most active and intelligent member was the other Oxford Burgess, Sir Robert Inglis, F.R.S., F.S.A., a popular and very influential Member, who had devoted much time to the work of the Commission on the Public Records, being the author of the report on them published in 1833, and who had been a Trustee of the Museum since 1834. Other active members were Sir Philip Egerton and Lord Stanley, afterwards Lord Derby. At the end of the first Session the Committee were unable to report, but the minutes of the evidence they had taken were printed, and attracted considerable attention, producing fresh witnesses for the reappointed smaller Committee of 1836; noteworthy among these was the young Edward Edwards. In both Sessions the Committee made a comprehensive investigation, taking evidence from the officers and from many men of letters and science outside, including the leading malcontents. The affair of Millard, which was not specified in their widely drawn terms of reference, did not occupy them long; he had not been prepared to face Madden's questions; in their Report to Parliament they contemptuously made no mention of him whatever. To the selection of Trustees, on the other hand, they devoted considerable attention. Nicolas and others put forward the view he had expressed in 1830; and the suggestion was made that the appointments might be made by learned societies, though the chief of them were already represented by their Presidents *ex officio*. Other witnesses, such as Olinthus Gregory, were of opinion that the societies were too much under the influence of coteries to exercise such powers with good judgment. Others held that there was good in the existing system. Panizzi, the most forcible mouthpiece of this view, declared that though the French system of government of the Royal Library by officials under a Ministry might suit the French, in an aristocratic country it was a good thing to have Trustees of the Museum in both Houses of Parliament; Trustees of high rank had helped to secure the King's Library.[3] Scientific men were "dogmatical and narrow-minded, and being infallible would never consult an officer." Even Sir Joseph Banks had done harm by meddling in the details of the Museum management.[4]

The Committee in their Report began by stating "that the great accessions which have been made of late to the collections of the British Museum, and the increasing interest taken in them by the public, render it expedient to revise the establishment of the Institution, with a view to place it upon a scale more commensurate with, and better adapted to, the present state and future prospects of the Museum" (par. 1). On the question of the Trustees they took a middle line. They made (pars. 2–3) no definite recommendation for a formal alteration in the system of government, such as would have required an Act of Parliament. But they suggested that when such alterations came to be made the opportunity might be taken of reducing the number of official Trustees; and also that in filling up vacancies it would be desirable that the electing Trustees should not in future lose sight of the fact that an opportunity is thus afforded them of occasionally conferring a mark of distinction upon men of eminence in literature, science and art (pars. 2–3). They recommended certain definite improvements in the organization. Those affecting the Library were: That the Departments be further subdivided (par. 6): That the office of Secretary be not combined with a Keepership (par. 8): That salaries should be revised, and officers hold no other paid appointment, it being found that a majority of the Assistants, of whom a number had recently been added to meet the growing work, were not regular officers on the establishment but supernumeraries; in short, that the Museum had outgrown the state in which it was staffed by the part-time work of beneficed clergy (pars. 11–13): That catalogues should be prepared and printed (they made no decision on the controversy between classification and the alphabet); and that objects entering the Museum should be registered

THE LIBRARY OF THE BRITISH MUSEUM

(par. 15). To these ends they recommended better Parliamentary provision for the Museum (par. 16).

The evidence on which these recommendations were based had been especially strong and full on two points: the printed catalogues and the funds devoted to the Printed Books. Witnesses had also dwelt on the bad condition of the Natural History specimens, some of which it seems were popularly known as the Museum's hobgoblins. Nicolas and others found, and not without reason, all the printed catalogues very imperfect. But the question on which the most various and most violent opinions were expressed was whether a new alphabetical catalogue or a classed catalogue was most needed. The printed alphabetical catalogue was from sixteen to twenty-two years old, and the folio volumes in the Reading Room, in which it had been expanded in MS., were congested and hard to use. For ten years, from 1824, a special staff under Horne had at a cost of over £5,000 classed the titles for two-thirds of the Library, 160,000 out of 240,000 books. But in 1834 it had been decided that the alphabetical catalogue was more urgent, and the titles were re-sorted into their alphabetical order, though marked so that they could be easily reclassed at need. Classifying was generally considered by witnesses, in proportion to their want of acquaintance with the matter, to be easy work: one of them declared that he could class a thousand books a day. The *Athenaeum* lent itself to the demand,5 and so did the scientific witnesses, who had a model to recommend in Jonas Dryander's classed catalogue of the Banks Library. But Panizzi (whose hand may surely be seen in the massacre of Horne's classed catalogue) was in both senses of the word hot from his trouble with the Royal Society, and declared that no two men would ever agree on a scheme of classification. The Committee, as noted above, made no recommendation on the point; and the classed catalogue was left in limbo.[6]

Many witnesses testified to the inadequacy of the Library of Printed Books. Sir Robert Owen stated (No. 1192) that the College of Surgeons had been forced to go to considerable expense in consequence of the gaps in the Museum's collection of zoological books, and that the Banks Library had not been properly kept up (as the Trustees had engaged to do), so that the position was relatively worse

TWO PUBLIC ENQUIRIES: GROWTH AND DISSENSION

in 1836 than it had been in 1824.7 Baber pointed out the poor funds with which he had had to make do for many years; at times he had under £200 a year. He added that the increased use of the Reading Room meant increased wear and tear, so that he had to spend £100 a year more on binding. And Edward Edwards produced a startling list of desiderata. But the most powerful evidence on this or any part of the Committee's enquiry was given by Panizzi; and it was now for the first time that the idea of a national public library, as we are familiar with it, found expression. Panizzi exposed the financial neglect of the Printed Books which had prevailed. The nation, he declared, had done almost nothing for the Library. Every other Department had had grants and assistance. He put his finger on the cause. "Public opinion is exercised only upon one of the purposes for which the British Museum was instituted: that is upon its establishment as a show place. Unfortunately as to its most important and most noble purpose, as an establishment for the furtherance of education, for study and research, the public seem to be almost indifferent." He drew the distinction between a national library and a library for education such as the celebrated library of the University of Göttingen (then, it is to be remembered, in the British Dominions), which nevertheless did buy rarities and exclude cheap and common books. The Museum, being the only library for the million-and-a-half inhabitants of London, was trying to be both and could never please everybody. There should be at least two public libraries for education.

Asked (No. 4795) "then the Committee are to understand that, in your judgment it is a very secondary object to keep up the library of the Museum, even if it could be done, with a full supply of all the modern British and foreign works?" he replied, "I would not say a very secondary object; but if I am to choose, I would say that it is of less importance for the library of the British Museum to have common modern books, than to have rare, ephemeral, voluminous and costly publications, which cannot be found anywhere else, by persons not having access to great private collections. *I want a poor student to have the same means of indulging his learned curiosity, of following his rational pursuits, of consulting the same authorities, of fathoming the most intricate inquiry, as the richest man in the kingdom, as far as books go, and I contend that Government is bound to give him the most liberal and unlimited assistance in this respect.* I want the library of the British Museum to have books of both descriptions; I want an extra grant for those rare and costly books which we have not, and which cannot be bought but upon opportunities offering themselves. Then the annual grant should be increased for modern books, that is books printed from about the beginning of last century. When Napoleon went to visit the King's library at Paris, which was then the beau idéal of a public library, and which had been got together by the unlawful means of which I have been speaking, Mr. Van Praet pleaded hard poverty, and he asked a grant of at least £40,000 to render the library complete. Napoleon said he should have it, and he actually ordered £5,000 to be paid on account; the political events which followed stopped the payment of the remainder. Now when you have given three times as much (say £100,000 in 10 or 12 years), then you will begin to have a library worthy of the British nation, but not if you continue to go on as hitherto."

These words, and especially those italicized, were almost a new language to the learned and governing world of 1835 in England, though the Reform Bill had been passed, nor by any means only in England. They remain the charter of our own and of other national libraries today, and it may well be that they will always remain so.

2. CHANGES AND APPOINTMENTS

The Trustees did not take such bold action as the Committee's recommendations might surely have justified. That had to wait another fifteen years and another Enquiry. But some improvements they did make. Of the six new members of their body elected in the next ten years, four, Henry Hallam (1837), W. R. Hamilton (1838), Sir John Herschel (1843) and T. B. Macaulay (1847), were decisively of the class of men eminent in science or literature. The Trustees, moreover, did divide the Departments somewhat further by establishing the Prints and Drawings (this did not now really concern the Library). But the real need, an Oriental Department, had long to wait. They followed one of the Committee's recommendations

TWO PUBLIC ENQUIRIES: GROWTH AND DISSENSION

literally, separating the Secretaryship from a Keepership, and appointing Forshall Secretary. They made the excellent and overdue reform of making their officers' posts full-time, and raising their pay, if not to anything adequate, at least by amounts that were relatively considerable; they forbade at the same time their holding other paid posts. (Panizzi, for example, now resigned his professorship of Italian in the University of London, and Baber, who was sixty, went to his country living, which he held for another thirty-two years. No longer could it be said, as Cobbett had said in 1816, "the establishment is in the hands of a few clergymen who keep poor curates to do their clerical work at their fat livings, while they are living in idleness and luxury at the Museum." They maintained the new Alphabetical Catalogue, and made no motion to revive the Classed Catalogue, which they rightly thought could wait to be a supplement to the other. Other catalogues were put in hand, and a system of registration of acquisitions was instituted.

This last change, necessary in itself, was unluckily rendered futile and vexatious by that regarding the Secretaryship, since Forshall, whose new office (even with control of the Copyright Receipt, which was allocated to him) gave him too little to do, gathered the work into his own hands and those of his immediate subordinates. Registration, carried out by even an able scholar who is not, as he cannot be, an expert in the work of every Department, is a mere waste of time.[8] With printed books, which may be required for use as soon as possible after their arrival in the House, the delay must have been intolerable. But, intolerable or not, registration in the Office was a relatively trifling matter. The new Secretary was a man of much energy, and the Principal Librarian was not. As the Commission of 1848–50 was to find, the inferior Officer was able to exclude his superior (the only statutory Officer in the House) from the Board's Meetings. He was also able to pack meetings, since there was no fixed Standing Committee in operation, any Trustee being free to attend any of its meetings, and Forshall summoned, as he said, any that he might know were available at the time. And of this Committee, in whose composition there was thus no continuity, let alone any impartiality, the Minutes were sometimes transmitted to the appropriate Keepers in a garbled version, and sometimes not at all. Panizzi declared, and with too much truth, that "it is impossible for an officer to know what the Trustees mean." It is impossible not to blame the Board's Chairman, Archbishop Howley, though he was perhaps suffering at the time when the trouble was at its worst from old age and some consequent failing of his faculties. There is no doubt of what Grenville meant (even if Panizzi had not suppressed the name) when near the end of his life he solemnly stated that there was someone who had great influence over the Archbishop and was no friend of Panizzi. Nor was Panizzi the only sufferer.

Many staff appointments were made. The Keepership of Manuscripts, left vacant by Forshall's transfer, went to Frederic Madden, who held it till 1866.[9] Forshall's transfer not only made a vacancy for a Keeper; it left the Manuscripts without an Orientalist. The Museum made a very good bargain in securing for the Assistant Keepership the young William Cureton, already a distinguished scholar, who had for four years been Sub-Librarian at the Bodleian. His future fame was to rest on his work on the Nitrian Syriac MSS., which is dealt with elsewhere (see pp. 108–10, 295–6). His first task was to make a classed catalogue of the Museum's numerous Arabic MSS., which was published in 1847 as Part II of the General Catalogue of Oriental MSS.[10] Holmes, who had been a supernumerary since 1830, became a regular Assistant at the same time, in conformity with the Committee's recommendation. He was a very good herald and records expert, and of general use in the Department. And in the next year the Department was strengthened by the appointment of another Assistant, who was to play a great part in the Library during the next half-century. This was Edward Augustus Bond, who came with five years' experience in the Record Office.

A word should be said of a remarkable Transcriber in the Manuscripts, appointed about this time, Richard Sims, who became a very competent genealogist and a great standby in the Department. He compiled two most useful books, *An Index to the Pedigrees and Arms*, 1849, and his admirable *Handbook to the Library of the British Museum*, 1854, part of which did something to supply the want of a Class Catalogue of MSS.

TWO PUBLIC ENQUIRIES: GROWTH AND DISSENSION

In the Printed Books too there were great changes. On Baber's retirement Panizzi was promoted to be Keeper over the head of Cary, who was regarded as disqualified by his age and notorious infirmity; he had recently recovered from a fit of insanity. Panizzi had only made application after learning from Cary that he had no objection to make. Cary, however, took offence and complained bitterly to the Lord Chancellor in his well-known letter of July 17th, 1837, which was published (presumably by himself) in *The Times* of the next day. He there urged that "my age, between 64 and 65 years, it was plain, might rather ask for me that alleviation of labour which, in this as in many other public offices, is gained by promotion to a superior place." Cary had not read the signs of the times, and luckily his successful rival was far from looking to promotion for alleviation of labour. Cary also complained that Panizzi was not only his subordinate and junior but also a foreigner, as if the Museum staff had not abounded in foreigners ever since the foundation. No such complaint had been made on the promotions of Maty or Planta; but vulgar nationalism had increased since Waterloo, and Cary had many ardent and injudicious friends who campaigned against the appointment. It must be admitted that Panizzi owed his appointment to the fact that he was a political refugee.

Cary was followed in 1838 as senior Assistant by the Rev. Richard Garnett (1789–1850), a very remarkable self-taught linguist and philologist, and now a retired country clergyman. Garnett's death in 1850 occasioned much sorrow, but it had its compensation, for it was the occasion of the very early addition to the staff of his young son Richard, afterwards to play so great a part in the Library. According to the son (in *D.N.B.*) the father was not active in the reforms instituted by Panizzi. He seems to have been of the type of pure scholar, though wielding a lively pen, which is not given to all scholars. He dealt principally with the Northern European and Oriental tongues, leaving the Romance tongues to Panizzi; his scholarship extended to many obscure tongues and dialects. Before him the Germanic tongues had been dealt with by Dr. Schier.

Just before Garnett there came in another linguist, and a member of a literary family,[11] the man who was to be Panizzi's adjutant and successor both as Keeper and as Principal Librarian, John Winter Jones (1805–81). Jones had the chief hand in framing the Ninety-One Rules for the Catalogue, and was a good all-round man. His special interests were geographical, and he played a considerable part in founding the Hakluyt Society and its long alliance with the Museum; we may attribute to him the development in the forties of the map-collection (see below, p. 216–20).

With them there entered William Brenchley Rye and George Bullen, who were both to be Keeper of Printed Books, Edward Edwards, John Humffreys Parry (afterwards Sergeant Parry) and in 1838 Thomas Watts, also to be Keeper.

Garnett and Jones were employed on the Department's chief labour, the preparation of the General Alphabetical Catalogue decided on in 1834. This and its predecessors and successors are dealt with elsewhere; but another burdensome labour was already casting its shadow before. The North Wing, as originally planned, was approaching completion, and the books (other than the King's) must be moved into it from the Old House. New hands were wanted for this work. Parry left for the Bar after five years, and Rye and Bullen were not prominent at this period, but the other three were. In 1835 Edwards, as a young man of 23, had come to the Library with criticisms, and had been kindly received by the amiable Baber, then near retiring.[12] He followed the Committee, then sitting, with passionate interest, and produced a valuable pamphlet on reform of the Library.[13] When the new Committee resumed the enquiry in the Session of 1836, Edwards proved to be one of the best witnesses and a strong supporter of Panizzi's ideas; he showed also considerable bibliographical knowledge in the list of desiderata he produced—a list in which Baber was only able to find one error. It was therefore natural that he should be brought on to the staff. He worked as a supernumerary on the Rules and on the Thomason Tracts, which had been covered in the existing Catalogue by a single title, and which were now for the first time singly catalogued. But he was of a difficult and independent temper and in 1846 he resigned his post. He continued to frequent the Museum as a reader, and took a leading part in the agitation for public libraries which resulted in Ewart's

TWO PUBLIC ENQUIRIES: GROWTH AND DISSENSION

Act of 1850; and in that year he became Manchester's first Public Librarian. This post also he soon resigned, and devoted himself to writing his *Memoirs of Libraries, Libraries and their Founders,* and *Lives of the Founders of the British Museum,* to which all later writers on the Museum are deeply indebted, and other works. He died in 1886.

3. WATTS AND THE REMOVAL: THE SURVEY AND THE PURCHASE GRANT: ACQUISITIONS

Of the group far the ablest was Watts (1811–69). He had from boyhood devoted himself to linguistic study, and displayed an extraordinary talent, adding languages to his repertory not singly but by groups.[14] In 1836 his attention, like so many others', was attracted by the Parliamentary Enquiry, and in 1837 he contributed to the subject a very intelligent article in *The Mechanics' Magazine,* which incidentally anticipated the idea of a round Reading Room; but this passed unnoticed, and his introduction to the Museum was effected by his recommendation of the purchase of a parcel of Russian books (in which language the Museum had hardly anything), which being approved by Panizzi, and there being no Slavonic scholar in the place, he was engaged to catalogue. This led to a regular engagement as a supernumerary, and later to an Assistantship. He catalogued the Banks Icelandic books, which had been in the Library uncatalogued since the eighteenth century, and such Russian and Icelandic books as were in the Banks and King's. He was also at once given much of the work of purchasing, and also charge of the removal of the books and their reclassification on the new shelves. This enormous labour Watts performed, beginning in 1838 and finishing early in 1840, with only the smallest assistance,[15] and his colossal memory for books found full scope. The move was so well organized that at no time were more than those actually in transit rendered unavailable to readers, a fact which was approached, but not equalled, almost a century later when the first quadrant of the new Ironwork was filled from the old. But all books had to be press-marked afresh, and the alterations effected in the copies of the catalogue, and this led Watts to devise what was called "the elastic system," i.e. numbering presses not continuously but with gaps, which could be filled by presses of later accessions. By this plan whole presses could be moved without any alteration of press-marks. The classification Watts adopted resembled, but was not identical with, that of "the Paris booksellers," but was divided into broad classes only.

Provision for placing accessions was to be very necessary. Panizzi had two aims, to build up a national library worthy of his idea, as expressed to the Parliamentary Committee, and to make it accessible by a properly constructed catalogue, neither of them things for which there was any model in existence. And though they had to be pursued *pari passu* the first was the more important.

There were in 1837 some 227,000 books, and outside the King's Library the collection was still very haphazard, as had been shown by the revelations of deficiencies made in 1835–36.[16] But the purchase fund had improved, being in this year £2,944, as compared with £1,032 in 1832, and that had included some hundreds of pounds from the sale of duplicates. In 1838 £1,000 was added to it. Moreover, from the year 1834-35 regular annual grants had taken the place of occasional special purchases by Parliament. As soon as Watts's reshelving of the books in classified order allowed, Panizzi set himself and his Assistant to work on a methodical survey of the library, comparing it section by section with such bibliographies as existed. This survey he submitted in January 1845 to the Trustees with a Report, sketching the growth of the Printed Books, exposing the inadequacy of the resources for purchase, and recommending application for a substantial annual grant. "The expense requisite [he said] for accomplishing what is here suggested—that is, for forming in a few years a public library containing from six to seven hundred thousand printed volumes, giving the necessary means of information on all branches of human learning from all countries, in all languages, properly arranged, substantially and well bound, minutely and fully catalogued, easily accessible and yet safely preserved, capable for some years of keeping pace with the increase of human knowledge—will no doubt be great; but so is the nation which is to bear it."

The Standing Committee sent this Report to the General Board,

TWO PUBLIC ENQUIRIES: GROWTH AND DISSENSION

which in May approved it. Then in the autumn the attention of the Treasury was called to the needs of the Library, and on 29th November the Chancellor of the Exchequer was present at a meeting of the Sub-Committee on Printed Books. Formal application was thereupon made and a grant of £10,000 received as the first of a series intended to continue till the deficiencies were made up; the Treasury is never able to promise outright grants for years beyond the current. The Report, with correspondence, was printed as a Parliamentary Paper on 27th March of the following year. This grant lasted, with occasional cuts, for just half a century, and was chiefly responsible for the Museum's pre-eminent position at the end of that period.

Even before this grant allowed Watts to begin his task, still kept up in the Library by a group of Assistants, of reading all the current and the chief of the antiquarian booklists of the world and marking in them, or at least in the former, for purchase the bulk of books of any real value, occasions had been taken of filling gaps. The foundation of the Library's vast Luther collection was laid. Large purchases were made from the Libri, Sussex and B. H. Bright sales in 1844 and 1845, for which special grants were obtained. From the Sussex came many rare Bibles; and from the Bright early English books, including the celebrated Roxburghe Ballads. In 1839 there were practically no American books in the collection, but a substantial order was then given. Still, four years later, there were only about a thousand of them. In 1845, however, a young man from Vermont "drifted in," as he expressed it, introduced by Mr. Jared Sparks. This was Henry Stevens, and Panizzi instantly perceived the use that might be made of him and set him on his great task of placing the Museum collection of Americana in the forefront of the world's, including American, libraries (see below, pp. 207–8). Maps and music also began to be bought. Orientalia, which had hardly gone beyond Hebrew, were more widely envisaged, and in 1847 the great Morrison library was bought, thus laying the real foundation of the Museum's Chinese collection (see below, pp. 317–19). An out-of-the-way European literature, Modern Greek, was also put on a better footing by the purchase of 627 volumes from Lord Guilford's sale in 1853. If one among the occasional purchases of this time is to be mentioned it may be a remarkable volume (C.20.e.13) of "agenda" format, in original binding, containing over sixty French mid-sixteenth century "sotties" or farces, nearly all of them otherwise unknown.

4. The Grenville Library

Many criticisms of omissions to take the opportunity of picking up rare old books had to be passed by in silence, because Panizzi could not reveal what he alone knew, that Grenville intended to bequeath to the Museum his entire and splendid collection, abounding in early printed books, in the literature of the romance languages and in some special chapters of English history (see below p. 193–8). This bequest, effected in 1847, of over twenty thousand volumes, all (even the unimportant books) very well bound, strengthened the Museum almost as much again as Cracherode's and the King's Libraries had, and was a triumph for Panizzi, to whose personal influence alone the bequest was due.

Not that the triumph did not involve troubles. Panizzi knew of Grenville's desire that the collection should be kept together, and the old struggle over the King's Library was renewed with Madden, who naturally wished the Grenville MSS. to be moved to his Department. The fight raged hottest round the body of the splendid illuminated volume of the *Triumphs of the Emperor Charles V*, then believed to be the work of Giulio Clovio. Madden obtained the transfer of this, but, as he told the Commission in 1848, four successive orders of the Trustees for the transfer of the other Grenville MSS. were ignored. He, on his part, entertained an equal disinclination to transfer to the Printed Books a Vérard volume which was among the Harleian MSS., but was not conscious of any inconsistency. Moreover, the room in which Grenville's books were eventually placed and (in peace time) still stand had been allotted to the Manuscripts, and therefore became a battlefield. For years the books lay on the floor in piles and parcels, a scandal which must have almost broken the heart of Holden, Grenville's devoted personal servant, who came with his master's library and was in attendance on it for many years thereafter.

TWO PUBLIC ENQUIRIES: GROWTH AND DISSENSION

5. THE COPYRIGHT ACT OF 1842: COLLECTION OF COPYRIGHT BOOKS

Copyright books were not coming in as was intended by the framers of the existing Acts, and when a new and comprehensive Bill was drafted the deposit clauses were more closely defined. Reprints of books of which copies of previous editions had not been deposited were claimable by the Museum. All books deposited were to be absolutely complete and in the same state as those offered for sale. The penalties for non-compliance were the price of the book, a fine not exceeding £5 and legal costs. The act (5 & 6 Vict., c. 45, "the Imperial Copyright Act") embodying these provisions was passed in 1842, but the administration was laxly performed by the Secretary, who told the Royal Commission in 1848 that publishers "on the whole cheerfully comply with the provisions of an Act which is of very dubious policy." It was not till 1850 that Panizzi obtained from the Trustees their power of attorney (subsequently given to every Keeper of Printed Books) to proceed in their name against defaulting publishers, cheap books being selected, in order to make light fines. He issued a circular, drafted by the Trustees' solicitors, to the trade, and then in 1852 issued summonses, first in London and then in the provinces; he also travelled round the provincial houses. By these means he secured for the national library the steady supply of current English books which Parliament had long intended, and which has been continued to the present day. He was indifferent to the fact that he also secured for himself extreme unpopularity in the trade and a flood of abusive attacks in the journals to which publishers had access; he was a public official, carrying out the provisions of an Act of Parliament, and, except for a letter in *The Times* (2nd February, 1853) he ignored the clamour, which died away, as ignored clamour generally does. In time it was realized that the Copyright Act did not differ from other Acts of Parliament in being optional. The effect may be seen from the figures. In 1851 the books received by copyright numbered 9,871, in 1858 they had risen to 19,578.

Activity in the Printed Books in this period was largely swallowed up by the General Catalogue, to which we shall recur later, and by the task of dealing with the growing volume of current accessions. Other special cataloguing was that by Edwards of the Thomason Tracts, already mentioned, of the music by Oliphant, who was appointed for the purpose in 1841, and after his retirement in 1850 by Edmund von Bach, and of the maps by William Hughes (1841–43) and after him by R. H. Major.

6. THE MANUSCRIPTS: ACQUISITIONS MADE AND ACQUISITIONS MISSED

Accessions in the Manuscripts were far less important than in the Printed Books in this period, though the resources for purchasing had been swollen by the Egerton and Farnborough Funds and the Department shared in the increased liberality of the Treasury to the Museum. Fixed at £700 in 1837, the grant was doubled six years later, and by 1848–49 had reached £3,000. Later it dropped to £2,000. A few notable gifts were made. The official papers of Richard, Marquess Wellesley, Governor-General of India, 1798–1805, were presented in 1842 by his Executors—to be joined much later by the mass of the personal papers of Warren Hastings; two years later two large collections of Welsh MSS. were given by the Governors of the Welsh School and by the Cymmrodorion Society. Considerable purchases of collections included Bishop Butler's MSS. (one of them a copy of Gregory's *Moralia*, written in the seventh century in Merovingian characters), bought in 1841; volumes of Sir Julius Caesar's papers (1838 and 1842), which formed a supplement to those in the Lansdowne MSS.; over 120 volumes from the Upcott sale (1846), consisting of the correspondence and papers of various Elizabethan public men such as Hatton; a large liturgical collection, both manuscript and printed, bought (1847) from a famous collector, the Rev. William Maskell, who also advised the Museum in its purchases in this field; and a selection relating to Anglo-French history, from the vast collection of documents assembled by the Baron de Joursanvault during the French revolution, which Ellis had inspected at Pomard in 1829 but (Joursanvault proving impracticable) had failed to buy; thereby bringing upon himself an incredibly spiteful and wounding attack by Harris Nicolas, in his *State of Historical Literature*, 1830, who ridiculed Ellis as a vain chatterbox, ignorant of French. Of the many single volumes of great value bought in this period at prices that now seem derisory, one, the very early copy of the Vulgate in Alcuin's revision, in Caroline minuscules, was much advertised before the Committees of 1835-36 by witnesses who blamed the Trustees for not buying it at the then enormous price of £1,500; it had first been offered for £12,000 by its hopeful owner. It was eventually bought for £750. More important was the magnificent Hours of John Duke of Bedford, bought for £3,000 in 1852, one of the very finest illuminated books in the Library. It had been in the Harleian Library, but had been retained by the Countess of Oxford in 1753 and sold at the dispersal of the Portland Museum in 1786.

Many great opportunities, however, were lost, generally for want of funds. The Treasury refused the £1,500 which Madden asked to bid with at the Duke of Sussex and B. H. Bright sales of 1844 and 1845, on the ground of the grants which had been made to other Departments. He wrote on the occasion a letter to the Trustees which Ellis declined to lay before them. In 1839 the Trustees refused the offer, at a low price according to Madden, of the 530 Pucci MSS. from Libri's collection. Seven years later they failed to secure a Treasury grant of £8,300, or even of £6,000, their second appeal, to buy the most valuable part of Libri's library, which had passed to the Duke of Buckingham at Stowe. Then in 1848, perhaps discouraged by their failure two years before, they made no application for funds to buy the 702 Barrois MSS., which Madden valued at £6,000. And when in the following year the Duke of Buckingham offered the whole of his Stowe MSS., valued by Madden at £8,300 (see below, pp. 257-9), and the Treasury gave the Trustees authority to treat further, some obstacle presented itself, for they were bought by Lord Ashburnham for just £8,000.

THE LIBRARY OF THE BRITISH MUSEUM

7. THE NITRIAN SYRIAC MANUSCRIPTS

On the Oriental side a gift of 74 MSS. in 1846 from the Church Missionary Society started the Ethiopic collection, and a large Chinese collection, including maps, sent by order of the Earl of Aberdeen did as much for manuscripts in that language as the Morrison collection did a year later for printed books. But the greatest acquisition of the Department, and, except for the Grenville Library, of the Museum in this period was that of the Syriac MSS. from the Nitrian Desert of Western Egypt.[17] There were then but few Syriac scholars in England, and little provision for teaching the tongue, in spite of its importance to the early Christian Church, and this acquisition and Cureton's use of it placed the study on a new footing.

The libraries of the Nitrian Convents had long been known of in the West. As early as 1678–79 the Oxford Orientalist Robert Huntingdon visited them and brought back some MSS. now in the Bodleian. Then, in 1707 and 1715 the cousins Elias and Joseph Simon Assemani were successively sent by the Pope, and they too brought back a number, now in the Vatican. But over a century passed before another Western scholar renewed the quest. Henry Tattam, Archdeacon of Bedford, the leading Coptic scholar of his day, was in search of texts for his grammar of some of the dialects and especially for his *Lexicon Aegyptiaco-Latinum*, 1835. On his behalf Lord Prudhoe in 1828 visited the Nitrian Desert and its convents. In one of them, that of S. Mary Theotokos, or Deipara, also called Souriani, or the convent of the Syrians, from its having been founded by the Syrians from Mesopotamia, though he did not secure the particular book, a Coptic-Arabic dictionary, which Tattam wanted (Curzon afterwards found it and had it brought to England), he did get a sight of an oil-cellar in which were lying neglected masses of apparently ancient MSS. Prudhoe reported his find, and the Souriani Convent was therefore one of the goals of the next English traveller who hunted for MSS. in the Levant. This was the Hon. Robert Curzon, of Parham, a young man of wealth, enterprise and infinite humour, who was collecting materials for a history of writing, and who also had an idea that texts of lost Greek

TWO PUBLIC ENQUIRIES: GROWTH AND DISSENSION

classics might be found in Eastern monastic libraries, such as those of the Nitrian Desert, the rock-pinnacles of northern Greece and Mount Athos.[18] This latter idea was to be disappointed. The monks of Mount Athos, whose large libraries had long before been examined, were under a threat of excommunication if they consulted any secular work whatever; and the ignorance of the Levantine monks in general, as experienced by Curzon and Tattam, was as extreme as that at St. Catherine of Mount Sinai when Tischendorf, not many years later, found the Codex Sinaiticus there. The monks of Souriani had, like the rest, fallen from the state of learning of their predecessors of the early centuries, and knew nothing of the contents of the books, which Curzon found lying in heaps in dust and decay. The abbot began by denying their existence, but by the aid of sweet pink rosoglio, a strong drink which he had had the wisdom to bring with him, Curzon was able to overcome this obstacle, and was shown the celebrated oil-cellar; it was empty, but leading out of it he found a door, and beyond it a smaller cellar filled to the depth of two feet with loose leaves of Syriac MSS. One large volume was mistaken by the monks for a box of treasure in another than the true sense in which it was one, and in their disappointment on finding that it was only an old book they sold it and a few more which Curzon had found used as lids of large empty jars.

Next year Tattam himself came out and methodically examined the Nitrian convents and bought a considerable quantity of the books from Souriani. The Syriac MSS. he sold to the Museum; and in some of these notes were found by Cureton stating that in A.D. 932 the Abbot of the time had brought 250 volumes from Mesopotamia. It was therefore obvious that most of these must still be in the convent. The Trustees put the case to the Treasury and Tattam was sent out in 1842–43. He wisely did not this time negotiate direct with the monks, who were by now aware of the value of their neglected books, but used the influence of the Patriarch and the Sheikh and the services of a clever native servant; he secured what was supposed to be the whole remaining library, which when sorted at the Museum proved to contain 317 volumes, mostly written at Edessa or Tekrit; the latest bore the date 1292, the earliest 411. But the monks had

THE LIBRARY OF THE BRITISH MUSEUM

kept back half the books. A few years after this one Auguste Pacho, acting at Cureton's suggestion, completely cleared the rest, and sold most to the Treasury for the Museum in 1847. But he in his turn swindled the purchasers, selling volumes on his way to England, and the final instalment was only bought by the Museum some years later. (For a note on the collection, see below, pp. 295–6.)

Forshall had before leaving the Department catalogued the Syriac and Karshuni MSS. from the Rich collection. The vast new accessions now made were not to appear in a published catalogue till Wright's of 1873; but Cureton (while engaged on the first Arabic Catalogue, which came out in 1847–52), had the fundamental task of sorting and identifying the fragments in which the Nitrian MSS. arrived at the Museum. When he entered the Museum he knew no Syriac, but became a master of the tongue, and made many important discoveries in the collection. His claim that the Nitrian copy of the Epistles of St. Ignatius to Polycarp, the Ephesians and the Romans is the only authentic text, over which controversy was vigorously conducted, has been given up; but the fragments of an unknown Syriac version of the Gospels, which he published, known as "the Curetonian Gospels," hold the place he gave them. He also found and edited for the Trustees a palimpsest copy of a large fragment of the Iliad (see p. 274).

In 1836 Forshall had told the Parliamentary Committee that there were in the Department some 4,000 uncatalogued MSS., and that it was difficult to find anything. The next fifteen years or so were to see most arrears cleared off. Music and maps, Syriac, Arabic and Ethiopic, the Arundel MSS., the Additionals from 1836 to 1853, and the few papyri, were represented by published catalogues; and though the gap in the Additionals between Ayscough's catalogue of 1783 and 1835 remained (as it still remains) uncovered, an Index published in 1849 went part of the way, and Madden mentioned as undescribed in 1848 only a number of the Indian MSS. Meanwhile, though in the ten years from 1838 and 1847 seven thousand MSS. had come in, the eternal task of folioing went on, the Lansdowne being only finished in 1860.[19] And Madden, besides his private work on the text of Wyclif, made much progress with the slow and difficult restoration of the burned Cotton fragments.

TWO PUBLIC ENQUIRIES: GROWTH AND DISSENSION

8. The Printed Books: The Catalogue

In the Printed Books the large accessions, especially from 1846, prevented much activity in the production of special catalogues, though (as in the Manuscripts) Music and Maps were taken in hand. The time was hardly ripe for them while the collections were in an early stage of growth, and only a part of the use of special catalogues is to call lacunae to the notice of possible benefactors. So a suggestion of a catalogue of early printed books made by Croker bore no fruit. But in both Departments advantage was taken of the new galleries (though not till 1851) for small exhibitions, which had been projected twenty years before but postponed for want of space.

The move to the new house and the work on the increasing accessions were doubtless laborious, but they were not controversial activities. It was far otherwise with the Alphabetical Catalogue. On 30th April, 1834, the Trustees had decided to suspend the Classified Catalogue which had for some time been languishing, owing to the greater need for the men in cataloguing accessions for insertion in the old octavo catalogue. The state of the staff and Reading Room copies of this was by now chaotic with erasures and interlineations; it was almost unusable. Moreover collections like the King's, Banks, Thomason and French Revolution were not included. The Trustees therefore rightly decided on a new alphabetical catalogue of the whole Library, in spite of their Principal Librarian's opinion that readers should depend for accessions on the Librarian's memory. But they inadvisedly rejected Baber's recommendation of putting the work under one competent general editor (i.e. Panizzi) and gave it to four inferior men, who had no head over them. The result of their work was negligible. Baber reported again, on 19th January, 1836, in a document which was certainly largely written by Panizzi, for it expounded his principles of cataloguing shelf by shelf. On 23rd February Panizzi himself put in a long and considered report, which anticipates the main principles of library cataloguing as now long understood by all librarians, and again, after his succession to the Keepership, he urged that on the old system there was no hope of a catalogue in any reasonable time. But Ellis was part-author of the old

Catalogue, and Forshall hated Panizzi. Nothing could move the Trustees, who merely reiterated their demand for a printed catalogue at the earliest date. It was not till 1839 that Panizzi obtained their authority for a revision of the rules, on receiving which he at once put before them his celebrated 91 Rules, which with Winter Jones, Edwards and Parry he had been for some time preparing on the basis of a simple code drawn up in 1834 by Baber and himself. The Trustees accepted the Rules at once, at the same time ordering Panizzi to deliver a catalogue "complete from press" by the end of 1844. Panizzi was helpless. Thoroughness gave way to speed, and Volume I, containing the letter A alone, appeared on 9th July, 1841, with the Rules prefixed; but Panizzi protested in submitting it that the rest could not appear in the given time, and that the volume was full of faults and also of omissions due to not cataloguing shelf by shelf, which would be the pretext for attacks on himself. In the next two years he reported again and again, and in 1844 expounded at a Trustees' meeting the impossibility of completing the work in time, but they took no notice. It was not till January 1846 that they asked Panizzi why no more had been printed. He replied that he had stopped the printing because it had become obvious (he might have said he had known from the first) that no alphabetical catalogue could be printed till the whole work was ready for press. The Trustees accepted the situation, but added that a report should be made to Parliament.

So ended the fiasco of the 1841 Catalogue. An attempt was made in the Board to have printing resumed in 1847, but it failed. It should be remembered that they had just had the striking success of Panizzi's report on the collections of his Department and the consequent grant, and they were probably influenced by this in bowing to the inevitable. But the episode does the Board small credit, though the ultimate responsibility no doubt rests on Ellis and Forshall.

9. The Royal Commission, 1847–49

The affairs of the Catalogue were soon to have abundant light thrown on them. The malcontents found powerful allies in the men

TWO PUBLIC ENQUIRIES: GROWTH AND DISSENSION

of science who felt that Sloane's intentions had been neglected and that the Museum had fallen into the almost exclusive control of men of literature and history. A number of leaders in science sent a memorial on the subject to the Prime Minister on 10th March, 1847, and a Royal Commission was appointed on 17th June, under the Chairmanship of Lord Ellesmere, who as Lord Francis Egerton (he was a nephew of the founder of the Egerton Collection) had sat on the Committee of 1835–36. A less happy choice was that of John Payne Collier, a violent and indiscreet partisan on the Catalogue question, to be Secretary.

The Commissioners, who reported in 1850,[20] patiently investigated the affairs of the whole Museum. The injustice to Natural History, surprisingly, engaged little of their attention, which was chiefly given to the bad administration of the Principal Librarian and Secretary, and most of all to the Catalogue. Their meetings in fact became a stage for a long-drawn-out contest between Panizzi and his critics. The two subjects were in fact closely allied, since under any good system of management the Catalogue would have been either dropped altogether or carried out on the principles which were again and again laid before the Trustees. They strongly condemned the excessive and irresponsible power of the Secretary, and his officious control, for example, of registration; they found that his register was "not only of no practical use, but in some cases destructive of responsibility." They recommended that the two offices of Principal Librarian and Secretary should be amalgamated.

Round the Catalogue the storm raged. The party who demanded a printed catalogue, without much caring about its quality, had full opportunities in the journals, and especially in the *Athenaeum*, and had undoubtedly influenced the Trustees. Panizzi had been necessarily silent, but now the critics were confronted with him, and one by one he destroyed them. His own colleague, J. E. Gray, the Keeper of Natural History, wrote and published two pamphlets attacking him.[21] This outrage he referred to the Trustees, who advised him to take no action; they did not reprimand Gray, but Panizzi had their sympathy. Collier also published an attack, Secretary of the Commission though he was,[22] and was so ill-advised as to produce a specimen of the system of simplified and accelerated cataloguing which in spite of his bibliographical experience he considered feasible, but which when examined by Winter Jones was found to contain in twenty-five titles "almost every possible error which can be committed in cataloguing books," and to be "open to almost every possible objection which can be brought against concise titles." Nor was the answer difficult to a Commissioner who asked Panizzi "What is the use of a title in Russian characters to an English reader?" Winter Jones proved a very useful supporter of Panizzi, and his evidence did much to drive off the field the many advocates of quick and easy cataloguing. Panizzi and Winter Jones found among the witnesses not only critics but valuable allies. Cureton spoke with his calm good sense and good feeling, and Edwards, though he preferred a classed catalogue, spoke well of the necessity of an alphabetical catalogue, each to support the other. But the best support came from Augustus de Morgan, mathematician and bibliographer. He declared his approval of Panizzi's Rules simply because they were rules, while most catalogues were made with none. He examined the recent and lauded catalogues of the Bodleian and the London Library; the former he found to be no credit to the University of Oxford, and the latter to be even worse than those produced by dealers. And to the views of amateur cataloguers he replied that he knew very few mathematicians whom he would trust to give an accurate description of a mathematical book.

The Commissioners entirely supported Panizzi on all points of the controversy. They believed that the Trustees were ill-advised in commencing the publication of the Catalogue and consequently in encouraging the expectations thus disappointed. Nor did they think that when the MS. was completed the Trustees would think the expense of printing worth while. Panizzi had estimated to the Trustees in 1847 that if the Catalogue were to be prepared to contain all books received up to the end of 1854, the result could go to press in 1860, and the publication could not be completed till 1895, or forty-one years later than the closing date of accessions. Publication was impossible during the preparation of the copy. Moreover they strongly condemned the Trustees' interference in the details of cataloguing,

TWO PUBLIC ENQUIRIES: GROWTH AND DISSENSION

an interference which they would not have attempted in such special subjects as Natural History or Antiquities. The delay in the production of the Catalogue they held to be simply due to the Trustees' desire to hurry on its printing.

They recommended no change in the General Board of Trustees, but suggested (not unanimously) an Executive Council, on which the Departments should be represented. The Board was too large, and the Standing Committee, consisting of members summoned according to the fancy of the Secretary (which might have been more briefly expressed), in spite of the Statutes of 1833 and 1839, meant "an abridgment of individual responsibility, productive of the worst consequences." The Reading Room they thought should be enlarged and should be available to young students and to persons engaged in "the manufacture of useful knowledge"; but they would see mere reading for recreation excluded. (It will be remembered that Ewart's Committee on Public Libraries was just about to meet.) They severely condemned the quarrels between high officers which had been revealed, and thought that Panizzi, who had been throughout attacked rather than attacker, had been too sensitive; his self-appointed critics' "proved want of judgment and perspicacity" was punishment enough, they thought. They made some useful recommendations on staff matters: the staff should be brought under the Superannuation Act and be pensionable; life tenure and temporary posts alike should be abolished. A separate Department of non-European MSS. should be formed.

10. ACTION ON THE ROYAL COMMISSION'S REPORT

The Trustees sent a grateful reply to the Commissioners' Report in general terms accepting their findings. This document was drafted for them by Peel, who vied with Sir David Dundas, Sir Robert Inglis, Henry Hallam and Macaulay in being the most zealous of the Trustees; it was his last act, being found on him after his fatal accident. They set up a Committee, and as a result of its report the Standing Committee was reconstituted under exact definitions of its composition and mode of election; and their Statutes of the same year gave effect to many of the views expressed. Though an Executive Council was not formed, the Secretaryship vanished, being merged in the office of Principal Librarian. This was facilitated by Forshall's retirement from ill-health at this moment.²³ The Principal Librarian was retained (the Trustees stated that they required a principal officer); he was to communicate the Trustees' orders to the officers and see them carried out and to report, and he was also given control (which he still has) of the Reading Rooms and admission to them. The Temporary Assistants were merged into the Permanent. The Keepers were to make (as they still do) monthly and annual reports of progress in their Departments. The Keeper of Printed Books, as noticed above, was to superintend and enforce delivery of Copyright books. By tacit consent Panizzi's system of examining all the books shelf by shelf before cataloguing was adopted, but the catalogue had already reached G.

V

THE READING ROOM AND IRON LIBRARY: PANIZZI, PRINCIPAL LIBRARIAN (1851-66)

1. The Reading Room and Iron Library

THE price of great acquisitions was as usual the need for enlargement of the building, especially since, as we have seen, Smirke drew his plans before the new ideas had arrived. In 1850 Panizzi reported that in view of the difficulty of storage he could only usefully spend £2,500, in place of the £10,000 voted in 1846, and this reduction held in the following year also. The Grenville books, and many others as well, were stacked on the floor, and by December 1852 a librarian's nightmare was realized; books were placed on the shelves three deep. Even the Catalogue titles could not be properly stored.

The Trustees had been for some time in favour of making their next expansion by buying the hither side of Montagu Street and erecting a wing for the Printed Books on the site, with the Reading Room at the North-East corner; they had applied to the Treasury in vain in 1846, 1848 and 1850. Not only was there no room for acquisitions of books, but the Reading Room was much overcrowded. In 1853 Carlyle agitated in vain for a separate room to read in.

Public attention having been called to the Museum's needs by the Royal Commission, William Hosking, Professor of Architecture in the University of London, put, first to the Commission and then, in 1849, to the Trustees, a plan he had drawn for turning the Northern half of the King's Library into the Reading Room and creating in the quadrangle a handsome domed rotunda for the exhibition of sculpture; and in this or similar ways there were many plans for filling the open central space of the existing buildings. The earliest of these, and the best, is that contributed by Watts to the *Mechanics' Magazine* in 1837. In 1852 James Fergusson published his *Observations* and a Parliamentary Paper appeared. Croker reviewed all these in the *Quarterly*.[1] Fergusson, like Watts, proposed a Reading Room in the centre of the

THE LIBRARY OF THE BRITISH MUSEUM

quadrangle, which everyone agreed was wasted, since it could only be seen from the ground floor through a hole specially cut in the North wall of the Entrance Hall.

Panizzi's plan was therefore not altogether original, nor was the use of iron construction at all new. From Abraham Darby's iron bridge in Shropshire down there had been many precedents, and the most striking was the most recent, Paxton's Great Exhibition, afterwards the Crystal Palace, which was designed and erected in Hyde Park in 1850 and was the sensation of the day. And in library architecture iron had been used, by Labrouste at the Sainte Geneviève, where the long Reading Room is like a Crystal Palace, but enclosed in stone, and at the Library of Congress, where T. N. Walter in 1851–52 built, not a true stack indeed, but iron shelving on a stone floor. And there were much earlier domed reading rooms at Wolfenbüttel and the Radcliffe at Oxford. Panizzi must have known of all these. But his plan, which he put before the Trustees in May 1852, combined the advantages of all the others and was far more practical. It was approved, worked out by Smirke, put to the Treasury, refused, vainly reported against in 1853 by Sir Charles Barry (who preferred a glass-covered sculpture hall in the quadrangle), then on a second submission accepted by the Treasury on 18th May, 1854, when it at once became one of the *mirabilia Londini*. The cost, £150,000, three times as much as Panizzi's first guess, was small by comparison with that of any other form of building.[2] Frescoes in the dome were considered but fortunately not carried out; in the reading rooms of other libraries where they are found they are both in themselves and as an attraction to visitors a nuisance to readers; in fact one of the great virtues of the Room is that it looks what it is, a library, with no decorations other than gold-lined panels and on the walls the bindings of books—real (the whole selection was specially rebound) or, on the doors, imitations. The decoration of the dome consisted of broad vertical bands of grey-blue alternating with panels of bright gold, which became so dingy that in 1939 no member of the staff could remember what the decoration had been before the redecoration of 1907.

The plan and fittings of the Reading Room were much admired

THE READING ROOM AND IRON LIBRARY

by Labrouste, who imitated some features in the Salle de Travail of the Bibliothèque Nationale at Paris. Panizzi's friend Prosper Mérimée said that it was "destiné à servir de type"; but though there have been circular reading rooms built since, there is none, except perhaps that at Leeds University, built only the other day, which repeats its best features.[3]

The bust of Panizzi by Marochetti, later placed over the door of the Room, occupies a place for which Smirke had suggested a bust of Minerva or, alternatively, of Queen Victoria.

The Trustees ordered that the Superintendent, who had, it will be remembered, previously been a selected member of the lower staff, should henceforward be the Senior Assistant Keeper in the Department. He is still always a Deputy-Keeper (the modern name for an Assistant Keeper) but not necessarily the Senior. Watts accordingly became the first Superintendent of the new Room, not much to his own satisfaction, since he was a rather shy man, and he did not wish to leave the work of Placer of books. He continued his work as chief selector of purchases, however.

The books in the Room were catalogued in a special catalogue. There had been since 1839 a MS. catalogue of those in the old Reading Room, but the new reference library was much larger and was a quite new selection.[4] Manuscripts as well as printed books were still sent into the one Reading Room, only what we call "Extra-select" MSS. being (inconveniently) seen in the Department, there being as yet no Students' Room. Madden suggested special Attendants to supervise readers of MSS., but did not get his way, and this was a more reasonable grievance than most of his. Nor was there at first any Reserve Room for rare books. And facilities for hand-washing were only provided in 1868.

The Iron Library was an even more remarkable achievement than the Reading Room itself. Apart from the reduction of fire risk an immense space was saved by eliminating brick supports and substituting metal. Never before, certainly at so small a cost, had there been erected shelving for nearly a million books. Modern stack-building has, of course, improved on it, substituting steel for cast-iron and economizing space; but the Iron Library is the honoured ancestor of every stack that has since been built. The acquisitions made since 1845 were moved into it at its opening.

The engineering was very thorough, great pains being taken with the foundations in particular.[5] When the roof of Charing Cross Railway Station fell in 1907, H.M. Office of Works tested the structure, then just half a century old, and found nothing wrong; and recently another inspection gave the same result.

2. Panizzi Principal Librarian

In 1856 Ellis at last retired, aged 79, to live another thirteen years, "full of geniality, urbanity and anecdote to the last."[6] There could be no doubt as to his successor—Madden, Hawkins and Gray were able men, but the ablest and senior of them, Madden, impossible —Panizzi received the appointment, so that when his Reading Room was opened he had been Principal Librarian for a year. He was succeeded as Keeper of Printed Books by Winter Jones.

Panizzi's Principal Librarianship lasted for ten years, years which after the preceding twenty must have seemed to him "calm after storm, port after stormy seas." Two important affairs, however, occupied his energies, which for some time were undiminished. The first, a comparatively simple matter, but one which was long overdue, was the inclusion in 1860 of the Museum Staff in the regular Civil Service, and the application to them of the Superannuation Act of the previous year. Panizzi had always been sympathetic and often personally generous to his juniors, who were even worse paid than he was himself. His first care on becoming Principal Librarian was to obtain from the Treasury some improvement in the salary scales, and he was able before he retired to see his men (at the price of an entrance examination, which so far limited the Trustees' right of nomination) secure of their pensions, which had been accorded of grace to Forshall and Ellis and never to anyone else in the Museum's history.

The second was a larger and thornier problem, the old problem of house-room. Hardly had the Reading Room and Iron Library been built when space became again a pressing need. This was the period of massive acquisitions of ancient sculpture from the Near East. And the intake of Copyright Books, stimulated by Panizzi's own activity,

THE READING ROOM AND IRON LIBRARY

threatened to fill the Iron Library, as it soon would have done, had not the sliding or swinging press been devised in 1886 (see below, pp. 137–8). Shelving had been provided for 800,000 volumes, but though the capacity proved to reach a million, the annual rate of increase also exceeded the estimate, which had been 20,000 a year, which would fill the space in forty years; actually by 1861 it had reached 35,000.

Nor were the Manuscripts better off. In 1860 Madden asked for six more Assistants, but confessed that if he were to get them he would not know where to put them. The grant was now £2,000 a year, and additions were coming in at the rate of a thousand a year. Something had to be done. On 26th November, 1859, the Trustees decided that the Library and the Antiquities (the latter with some limited exceptions) should stay at Bloomsbury, and on the following 21st January they made, but only by a majority of one, the consequent decision to remove the Natural History. In October they applied to the Treasury for funds for the purchase of land. The Treasury decided for South Kensington, where the Government already possessed the Great Exhibition area. Smirke in 1857 had recommended building on the south side of Montague Place, to the North of the Museum. A proposal made at this time to take the line of narrow Exhibition Galleries on the upper floor of the North Wing into the Printed Books was not acted upon. By 1858 Panizzi had already seen and reported to the Trustees that to keep the Museum intact it would be necessary to buy and build over the whole island site. The Museum was not kept together; the Natural History Departments were moved, though not till 1880–83, since the Bill was rejected in 1862, and authority was only obtained in 1878; yet forty years after Panizzi's report the rest of the island site was secured.

At the end of 1862 Panizzi had a break-down in health, and Winter Jones, though far from being Senior Keeper, acted as Deputy during his four and a half months' sick-leave. In 1865 Panizzi expressed a desire to be superannuated, offering unpaid assistance to his successor for a while. In 1866 he and Madden both retired. Madden, a very great scholar and palaeographer, had done much for the Museum's collection of manuscripts, but what he had done had been chiefly the direct result of his own scholarship and his own energy; he cannot be said to have organized his Department well, still less to have conducted its relations with the House as a whole in such a way as to have benefited both.7 Panizzi, contrariwise, was very soon after his arrival taken away from his scholarly work in literature, which he loved, and immersed in administration.

As a library administrator he has never had a rival; he throws Bignon, Korf and Delisle into the shade; perhaps his nearest competitor is Dr. Herbert Putnam. But it must be admitted that he was *felix opportunitate vitae*. He arrived at the time of the meeting of the old and new, crystallized in England by the Reform Bill. He found a library of 115,000 printed volumes, not counting the King's Library, which was not actually received till after his appointment. And this library not only stood low among the greater libraries of Europe, disgracefully low considering the position of the country, whose national library it nominally was, but it was a haphazard accumulation of benefactions, useful no doubt for historical scholars, though not as useful as methodical purchasing could have made it even to them, and to students of modern subjects of practically no use at all. Playing on the national vanity, as a foreigner could so well do, and using in his later days his considerable political influence as an unofficial intermediary between the Government and Continental Liberals, he obtained national funds and left a methodical collection (apart from the Grenville bequest, which was solely due to himself), properly supplied by copyright and purchase, of close on a million books. The manuscripts, with which he was not concerned till he became Principal Librarian, had, of course, from the first been of high importance; the Printed Books were a neglected appendage to them till his Keepership.

To books a catalogue is necessary, and to a catalogue a code of rules. Panizzi's long and exasperating battle with journalists and with a Board unduly influenced by them, to secure a worthy catalogue, has been lightly sketched above. His Rules were the first thorough code ever drawn up. And he secured house-room for books and seats for readers on a scale never before imagined. In all these four things, collection, shelving, catalogue and reading room, the standards which we use today to judge him were of his own invention.

THE READING ROOM AND IRON LIBRARY

Panizzi's personal character was chivalrous, that is combative and generous. Nothing could have been more foreign to *le flegme anglais*. To introduce him into the quiet Museum was to attempt to acclimatize an Italian volcano in a Dutch garden. In money matters he was remarkably disinterested, for example declining Grenville's offer to share the expense of his Boiardo and Ariosto, which he had dedicated to Grenville as having generously lent him, an unknown foreign scholar, unique copies of original editions. And he made warm and true friends not only among political and social leaders in London, but also in the commercial society of Liverpool, where at the same period Hazlitt (in *Table Talk*) thought nothing of the kind possible; so much do men find others differ according to the difference in themselves. But Panizzi was impatient of incompetence, and even more of incompetence combined with shiftiness and arrogance, such as he encountered in the Royal Society when he undertook their catalogue in 1833. Such impatience was no more than not to suffer gladly fools who were also knaves, no great failure in charity. But Panizzi owed to this experience an unfortunate life-long dislike of scientific men, which went much beyond his preference at any time (according to Macaulay) of one Aldus to three mammoths. He was no doubt unduly sensitive, as the Royal Commission found in their Report of 1850, and as he himself felt when on retiring he wrote to his colleagues, "if I have ever given unnecessary pain to anyone I regret it most sincerely, and trust that credit will be given me for having been uniformly influenced solely by a sense of duty."

The vulgarity and pertinacity of the personal attacks made on him, which were even repeated in Parliament on his retirement,[8] are the more remarkable that he seems never to have started a quarrel. He was, in truth, that vicious animal which defends itself when attacked. Inside the Museum he was certainly a martinet; on one occasion he reproved even the valued Watts for late appearance on duty, and in his later days he was much feared by juniors, Gosse, a Transcriber, going so far as to recall him as "a thorough-going tyrant,"[9] while the late Dr. Percy Gardner, who had been an Assistant in the Department of Coins and Medals when it was formed out of the Antiquities in 1861, described him as "a steam-roller." But he formed high opinions of, and showed much kindness to, some of the young men, such as Deutsch, Major, Rieu, Ralston [10] and Maunde Thompson, who will figure in later pages; and it must be said that in these cases anyhow he showed sound perception.

The formidable aspect of him is well shown in the fine portrait in the Board Room, painted by G. F. Watts shortly before his retirement. With, and really some time before, Panizzi's departure the age of stress and revolution in the Museum, and especially in the Library, ended. Later Principal Librarians and Keepers, some of them men capable of work like his, have, except in the printing of catalogues, had less opportunity; he had laid down the lines for them. The Museum does well to hold him in honour.

VI

INTERLUDE: WINTER JONES, PRINCIPAL LIBRARIAN (1866-79)

1. Winter Jones, Watts and the Printed Books

Of the men whom Panizzi had trained in the Printed Books and who had carried out his reforms, Winter Jones was one of the most useful. Though he had considerable scholarship, doing solid work for the Hakluyt Society, he was not a specialist, as Watts was on languages or Major on cartography. Rather he was Panizzi's right-hand man and adviser on all details, whether of the Catalogue, of which he was principal reviser, or of the building of the Reading Room and Iron Library. He had not obtained the special promotions previously recommended for him, but on the elder Garnett's death in 1850 he succeeded naturally as senior to the vacant Assistant Keepership, and as naturally followed Panizzi as Keeper in 1856. He thus had the move into the new Room and Iron Library to organize, and very well it was done. The new space having justified the restoration of the full purchase grant, he also had during his Keepership the task of making up the arrears of the previous years, during which the grant had been, on Panizzi's own reports, cut down for want of shelf room.

On Panizzi's retirement from the Principal Librarianship ten years later, Jones again followed him. Not so striking a character as his master and predecessor, he was nevertheless a good Principal Librarian, in one point perhaps better than Panizzi, for he interested himself deeply in the work of the Antiquities. In 1877 he had presided over the Congress which led to the formation of the Library Association, and he became the Association's first President in the following year, thus setting a precedent which has been followed by many of the Museum's leading figures. His great achievement was to secure in 1877 a further improvement in the pay and conditions of service of the Staff, though they still remained at a lower level than those of other Civil Servants. With a curious want of imagination Gladstone is said to have stated in the Commons that the work of an Assistant in the Museum was so attractive that it required no added material attraction of pay. The long struggle with the Treasury over this matter, and the negotiations which led up to the removal of the Natural History Department to South Kensington, were the chief cares of this period. The former in particular wore Jones's health out, and he retired in 1878.

During Panizzi's and Winter Jones's Principal Librarianships there entered several men who were to come to the front in the later years sketched in this chapter, notably, in the Printed Books, Douglas, Fortescue and Miller, and in the Manuscripts Maunde Thompson and Warner. Douglas was to be transferred to the new Oriental Department.

In the Printed Books Winter Jones was naturally succeeded by Watts, who was only just his junior and had played a part hardly second to his in the period of stress and reform. But Watts's Keepership lasted only three years, for he died suddenly in 1869. No great events occurred in the Department in that short time, except the separation of the Maps from the Books in 1867. The preparation of the Catalogue in MS. went on, the idea of printing it having been abandoned since the forties, to be reintroduced and carried through thirty years later, as will be recorded. Watts pushed on with his great ambition of collecting the best of the world's literature. Not only European languages were collected, since the Oriental books were not separated for some while yet. Thus, just as the Michael Hebrew and Morrison Chinese libraries had been acquired by his activity under Panizzi at the end of the forties, he added during his Keepership the Siebold Japanese collection and two, the Fischer and Andrade, of Mexican books.

Watts has been overshadowed by Panizzi, but he was a very remarkable man. He is said to have seen and handled while Placer over 400,000 volumes of accessions. Something of his achievement is shown by him in his well-known report to Panizzi of 1861. In the previous decade he had ordered 80,000 books and examined 600,000 titles, maintaining not only in each of the greater, but more remarkably in the lesser literatures also, Panizzi's and his own ideal of the second-best library in the world. "In Russian, Polish, Hungarian, Danish and Swedish," he said, "with the exception of perhaps fifty volumes, every book that has been purchased by the Museum within the last three-and-twenty years has been purchased at my suggestion. Every future student of those literatures will find riches where I found poverty." It is no bad epitaph. An uncommunicative eye and a certain brusquerie made Watts difficult of access to strangers—a quality which unfitted him for the Reading Room—but he was really a very warm-hearted (and, it seems, also sometimes warm-tempered) man, and inspired much affection among his colleagues. His astonishing memory, which had enabled him to master so many languages and literatures, also made for a richness and charm of conversation which Garnett has compared with that of his famous contemporary, Macaulay.

Watts was followed in the Reading Room by George Bullen, who filled the Superintendentship through the following Keepership as well, in fact till he himself became Keeper in 1875. Bullen, who had come in with Rye and the elder Garnett in 1838, and had assisted Watts in the removal from old Montagu House, was no such scholar as his predecessor, though the Aristotle heading in the 1841 Catalogue, which was allotted to him, was a more than creditable piece of work. But he had what Watts lacked, an easy and genial way with readers; Barwick describes him as a "jovial Irishman"—he was born at Clonakilty, co. Cork. The foundation of the Reading Room's reputation for hospitality and absence of unnecessary discipline has often been attributed to Garnett, but it seems fair to give the first credit to Bullen.

One stiffening of the regulations of the Room had taken place while Watts was Superintendent. The age limit for admission had been a very nominal eighteen. But the Room was often crowded, and in 1862 the Trustees laid down the rule, still in operation, that "to preserve to the uses of those best entitled to them the advantages and facilities afforded by the Library and Reading Room of the British Museum," they "though with great reluctance" were "compelled to raise the limit of age at which persons shall be admissible from eighteen to twenty-one years, unless in special cases, which will be laid before the Trustees at their next meeting."

THE LIBRARY OF THE BRITISH MUSEUM

Watts was succeeded as Keeper by W. B. Rye, who held the office however for only twice the length of time, being succeeded in 1875 by Bullen. Rye was not a man of the calibre of Jones or Watts, let alone of Panizzi, and shyness handicapped him; but he was one of those useful competent men without much initiative whom seniority brings to the top, and he was a sound antiquary. He had come in 1838 and assisted Watts, and had then acted as chief proof-reviser of the 1841 Catalogue. Panizzi had put him on to the arrangement of his beloved Grenville books and the cataloguing of those which Payne and Foss had left uncatalogued (see p. 197), which argues a high opinion of his quality; and Rye also made the first selection and catalogue of the books of reference in the new Reading Room. Not much of note happened during his Keepership, but many good purchases continued to be made, especially of early printed and old English books; in 1870 a large collection from the suppressed monasteries of Portugal was secured. Panizzi had long before suggested that they should be searched.

The most eventful part of Bullen's Keepership fell in the Principal Librarianship of Bond and will be described later.

Two men of very high talent adorned the Department in the middle of the century but had disappeared before their time for command arrived. Coventry Patmore was appointed in 1846 and remained in the Museum, doing excellent work there, as well as making his reputation outside as a poet, till 1862, when the death of his first wife and his own health sent him abroad.[1] An even more remarkable man was the great Talmudic scholar Emanuel Deutsch. "Seldom," wrote Lane-Poole in *The Dictionary of National Biography*, "has the Department of Printed Books acquired the services of so variously accomplished a man," and even if this remark betrays an attitude towards the Printed Books which is not quite unique, it is true, and would also be true if for the Printed Books we were to read the Museum. It was as a Hebraist that Panizzi in 1855 secured Deutsch through the Museum's German agent, Asher, but he was also a fine classic and learned in other Oriental tongues and early German, and had withal the mind of a poet. "For fifteen years," says Lane-Poole, "he did the work of a helot"; but he was able to make important

INTERLUDE: WINTER JONES, PRINCIPAL LIBRARIAN

contributions to Hebrew and other learning in such publications as Smith's *Dictionary of the Bible*, while seldom has a periodical article created such a reputation for its author as Deutsch made by his on the Talmud in the *Quarterly Review* for October 1867. But he was the victim of cancer, and went to Egypt in 1870, dying there three years later, with no great work to his name such as he might have accomplished.

The Far Eastern Collection had acquired importance with the acquisition of the Morrison and Siebold collections of Chinese and Japanese books. Robert Kennaway Douglas, who entered in the early sixties, was in charge in the Printed Books of this part of the Library, and also, after Major's retirement in 1885, of maps; he was transferred in 1892 with all the Oriental Printed Books to the Department of Oriental Printed Books and Manuscripts, as it then became.

2. THE MANUSCRIPTS: BOND FOLLOWS MADDEN

In the Manuscripts Madden's obvious successor was Edward Augustus Bond. When John Holmes died suddenly in 1854 he had followed him as Assistant Keeper of the Department under Madden, and for the next dozen years was its backbone, struggling against the arrears into which the work of the Department was falling, and forming ideas and plans which were later to bear fruit. He was also used as a necessary intermediary between his Keeper and the Principal Librarian, who were not on speaking terms; and he thus acquired a sense of the Museum as a whole. When he became Keeper and found himself invested with the necessary authority he set about reforming the Department. Edward Maunde Thompson had been in it for about four years, and five years later he acquired another first-class man in George Frederic Warner. With these lieutenants he brought up to date the cataloguing of the Additions, the Department's standing first duty. Nothing received in the previous twelve years had yet appeared in a published volume. Bond postponed publication of the Additional Catalogue, however, to the Class Catalogue (of which more is said below), with the expressed intention of following it up with full special catalogues; and after a long interval two stout volumes, covering the period 1854–75 were brought out in 1875–77, while his successor saw through the press a great Index to them, published in 1880; and until the interruptions of European wars made delays inevitable the prompt and regular appearance of quinquennial volumes of the series was thereafter maintained.

Bond also re-started the Department's output of special catalogues and facsimiles, which had languished, never in fact having been of much bulk or importance, with the Autotype *Facsimiles of Ancient Charters* and the *Catalogue of Spanish Manuscripts*, by Don Pascual de Gayangos (1875–93). With Thompson he settled for good in 1872–74 the controverted question of the age of the famous Utrecht Psalter, once in the Cotton Library, for which a date as early as the sixth century had been claimed, they placing it by arguments which have held their ground not earlier than the late eighth or the ninth century: this enquiry led to the two men together forming the Palaeographical Society, the publications of which (1873–95) proved of immense educational value to younger palaeographers both in and outside the walls of the Museum.

Valuable as these pieces of work were, Bond was responsible for another, almost more valuable and so far without a predecessor. Nearly half a century before this voices had been heard desiderating a subject catalogue of the Manuscripts as well as of the printed books. Bond was convinced of the need of some such guide to the contents of his Department, a necessarily inadequate attempt at which, however praiseworthy, was made by Richard Sims in his *Handbook* of 1854, and he set about making a Class Catalogue, Thompson undertaking some of the more massive headings. The existing catalogues were cut up and the entries arranged in classes, and to these were added manuscript entries and notes. The Class Catalogue has never been printed and is in a constant state of growth and revision; but even so it is one of the most valuable tools that are at the service of the Department or of students of the many branches of learning it represents.

Another of Bond's great services was to set the example of punctuality and regularity in attendance. This enabled his successors to establish it as a firm tradition.

INTERLUDE: WINTER JONES, PRINCIPAL LIBRARIAN

3. THE MAPS AND THE ORIENTAL MANUSCRIPTS

During Winter Jones's reign the Trustees took two steps in the further subdivision of Departments, establishing in 1867 Departments of Maps and of Oriental Manuscripts under R. H. Major and Charles Rieu as Keepers. The former never comprehended the manuscript maps already in the Museum, though it acquired a great many for itself; and when Major retired in 1880 it lapsed back into the Department of Printed Books, from which it had been chiefly drawn (see p. 216). The latter, which had long been a need, was permanent; but it was not till 1892 that the obvious complementary step was taken of transferring to it all the Oriental Printed Books. In 1836 John Holmes had told the Parliamentary Committee that, apart from Forshall's exceptional knowledge of both, Eastern and Western MSS. should be divided. Rieu had come as a supernumerary in 1847; he already had a wide reputation as an Orientalist, having studied with much honour under Silvestre de Sacy at Paris and in other continental universities. He had an even more brilliant Assistant in William Wright, who was, however, only in the Museum for nine years, retiring in 1870 to become Sir Thomas Adams's Professor of Arabic at Cambridge, a post in which he was later followed by his former Keeper. The son of a Captain in the East Indian Company's service and of a mother who was herself no mean Oriental scholar, he also came to the Museum with a high reputation. His chief works for the Museum, published on and after his retirement, were the Catalogue of Syriac MSS. acquired since Forshall's catalogue (i.e. since 1838, and thus describing the Nitrian, as Forshall had described the Rich collection), and the catalogue of Ethiopic MSS. He died in 1889.

VII

BOND, PRINCIPAL LIBRARIAN: PRINTING THE GENERAL CATALOGUE (1879–88)

1. The General Catalogue

PANIZZI had had the courage of his own opinions; Bond had an almost equal and certainly a rarer virtue, the courage of the opinion of others. He was preternaturally quick to see the merits of reforms proposed to him by his subordinates, and energetic and tenacious in negotiating their translation into fact. Winter Jones had possessed little initiative, and as Keeper and Principal Librarian had needed little, since after a period of violent stress a period of repose must follow to consolidate the reforms. But now it was time for fresh growth, and Bond had shown in his Keepership that he had initiative of his own, as he was to show that he had a receptive ear.

When Winter Jones was absent from illness for four months in 1878, Charles Newton, Keeper of Greek and Roman Antiquities, and the Museum's most striking figure, acted as his Deputy. He was the natural successor, but did not wish to give up his archaeological work for administration, and the world was surprised when the comparatively unknown Keeper of Manuscripts, a shy and reserved man, known to few outside the Museum, was given the appointment.

His first action was to introduce electric lighting into the Museum, which was done in 1879, and though the first experiments were not altogether satisfactory, as was natural, seeing that electric lamps and wiring were then and for long after in process of improvement by inventors, he persevered, and the improvement became permanent. It was a vast boon. Till then (gas being banned), if a fog were to come on, not only was the Reading Room closed, but the entire staff went rejoicing home. Thereafter a working day meant a day's work.

But Bond's most important achievement was the application of print to the General Catalogue of Printed Books. Here we must look back a little over ground already touched.[1]

The one volume of the abortive Catalogue of 1841 possessed the faults which the method of production forced upon Panizzi made inevitable, and which he himself proclaimed. Apart from faults due to haste, when A had been printed multitudes of titles turned up which should have appeared under it, discovered as the later letters of the alphabet were examined. It seems indeed to us insanity to have allowed any other method than that recommended by Panizzi, i.e. a complete preliminary investigation of the books shelf by shelf, but what is obvious to all now was not even obvious to all professionals then, still less to amateurs. Panizzi calculated that by the time this was done, and the Catalogue made, revised and printed, it could at its completion only represent the Library as it had been some forty years before, a ridiculous result. Before the Royal Commission endorsed it, this judgment against printing had won the day, and the Trustees had allowed the matter to lapse till in 1846 they called for a report on it.

Now up to a point and in the actual circumstances Panizzi was right. In a rapidly-growing library any published catalogue must be far out-of-date as soon as it is published unless the accessions can in some way be incorporated, and the printing kept up *pari passu* with the intake of books. And the Museum Library, owing to Panizzi's own activity, was increasing at a rate whose only precedent was perhaps the vast increase of the Bibliothèque Nationale at Paris from the dépôts littéraires during the Revolution, and that was not a continuing process but a single cataclysm.

So Panizzi's original ideal was pursued. The Catalogue was made in manuscript; the titles of all accessions and by degrees those of the older stock were copied by the Transcribers appointed in 1847 and later years and reproduced in four copies by the "carbonic process," one set forming, as now, a shelf-list; the other sets were inserted by the moveable method in the Reading Room and Staff copies.[2] For long there were two catalogues side by side, the "Supplementary" containing the accessions, and the "New General"; they were gradually amalgamated.

But Panizzi failed to see the fatal drawback to manuscript, its relative bulk. In a comparatively small library this did not much matter; but the Museum Library as he himself had conceived it and set it on the way to becoming, was vast. No special pains were taken to instruct the Transcribers to economize space. And the slips swelled the bulk of the volumes, which had to be broken up and rebound. In 1850 a hundred and fifty volumes of the Catalogue were placed in the Reading Room; by 1875 the number was 2,250 and the future numbers could be foreseen. There were also the Catalogues of Music and Maps, kept up in the same way. In fact the Reading Room would in due time contain the Catalogues and little else, a position which was half a century later to be repeated in the world's second great circular reading room, that of the Library of Congress.

Not only was the bulk becoming intolerable. The cost of shifting and relaying titles involved ever more work to be performed (as it is to-day with the printed slips) by the binder's staff, and the mounting expense of this, and of breaking up and rebinding volumes, brought repeated communications from the Treasury. In 1875 Garnett had become Superintendent of the Reading Room, and was in a position to report with authority what had long been plain to him, that the Catalogue, or at least some part of it, must be printed to save space. Some of the seniors, influenced by their memories of 1841, or by their veneration for Panizzi, were at first unconverted. But in Panizzi's time the system of movable slips, so great an improvement on the old manuscript intercalations, seemed to have solved the problem for as long as could be foreseen.

Garnett represented the same facts again in 1878, when Sir Charles Newton, acting as Deputy Principal Librarian, showed himself very favourable to the plan of printing. Action, however, had to wait for Bond's accession. He, like Garnett, had long been of opinion that the Catalogue should be printed, though his opinion was naturally based on literary, as Garnett's had been on administrative, grounds. He seized on the Treasury's discontent and negotiated so effectively that in 1880 he obtained consent to the printing thenceforward of all accessions. And in the following year he further obtained the first further annual grants for printing the most unwieldy volumes of the existing Catalogue. This accounts for the fact that some parts of the alphabet appear in a more primitive state than others, improvements having been introduced during the printing. Some large headings,

BOND, PRINCIPAL LIBRARIAN

England, France, Germany, Great Britain and Liturgies, were reserved till the end, England (including Great Britain) being revised by Barwick and Liturgies by Jenner and Proctor. The grants, which at first seemed precarious, presently became regular, and the printing of the Catalogue occupied part of the Department's staff for the next twenty-five years. The main alphabet was followed by a supplement, completed in 1905, and the whole represented the Library as it was on the last day of the nineteenth century. This was the first general catalogue of one of the world's great modern libraries to be given to the world outside its walls by the medium of print; it contained four-and-a-half million entries. When the printing was commenced there were 1,300,000 books in the Library.

Garnett was the chief editor, and, dying in 1906, he just achieved his wish of seeing it completed. He was transferred from the Reading Room in 1884 in order to devote himself to the work, and then, and still more after he became Keeper in 1890, his principal sub-editor was Arthur Miller, a reserved but most lovable man, of great learning, who made the Catalogue his life work, and effected during its progress the improvements in the old Rules which made extensive headings easier to search. Garnett, Dr. Pollard tells us, was for speed, Miller for perfection.[3]

Printing the Catalogue meant that the Transcribers' occupation was gone. This grade had been employed from 1830 to make intercalations in the official copies of the old octavo Catalogue; and fresh members were recruited in and after 1847. One of these was the late Sir Edmund Gosse, who has left a bitter account of the conditions of work in his time and of the idleness of some of the staff.[4] The Transcribers remaining in 1880 were drafted into the ranks of the Assistants. The late Cyril Davenport, well known as a fertile writer on bindings and other artistic and heraldic subjects, who had charge of the Museum's binding, and Henry Mayhew, a most competent controller of current foreign purchases, were among these.

2. The Subject Index

It had long before been suggested that the system of duplicate carbon titles, used for the shelf-catalogue, might also be used for special catalogues. With printing this was obviously still easier, and Bullen had the titles of English books printed before 1641 (a date chosen by Edward Arber in 1875 to close his published transcript of the Stationers' Register, and frequently adopted by later bibliographers as convenient) picked out from the mass, expanded and printed in advance. They were provided with indexes of printers and subjects and published in three volumes in 1884, the first of the Museum Library's special catalogues of periods.

Garnett's successor in the Reading Room, George Fortescue, who had entered in 1870 and had, like so many other Superintendents, been Placer, was soon struck with the fact that while the Catalogue, once understood, answered all enquirers who knew their book's author and title, there was little beyond Watt's *Bibliotheca Britannica*, now old, to help those who wished to find what the Library possessed on any given subject, and nothing whatever when (as was increasingly the case) it was a modern book that was wanted.

A Class Catalogue of the Library had been begun, as we have seen, only to be abandoned, just fifty years before this, but the dream had haunted many brains. Of one subject a classified list had been lately privately produced by a Museum man, John Parker Anderson's *Book of British Topography*, 1881, and another was F. B. Campbell's *Indian State Papers*. In 1879 the bibliographer William Prideaux Courtney desiderated a class catalogue, and so did others of less experience. Fortescue, however, was the most practical of men. He observed that the part of a classed catalogue which showed most signs of heavy use was always the alphabetical index, and he drew the obvious inference. Spending much of his own time on the work, by using the printed monthly Accession Parts he arranged the titles of all books that had entered the Library since 1880 under their subjects in order of the alphabet. Bond was much interested in his younger colleague's single-handed enterprise, but was prejudiced as to its form by his experience in making the Class Catalogue of the Manuscripts, and this led Fortescue, against his better judgment, to adopt certain large comprehensive headings in his first volume, which appeared in 1886, and covered the books of 1880–85. Fortescue produced three more quinquennial volumes, which were amalgamated into one alphabet and published in 1902–3; and the series has been continued at the same intervals without a break till today, and its preparation is one of the standing tasks of the Department.

It has been argued that it is now time to amalgamate the Subject Index into a single alphabet, and so save the search in a number of volumes when the date of a book is not known; but it is doubtful whether, in view of the number of bibliographies now existing, this would be worth the expense. The vastly larger proposal for a complete subject, or classed, catalogue of the whole library has also been made by librarians of modern libraries, but hardly ever, if ever, by one who has had the experience necessary to give his views weight. There were newspaper agitations in this direction in 1900 and in 1912 (in *The Morning Post*), but they were unsuccessful and for good reason. Such a catalogue would include huge and useless headings; and if the Trustees could ever obtain the necessary money, they would certainly need it much more for some other purpose.

It is difficult to realize that Garnett was Superintendent of the Reading Room for no more than nine years, for in that time he earned a reputation which is still alive. He came to it, as we have seen, with the invaluable experience of Placer, and his great memory for the books which he had placed made him a walking Subject Index, in fact almost a realization of Ellis's theory of a librarian as one whose memory is the only record of accessions. He was, moreover, gentle and unassuming, accessible, and always ready to put his great learning at the disposal of the humblest enquirer. In Samuel Butler's *Notebooks*, and in many other writings of the time, there will be found appreciative accounts of Garnett. He certainly did much to make the Room the least official of official institutions.

3. BUILDINGS: THE SLIDING PRESSES: THE WHITE WING

The problem of space had yet again become pressing before the end of Bond's reign. That it was solved, for another half-century, at least for the Printed Books, the Museum is indebted to one of the Public Libraries of London, then new, and to the interest taken in them by

Museum men. Some slightly earlier experiment had been made at Bradford Free Library, but it was at Bethnal Green in 1886 that Garnett, attending a celebration in the renovated Free Library, was shown some supplementary sliding presses, invented by that Library's founder and chief benefactor, Dr. Tyler, to house the specifications of Patents annually presented to public libraries by the Patent Office. Garnett told the Placer, Henry Jenner,[5] of this invention; Jenner went, saw and was convinced. His problem was to adapt the idea to the grated iron of the Museum Ironwork, and this he did by the plan, entirely original, of suspending the presses on rollers from the flooring. Bond instantly perceived the economy represented by this device, which saved new building; a model was made by the Museum's locksmith of the day, Sparrow, and shown to the Trustees. They were persuaded, and so were the Office of Works and the Treasury; the first sliding presses were ordered in 1887.[6]

New building had been made possible just before this by the bequest by William White in 1823 of money for the improvement of accommodation in the Museum. Mr. White was a neighbour and had seen the state the old House was in. At just this time the King's Library came and the consequent building postponed the need for the bequest, which took effect in 1879, realizing about £65,000. Bond, then taking up office, was able to provide, not only the Mausoleum Room, but expansion for the Library Departments. The White Wing, opened in 1885, was erected to the East of the Manuscript Saloon and of the Middle Room of the Department adjoining the Saloon on the South. It covered ground including part of the Principal Librarian's garden, which Panizzi had formerly offered and Bond offered afresh, and reaching to Montague Street; the old building standing on it and used partly for a guard house and partly for a bindery was abolished and the present Bindery built on the ground North of the Supplementary and Arch Rooms. The new wing's ground and mezzanine floors were given to the Library. The Manuscripts acquired working-rooms for the staff and also a Students' Room, so that for the future there was no need to send MSS. into the Reading Room. Working-rooms and storage were found for the Oriental Manuscripts and (a few years later) Printed Books, while the Reading Room was further relieved by the opening of a Newspaper Reading Room with thirty seats.

Some space, but chiefly in the Antiquities, had been freed by the removal of the Natural History Departments to South Kensington. After long delays the building there had been commenced in 1873, but the Act (41 & 42 Vict. c. 55) sanctioning removal was not passed till 1878, and the collections were transferred in 1880–83. Exhibited specimens were removed from the King's Library, new cases were made, and a selection of books for exhibition, the basis of that shown today, illustrating the early history of printing, was made by Stephen Aldrich, one of the Library's best historical bibliographers of the period before the great modern development of that study.

4. THE MANUSCRIPTS

The new space was to be very necessary to the Manuscripts. In 1883, after four years' anxious negotiations, Bond had persuaded the Treasury to buy the very important Stowe MSS., amounting to well over a thousand volumes (see below, pp. 257–9), while in 1886 began the gifts of the vast and famous collection of the Newcastle and other papers of the Pelham family, which was to be followed in later years by similar gifts of the private and semi-private archives of nineteenth- and twentieth-century statesmen. The accession (in 1872) of 264 volumes of the personal papers of Warren Hastings enabled Bond to edit the famous trial.

Bond's successor as Keeper, Maunde Thompson, more than kept up the output and quality of work produced by the Department under his predecessor. In spite of these great accessions the volumes of the Additional Catalogue were steadily produced. Photography had first been used in the Museum in 1851 for Cureton's facsimile of the Epistles of Clement in the Codex Alexandrinus; and Bond had used it for reproducing the *Ancient Charters*, and for the facsimile of the Codex Alexandrinus, which he initiated. Thompson completed this and, using the experience gained in the Palaeographical Society, produced in 1881–84 the two parts, Greek and Latin, of *Ancient Manuscripts with autotype facsimiles*. He also started large catalogues, completed by his successors, of Romances, by Harry L. D. Ward, and of Seals, by Walter de Gray Birch, son of Samuel Birch, Keeper of Antiquities, of Spanish and of Irish MSS., thus fulfilling Bond's intention when he dropped the Additional Catalogue for a time in favour of the Class Catalogue.

Accessions acquired during Thompson's Keepership included some of the earlier of the flow of classical and other Greek papyri then beginning to come out of Egypt, with a large number of striking single volumes, such as one of songs by Henry VIII and members of his court (Add. MS. 31922), the Household Book of the same king (Egerton MS. 2604), and Milton's family Bible (Add. MS. 32310); Madden's Hampshire and especially Portsmouth collections (he was a native of that town) were also bought at this time.

Bond retired in 1888, carrying with him the regard and respect of all his colleagues, who had perceived behind a cold and reserved manner "a most kind heart and a truly elevated mind, far above every petty consideration, and delighting to dwell in a purely intellectual sphere."[7]

VIII

MAUNDE THOMPSON, DIRECTOR AND PRINCIPAL LIBRARIAN (1888–1911)

1. Staff Reorganization: Copyright: Building

So in 1888, Bond having retired, Maunde Thompson ruled in his stead, and a ruler of great power he proved, as had been anticipated by those who knew him as a Keeper. Under him the Departments continued to turn out important catalogues, of which more in their place. Obtaining the appointment in 1898 of a strong Treasury Committee to examine the salary scales of the higher Staff in relation to the Staffs' scientific output, he thus carried through a further improvement of salaries, under which, for example, the salary of entrants to the Assistants' Grade was raised from £120 to £150, and the seniors accordingly; by this rearrangement the facts of his own dual position were recognized and he and his successors became not plain Principal Librarian, but Director and Principal Librarian; of late, it being an age of abbreviations, the original half of the title has tended to be dropped.

Except for a difficult controversy over the Natural History Museum towards the end of his time, which strained even his great strength of will and constitution, Thompson's chief care was the eternally recurrent problem of space, and he was able when he retired to leave the Museum not only with large new buildings but also with land which should provide for all needs for any period that could be contemplated.

In the Library the cause of pressure was, of course, the bulk of the annual copyright intake. Not only had the national production, and with it the proportion of books deposited, continued to increase since Panizzi's campaign of 1852 and following years.[1] In 1869 the Newspaper Printers and Reading Rooms Act (32 & 33 Vict. c. 24) had put an end to the system by which newspapers were delivered to the Inland Revenue at Somerset House, and there remained, for nearly three years on the average, to be consulted by the public on payment of a fee, before transfer to the Museum.[2] Henceforward the publishers were to deliver direct for the Museum, Messrs. Lethbridge, large newsagents, and after their abandonment of the commission in 1873, Messrs. W. H. Smith and Son, being appointed Collectors for the Trustees. And newspapers are many times as bulky as books. The accumulations, which had to be dealt with by employing two boy sorters, so appalled the Trustees that they decided that the newspapers should be separated from the Library. Moreover, effective deposit had begun to spread to the British Empire. The Act of 1842 had provided that books produced in the Dominions and Colonies should be deposited in the privileged libraries, the delay allowed being twelve months as against one allowed to publishers in the United Kingdom. But no penalty was provided for non-compliance, nor would recovery by law have been easy or acceptable. Giving evidence before the Royal Commission of 1847–49 Panizzi said that Colonial books did not come in by copyright, and he did not feel justified in purchasing them, the result being that the Museum lost them. The Royal Commission on Copyright reported in 1878 that in their opinion the Museum should buy Colonial books; and the International Copyright Act of 1886 further complicated the legal situation. Nevertheless, deliveries were no longer non-existent. In 1894 Maunde Thompson wrote to the Secretary of State for the Colonies, complaining that while books were delivered from India (since 1890, when the system of sending the Provincial lists of new publications to the Museum for marking had begun), from the Cape, and from several Crown Colonies, none came from Canada; representations were made to the Governor-General, with good results. Thompson also gave evidence on the same subject before the Select Committee of the House of Lords for the abortive Copyright Bill of 1898. Imperial Copyright deposit was regularized by the Act of 1911 in the first years of Thompson's successor.

Before the end of the century the Trustees were making application to the Treasury for funds for building. They had in hand £50,000 bequeathed to them by Vincent Stuckey Lean (son of James Lean of Bristol, one of the founders of Stuckey's Bank) "for the improve-

MAUNDE THOMPSON, DIRECTOR

ment and extension of the Library and Reading Room." And in 1894, it is said owing to the chance presence at a Board Meeting of the Chancellor of the Exchequer, Sir William Vernon Harcourt, the Government had taken the important step (under the Act 57 & 58 Vict. c. 34) of buying from the Duke of Bedford the whole of the rest of the island site, reaching on the South-West to Great Russell Street, on the West to Bloomsbury Street and Bedford Square, on the North to Montague Place, and on the East to Montague Street, thus providing sites for any further expansions of the Museum buildings that could possibly be foreseen.3 But the South African War was in progress, and the country, having no recent experience of what wars could cost, felt poor; money was not to be had.

A Bill was accordingly brought into Parliament against the Trustees' wish, which was designed to solve their problem and the Treasury's, not by increasing house-room but by diminishing the possessions to be housed. This Bill provided that the Trustees might be authorized to transfer their files of local newspapers or other material, of dates not earlier than 1837, to the charge of boroughs or counties in England and Scotland, and might destroy any valueless material, whether duplicate or not, not earlier than 1660.

Excellent service was done by the late Sir Sidney Lee, who by a letter to *The Times* of 5th May, 1900, called the attention of Parliament and the student public to the dangers of such liberty to disperse and destroy. Various members of Parliament and many writers in the press took the matter up. There was little prospect that many local authorities would accept the files of newspapers, of which many would be duplicates, and which would, if refused, presumably join the classes of printed matter to be destroyed; while even if accepted they would be far less accessible to students than if assembled in one place. And no historical student could view calmly a proposal to give such wide discretion to destroy the small pieces which become so valuable by lapse of time. The storm rose, in spite of the preoccupations of the war in South Africa, till John Morley, himself a Trustee, who had charge of the Bill, withdrew it.

The only alternative was to build. The Treasury naturally shrank from so soon using any of the land provided for future needs and thereby losing useful rents. But a cheaper alternative was found.4 An Act (2 Edw. VII, c. 12) was passed in 1902, empowering the Trustees to remove and store, but with facilities for consultation at Bloomsbury on notice given, newspapers and other printed matter appearing to them to be rarely required for public use. Land was bought at Hendon, in the North-West of London, and a purely utilitarian store, with a Superintendent's house, erected on it; ample space was left for future enlargement, which, as we shall see, was to come thirty years later. The building was in use by 1905, all the provincial newspapers later than 1800 being moved into it, with a few other classes of little-used documents. A supplement to the General Catalogue, then being completed, was printed at the same time, listing both London and provincial papers from 1801 to 1900. The arrangement for consultation of the papers at Hendon was that any asked for were brought up to the Museum by a weekly delivery and there read in the Newspaper Room as before. It may be imagined how inconvenient the delay of anything up to seven days between request and access often was to readers.

As soon as the financial burden of the War was lifted the Government provided, under the Public Buildings Expenses Act of 1903, a sum of £150,000, to be used in conjunction with the £50,000 from the Lean bequest. The Treasury had previously refused to do this until the Trustees should have attempted to reduce the bulk of their collections. Sir J. J. Burnet was appointed architect, and he drew plans for a completion of the Museum buildings on the three remaining sides, the portion to be immediately taken in hand being the North side, covering the sites of the houses on the South side of Montague Place. On 7th June, 1907, King Edward VII laid the foundation stone of the wing which was to bear his name. As the King Edward VII Building was not to be completed till the time of Maunde Thompson's successor, it will be described in the next chapter.

2. THE ORIENTAL LIBRARY

In 1892 Rieu retired, and soon afterwards went to Cambridge as Adams's Professor of Arabic.5 As that great Orientalist William

MAUNDE THOMPSON, DIRECTOR

Wright had not stayed long in the Museum, the next senior man in the Museum suitable by scholarship was Robert Kennaway Douglas, afterwards Sir Robert Douglas, who since Major's retirement and the re-incorporation of the Maps into the Printed Books in 1880 had as Assistant-Keeper in that Department taken charge of the Map Room as well as of Chinese and Japanese books, of which, together with the MSS. in those languages, he produced the catalogue in 1877. His interests were in fact rather in Far Eastern literature than in cartography. The opportunity was now taken by Maunde Thompson to transfer Douglas to be Keeper in succession to Rieu, and with him all the printed collections of Indian and Near as well as Far Eastern literatures. The Trustees took the decision on 9th May, 1891, and the Department became that of Oriental Printed Books and Manuscripts. The change seems to have been obviously desirable long before this; but very often organization depends on the chance of the right man being available at the right moment.

Douglas had under him a grandson of Sir Henry Ellis, Mr. A. G. Ellis, who entered in 1883, retired in 1909 and died in 1942, a scholar in the Semitic tongues; the Rev. G. Margoliouth, a Hebraist; and Dr. Lionel D. Barnett (entered 1899, Keeper 1908, retired 1929), who added to wide classical, Hebrew and modern language scholarship an exceptional knowledge of the tongues of India; and rather later Dr. Lionel Giles (entered 1900, Keeper 1929, retired 1940), who was to replace Douglas as the Museum's Chinese scholar. Between them these men added to the Museum's publications a number of new, and supplements to the old, catalogues. Ellis's catalogue of Arabic books is spoken of as "a monument of sound learning." The Department also began the valuable practice of introducing external scholars to deal with some of the many tongues it covered. Not only did Nubian and Coptic texts begin in 1909 to be published by Wallis Budge, Keeper of Egyptian and Assyrian Antiquities, but Dr. W. E. Crum made the very important *Catalogue of Coptic Manuscripts*, published in 1905.[6]

THE LIBRARY OF THE BRITISH MUSEUM

3. The Printed Books and the Reading Room: Garnett and Others

When Bullen retired in 1890 Garnett became Keeper, the Assistant Keepers under him being Douglas, Russell Martineau and William Younger Fletcher, promoted on the deaths of Roy and G. W. Porter in 1884 and 1888 respectively, and Fortescue, who succeeded Garnett in 1890, while remaining Superintendent of the Reading Room. Garnett's chief energies, as we have seen, were absorbed by the effort to produce the great General Catalogue punctually. But his wide literary knowledge now had fuller scope than before to influence the Department's purchases of important original editions and of early printed books, as may be seen in the volume of *Three Hundred Notable Books*, produced in his honour on his retirement. Garnett enhanced the Library's prestige in its strongest sections, and raised one weaker one, that of early Spanish books, to the level of the rest.

In this, the most attractive part of a Keeper's work, he had the help of Dr. Alfred William Pollard, who joined the Staff in 1883 and is fortunately still with us, so that no account of his career, other than what is necessary to the narrative, falls to be given here. And just ten years later there arrived a very remarkable Assistant, who was both largely to increase and completely to organize the Museum's already very large collection of incunabula. This was Robert George Collier Proctor. Proctor had almost born with him a passion for investigating early printing. While an undergraduate at Corpus Christi College, Oxford, he had examined the bindings of the early books in the College Library (it must be admitted considerably to their detriment) and found in them a number of fragments of unknown books, used as binder's waste. From this he proceeded to examining and noting under their printers, in many cases identifying them by their types, all the books in the Bodleian printed before 1501. On entering the Museum he could not, of course, at once devote his official hours to the early printed books there. Like all other junior Assistants he had to learn the art of cataloguing by the copyright books, which provide far more exceptions and conundrums

MAUNDE THOMPSON, DIRECTOR

than do the foreign books, and it is remembered that he did his full share of this and the other routine work of the Library. Day after day, however, he stayed on after his colleagues had gone home, and searched the Catalogue for titles of incunabula. He is in fact, with the exception of its editors, Garnett and Miller, probably the only man who ever read the entire Catalogue through. Though in correspondence with incunabulists all over the world, and much influenced by his friend Francis Jenkinson of Cambridge and by Gordon Duff, he was a man who went his own way, and it was as a private venture (being possessed of some private means) that he published between 1897 and his death his *Index of Early Printed Books in the British Museum, with notes of those in the Bodleian*, completing the first Part, which describes the incunabula, and commencing the second Part, describing books of the following twenty years.

The knowledge and insight shown in the first section (Germany), and the illuminating arrangement he adopted, by countries, towns and presses (since known as "Proctor order"), made Proctor famous in the bibliographical world. He was given authority to assemble the incunabula in presses occupying the Westernmost two pairs of bays of the Arch Room, which he insisted on doing with his own hands, but to his regret he was not allowed to include among them the books in the King's and Grenville Libraries.

Minute examination of types ruined Proctor's eyesight, and he was in imminent danger of blindness when in 1903, on a holiday (for the first time without the company of his mother), he walked, *more suo*, all alone and asking no question of anyone,[7] over a pass in the Austrian Tirol after fresh snow. His body was never found, though Maunde Thompson, learning that he had no active relations, took the step, strongly disapproved by the Treasury, of persuading the Trustees to send at their expense one of Proctor's colleagues, who knew the district, to search for him. (For the Incunabula see below, pp. 202–4.)

Proctor had been dead some little time, and Pollard and Henry Jenner had completed the arrangement of the books which he had left in progress, before the Trustees decided to publish a full-dress catalogue of the Incunabula on the basis of his work. This great

THE LIBRARY OF THE BRITISH MUSEUM

catalogue, which is still in progress under the editorship of Dr. Victor Scholderer, was commenced by Dr. Pollard.

After all but half a century of service, for he had entered as a mere boy on the death of his father in 1850, Garnett retired in 1899, and the Museum lost its best-known figure of that or perhaps any generation. The Museum nearly lost him in his early days, as it has lost other good men. First Roy was promoted over his head; Garnett was offended, but placated when it was put to him that Roy, though two places below him, had not only ten years more service, but had rendered exceptional service—his case had been one of Panizzi's dreadful examples in support of improving staff pay and conditions. Then the offence was repeated when Ralston was promoted, and this time there was less excuse and Garnett all but resigned. That he never showed any animus in his numerous references to Panizzi is one of many evidences of his generous nature. His memory was wonderful—Fortescue remembered having heard him on the same day recite the names of the Popes of the seventeenth century and of the Derby winners from 1850 to 1860—while his knowledge of literature was very wide, with special interest in Italian and in the English romantics; and he put his memory and knowledge of books, much helped by his experience as Placer, at the service of all who asked. He wrote much, some of it no doubt merely to add to his income and maintain a growing family, but he was the first of the writers who have made many really poetical translations from the best epigrams in the Greek Anthology, setting the fashion with his *Idylls and Epigrams*, 1869, and he was the author of two strikingly original works, one a little sheaf of aphorisms on love, entitled *De Flagello Myrteo*, the authorship of which was not revealed till the end of his life, the other the well-known volume of bizarre and ironical stories, not altogether unlike Anatole France but really quite individual, *The Twilight of the Gods*. This latter was at first a failure, and was remaindered; Dr. Pollard records that it was only when the remainder-dealer received from the Museum an order for no fewer than twenty-five copies of it from his catalogue that the book was restored to the land of the living. Of Garnett's quaint humour there are many stories, and it may account for his interest in astrology, which he

MAUNDE THOMPSON, DIRECTOR

actually practised, to the very natural disapproval of Samuel Butler, who held him otherwise in high regard; and indeed in his position it was a vagary *pessimi exempli*. But he was individual in all things, and a striking refutation of the absurd popular idea of a librarian; he has been called "the most living of men."[8]

George Fortescue was Garnett's successor as Keeper.[9] He had left the Reading Room in 1896 to devote himself to the Subject Index, to the analysis (it is not a detailed catalogue) of the Croker French Revolution Tracts, published in 1899, and to helping the Keeper in the general administration of the Department, a task which of course far exceeds that in any other Department, and is about equal to that in all the rest taken together, which is perhaps why some of the Keepers and a number of the Deputy Keepers of Printed Books have left names remembered only inside the Museum or even inside the Department itself. In the Reading Room Fortescue was followed for four years by one of these little-known men, William Robert Wilson. Wilson was no great scholar, but both in the Reading Room and in the general administration, to which he was later transferred, he had many of the qualities of Winter Jones, calm good sense, which caused him to be highly valued by Maunde Thompson, and a kind heart, which served as a lubricant, sometimes needed, in the working of the Library. This latter quality contrasted with the would-be stern but in practice often very ineffective discipline practised by some seniors in his own junior days, which he was sometimes heard to speak of with contempt. In 1900 his place in the Reading Room was taken by George Frederick Barwick, a man of more striking ability and of much scholarship, whose administration of the Room has left a tradition ranking with Garnett's and Fortescue's. After his retirement from the Museum Barwick employed his leisure in writing what is the standard book on the Reading Room.

During Barwick's time as Superintendent occurred the closing of the Reading Room, which has been referred to in an earlier chapter. In 1907 the barrel roof of Charing Cross station suddenly collapsed. The Trustees were naturally concerned as to the state of the similar structure of the Reading Room, which had then had exactly half a century of use, being a little older than Charing Cross. They had the structure tested, with most satisfactory results, and took the occasion to have the interior decorated. The re-decoration included a much-criticized feature; in the panels below nineteen of the twenty windows (that under the twentieth being occupied by the clock) there were painted the names of a series of great English writers. During these proceedings, which lasted for six months, the Room was closed, select readers being with difficulty accommodated in the Large Room and the Catalogue Room. They were rationed in days and hours in proportion to the apparent value of their studies, a task which required a strong as well as a tactful judge to carry out; there was no loud complaint. The opportunity was also taken to revise the books of reference, all of which had necessarily been moved out of the Room; the 4th (and latest) edition of the Catalogue of them was produced in 1910.

In spite of the cares of the Keepership Fortescue continued to edit the Subject Index, and he carried out a task long overdue, the *Catalogue of the Thomason Tracts*, which had been in the House since 1762; it appeared in two volumes in 1908. Fortescue thus acquired a remarkable comparative knowledge of the two Revolutions—and incidentally a considerable contempt for the revolutionary type—which it is a pity he did not elaborate in more than a couple of papers to the Bibliographical Society. Of Napoleon, whom he considered the key to the understanding of all modern history, he had an equal knowledge. He also, like Garnett, with the help of Dr. Pollard, pursued the policy of filling up gaps in the early English books and in the incunabula, revealed by Bullen's "1640 Catalogue" and by Proctor's *Index*. Older foreign literature, like English literature after 1640, tended to be postponed to these two classes and neglected till American intelligence and competition made acquisitions difficult, especially in the latter field; but it received a very useful addition in the shape of Henry Spencer Ashbee's library, rich in French and Spanish (especially Cervantes), which was received by bequest in 1900.

Fortescue was followed as Keeper by Miller, who had but two years, and Miller in 1914 by Barwick, whose term of office exactly covered the years of war.

MAUNDE THOMPSON, DIRECTOR

4. THE MANUSCRIPTS: WARNER AND OTHERS

In the Manuscripts Warner had been Thompson's right-hand man, but he was junior by eight years to the Assistant Keeper, Edward John Long Scott. Scott, who now became Keeper, joined in 1863, in part at least as an Orientalist, since he was not only a good classic but had been Boden Sanskrit Scholar at Merton, though he was not transferred to the new Department of Oriental Manuscripts in 1867; as Wright was transferred with Rieu, Scott could probably not be spared. He supervised the Stowe Catalogue (1895-96), and made the Sloane Index (1904), but his chief interest was in Charters, a very important section of the Department's collections which had been neglected, so far as publications were concerned, except for the series of facsimiles started by Bond. The *Index (Locorum) to the Charters and Rolls* acquired up to 1881 (1900) and the *Facsimiles of Royal and other Charters* (Vol. I; William I–Richard I) (1905), were among the publications issued under his Keepership. When he retired he became Keeper of the Muniments at Westminster Abbey, and it was in the Abbey Muniment Room that he died suddenly in 1918, as a tablet to his memory erected there recorded. The general management of the Department, the selection of acquisitions and the editing of the Additional Catalogue, which was kept up to date, he left to Warner, whose position in the Department was almost that of Keeper before he succeeded to Scott.

Warner was Keeper for seven years (1904-11), retiring two years after Thompson. Though he never allowed himself to become a mere specialist, but had a thorough knowledge of all the chief classes of manuscripts, he was, as we have seen, a first-rate scholar in ancient palaeography, and he took a special interest and delight in illuminations; he was the master of his successors in special charge of the Museum's illuminated MSS., Mr. John Herbert and Mr. Eric Millar. His first publication in this field (1894) was a volume of facsimiles of miniatures and borders from the splendid Milanese manuscript, the Sforza Book of Hours, which had been presented by John Malcolm of Poltalloch the year before. In 1900-3 he edited the Museum's first facsimiles in colour, the series entitled

Illuminated Manuscripts, reproducing specimens from the Museum's best MSS. in this class, and he followed it up by five series of facsimiles ot autographs, and by starting in 1907 a less costly and more copious selection of *Reproductions from Illuminated Manuscripts*. After his retirement there appeared a volume of reproductions of all the illuminations and drawings in *Queen Mary's Psalter*, with an introduction by him. But his chief publication was the monumental *Catalogue of the Royal and King's Manuscripts*, which he commenced in 1894, but which was completed by J. P. Gilson in 1921.

Outside the Museum too Warner was active. He had travelled over Europe with Thompson, examining ancient MSS., and was one of the leaders of the Palaeographical Society, which he revived in 1903 as the New Palaeographical Society. For the Roxburghe Club he edited facsimile editions of the Benedictional of St. Æthelwold in the Chatsworth Library, of the famous twelfth-century roundel drawings of the life of St. Guthlac, from Crowland Abbey (Harley Roll Y. 6), and an edition of Mandeville's Travels, which by immense research he showed to be a French fiction. His detective ability was also exhibited in a catalogue of the muniments of Dulwich College, in which he was the first to expose the forgeries relating to Shakespeare. His edition of *The Libelle of English Policy* is another first-class piece of work.

It is difficult to speak without hyperbole of Warner, whether as scholar, Keeper or friend. Immensely thorough, "he habitually understated rather than overstated the certainty of the results to which his researches led him, and never declared to be certain that which he had only shown to be extremely probable." Great scholar as he was, he meticulously kept every side of the work of his Department up to the mark throughout the long period of his command in it, yet, however well he made his men work, it is recorded by one who knew him perhaps as intimately as anyone that "it is probably safe to say that no one ever saw him out of temper."[10] He had the inevitable reward of these qualities in the admiring affection of all Museum men of his time.

He was succeeded as Keeper by the Senior Deputy Keeper and the Department's chief mainstay, Gilson.

MAUNDE THOMPSON, DIRECTOR

Some remarkable acquisitions were made in Scott's and Warner's Keeperships. Letters of Keats and Shelley, Sterne's Journal, Nelson's Trafalgar Memorandum, several collections of autograph works by great musical composers, the papers of General Gordon, and the economic papers and collections of Francis Place, rich in the history of the early trade unions, may be mentioned; while George Eliot started a fruitful tradition by bequeathing the autograph copies of some of her chief works. The gift of the Sforza Book of Hours in 1893 has already been mentioned, and six years later came the bequest of Baron Ferdinand Rothschild, M.P., of fourteen volumes, nearly all of them splendidly illuminated. One contained a series of drawings of sixteenth-century English royal and noble funeral processions. One of the illuminated MSS. (No. ii) proved to be the missing first volume of a Breviary in the Harleian Collection (Harl. MS. 2897), executed for Jean sans Peur, Duke of Burgundy (*d.* 1419); its existence was unsuspected till the Rothschild books were unpacked by Warner, whose delight may be imagined.[11] And at the end of Warner's time came the bequest by Alfred Huth of fifty volumes from the famous library collected by his father Henry Huth, which included thirteen illuminated MS. of the highest quality. Of equal importance with any of these was the Psalter of Lothaire, bequeathed by Sir Thomas Brooke in 1908.

Historical and literary autographs and illuminations were classes in which the Museum had always been pre-eminent. Another class, not entirely new, was now soon to take rank with them. Systematic excavation began to produce great masses of books and documents, mostly fragmentary, written on papyrus and marvellously preserved by the dry sands of Egypt; hitherto only scattered examples and one or two large finds had appeared. At the end of the century the Graeco-Roman Branch of the Egypt Exploration Fund (now Society) was formed, and Grenfell, Hunt, Hogarth and others began to dig, the Society distributing its finds thus made to various libraries, the Museum receiving a generous share. Classical and Biblical studies, and the Museum's material for such studies, have been greatly enriched by these gifts, and also by purchases of papyri (see below, pp. 267–71). Among the earliest to be acquired when the rush began in the last fifteen years or so of the nineteenth century were the lost books of the *Mimes* of Herodas, large parts of twenty Odes of Bacchylides, parts of the *Antiope* of Euripides, and, even more important than these, Aristotle *On the Constitution of Athens*, a work famous in antiquity but since then known only from early quotations. The *Antiope* fragments, and some of Plato's *Phaedo*, were of the third century B.C., and were the most ancient Greek texts then known; though a very few more ancient still have since been found.

Scott and Warner entrusted work on papyri to Mr. (now Sir Frederic) Kenyon, who had joined the Staff at the right moment for it, in 1889. Thompson persuaded the Trustees to embark on a policy of publishing the papyri, a policy which is still maintained. Kenyon edited texts and facsimiles separately of the three most important single books, the Herodas, the Aristotle (both in 1891–92) and the Bacchylides (1897–98), and in 1893 commenced two publications, a Catalogue and a series of facsimiles. And, ancient MSS. other than papyri falling in his field, he edited facsimiles of Biblical MSS. (1900) and just as he was leaving the Department (1909) initiated a new facsimile of the Codex Alexandrinus in smaller and handier form and in collotype, which had now become available and had superseded the old autotype process.

5. Maunde Thompson

Thompson retired in 1909, to live for another twenty years. He was a man of commanding power, as he was of commanding presence, with aquiline features and piercing blue eyes. The Trustees had entire confidence in him, and rightly, and he was especially valued by King Edward VII, who was for a number of years before his accession in 1902 the Royal Trustee. Thompson was a disciplinarian. A tremendous worker himself, he would not tolerate the idleness which had been common in the place in his own early days; but if more than a little terrifying to juniors, he was very friendly to those (like, for example, Sir Frederic Kenyon and Dr. Pollard) who had earned his good opinion and regard. Nor was he, Sir Frederic records, at all impervious to suggestions from others, however decided his

MAUNDE THOMPSON, DIRECTOR

own mind. He devoted much thought and energy to the improvement of the Staff's pay, and at the end of his official time was still engaged in doing for the lower grades something comparable to what he had done for the higher Staff in 1898; his efforts bore fruit after his retirement. He was, wherever occasion allowed, bluff and genial. He certainly received the present writer, when he first called as a very shy youth to be interviewed for an Assistantship, in a way which set him at his ease and earned his gratitude. In its external relations the Museum has never had, even in Panizzi or in his own successor, a more impressive figure-head. He came to carry great weight in Governmental circles, thus being enabled to secure from the Treasury the funds necessary for his Staff reorganization, for the purchase of land and for building. He was no mere administrator, the cause of scholarly work in others; he himself made both officially and in his private time very solid contributions to palaeographical and historical scholarship. He edited no fewer than five of the medieval chronicles of England, the anonymous St. Alban's Chronicle, Adam Murimuth, Robert of Avesbury, Adam of Usk (from the unique MS., discovered by himself in the Museum) and Geoffrey Le Baker, and also several more modern texts and series of papers of historical importance. Out of his work for the Class Catalogue he found the material for articles, afterwards published as a book (1895), on *English Illuminated Manuscripts*, and he was after Bond the guiding spirit of the Palaeographical Society. But of classical palaeography he was an even more eminent master. His *Introduction to Greek and Latin Palaeography* (1912), originally an article in the *Encyclopaedia Britannica* (ed. 1895), is the standard work on its subject. With Warner to help him he produced the *Catalogue of Ancient Manuscripts*, in which all the Museum's Greek and Latin MSS. of dates up to the end of the ninth century were described with many facsimiles; and he edited full facsimiles of the Utrecht Psalter (1874) in connection with the controversy over its date, which Bond and he settled, of the Codex Alexandrinus (officially, 1879–83) and (with Sir Richard Jebb) of the Laurentian Codex of Sophocles (1887). At the end of his life he published a book on the handwriting of Shakespeare, including a study of the passage in the play of *Sir Thomas*

More, claimed to be not only by Shakespeare but in his autograph. All this would be a notable lifework for a scholar with no official administrative duties. But Thompson was a man who in brain and will power as well as in body, was cast in heroic mould.[12]

IX

THE LAST THIRTY YEARS

1. Sir Frederic Kenyon, Director and Principal Librarian: the King Edward VII Building

Sir Frederic Kenyon succeeded Maunde Thompson in 1909. As Sir George Warner remained Keeper of Manuscripts for another two years (he had a year's extension), Sir Frederic had the unique experience of stepping straight to the Directorship without having done the work of a Keeper.

When he took office the King Edward VII Building was rising, and its erection occupied the first five years of his Directorship. It was opened by King George V in 1914. It is a curious coincidence that the opening of the King Edward VII Building of the Museum and of the new buildings of the Royal Library of Berlin were the last State ceremonies performed before the War by King George V and by Kaiser William II alike.

The new wing housed on the upper floor the Exhibition Gallery and Students' Room of the Prints and Drawings, and on the main floor the Exhibition Gallery of the British and Medieval Antiquities. Between these a Mezzanine floor took the workrooms of the Prints and Drawings and also the Music and Map collections and workrooms, with accommodation for students. The Sub-ground Floor and the Basement were also given to the Printed Books, and took the Copyright Office—which needs separate access from the street—and large storage for books and newspapers, which were again threatening to overfill their house-room.

The main building was joined to the new wing by an extension Northwards of the Large Room, meeting it in the middle of its length. The room, so enlarged, was paid for by Mr. Lean's bequest, in accordance with the terms of his will, and was renamed the North Library. It was much loftier than its predecessor, and the walls took two galleries of books; the lower of these was wide, with bays, and under it ran a service passage, thus diverting the traffic which used necessarily to pass through the Large Room, but at the same time cutting the long vista from the Arch Room at the West to the Catalogue Room at the East. A deeply and elaborately coffered ceiling and pairs of square white stone and round black columns standing forward of the gallery along the sides of the room added to its architectural dignity, while the columns reduced the span of the girders carrying the floor above; but it cannot be denied that both reduced the space and were in contrast with the plainness which is the distinction of the Reading Room.

A Photographic Studio, much larger than its predecessor and fitter for the increasing demand, was contrived on the roof of the King Edward VII Building.

2. The Copyright Acts, 1911 and 1915

The International Copyright Conventions of 1886 and 1908 called attention to the lack of uniformity in the copyright laws of the countries of the British Empire, and the subject was discussed at the Imperial Conference of 1910; a special Imperial Copyright Conference was called which also insisted that uniformity should be achieved throughout the Empire, of course with the assent of the legislatures of the self-governing Dominions. The result was that in 1911 a new Imperial Copyright Act was passed (1 & 2 Geo. V, c. 46). The clauses providing for deposit at the Museum repeat those in the Act of 1842. After a fierce fight the claim of the University Libraries was retained, and the National Library of Wales was added; but these points do not concern us here. The primary intention of the Act, and the chief novel provision, dealt with the Empire. By the International Copyright Act of 1886 the depository libraries had lost their right to Colonial books, which, as we have seen, were very irregularly supplied. The new Act extended to all His Majesty's Dominions, subject to the legislative confirmation of the self-governing Dominions. And His Majesty was empowered, by an Order in Council, to apply it to territories under his protection and to Cyprus. The self-governing Dominions gave effect to the Act by local Acts

THE LAST THIRTY YEARS

passed in the next years; an Indian Act was passed in 1914. And by an Order in Council of 24th June, 1912, the Act was applied to the Crown Colonies and to Cyprus.

The section providing for deposit, however, applies solely to books published in the United Kingdom, though high authority has held that the clause applies by inference to the other countries of the Empire. It is by force of the local legislation rather than of the Imperial Act that the Museum and the other libraries receive books published outside the United Kingdom. Local legislation, which excludes Government publications in general from deposit, orders the delivery of Acts, Ordinances and the like.

Delivery at the Museum from the Dominions and Colonies is not complete, but is nevertheless fairly well observed. Cypriot Greek pamphlets celebrating minor local events in Saturnian verse (the metre of "the king was in the counting-house") became after 1911 a frequent and amusing feature of the cataloguer's day. But were copyright not so thorny a subject, there would seem to be a case for an amending Act to rectify the imperfect drafting of the Act.

By another oversight in drafting, trade advertisements were not excluded by the Act from deposit with books and papers. As no other form of registration was provided, that hitherto, and latterly very irregularly, provided by Stationers' Hall having been dropped out, many trade firms conceived the idea that they could obtain registration, and free registration at that, by the simple process of delivery at the Museum, whose receipts would serve the purpose. Floods of worthless leaflets and labels poured in, and some, bearing the Museum's dated blue copyright stamp, reached the tables of cataloguers, who gazed at them in despair and (official conscience forbidding them to remove and destroy them secretly) slipped them under books and papers where they could be quietly forgotten. A protest was made by the Keeper, and at the Trustees' instance the Copyright (British Museum) Act (5 & 6 Geo. V, c. 38) was passed in 1915, exempting the Museum from the duty of receiving such matter, the copyright in which under the Act of 1911 was, however, left undisturbed.[1]

By the Act of Separation of Southern Ireland from the United Kingdom in 1921 the reciprocal obligation of deposit was retained:

but in the absence of any provision for registration authors publishing in Ireland were left unprotected. It was not till 1927 that, after heated debates, the deposit of copies of Irish books in the libraries of Eire and the United Kingdom was satisfactorily established by the Eire Industrial and Commercial Property (Protection) Act. No fewer than ten copies were to be delivered, those for the five Irish libraries and the British Museum automatically, the rest on demand. It cannot be said that the obligation to deposit books in Trinity College, Dublin, is cheerfully complied with by the publishers of the United Kingdom, and apart from their view, the Free State certainly gets much the best of the bargain, seeing how much greater is the mass of books produced in the United Kingdom. But from the point of view of the Museum, either free deposit of books from Eire or sufficient funds to buy most of them is necessary. Eire is historically and, it may be added, emotionally, in a different position from the other self-governing Dominions of the Empire, which deposit books in the Museum, but receive no deposit in return.

It may be observed that British legal deposit differs from that of other great countries. For example, French law requires two copies, one from the publisher and one from the printer, thus covering privately printed matter; while in the United States there is no provision for retaining in the Library of Congress, as there is for registering, everything published.

3. The Four-Years' War

With the King Edward Building ready, the nuisance of the Copyright infima removed, and a flow of important catalogues in preparation, a period of fresh prosperous growth seemed to be at hand; but like all other intellectual activities the Library's was to be sadly set back by four years of world war.

The Trustees had long encouraged their staff to be Territorials, and a Rifle Club, whose membership covered both Museums, had flourished for a number of years. The Director himself was in a Territorial camp at the moment of mobilization, and he crossed to France on the first ship carrying the British Expeditionary Force, on 9th August, 1914, four hundred and ninety-nine years to the

THE LAST THIRTY YEARS

day, as he recalls,[2] since the last British Force, Henry V's army sailing for the Agincourt campaign, had made the crossing from Southampton to Le Havre.[2] He was recalled just a month later, to take charge of measures for the Museum's security, and thereafter, except for visits to France as a member of the War Graves Commission, served at home with the Inns of Court O.T.C., at Berkhamsted, spending about a week each month at the Museum and attending all the meetings of the Trustees, but otherwise conducting the Museum's affairs by correspondence. The Assistant Secretary, Mr. A. R. Dryhurst, carried the extra load of work and responsibility.[3]

In all, out of a total staff of 384 (of which the Library accounted for perhaps half), 137 joined the armed Forces, while 44 were lent to other Government Departments, such as Intelligence and Censorship, in which a knowledge of foreign languages was needed. Every man served except those over military age or rejected or a very few claimed as indispensable; there was one conscientious objector, and he took work allowed as of national importance. Ten of the fighting men were killed or died of disease on active service; their names were carved by Eric Gill under a laurel wreath, not on a tablet, but in the stone of the building itself, a pilaster under the colonnade by the main Entrance, and with their names the famous four lines from the poem "For the Fallen" by the late Laurence Binyon, himself a member of the Museum (Print Room) Staff and afterwards Keeper of Prints and Drawings. Below it on Armistice Day in the following years the Staff, with readers and visitors, and sometimes also the Trustees, assembled for the two minutes' silence.

The Roll of Honour of the Librarians of the British Empire, made by the Library Association, was placed on a wall of the passage leading to the Reading Room.

In the early stages of the war the Trustees did not close the Exhibition Galleries or evacuate any objects from Bloomsbury, but in the first six weeks portions of the basement were converted into strong rooms and the most precious books and manuscripts, with the smaller antiquities, were stored there in safes. The nearest bomb exploded in Bedford Place, about 150 yards off, on 13th October, 1915, and the only damage directly done to the Museum was due to a fragment of a British anti-aircraft shell which entered the Iron Library and stripped the backs off two books. The most serious damage may have been hastened by the concussion of neighbouring explosions, but would have happened in any case before long; the heavy coffered ceiling of the First Supplementary Room fell one morning. Luckily little damage was done to books and none to the Staff, as a few hours' warning had been given; but fifteen tons of timber and plaster knocked the solid bay-presses about and buried everything. The similar ceiling in the Second Supplementary Room was taken down as a precaution.

The bombs used by the enemy in the earlier part of the war were of a light type which exploded in the upper storeys of buildings hit; but heavier bombs began to be used later, and in the summer of 1917 the Trustees accepted offers by the Governors of the National Library of Wales, communicated by the late Sir John Ballinger, the Librarian, of storage in the unoccupied new building of the Library for printed books, manuscripts, prints and drawings, and another by Mr. C. W. Dyson Perrins, a collector and friend of the Museum Library, of the strong room in his house at Davenham near Malvern for specially important volumes. Mr. Pollard went to Davenham with some eight hundred volumes, the cream of the printed library, while a mass went to Aberystwyth. In the latter place one Keeper was always in charge and was helped by one representative of each of the Departments concerned. The evacuation of 1917 was but a faint foreshadowing of that of 1939–40, of which our story will stop short, but of which it may be said here that the hospitality of the National Library of Wales was repeated on a very much larger scale.[4]

Early in 1916 the Government made a call for economy, and a memorandum was submitted, showing the following possible savings: without closing the galleries £11,400, by closing them another £10,000, and by closing the Reading Room, £7,000; £53,000 had already been saved. The Reading Room, it was urged, could not be closed without serious public as well as private injury. The Treasury suggested imposing fees for the use of the Reading Room; but the Law Officers of the Crown were of opinion that this could not be done under the Museum's Act of Incorporation, and the suggestion

THE LAST THIRTY YEARS

was withdrawn. The Reading Room and the Manuscript Students' Room were left open, some economy being effected by the employment of a few young women in the former. The Galleries were closed on 1st March, at a saving, it was reckoned, of the cost of the war for two and a half minutes, and certainly at the cost of much derision by the enemy, who never closed a museum or library or even reduced a purchase grant throughout the war, whereas the British Museum's purchase grant, like that of other national museums and galleries in this country, was suspended, except for grants for the purchase of necessary printed books, and especially periodicals, amounting to £2,000 in 1915, £3,500 in 1916, £3,000 in 1917 and the same in 1918. The Manuscripts were reduced to the product of the Egerton and Farnborough Funds.

The greatest danger to the Museum throughout the war, however, was neither hostile action nor economy. In 1916 the Air Board demanded that they should occupy the Museum buildings, which would not merely have put them altogether out of action for their proper use, but would have made the great extent of roof not only an easy but a legitimate target for German bombs; for in the first World War the German Air Force drew that distinction. The Trustees protested vigorously and Sir Frederic Kenyon attended a meeting of the War Cabinet, but to no purpose; as he records, "with one exception, the members of the War Cabinet showed complete indifference to the interests of the Museum or the effect which the proposed action would have on the good name of the country," and the Air Board's claim was allowed. The Trustees protested anew that the building was unsuitable (which had been the impression even of some of the Air Board's officers) and that it was impossible to move the collections out in time. Their protest might have been unavailing, but for the Press. Two well-known scholars, Sir John Sandys and Sir Arthur Evans, protested simultaneously; the former wrote to *The Times*, where, as also in other papers, he was followed by many influential men and by learned societies. The public condemnation of the Air Board's proposal was so strong and general that the scheme was dropped.[5]

During the war there were issued a few important publications, the main cost of printing which had been incurred in peace-time; among these were the fifth volume of Greek Papyri, the fourth volume (Subiaco and Rome) of the Catalogue of Fifteenth Century Books and sections of the Catalogue of Hebrew and Samaritan MSS. But no fresh printing was undertaken. The Treasury, as we have seen, cut only the portion of the grant normally allocated to "museum" purchases—if any library acquisitions can be rightly so called. And the four years were by no means barren in gifts of books and MSS. On the whole the Library came through the war better than it might have done.

4. Between Two Wars

The twenty-one troubled years of peace which followed were troubled for the Museum by congestion and recurring difficulty in obtaining funds. Yet much was accomplished in them.

A beginning was made by the installing of the Map and Music Rooms as well as of the Copyright Receipt Office in the King Edward Building, improvements which the outbreak of the war had postponed. But the basement of that building had to be used for the temporary storage of newspapers, since the Repository which had been opened at Hendon in the North-West suburbs of London in 1906 was full by 1921, many years before the estimated date. And the old Iron Library shelves were also full. The five years of Dr. A. W. Pollard's Keepership (he succeeded Miller in 1929) were no easy ones.

The Office of Works began with the latter, and as was thought the easier and cheaper, job. A fourth storey was added in 1920 to the South-Eastern quadrant of the Iron Library. But in the process the structure below was found to be too light; so the other quadrants were left alone. Still worse, the Office of Works insisted on the removal of two hundred and fifty of the hanging presses, holding 88,000 books, which had to be stacked for the time with the recent intake of newspapers. Novels, which are often singled out as a needless burden, are not in fact a great problem.

The Trustees in despair appealed to the Government for leave and funds to use more of their site. But similar appeals were arriving in

THE LAST THIRTY YEARS

Whitehall from other national museums and galleries of science and art. In 1927 there was appointed a Royal Commission to investigate the state of all these institutions, and above all to find, if possible, some way of economizing on building without crippling them.

The Report, which appeared in two parts, Interim and Final, with the Evidence, in 1928–30, is a pleasant contrast to the two previous public enquiries into the conduct of the Museum. Not now is a backward and sleepy institution goaded, as in 1835–36, into a recognition of modern needs. And not now, as in 1847–49, is there a voluminous public washing of dirty domestic linen. The attitude of the Commissioners is throughout friendly and helpful. In the Evidence will be found an admirable summary account of the Museum's history, government and economy, by Sir Frederic Kenyon.[6]

The Final Report only touched the Museum Library on one point. So recently as 1927 the Board of Education's Committee on Public Libraries, under Sir Frederic Kenyon as Chairman, had dealt with the keystone of the whole arch, the Central Library for Students, as it was then still called, now the National Central Library, which exists to organize mutual lending between libraries, as the Berlin Leihverkehr had long done for those in Germany. The Committee recommended that the Library should be incorporated as a Department of the Museum. The Trustees, when this was put to them, foresaw difficulties. They had not enough knowledge of the Public Libraries; and the correlation of the two staffs would be a problem. The Royal Commission agreed with them, and recommended as an alternative that the Central Library's constitution should include representation of the Museum in its governing body; and this was done. We have in these two libraries the two halves of a national library system: on the one hand a stationary reference library which does not lend; and on the other an organization of all those libraries which do.

In their Interim Report the Commissioners dealt at large with the Museum. They found that the problem of outstanding urgency for the Museum was that of the Library. It could not stand still, but must be kept up to date. Agreeing with the learned societies which had given evidence, they were against any diminution of the Library's

THE LIBRARY OF THE BRITISH MUSEUM

right to legal deposit, whether by transfer of books on special subjects to the appropriate special libraries, a plan which would destroy the Library's universality, or by selection. No selection would save more than a fifth of the bulk, or could fail to be costly and to involve irreparable mistakes. They endorsed a scheme prepared for the Trustees by Sir Richard Allinson, the Chief Architect of the Office of Works. The Iron Library should be completely reconstructed, quadrant by quadrant, in modern space-saving stack-building style in steel (whereas the old structure was of cast-iron) and fireproofed and air-conditioned. Meanwhile the two Supplementary Rooms of the Old Library should be filled with floors carrying stacks, and an annexe should be built in the quadrangle, to take the initial displacement. The Newspaper Repository should be enlarged to take all newspapers later than 1800, with some other classes. All this would cost £283,500, occupy twelve to fifteen years, and provide for the intake of over half a century, beyond which period it is hard to expect library builders to look.

Economic blizzards, wars and rumours of wars, have played havoc with this programme, at least with its time-table. But the Supplementary Rooms were filled, and two quadrants rebuilt and one fitted, including a mechanical book-carrier, and filled; the Newspaper Repository at Hendon[7] was enlarged and reopened in 1932 as the Newspaper Library, complete with Reading Room, bindery and photostat, while there is a State Paper Reading Room in the King Edward Building—State Papers used to be read in the Newspaper Room—and the Newspaper Room, thus freed, was turned over to the Oriental Library for a Students' Room, newspaper shelving space adjoining being divided between the Manuscripts and the Oriental Library; floors were inserted in the wastefully lofty rooms of the North Wing, once the Reading Rooms, and the North Library gave up similar top space to the Egyptian Department above it for storage, and was remodelled and refitted, in a very modern style, but with a great improvement in the lighting. A small Bible Exhibition Room was rather later contrived, adjoining the South-East angle of the Manuscripts Saloon.

Though financial stress and finally war have prevented the punctual

THE LAST THIRTY YEARS

completion of the scheme, its conception was prompt and was due to a benefactor. The late Lord Duveen, then Sir Joseph Duveen, immediately on the appearance of the Interim Report, offered to build certain much needed art galleries for the Museum, the National Gallery and the National Portrait Gallery; and he made the sole stipulation that the Government should carry out the Commission's recommendations on the scientific and library side. He fulfilled his part of the bargain; the Government have done their best to carry out theirs.

A suggestion had been put forward before 1917 that a Twentieth-Century Catalogue should be published as a supplement to the General Catalogue. Meanwhile that great work rapidly went out of print and became rare, while the vast development of libraries on both sides of the Atlantic, but particularly in the United States, made competition, and very high prices were paid for sets. Robert Farquharson Sharp, who succeeded Dr. Pollard as Keeper in 1924, put to the Trustees a scheme for a more or less mechanical incorporation of accessions and reprint of the whole, calculated to take a dozen years or so, and this was approved. But when work began this plan was found so unworthy of the Museum that it was expanded to include thorough revision. The old catalogue was full of errors, due to speed in printing, for Garnett, as we have seen, had sacrificed perfection to punctuality in the appearance of the fascicules. The Treasury naturally hesitated, but was persuaded, and a new grade of twenty Assistant Cataloguers, of the same type as the Assistant Keepers, was recruited. The Rockefeller Foundation helped nobly, especially by providing for a discount to be given to the first hundred American libraries to subscribe. The first volume of the new Catalogue appeared in 1931. It goes on, though much hindered by the war, since many of the Staff are in the Army, for it is an obligation. But it will take perhaps four times the original estimate of a dozen years, and it will be in many more volumes.

Sir Frederic Kenyon retired at the end of 1930. It is fortunate that as all but the first five years of his Directorship were to be a time of such difficulty, the Museum was destined to have at its head during them a man of power to face and overcome difficulty. More

THE LIBRARY OF THE BRITISH MUSEUM

than that could not be fittingly said here, but it may be mentioned that in 1921 Sir Frederic secured from the Treasury substantial improvements in the pay of the Staff, improvements which carried with them the change from the titles of Assistant Keeper and Assistant to Deputy Keeper and Assistant Keeper; and that he followed this up in 1927 by a further reorganization of the Clerical and Attendant Staff by which a ladder was provided through the grades of Attendant and Second, First and Higher Grade Library (or Museum) Assistant.

He was succeeded by Dr. George Francis Hill (Sir George Hill), who had long been Keeper of Coins and Medals, and who was the first Director and Principal Librarian not to have been trained in one of the Library Departments. And about the same time came two other changes; in the Printed Books-Mr. Sharp retired and was followed by Mr. Wilfred Alexander Marsden, and the Manuscripts lost Gilson by sudden death, Dr. Harold Idris Bell, who is still Keeper, succeeding him. Gilson's profound and multifarious learning can be seen in the published catalogues—and notably that of the Royal MSS.—and in the Class Catalogue. With learning, and perhaps, as an aid to it, he had a remarkable gift of silence; but he will be long remembered for the readiness with which he followed the Museum's tradition and placed his knowledge at the disposal of all who sought it.[8]

Sir George Hill's period of office was brief, for he came to it late. He retired in 1936 and was succeeded by the present Director, Sir John Forsdyke, previously Keeper of Greek and Roman Antiquities. The chief events in the Library in Sir George Hill's time as Director were the purchases of three manuscripts, the Luttrell and Bedford Psalters and the Codex Sinaiticus. The two former were secured by the extraordinarily generous action of Mr. John Pierpont Morgan in lending the whole price, £64,000, free of interest for a year; but the effort to raise the money, which was accomplished by the help of the Government, the National Art-Collections Fund and friends, was a considerable strain. Two years later came the even greater effort needed to secure the Codex Sinaiticus of the Greek Bible, undoubtedly the most valuable single acquisition ever made by the Trustees, whether it be valued by the standards of the market-place or of the study. The history of this celebrated manuscript is well known. It is datable by its uncial script to the fourth century, and is a sister of the Vaticanus.9 It was found in 1844 by Tischendorf in the monastery of St. Catherine on Mount Sinai in a heap of parchment leaves thrown on one side by the monks for destruction. Tischendorf took 43 leaves and presented them to the King of Saxony, and they are in the University Library of Leipzig. In 1859 he induced the monks to give the remainder to the Tsar—in return for 9,000 roubles and honours, with which they were well content. Some 390, out of about 730, beautifully written four-column leaves, thus passed into the Imperial Library at St. Petersburg. In 1933 these leaves, still unbound, were offered by the Soviet Government for £100,000. Towards this great sum, unexampled for a single purchase for the Library, the Trustees could produce from their reserve £7,000. The Government, under Mr. Ramsay MacDonald, and at the instance of Sir Frederic Kenyon and the Archbishop of Canterbury, lent the sum needed and offered to give £1 for every £1 subscribed by the public. In the end the Government was left to pay rather over £30,000, but the process of obtaining the balance from the public is one which those engaged in it will never forget. On the day in December 1933 on which the Codex was received the Entrance Hall overflowed with enthusiastic sightseers, and for months the Museum was flooded with visits and correspondence. A great sum was received in small coins left in a box in the Hall, while collections were made in churches and lecture halls all over the country. The task, it may be added, was complicated by the activities of a section of the London Press, which, apparently inspired by political animus, violently attacked the proposed contribution from public funds, and spread ludicrous rumours about the Codex.

But very shortly afterwards the same sum had to be raised by the British and Victoria and Albert Museums in conjunction to secure the late Mr. George Eumorfopoulos's Chinese antiquities.

Sir John Forsdyke had very early in his Directorship a similar problem. Thomas James Wise died in 1937 and by his will instructed his trustees to offer the Library to the Museum, at a price to be fixed by his widow. It is by her public spirit that the price fixed was quite uncommercial. But even so it could only be paid by a series of annual instalments, which swallowed all and much more than the amount which the Printed Books might have had to spend on old books. (See below, pp. 199–201.)

Great gifts have perforce grown scarce; but 1941 saw one in the grand manner, when 47 illuminated MSS. from the famous collection of Henry Yates Thompson were presented, in fulfilment of his widow's desire, by her executors.

Even before the present Director was appointed rumours of war were in the air, and the first steps towards evacuation had been taken. As time went on these were elaborated, and at the Munich crisis of September 1938 were all but put into operation. And to them were added the even more elaborate precautions against air raids. The building of the new Parthenon Room, though it is outside the scope of the present book, must also be mentioned as one of the major cares of these last years.

The years between the wars were, considering the troubles of the time, as fruitful as any. The publications, not counting the new General Catalogue, were of as high number and quality as in any other twenty years in the Library's history, now nearing the end of its second century. If the Catalogue of the Royal MSS. and the facsimiles of the Lindisfarne Gospels and the Luttrell Psalter are the finest of the three Departments' recent publications, fruitful new moves, which it is to be hoped will reach far, are to be seen in the series of short-title lists of the printed books of countries and centuries, and in the extension to the Map Room of the Museum's old tradition of publishing facsimiles of its chief treasures. Except in the depression at the beginning of the thirties, which alone caused the offer of the Codex Sinaiticus to fail in America and to reach London, prices ruled high. But apart from the sensational purchases which have been mentioned, the standard and number of acquisitions were kept up better than might have been expected, and the Treasury increased the purchase grant to £30,000, only to have to withdraw it on the outbreak of war. In the Manuscripts the Luttrell and Bedford books, for example, were only the chief of a series, described below (pp. 278–80), of notable specimens of English illumination

THE LAST THIRTY YEARS

acquired in these years. In the Printed Books additions were made even to the Caxtons, while the stores of later Tudor literature were continually increased, though at the Britwell Sales little success was obtained against the competition of Mr. H. E. Huntington. And such gifts have been received as that of Rudyard Kipling's "file" of his books, given by his widow in 1940, and Canning's copy, annotated by him with the names of contributors, of the prospectus and original 36 numbers of the *Anti-Jacobin*, given by Mr. Julian Moore in 1936. Both Departments had great help from the Friends of the National Libraries, founded in 1931 under the Chairmanship of Sir Frederic Kenyon, and the Manuscripts (for illuminated or other artistic MSS.) from the National Art-Collections Fund.

A great deal was done in this period to spread public interest in the Museum. *The British Museum Quarterly*, founded in 1926, has published illustrated accounts of accessions. Much earlier in his Directorship Sir Frederic Kenyon established a bookstall, at which not only larger publications, but beautiful cheap reproductions, especially of MSS., enjoyed large sales. Official Guide-Lecturers were another of his devices for (in the right sense of the term) popularizing the Museum.

In the Reading Room little remains to be recorded. G. F. Barwick, one of the best and longest in office of its Superintendents (1900–15), and author of the one useful book (apart from handbooks), yet written on it,[10] was succeeded in turn by Mr. R. F. Sharp, Mr. F. D. Sladen and, last, the present Superintendent, Mr. A. I. Ellis.

From about 1926 the rules for admission of readers were less casually, though it is hoped never illiberally, administered. While the age-limit has often been waived with the Trustees' previous or subsequent sanction, generally in favour of young students engaged on post-graduate theses, other libraries in London, both special and public, have been so developed and their resources made known in such works as R. A. Rye's *Student's Guide to the Libraries of London*, that the Museum Reading Room is not now, as formerly, the only or even always the best resource for all and sundry readers, who are moreover multiplied beyond the Room's capacity and also beyond the preservation of the books. An applicant, if not admitted, is advised of the library most suitable to his needs. It will doubtless be long before the public generally understands the position. The penalty of the Museum's celebrity is that the average person needing a book not in his own possession nor new enough to be available in the commercial circulating libraries, turns first to Bloomsbury. A very few of those not admitted but referred elsewhither, resent it, wrongly regarding admission as the unconditional birthright of an Englishman—or at least of a taxpayer—and indignant at seeing it given to foreigners. The standard and convincing reply to these is that their taxes maintain not only the British Museum, but also the Houses of Parliament, not to speak of prisons and lunatic asylums, and that for all that they presumably do not claim entry to these places. Most, however, are well enough content. A pleasing example was that of a middle-aged man who had spent many years in Central Africa and applied for a ticket in order that he might read again a favourite book he had not seen since his youth in England. On enquiry the book proved to be Bacon's *Essays*, and he was delighted to hear that he could not only see a copy in any public library, but could probably buy one for sixpence or a shilling within a hundred yards of the Museum.

The cumulative effect of such a Library as the Museum's is impossible to estimate. It has the function, at first its only function, of preserving the printed and written records of civilization. But, beyond that, it is a seedbed from which grows the forest of modern knowledge, specially but not only in its historical field. No proof can well be offered, but surely the Library fulfils the second function as well as it fulfils the first, though not all its users nor all its servants be worthy. The end and essence of its work is to preserve and to disseminate truth. Hardly any other life-work can more thoroughly make an integral part of the mind a patient respect for fact.[11] It is a discipline for which no one who has been through it can fail to give thanks to the company of his predecessors who created it, or to be proud of the old title, "a servant of the Trustees of the British Museum."

PART II

THE COLLECTIONS AND THEIR CATALOGUES

I

THE PRINTED BOOKS

In the following sections the special collections and some important classes will be summarily described, with notes of their catalogues. The large bulk of the approximately five million printed books is composed of those received under the Copyright Acts. Most of the largest libraries of the world are swelled by legal deposit, and such a library as Harvard's, which reaches three million without it, is therefore the more remarkable. Foreign books are acquired by the Museum in very large quantity, the books being ordered from the national trade lists on publication; the work of selection is divided among the Staff, not by subjects but by languages. Each man so detailed is expected to become expert in the literature chosen, and to be a sort of liaison officer to the scholars and bibliographers of the country. This system in a way obviates the need for consulting experts such as were added by Dr. Putnam to the Staff of the Library of Congress. Many of the Staff have in fact taken high rank as scholars, though others who might have done so within the Museum's walls have been lost to it; Edmund Gosse, for example, carried elsewhere those studies in the Scandinavian literatures, as well as in the English Restoration drama, which, chastened by the atmosphere of the place, would have been so useful there. It would, however, be a valuable addition if there were some advisers in subjects—such as Law—which the Museum's own scope does not cover.

With funds limited not only relatively to what is needed but also relatively to those of rapidly expanding libraries on the other side of the Atlantic, it has not been possible to maintain the ideal of universality in collecting. Nor has it, fortunately, been so necessary as in the past. Special libraries in London have vastly increased in number, importance and accessibility to students. This is particularly the case with the physical sciences. Buying in these fields can therefore be confined to the more important works, while in others, in which special libraries do not abound, such as foreign literature, history and topography, the Museum still endeavours to be exhaustive.

For natural history the Sloane and Banks libraries had provided a solid foundation. When the Natural History Departments were removed to South Kensington the Trustees considered a proposal to send after them the appropriate sections of the general library. This they declined to do (as they have declined similar proposals for the deposit of special books in other and special libraries), with the result that they had to start afresh building up a special library at South Kensington, with what success is known to all users of its Catalogue. It includes among much else what is perhaps the finest Linnaean collection in existence.[1] For natural history, thenceforth, as for inorganic science and technology, which are provided for in detail by the Science Library and that of the Patent Office, the General Museum Library could dispense with buying all but the outstanding books and (still more) periodicals.

Of periodicals, indeed, the swelling, and as many think absurd, number was first clearly revealed in *The World List of Scientific Periodicals*, 1927, compiled in the Museum, though not published by the Trustees. Hesitation to add to the number of journals filed has had its good reasons not only in limits of funds, but also in those of space, for the length of time any periodical will run, and consequently the amount of shelf-room it will require, are uncertain quantities, and in the case of many of the chief German scientific periodicals the annual bulk and also cost have been certain only to rise.

The Museum has never purchased whole libraries and sold all books from them which it did not need, a practice which has been found very profitable by some of the greater American libraries, but one which needs either available capital or easy access to large and possibly speculative grants of money. Nor has it sent out travelling collectors. Many of the best dealers, however, knowing its special interest of the moment, report likely finds, and are very friendly in their dealings with it. At the risk of invidious omission mention may be made of Bernard Quaritch and his successors, who have for very many years not only been agents for the Trustees' publications but have acted for them in the auction-room and in other ways have helped the collections.

THE PRINTED BOOKS

It cannot be often enough repeated that no serious library buys old books for their rarity or as curiosities, or for any other reason than to preserve and make available such knowledge as they may have to convey.

1. THE SLOANE LIBRARY

There is little that can be said about the library of Sir Hans Sloane, which formed the groundwork and for half a century and more the bulk of the Department's collection. The books have been mixed with the later acquisitions which formed the Old Library, i.e. up to the middle of the nineteenth century, by the successive shelf-arrangements. Sloane's MS. press-marks by which they can be identified have only recently been traced.[2] Nor is there a printed catalogue; but there is an incomplete one in manuscript (Sloane MS. 3972 C). The number of volumes was at the time of the foundation stated at 50,000 volumes; there were really 40,000. There is no doubt that quantities of so-called duplicates were sold from among them in the Sales up to 1805.

Sloane collected, as might be guessed, medical and scientific, and especially botanical literature, both practically and historically, and was rich in the publications of continental academies. But he threw his net wider, and was in fact omnivorous. So far as is known, the Museum owes to Sloane few if any of its rarer monuments of literature or typography; but it does owe to him a very solid foundation-stone of a great library of universal scope.

2. MAJOR EDWARDS'S LIBRARY

See below, p. 352, n.11, for the Library bequeathed (with money) before the Foundation by Major Arthur Edwards.

3. THE OLD ROYAL LIBRARY

The chief importance of the Old Royal Library presented by George II to the Museum by Letters Patent of 6th August, 1757, lies in its manuscripts; and accordingly some account of the history of the Library will be found below, under the Collections of that Department (pp. 240-48).

The first printed books to be acquired by an English sovereign appear to be a long series of copies on vellum of books printed at Paris by Antoine Verard. They were bound in crimson vellum (renewed in modern times) of the sort alluded to by Leland when he said that "unless trueth be delicately clothed yn purpule her written verities can scant find a reader." They have often been spoken of as a treasure; but in their own time they were merely cheap imitations of French illuminated MSS., with the woodcuts smothered in coarse colour, such as an economical king like Henry VII would naturally prefer. His successors up to James I collected comparatively few printed books, but many of those that did enter the Royal Library in the sixteenth century are bound in fine armorial bindings, and some bear personal notes of great interest. Paul Hentzner, who visited Whitehall in 1598, noted in his *Itinerary* that Queen Elizabeth had many books finely bound in embroidery and jewelled bindings. Henry VIII, who during his elder brother's lifetime had been trained for the Church, with a view to an Archbishopric, had a number of standard books of value in theology and common law. One of these, Augustinus de Ancona, *Summa de potestate ecclesiastica* (Cologne, 1475; I.B. 3131), bears notes in the King's hand showing close study. Apparently at the time of the Divorce he turned to his books again; for many of the sections marked have relevance to the Pope's powers of dispensation and the like; and on that dealing with dispensation for marrying more than one wife, against the sentence in the text "Est dicendum quod plures uxores habere non fuit contra naturam in antiquis patribus" he commented succinctly, "Ergo nec in nobis."

Strype's statement in his *Memorials of Cranmer*, that Martin Bucer's library was bought for Edward VI appears to be unfounded. Such an action would have been far from characteristic of the Protector Somerset.

James I, as befitted a scholar, made very large additions with the aid of his librarian, Patrick Young. The greatest accession of his reign was the purchase for Henry, Prince of Wales, of the library of

THE PRINTED BOOKS

Lord Lumley, son-in-law of Henry Fitzalan, last Earl of Arundel of the name, who had bought a good part of the library formed by Archbishop Cranmer; very many incunabula and MSS. bear the signatures "Thomas Cantuarien" and "Lumley." James I also bought part of the library of Isaac Casaubon, with whom Young was on friendly terms, after the great scholar's death in 1614.

Acquisitions made under Charles I were far less numerous, but included some notable gifts, such as those presented by the community of Little Gidding of books made and bound there.

During the Civil War and Commonwealth there was some pilfering, and many books in fine bindings of earlier sovereigns are to be found in various libraries today. Some notable examples came to the Museum among Cracherode's and the King's books; there is also a considerable series in the Library of Worcester College, Oxford, most of them having been taken, presumably in 1649, by William Clarke, the Assistant Secretary to the Army Council in England, who paid £20 to settle the matter; his son George was Worcester's benefactor.[3] But the Royal Library luckily escaped the dispersal by sale which befell Charles I's pictures. It was not to be expected that any considerable additions would be made in the period, though John Durie, Young's successor from 1650, entertained ideas of librarianship in advance of his time. His successor at the Restoration, Thomas Ross, though not a man of the same calibre, was able during his five years' tenure of office to make at least one large acquisition, the library, chiefly printed, of John Morice ("Mauricius"), which is rich in incunabula.

Under Charles II the Library received considerable additions, though the chance to buy the Thomason Tracts was missed, and the Licensing Acts of 1662 and later years provided a new if not very fertile source of supply. The fashion which made Whitehall, like other European courts, a miniature copy of Versailles, probably had its influence, and especially in binding, for which Charles gave large orders to his stationer and contractor, Samuel Mearne; the bills survive for a series comprising scores of volumes bound through him in red Turkey morocco with the King's cypher. But Mearne, like other contractors to the Crown at that time, often had difficulty in obtaining payment; and 180 Hebrew books, nearly all printed, remained on his hands till he sold them to Solomon da Costa, who presented them to the Museum at its opening (see below, pp. 297, 373). These were clearly the Oriental books which Evelyn, who visited the Library in 1680 and 1681, mentions as remaining at the binder's. Franz Burman, who saw the library about 1710, speaks of piles of unbound books, which must have been those delivered in sheets from Stationers' Hall. Bentley stated in the preface to his *Phalaris* that he found that books were not delivered by copyright; he applied, and received a thousand from the very reluctant booksellers. In his *Proposal for building a Royal Library* he said that there had been "no supply of books for sixty years past, nor any allowance for binding" and that the thousand books received were "brought in quires to the Library, as due by the Act for printing" and so were all unbound and useless.

No notable additions were made between this time and 1757. When the Royal library reached the Museum the printed books numbered about 9,000. Panizzi described them in his survey of the Printed Books made in 1843-45 as consisting mainly of English history, Divinity, Latin classics and Spanish and Italian history and poetry. The Library was when at Whitehall arranged according to the Sovereigns by whom the books had been acquired. In the Museum shelf-arrangements of 1793 and later they were mixed with Sloane's and other books. But of late years a number bearing Royal armorial bindings have been picked out and arranged according to the original plan.

There is no modern catalogue including the printed books. In the series of inventories drawn up and signed by Durie and Ross, the outgoing and incoming Librarians, between 1661 and 1666, the books are listed by languages (Royal MS. App. 86). An old MS. catalogue of books is preserved in the Department of Printed Books.

THE PRINTED BOOKS

4. THE THOMASON TRACTS

The Thomason Tracts, or King's Tracts, as they were long called, even after the large collection in the King's Library had made the latter term somewhat equivocal, were the first important gift after that of the Old Royal Library, being presented in 1762 by George III, who surely showed thereby a notable public spirit, seeing that he was himself then beginning to form his own great library.

Their collector was George Thomason, bookseller, of the Rose and Crown in St. Paul's Churchyard (born not after 1602, died 1666). On 3rd November, 1640, Thomason began to act systematically on the profoundly true conception that the fugitive literature of the period of strife and crisis which he foresaw would be of great value if collected and preserved. From that day till the coronation of Charles II on 23rd April, 1661 (with a few additions to December of that year) he purchased, or occasionally received by gift, every small book, pamphlet or newspaper that he could come by published in London or the provinces, or even abroad if English. Folios he disregarded as having no topical interest, but quartos *et infra* he accepted whatever their contents.

The history of the collection both during its formation and during the century which elapsed between its completion and its final arrival in the Museum was far from uneventful. After the Restoration, Thomason was, like so many others, at pains to represent himself as a Royalist and even as having formed his collection at Charles I's command and for his use. Fortescue proves beyond any doubt that he was really a Presbyterian, having even been implicated in the Love Plot of 1651 to restore Charles II as a Covenanting sovereign. Whether Royalist or not, he was certainly an enemy of the Independents, and it is likely enough that the Advertisement issued is to be believed in stating that Thomason concealed the collection and at times sent it into Essex and Surrey. There is no doubt that he sent it to be cared for by Thomas Barlow, afterwards Bishop of Lincoln, at the Bodleian, to which he was a large regular purveyor of books. It thus escaped the Fire of London. Barlow tried to find a benefactor to secure it, but in vain, and sometime after 1676 it passed to Mearne,

THE LIBRARY OF THE BRITISH MUSEUM

the King's Stationer, who presumably issued the printed Advertisement referred to. In 1683 Mearne died, and on the 15th May of the following year the Privy Council approved his widow's petition for leave to sell the collection, a petition which she had clearly made in the belief (perhaps sincere) that Thomason had acted for the King.

The books passed to Anne Mearne's son-in-law Thomas Sisson and his descendants, who made many endeavours to sell them; it seems curious that Robert Harley did not buy them to add to his great collection of historical pamphlets. In 1761 Thomas Hollis, the well-known crank, who himself made a number of gifts to the Museum in its earliest days, came to know of the collection and directly or indirectly advised Bute to buy it, which he did for £300; the King is stated to have refunded this money, and Bute made the gift to the Trustees in the King's name on 22nd July, 1762.

The Thomason Tracts were rebound after their reception in the style and order of the original volumes; this binding has been replaced, still in the same arrangement, in recent years. Fortescue calculates the collection to contain 22,255 pieces bound in 2,008 volumes; these figures including 7,216 numbers of newspapers and 97 manuscripts.

Thomason thus preserved for us a great number of pieces which would otherwise have probably disappeared, and by his practice of arranging them chronologically and also dating them exactly in MS. he has enabled us to follow the movements of opinion from day to day through fateful years. Carlyle spoke not too strongly when before the Royal Commissioners of 1847-49,[4] he called the Thomason Tracts "the most valuable set of documents connected with English history; greatly preferable to all the sheepskins in the Tower and other places, for informing the English what the English were in former times."

It is hard to say how successful Thomason was in his endeavour to be complete. Fortescue shows that little attempt was made to secure numerous editions of a book or, in particular, to buy all the many Quaker tracts appearing.[5] As to provincial books, Falconer Madan revealed that very many Oxford printed tracts with false Lon-

THE PRINTED BOOKS

don imprints were bought by Thomason, though Fortescue's catalogue did not so describe them.

A special Catalogue of the Tracts, whose titles were only then for the first time being incorporated into the General Catalogue, was considered in 1847; but nearly half a century more was to elapse before it was undertaken. Fortescue's catalogue, it may be thought a belated performance of a duty of the Museum's, appeared in 1908. It follows Thomason's chronological arrangement. The newspapers follow the tracts in a separate section. There is a large index, which, however, is historically rather than bibliographically arranged and is not a perfect guide to the presence or absence of any particular piece. Mr. W. G. Hiscock, Sub-Librarian of Christ Church, Oxford, is at present at work on Thomason and on this Index.

Catalogue of the Pamphlets, Books, Newspapers, and Manuscripts relating to the Civil War, the Commonwealth, and Restoration, collected by George Thomason, 1640–61, 1908. 2 vols. (Edited, with preface by G. K. Fortescue.)

There is a MS. catalogue, drawn up for Thomason himself, in twelve folio volumes.

5. THE CRACHERODE LIBRARY

The Rev. Clayton Mordaunt Cracherode (1730–99) was a private scholar and collector, and played no part in public affairs. Westminster School, Christ Church, Oxford, the Society of Antiquaries and the Museum shared with a few scholarly friends and the formation of his own collections the whole of a determinedly private life, except for a few early years spent in the curacy of Binsey, near Oxford. Dr. Samuel Denne, indeed, in a letter of 19th April, 1799, printed by Nichols,[6] calls him a sleeping partner of the Antiquaries, and says that he could get so little out of him that he wonders whether his scholarship was really anything much. Of his shyness some well-known stories are told, how for example he never saw a celebrated chestnut tree growing on land of his no farther from London than Hertfordshire, how he had never mounted a horse, and how his life was darkened by the dread of having to act as the King's Cupbearer at a Coronation, which seemed likely to be not so distant, as duty by tenure of grand-serjeantry of his manor of Great Wymondley. All his changes were from the blue bed to the brown, from Elmsley's bookshop in the Strand to Tom Payne's at the Mews-gate (Charing Cross), where there was a "literary coffee-house," of which, according to Mathias in the *Pursuits of Literature*, "mild Cracherode" was a leading ornament, visiting both almost daily; he is reported to have travelled as far as Clapham.

He began collecting early. Denne relates that he had often seen him above forty years before, i.e. in the seventeen-fifties, in Tom Payne's Literary Gallery. But his father's death in 1773 put him in possession of ample means, and as he never married, he became a power in the book market, sharing with the King the dominance over the market for fine and early books, especially after the death of William Hunter in 1783. Though he protested at the high prices which came in late in his life, he bought up to the end. As he generally noted (with his neat monogram) the date of purchase in his volumes, it can be seen how he developed, and how the opportunities created by the French emigration at the Revolution helped him.

Whereas the King formed a library, Cracherode in the main collected a cabinet of fine volumes, as he did of prints or gems. His books numbered 4,500, and though they include working books of no great age, rarity or importance, the collection is distinguished not only by its treasures, but by the lovely condition of the copies, enhanced in most cases (though at the cost of the knowledge which no doubt perished with the original covers) by being bound by Roger Payne with Cracherode's beautiful armorial stamp centred in panels of the tooling of the greatest of English bookbinders. But Cracherode preserved fine early bindings, such as that of his Aldine Aristotle.

Cracherode was, *pace* Denne, a scholar as well as a man of taste, and he paid special attention to early editions of the classics and the Silver Age of Latin, as well as to early printing as an art. Copies of such books as the Mainz *Catholicon*, the Subiaco Lactantius, *editiones principes* of classics from the first presses of Rome and Venice. Its first and finest copy of the 1481 illustrated Divine Comedy, in which the Museum was then very weak, came from him. The Museum was later to obtain duplicates of many of his books from the King's and Grenville Libraries, but not only were hardly any of his copies then duplicates; they abound in beauty and often in variants. He bequeathed to Shute Barrington, Bishop of Durham, his copies of the Complutensian Polyglot Bible and Aldine Septuagint and Greek New Testament, and to Cyril Jackson, Dean of his old College (of which he remained a Student till his death) his *editio princeps* (Florence, 1488) of Homer, for whom Jackson had a supreme admiration; both legatees returned the books to their friend's collection in the Museum.

Cracherode's library has from the first been kept separate. Till the destruction of Old Montagu House it filled Room II; in the new building it has filled part of the room, named the Cracherode Room, adjoining the First Supplementary Room. Incunabula were moved about 1900 to their places in Proctor order in the Arch Room.

There is no special printed catalogue, but Cracherode's own MS. Catalogue is preserved (Add. MS. 11360); and there is a transcript, with additions not entered by Cracherode, marked by Ayscough (King's MS. 387).

6. THE CROKER FRENCH REVOLUTION TRACTS

These three collections comprise in all 48,579 pieces and sets of periodicals, being thus over twice as numerous as the Thomason Tracts, though, being mostly slighter, they are bound in fewer volumes—1,961 against 1,983.

The first series, press-marked "F," was collected chiefly by M. Colin, Marat's publisher, and bought in 1817 on John Wilson Croker's recommendation. They represented the early years, yet do not include Marat's own writings, as might be expected; but a large set of these, and of works relating to him, bound in seventy volumes, was presented in 1898 by François Chevremont, Marat's biographer; these last are not included in the collection, the production of the list of which in the next year was, however, doubtless occasioned by their acquisition.

Stimulated by his find, Croker, who from boyhood had studied the Revolution, and was, as is shown by his *Essays on the Early Period*

THE LIBRARY OF THE BRITISH MUSEUM

of the French Revolution (1857, reprinted, after his death, from the *Quarterly Review*) the best English authority on it, began to collect for himself, completing the first series not only by publications of the later Revolutionary years, but by filling gaps in the earlier. These two collections, sold to the Museum by Croker in two parts in 1831, and (shortly before his death) in 1856, are press-marked respectively "F.R.," and "R." Their value is greatly enhanced by the notes which Croker wrote on many of them.

The first series was bound after reaching the Museum; and Panizzi's first Museum task was to catalogue them, a task which he was not able to complete, and which was only accomplished in the early seventies. The F.R. and R. Tracts, on the other hand, remained not only uncatalogued and unbound, but even unsorted till the nineties, and Carlyle had excuse for his often-quoted and characteristically violent and picturesque exclamation, before the Commission of 1848, that "for all practical purposes they might as well have been locked up in water-tight chests and sunk on the Dogger Bank." Their titles were then incorporated in the General Catalogue, and a summary by classes, with a subject index (not a catalogue) of all these collections, whose title is given below, compiled by George Fortescue and published in 1899.

Fortescue amplified his preface to his *List* in two papers read to the Bibliographical Society in 1905 and 1906,[7] but unfortunately not printed in extenso; in the former he compares the French and English Revolutionary Tracts.

List of the Contents of the three Collections of Books, Pamphlets and Journals in the British Museum relating to the French Revolution. By G. K. Fortescue. 1899.

7. THE BANKS LIBRARY

Sir Joseph Banks, the botanist and zoologist, laid the foundation of his great natural history collections when, in 1768, as a young man of fortune (he was then twenty-five), he equipped and accompanied Captain Cook's voyage of exploration in the *Endeavour*. Elected President of the Royal Society in 1778—an office which he

THE PRINTED BOOKS

held till his death—he became an official Trustee of the Museum, and was one of the most active and influential members of the Board. He was indeed a man of such force of character that he dominated all societies, and exercised an unquestioned ascendancy over the Royal Society, quelling an attempted revolt when he had been for five years in the Chair. His house in Soho, with its collections, was the centre of the scientific world in this country, and he gave ready access to it.

In 1772, accompanied by his librarian Dr. Daniel Solander, who had been an Assistant Librarian in the Museum's Natural History Department, he visited Iceland, climbing Hecla; and to this visit and to Solander's Scandinavian origin we may attribute his gifts of Icelandic books to the Museum, which are mentioned elsewhere (pp. 205, 207). He himself began to form a large collection of books of botany and zoology, and of travel and exploration. Among his books is a copy of Wynkyn de Worde's *Bartholomaeus Anglicus*, 1495, celebrated as being the first book printed on paper made in England. After Solander's death in 1782, another Swedish scientist, Dr. Jonas Dryander, librarian to the Royal and Linnaean Societies, became his librarian and produced for him in five volumes, 1798–1800, a catalogue which has been generally regarded as a model of classification for its date, and also of accurate bibliographical detail.

Dryander died in 1810, and was followed by Robert Brown. Banks died ten years later, bequeathing his collections and library to Brown (with an annuity of £200 a year), and the reversion to the Museum. Brown quickly gave the Museum the collections and books, and himself came with them, when space could be found, which was not for some years.

The Banks Library occupies a small room, the pair of the Cracherode, adjoining the Old Music Room on the South; the scientific collections are, of course, at South Kensington. Lawrence's portrait of Banks is, with the exception of a cast of a cameo of Macaulay, the only portrait of a member of the Board which adorns the Board Room; and it is the finest work of art there.

THE LIBRARY OF THE BRITISH MUSEUM

8. The Burney Library

In 1818 the family of Charles Burney, D.D., classical scholar and son of the musician, petitioned Parliament to buy his library for the nation. The price asked was £14,000, but the Special Committee of the House of Commons abated this by £500 when recommending the purchase, which was accordingly made and the library transferred to the Museum.

It consisted chiefly of some 13,000 printed editions and manuscripts of classical Greek and Latin authors. (The collection of manuscripts is noticed below, p. 251.) Of the printed books many are distinguished by the MS. notes of celebrated scholars, among them Henri Estienne and Richard Bentley; of the latter's adversaria the Museum already possessed a collection, purchased in 1807 from Bentley's grandson, Richard Cumberland, for 400 guineas. Burney's classical books are not kept together as a collection.

Burney's library also included a collection of newspapers (noticed below, pp. 208–10), and a collection, in 349 volumes, of cuttings, playbills, portraits, etc., illustrating the history of the English stage.[8]

9. The King's Library

While yet Prince of Wales, King George III possessed enough books, some inherited from his father, Frederick Prince of Wales, some acquired by himself, to need a librarian, a post to which he appointed Richard Dalton. When he came to the throne the shelves of the Royal Library were empty, if indeed they remained at all, since three years earlier King George II had presented it entire to the Museum—perhaps apart from a few volumes identifiable as having belonged to it which are among the King's MSS. The new King at once set about collecting books and laid the foundation of his Library by purchasing on 28th January, 1763, for £10,000, the whole "Bibliotheca Smithiana," or library of Joseph Smith, merchant and British consul at Venice, of which Smith had in 1755 printed under that title a catalogue compiled by G. B. Pasquali. This was the second of the three collections formed by him; the first he had

THE PRINTED BOOKS

sold to Lord Sunderland in 1720, and the third was sold by auction in London after his death. That which the King bought is rich in classics, and, as might be expected, in Italian history and literature. Volumes from it may frequently be identified by eye as one walks through the King's Library today by the white vellum bindings then and much later common on Italian books.

Shortly after this Dalton was transferred to the Keepership of the Royal pictures and antiquities, for which he was much better qualified by his training as an artist and his work as a draughtsman of monuments in Greece and elsewhere, even if it is not true, as stated in the *Gentleman's Magazine* (lxvi, 746, quoting Dr. Thomas Morell) that he "in garbling H.M. library threw out several Caxtons as things that might be got again every day." In his place the King appointed his natural half-brother Frederick Augusta Barnard.[9]

It is not known how Johnson obtained admission; but it was while he was working there that he had in February 1767 his celebrated interview with the King, which occasioned his observation that "it was not for him to bandy civilities with his Sovereign." The King's policy was one of liberally admitting scholars, even if distasteful to himself. Thus in 1779 he allowed access to Priestley, with the words, addressed to Lord North, "If Dr. Priestly [sic] applies to my Librarian he will have permission to see the Library, as other men of science have had. But I can't think his character as a Politician or Divine deserves my appearing at all in it."

The King's lofty view of his duty is even more strikingly shown by the instruction which he gave to his bookseller not to bid at auctions against any scholar who was buying books for use. It is a good comment on Horace Walpole's remark, "that any of the [royal] family should have a real taste for letters or the arts would be little short of a miracle."[10]

Johnson was a valuable reader in the Library at the Queen's, or Buckingham House, for he gave excellent advice on the formation of the collection in his well-known letter to Barnard of 1768, written before Barnard's start on a book-buying tour on the Continent. Barnard withheld this letter from Boswell, and printed it himself in 1820 in his introduction to the Catalogue of the Library; it has since been often reprinted[11]; and Barnard elsewhere spoke of Johnson's kindness (characteristic, as we know) to so young a man as he then was. Johnson wrote in the same year two letters relating to the Library to Mr. Weston, perhaps Stephen Weston, though the latter was then a very young man. These three letters are now in the Museum, having been presented in 1916 by Lady Wernher. In that to Barnard Johnson, while advising on the classes of literature which might be best sought in each of the countries he was to visit, dwelt on what was to become one of the distinctions of the King's Library, the beginnings of typography, and says that of frequently published books "a royal library should have the most curious edition, generally the first (he might have said that the first was often the most accurate also) the most splendid, and the most useful, generally one of the latest." And he recommended feudal and civil law, calling the latter "a regal study." Each literature must be sought in its own country; the classics might be found anywhere. Maps should be collected locally.

Barnard followed Johnson's advice. The subjects to which he was advised to pay attention are just those in which the King's Library is strong. The geographical section grew to great size, and required a separate catalogue. The incunabula were very numerous and included a large proportion of works from the first presses, in very good copies. The King received gifts of early English printed books, an especially fine one in 1782 from Jacob Bryant, the antiquary, who was his friend and neighbour at Farnham Royal; and the only perfect copy of Caxton's *Aesop* was bequeathed to him by a Mr. Hewett of Ipswich. At West's and Askew's Sales in 1773 and 1775 he bought largely; from the former he obtained several of his fine series of Caxtons and the Mainz *Catholicon*, and from the latter early Italian books.

It was stated in the House of Commons report at the time of the transfer that the King's Library was richest in classics, English history, Italian, French and Spanish literature and in early printed books. It had been reported by the Trustees that the Museum Library, then amounting to about 125,000 volumes, would be greatly strengthened by the addition of the King's Library in the

THE PRINTED BOOKS

history of printing, in geography, heraldry, antiquities, theology, various branches of *belles lettres*, in grammars and dictionaries, in Italian and Spanish literature, and in general history. The English historical pamphlets, moreover, were an important section; they were much used by Macaulay, who sat close at hand, at a table which is still preserved in the King's Library. There were, besides the 65,259 volumes and 868 boxes of pamphlets (bound under Panizzi), of which the Library was found to consist when received and counted,[12] a separate geographical collection, consisting of maps, charts, plans and topographical drawings. Here, as in early printing, the King was glad to receive gifts from his subjects, and an important addition of prints and drawings of Scottish places was made through Barnard in 1786 by the Earl of Buchan.[13] The Geographical Collection incorporated that formed for military purposes by the Duke of Cumberland.

In English literature, which Johnson observed must be sought at home, and especially in the Elizabethans, the King's Library for the first time gave strength to the Museum collection; playbooks abounded too, but in those the King had been anticipated in the Museum by his contemporary collector Garrick; otherwise in them too he would have given it a new start.

The great bulk is, of course, made up not of rare and early editions, but of the standard books of the day such as are always necessary to a large working library; and among them are many periodicals. These are often duplicate copies which are, and were in 1823, in the Museum; but it is most useful to have well-bound second copies of such sets as *The Gentleman's Magazine* or *Archaeologia*.

An average of £2,000 a year was spent on the King's Library, and this was maintained by his private trustees during the Regency; and George IV as Regent sanctioned not only this but the extra expense necessary for printing the catalogue. But when he came to the throne he employed Nash to remodel Buckingham Palace, and probably found the books in the way. The room and octagon building holding them are illustrated in Vol. I of the Catalogue. The King wrote on 15th January, 1823, to Lord Liverpool, the Prime Minister, expressing his intention of presenting the library formed by his father to the nation, and "by this means of advancing the literature of my country." This letter has been the subject of much controversy. In an article in the *Quarterly Review* of 1850 a writer retailed (as from Richard Ford) a story that Richard Heber, the book collector, hearing that the King had offered to sell the Library to the Czar of Russia, went to Lord Sidmouth, who arranged to pay the King the amount from public funds (the Droits of Admiralty); or, alternatively, it was said that through Princess Lieven, Lady Spencer and T. F. Dibdin (Earl Spencer's librarian at Althorp), Lord Liverpool was approached. But the story was quickly denied by J. W. Croker, who would have known, and Princess Lieven also denied any knowledge of the transaction. The origin of the tale was probably the Duke of York, who was at odds with his brother over the disposition of their father's property; he told Greville (*Diary*, 10th January, 1823) that George had wished to sell the Library, but had been prevented.

The Prime Minister consulted the House of Commons and also the Trustees, and the verdict of both was for the addition of the King's Library to that of the Museum. It was laid down that it was to be kept separate and entire, and that any duplicates sold should be the General Library's and not the King's copies. These duplicates were reckoned at 21,000, but by excluding differences of large or fine paper, or other points, the figure was reduced to 12,000. It being reported that Montagu House was "in a decaying state," and so full that the Banks Library was still awaiting reception, funds were voted and a new wing was built, including the ground-floor gallery, which was calculated to hold the books exactly, as related above in Chapter III. The transfer was made in 1828 and the books made available in the next year. The Trustees had in their reply to the Treasury stated that extra staff would be needed; that of the King's Library, except Barnard, who retired, was taken over. The manuscripts were moved in 1840 to the Department of Manuscripts after furious controversy between Madden and Panizzi. The Geographical Collection, however, printed and manuscript together, remains in the King's Library and in the custody of the Keeper of Printed Books, and under him of the Superintendent of the Map Room.

THE PRINTED BOOKS

When the transfer was made, thirty choice books were specifically reserved, and these are now at Windsor Castle. There exists a transcript by Carlisle, the senior Assistant, of a memorandum by Barnard listing them.[14] They include the 1457 Mainz Psalter, bought by George III from the University Library of Göttingen (founded by his grandfather), Caxton's *Aesop*, mentioned above as having been bequeathed to him, Charles I's copy of the 1632 Folio of Shakespeare, with autograph note and motto—this is noted as having been "bought at Askew's sale (from Mead's) at the enormous price of Five Pounds, ten shillings," and the Subiaco Lactantius, with Caxton's *Doctrinal of Sapyence* and twenty-five other incunabula given by Jacob Bryant. These reserved books, with the rest of the Windsor Castle Library, were entailed by William IV on his descendants.

The catalogue of books and manuscripts was commenced by Barnard and his staff, and completed for the Trustees in the year of the transfer. Vol. I has an introduction by Barnard:[15]

Bibliothecae Regiae Catalogus. 5 vols. 1820–29.

There is also a manuscript classed catalogue in 12 folio volumes.

The Geographical Collection was separately catalogued:

Catalogue of Maps, Prints, Drawings, etc., forming the Geographical and Topographical collection, etc. [With classed index.] 1829. fol.

Copies of the two printed Catalogues were presented, but none were sold. There is also a manuscript Catalogue of Charts.

The manuscript maps, etc., were included in John Holmes's *Catalogue of Manuscript Maps in the British Museum*, 3 vols, 1844–61.

(For the King's MSS. see below, pp. 251–52)

A fine collection of coins and medals was transferred with the Library, and was placed in the Department of Antiquities. It probably included the remains of that in the Old Royal Library, dispersed in 1649–50.

10. THE GRENVILLE LIBRARY

With the long political life of Thomas Grenville (1755–1846) we are not here concerned, except to observe that as a young man, after Christ Church and a few years in the Army, he sat in Parliament for thirty-eight years, retiring in 1818, and in that time served a number of public offices and missions. From his early days he was an ardent student and book-collector, and his long retirement was devoted to these two passions. The period was a good one, and Grenville bought with judgment at most of the great sales, such as Count MacCarthy's, Bindley's, Sir Mark Masterman Sykes's, Hibbert's and Heber's. He was far from the commonly supposed type of bibliophile, never collecting for mere rarity, but considering the value of texts and positively avoiding books printed on vellum, which he considered ugly, though buying them when he could not find the same book printed on paper, as for example the forty-two-line Bible, of which he secured the fine Girardot de Préfond copy, and the Greek Anthology of 1494. Nor did he attempt to assemble bibliographically complete sets of the editions of authors.

His favourite classical authors seem to have been Homer and Aesop, of whom, and especially of the latter, he had many rare editions. The small Aldine Virgils of 1501 and 1505 he obtained, the former as the first book printed in italics, the second perhaps for once because it is the rarest of Aldus's productions, the King's copy of which had not come to the Museum but had been retained by the Crown for the Windsor Castle Library. The unique complete copy of Azzoguidi's first (Bologna, 1471) edition of Ovid Grenville considered the gem of his library, though he did not improve it by causing a capital and border, with his arms, to be painted on the first page of the second volume, in imitation of that, contemporary with the book, on the first page of the first volume. The rare Moschus printed at Alcala de Henares was also a favourite of his, as he greatly admired Cardinal Ximenes, for whom it was printed, and who was also the patron of the great Complutensian polyglot Bible of 1514–17 —also, of course, like the Ἐρωτήματα of Chrysoloras from the same press, represented in the collection by a fine copy. While he collected primarily as a student of literature and history, his library was also rich in monuments of early printing as such; it is to him for example that the Museum owes its only copy of the Mainz Psalter of 1457, the King's copy of which, like the 1505 Aldine Virgil, had been retained in 1823. But his fourteen Caxtons were nearly all selected for their importance as literature.[16]

THE PRINTED BOOKS

The English Bible was another of Grenville's chosen fields, and here his luckiest find was the only known fragment of Tyndale's English New Testament printed by Quentell at Cologne in 1525. Of the greater English poets he collected outstanding editions rather than rare separate pieces. Chaucer was one of his loves, and his copy of the First Folio of Shakespeare was for long regarded as the finest extant copy; he also had the *Sonnets*, 1609, and *Lucrece*, 1594, but no quarto plays. In British history he specialized in the voyages and travels, especially of the sixteenth century, out of which the Empire grew, his set of de Bry's Hariot's *Virginia* in four languages being noteworthy. The Spanish and Portuguese voyages are equally well represented. He also collected tracts relating to the divorce of Henry VIII, to the Armada, and to Ireland.

But perhaps his greatest contribution was in Italian and Spanish poetry and romances. Of Italian romance poems no Italian library or collection had so fine a series. Ariosto was the crown of it, and the gem the hitherto previously unknown first edition (1482) of the *Morgante Maggiore*. And we may remember the original editions of Boiardo, the loan of which occasioned Panizzi's earliest introduction to the collector.

The Museum's collection of Spanish and Portuguese poetry and romances was also vastly strengthened by Grenville. Here his choicest volume, at least in Grenville's and Panizzi's eyes, is the beautiful copy of *Tirant lo Blanch*, Valencia, 1490, of which only one inferior copy, in the library of the Sapienza at Rome, was known. It is thanks to Grenville that the Museum possesses its only specimen of the press at Goa.

Grenville did not collect MSS. as such, but possessed a few. The only really notable volume, other than printed books, contains no text but twelve splendid drawings of the Triumphs of the Emperor Charles V; it was once in the Escorial. This is the volume over whose custody such war raged between Panizzi and Madden, the former standing on the promise given to Grenville (though not a condition of the will) that the collection should be kept together, the latter claiming it as a manuscript. It is now in the Department of Prints and Drawings.

THE LIBRARY OF THE BRITISH MUSEUM

Nor did he collect bindings as such; but he preserved a certain number of the finest old bindings on books acquired by him, including some bound for Grolier and a number for de Thou. Would that he had done so far oftener; but like most of the collectors of his generation he rebound in sumptuous full morocco, stamped with his arms, nearly every book he bought, including the First Folio of Shakespeare, which reached his hands in its original binding. It is lamentable to think how much knowledge perished in the binders' shops of London between 1750 and 1850. Nor are the bindings made for Grenville really beautiful, though of excellent workmanship; the art had degenerated in his later days, and he did not employ Roger Payne in his earlier.

If Grenville detracted from the value of his books by rebinding them, he added to it by attaching neat little notes on their provenance, letters, etc.; some of these are from Panizzi, in copies of books which the latter picked up in Italy and presented to his friend.

The collection numbered about 16,000 works in 20,240 volumes. But it must be remembered that it includes great numbers of books of small rarity and value, being an entire library and not a mere cabinet of rare books. Thus it is rich in the publications of the learned societies of the time, and Grenville bound in the same lordly style as his Ariostos and placed on his shelves such pieces as the Statutes of the Museum and Panizzi's Report on the Library of 1845. These common books provided useful duplicates, and were a welcome supplement to the primary wealth of the collection. As Panizzi told the Trustees, the Grenville Library, the greatest accession except the King's received by the Museum Library, placed it in some classes at the head of all libraries, and in others second only to the Royal Library at Paris. The library was stated by its collector to have cost him nearly £50,000 and it was held to be worth more.

Grenville had originally bequeathed the library to his nephew Richard, the second Duke of Buckingham. It is very fortunate that he did not, since within two years of Grenville's death the Duke, who was impoverished, put up the Stowe MSS. collected by his father for sale by auction, from which fate they were saved by the

THE PRINTED BOOKS

Earl of Ashburnham, and the Grenville books would certainly have been sold also. Some MSS. he did leave to the Duke; but by a codicil he revoked the bequest of his library as a whole and left it to the Museum. There is no doubt that this was largely due to Grenville's love and admiration (sincerely returned) for Panizzi. But they were also due to twinges of conscience characteristic of the new age, which would never have occurred to an eighteenth-century collector. As far back as 1800 he had been appointed to a sinecure office, that of Chief Justice in Eyre South of Trent. Without the salary from this, he told Panizzi, he could not have formed such a library (though it afterwards appeared that he had been characteristically lavish throughout life in charities and generosities of all kinds). "I have therefore," he said, "determined to bleach my conscience, and to return to the Nation what I got from it, when I could have done without." His generosity in lending rare volumes to students was, it seems, constant; Panizzi was merely one instance.

The books fill the walls of the room named after Grenville, a result not achieved till they had been lying in piles on the floor for over two years, owing to the claim of the Department of Manuscripts for the room, which had been originally designed as part of it. They were arranged in 1849–50 by Rye. The Grenville Room contains a poor bust of the collector by his friend and fellow-Trustee, Sir David Dundas.

Grenville copies are distinguished by the press-mark G; they are not issued to readers without special application unless they are the Museum's only copies.

In Grenville's lifetime a selective catalogue was commenced by the booksellers Payne and Foss, one part in two volumes appearing in 1842. After his death the Trustees took over responsibility for the second part, which the same compilers had begun in 1843 but had discontinued. This they completed in a third volume. Part the third, compiled by Rye and published officially twenty-four years later, described the books discovered after arrival at the Museum not to have been described by Payne and Foss. A general index also picked up inadequacies observed in their work, such as the five hundred Civil War tracts which they had catalogued in a single entry.

THE LIBRARY OF THE BRITISH MUSEUM

Grenville's own record of his purchases is preserved.

Bibliotheca Grenvilliana, or bibliographical notices of rare and curious books forming part of the library of the Right Hon. Thomas Grenville. By John Thomas Payne and Henry Foss. 2 vols. 1842.

―― *Part the Second, completing the catalogue of the library bequeathed to the British Museum by the late Right Hon. Thomas Grenville.* By John Thomas Payne and Henry Fosse. 1848.

―― *Part the third. With a general index.* [By W. B. Rye.] 1872.

11. THE HUTH BEQUEST

It is rarely now that a complete library can be acquired, however choice, without producing a great number of duplicates and triplicates of important but well-known books. This was the case with the Grenville and even with the King's, and much more would it have been so by 1900 with almost any collection. A new form of bequest, adapted to the new conditions, was devised by Alfred Henry Huth. Under his will, dated 14th January, 1903, he bequeathed to the Trustees their choice of any fifty volumes from the great library chiefly formed by his father, Henry Huth. The terms of the will also allowed them to exchange a copy of a book for a finer one, but any such book taken by exchange was to count as one of the fifty.[17]

Thirteen of the fifty chosen are MSS. All but one are illuminated, the exception being (No. X) a Dutch Hours, remarkable as containing impressions of engravings by the Master of the Berlin Passion. Only one (No. III), a fine Psalter of the late thirteenth century, represents the English School, in which the Museum was already naturally very rich; the French Schools are the best represented, and notably by the splendid Bible in two volumes (Nos. I, II).

The printed books are relatively more important. The Museum's set of the first editions of the pre-Folio Quartos of Shakespeare were completed (bar the doubtful and unique *Titus Andronicus*) by *Richard II*, 1597, *Richard III*, 1597, and *Merry Wives*, 1602, and were supported by three contemporary sonnet-cycles, a group of Shakespeare's source books, and, notably, the Daniel-Huth half (70

THE PRINTED BOOKS

sheets) of the celebrated Helmingham collection of Elizabethan ballads; the other half was later unsuccessfully bid for by the Museum at one of the Britwell Sales and is now in the Henry E. Huntington Library in California. As each ballad was entered separately in the Huth Catalogue, this collection could only be counted as a single volume by giving up the claim to two books of high money value of which the Museum possessed other issues, the *Hamlet* of 1604, identical apart from the date with that of 1605, and the "anopisthographic" *Ars Moriendi* blockbook. Foreign books selected among the fifty were of equally high quality. There were, for example, two originals of translations by Caxton (*Eneydos* and *Fierabras*), two fifteenth-century editions of the *Danse Macabre* (Paris, 1492, and Lyons, 1499) with remarkable woodcuts, and the first edition of Cervantes' *Galatea*, 1585, which completed the Museum's set of that author's original texts.

To signalize their gratitude for this noble bequest the Trustees published a large illustrated quarto catalogue of it.[18] The printed books were shelved together, and to them were added such books as the Museum's funds, thus relieved of the onus of buying such prizes as these, secured at the Huth sales, and any acquired later.

Catalogue of the Fifty Manuscripts and Printed Books bequeathed to the British Museum by Alfred Henry Huth. (Edited by A. W. Pollard.) 1912.

12. THE ASHLEY LIBRARY

Thomas James Wise (1859–1937), a manufacturer of scents, was possessed from boyhood with a passion for the English poets. He began with Shelley and Browning. As Wise developed so did the scope as well as the value of his collections. Shakespeare quartos, unprocurable except by a really wealthy man, which he never was, he left alone, and except for a handful of sixteenth-century plays and poems, many from Swinburne's library, he went no farther back than Shakespeare's immediate followers. But for all periods from the end of the first quarter of the seventeenth century he secured original editions of all the major and many minor English poets, their prose works as well as their poems. The slighter and rarer pieces were his special quarry, and he took particular pains to secure copies in fine and original condition, those from the late eighteenth century down in boards with labels or other cover as issued; to this end he often turned out an inferior copy when he could replace it by a superior. Where differences of issue, cancels, and the like, existed, he tried to secure all states, and his series of issues of some works, such as *The Dunciad*, are extraordinarily complete. The greater Romantic poets are exhaustively represented in the Ashley Library, and so are Rossetti and Swinburne; he was indeed described by Gosse as the literary heir of the Pre-Raphaelite poets. Of the poets of both these periods, and especially of the latter, he also gathered important collections of manuscripts, including their correspondence and other biographical matter. A word should be said of his reprints. For many years, with Buxton Forman, he conducted the Shelley Society, and was responsible for a number of reprints of rare poetical pieces.[19] Of his own collection he published catalogues, comparison of which shows the growth of the collection. In them he entitled it "The Ashley Library," from his London home; in his later years he lived in Hampstead, where he was a near neighbour of his friend Edmund Gosse and also of George Aitken, the collector of Pope, and he did much to help the Keats House and its collection. The latest *Catalogue of the Ashley Library* appeared in eleven volumes from 1922. The whole of the work of cataloguing, with full bibliographical descriptions, was his own work, with the assistance of his wife. Of certain large headings he published even fuller catalogues: *A Shelley Library, A Byron Library, A Swinburne Library,* etc., and he contributed to the publications of the Bibliographical Society similar bibliographies of Landor and Coleridge, besides publishing full-dress bibliographies of Swinburne and others.

From his early days Wise had derived great help and inspiration from Richard Garnett's knowledge of poetry, especially of Shelley's, and he gave the Museum not only most of his countless privately printed reprints but also duplicates of scarce pieces. He intended, as he was childless, to bequeath his library outright to it. But the economic distresses of his later years did not leave him unscathed,

THE PRINTED BOOKS

and he found this impossible. He left it to his Executors to offer it to the Museum at a price to be decided by his widow after his death in May 1937. Mrs. Wise displayed great public spirit, and accepted a sum which she was unwilling to make public, but which was not half of what might perhaps have been obtained.

A room off the King's Library has been prepared to take the Ashley Library. Titles will in due course be incorporated into the General Catalogue; meanwhile a copy of the latest edition of Wise's own catalogue has been press-marked for use.

It has been remarked in criticism of the purchase that such a collection must to a considerable extent duplicate copies already in the Museum. Undoubtedly it does; yet the Ashley duplicates will be of the greatest service. Early publications of writers who subsequently became famous are generally printed in small editions. At first the Museum's copyright copies of the more modern of these are neglected. Then the writer attracts attention, and, though still not regarded as important enough to be placed in reserve cases, they are worn by much use in the Reading Room and are rebound. By the time of the author's centenary they are unworthy of being exhibited. For this purpose fine reserve duplicates are of value. Moreover, Wise's copies are in original condition, in which details of make-up, cancels and the like, can be examined; and this is especially true of his middle period, about 1800, books of which are rarely found in mint condition, but are generally bound in calf and cut down.

The Ashley Library: a catalogue of printed books, manuscripts and autograph letters, collected by Thomas James Wise. 11 vols. 1922–36.

The main alphabet ends in vol. viii, and the main index occupies vol. ix, vols. x and xi being supplementary.

THE LIBRARY OF THE BRITISH MUSEUM

13. INCUNABULA

There were naturally many incunabula in the foundation collections, where they figured, like other books, solely for the value of their contents. A large number were collected by Archbishop Cranmer and came into the Royal Library. Cracherode added a number of very beautiful copies of chosen books, mostly acquired from the libraries of such of the émigrés as had been able to export their books from France; and from George III and Grenville came many more, and all good copies. These collectors and others of their period had perceived an additional interest in early printed books, regarding them not merely as classical texts, or works on theology, law, medicine, or other subject or study, doubtless by then chiefly historical, but still living; they saw in them monuments of the invention and pioneer period of the art of typography. Theirs was not the first generation of collectors and antiquaries to interest itself in the earliest books. While in the early days of the Bodleian doubt could be expressed whether a volume were printed or manuscript, Pepys's omnivorous curiosity touched on old printing, and the word *incunabula (artis typographicae)* was coined in that period by C. à Beughem. Seventeenth-century owners often showed their interest by writing little sums below the date of imprint, in which it is subtracted from the date of writing, thus yielding the volume's age. And early eighteenth-century collectors such as Harley, Sunderland and Mead took early printing, and especially early editions of the classics, into their embrace.

On the foundation so laid continuous attention began to be paid to early printing, to the study of which a notable impulse was given in 1868 by the publication of J. W. Holtrop's *Monumens typographiques des Pays-Bas*. Just before this the sale of duplicates from the Hofbibiliothek at Munich, largely from the suppressed monasteries of Bavaria, had yielded a rich haul of books from German presses of the fifteenth century, and Rye's Keepership saw also the acquisition of the Weigel blockbooks, thus putting the Museum in a strong position for what is perhaps the rarest class of books in existence; and under Bullen, Garnett, and their successors the buying became systematic. The current lists of the antiquarian book-sellers were

THE PRINTED BOOKS

drawn on, while the chief sales, such as the Hérédia, Ashburnham and Dunn, were turned to account. George Dunn had intended to bequeath his books between the Museum, the Bodleian and Cambridge, but died before providing for the bequest. The Museum, however, was enabled to secure many of Dunn's very rare and obscure early printed books at his sale. The law-books went to Harvard.

System in buying a special class of books is impossible without a preliminary survey and at least the assemblage of material for a special catalogue or hand-list. And with a difficult class like this these necessaries in their turn depend on the man. We may here be allowed to recapitulate our account in Part I of how this happened. In 1893 Robert George Collier Proctor joined the Staff. Proctor, who had been one of Thomas Dunn's pupils at Bath College, had in full measure learned that great teacher's lesson of patient and accurate work, thus, it may be observed, doing something to redeem the reputation of the family, since he was a relative of John Payne Collier, whose industry was not always paired with integrity. He did his share of the modern work of the Library, but was soon allowed to specialize and presently to segregate the incunabula from the general library into the Arched Room and there arrange them by what has since become known as "Proctor-order," i.e. by countries, towns, presses and (as last subdivision) chronology. He began to do the same with those in the Grenville and King's, but was restrained by authority. For this purpose he read through the entire General Catalogue, the printing of which was then approaching completion. In 1897 he printed his *Index to Early Printed Books in the British Museum to 1500*, with notes of those in the Bodleian, in which the scheme was followed.[20] He acquired by practice an astonishing eye for types and their small differences, "and knew immortal Hain by heart," or so one is tempted to believe. But he acquired it at the cost of his eyesight, and his early death in the Alps in September 1903 probably saved him from half a lifetime of blindness. His loss was due to his own characteristic self-reliance and rashness; but it seemed a fitting end for one who had in ten years scaled such a peak as the Museum Catalogue and had made so great an addition to knowledge and to bibliographical method.

THE LIBRARY OF THE BRITISH MUSEUM

On the basis of Proctor's *Index* and arrangement of books in the Arch Room, the latter completed by Henry Jenner, systematic buying went on under the supervision of Alfred Pollard. Before long Fortescue, then Keeper, persuaded the Trustees to embark on a full-dress catalogue, illustrated with facsimiles of types, of the Museum's incunabula, now approaching 10,000 in number, and very rich in the first presses. Pollard took charge and the first volume appeared in 1908. Seven have appeared, and Germany and Italy, the chief bulk, are completed; France is in hand, and the smaller countries remain. England has in effect been done for the Bibliographical Society by Gordon Duff, and the Low Countries should not be difficult, what with the work of the Dutch and Belgians and also that of Bradshaw and Jenkinson at Cambridge.

Croker first suggested to Panizzi the production of a catalogue of fifteenth-century books; but it was well that the idea had to wait till the collection had been built up.

Catalogue of XVth Century Books. [With facsimiles. By A. W. Pollard, J. V. Scholderer and others.] 1908–

Facsimiles from Early Printed Books in the British Museum. Selected pages . . . exhibited in the King's Library. [With descriptions. By A. W. Pollard.] 1897

The Guide to the King's Library Exhibition had before this constituted a brief sketch of early printing.

14. EARLY ENGLISH BOOKS

Early English books have long, and rightly, been a chief charge on the Department's funds for antiquarian buying. The year 1640 was chosen in 1875 by Edward Arber as the conclusion of his published *Transcript of the Registers of the Stationers' Company*, and this date, so convenient as excluding the pamphleteering of the Civil War, was quickly adopted by other bibliographers. Accordingly when the opportunity of the titles being assembled for the printing of the General Catalogue presented itself, it was taken. The Keeper, George Bullen, assisted by Gregory Eccles, collected copies of all titles for

THE PRINTED BOOKS

books printed in the British Isles, and also for English printed abroad up to and including that year. The result, "the 1640 Catalogue," was published in 1884, in three volumes, the third including indexes of printers, titles and (very usefully) of classes, such as poetry, drama, herbals, etc. The titles in the Catalogue were taken over from the General Catalogue, with some expansion of title and imprint. The indexes give bare reference to headings, and are usable with difficulty.

The Catalogue is long out of date, large later additions having been made to the collection, but a new edition is hardly worth while in view of the Bibliographical Society's *Short Title Catalogue* of 1927, a union catalogue covering the same field for a large number of libraries.

Catalogue of books in the Library of the British Museum printed in England, Scotland and Ireland, and of books in English printed abroad, to the year 1640. 3 vols. 1884.

15. EARLY FRENCH, SPANISH, PORTUGUESE AND ICELANDIC BOOKS

In the following year the titles for Icelandic books from 1578 to 1880 (the collection of the earlier part of which was founded by Sir Joseph Banks's gift), were picked out and issued rather inconveniently in the same folio form as the General Catalogue.

The 1640 Catalogue of 1884 was the first of a series. So early as 1848, in evidence before the Commission of that year, a desire had been expressed by Carlyle for special catalogues of the Museum's books, so that one could buy them and consult them at home, a need which the printing of the General Catalogue had certainly not filled. Not only do portable octavo special catalogues answer the purpose of such students as Carlyle; they enable gaps to be readily found and filled by comparison with auctioneers' and dealers' lists. But for this and for the essential of portability such full titles as those in the 1640 Catalogue are not needed. The following volumes, therefore, are short-title lists, and they have no indexes. But they follow the lead in being devoted to a country and a period. The short-title form for such lists was first suggested by Dr. P. S. Allen, an eminent example of the type of scholar to whom they would be most valuable.

The first, by Dr. Henry Thomas, was a list of the Museum's early Spanish books, other than Spanish-American. It revealed that though the Museum possessed perhaps not more than a sixth of the books in this field known to exist, those of importance were (thanks largely to Grenville's love of Romance literature) much more nearly complete. Five years later Dr. Thomas supplemented his European Spanish list by a similar one covering in two lists the smaller ground of Portugal and Spanish America for the same period. The lists were published in the *Revue Hispanique*, and were republished together in London. The Portuguese section (the bulk) of the latter was brought up to date and republished officially in 1940. An exceptionally important accession recorded in this last list, the hitherto unknown *Carta das Novas*, or first account of Abyssinia in 1520, given in 1926 by the Friends of the National Libraries, was published two years later.

But a larger contribution to the series, which appeared between these two, under the same editor, was naturally that for fifteenth- and sixteenth-century French books. It records nearly twelve thousand editions, and though these do not include more than a fifth of those known to have come from the presses of Paris or a sixth of those from the provinces of France, among them are many very rare and certainly some unique books.

Further volumes in the series were planned, and some work done towards them; but the production of the new edition of the General Catalogue absorbed all available hands. The obvious next desiderata are lists for other countries to 1600, and a supplement to the Thomason Catalogue listing by the same chronological methods other English books from 1641 to 1661, or, better, to 1700, a date which would include other fruitful public controversies. A further short-title list, 1641–1700, was projected. But the General Catalogue and the War have intervened, and a bibliography of the period is being compiled by an American scholar, Mr. Donald G. Wing.

THE PRINTED BOOKS

Catalogues and other publications are:

Short-title Catalogue of Books printed in France and of French Books printed in other countries from 1470 *to* 1600 *now in the British Museum.* [By H. Thomas.] 1924.

A Short-title Catalogue of Books printed in Spain and of Spanish Books printed elsewhere in Europe before 1601 *now in the British Museum.* By Henry Thomas. 1921.

Fray Ambrosio Montesino: *Coplas sobre diversas devociones y misterios de nuestra Santa Fe Catolica.* Reproduced in facsimile from the only recorded copy of the original impression. Toledo, *c.* 1485, now in the British Museum. With an introduction by H. Thomas. 1936.

El Comendador Roman: *Coplas de la Pasión con la Resurrección.* Reproduced in facsimile from the only recorded copy of the original impression. Toledo, *c.* 1490, now in the British Museum. With an introduction by H. Thomas. 1936.

Short-title Catalogue of Portuguese Books and of Spanish-American Books printed before 1601 *now in the British Museum.* By H. Thomas. (Unofficial: Quaritch.) 1926.

Short-Title Catalogue of Portuguese Books printed before 1601 *now in the British Museum.* By H. Thomas. 1940.

The Discovery of Abyssinia in 1520: *a facsimile of the relation entitled Carta das Novas que vieram a el Rey Nosso Senhor do discobrimento do Preste Joham* [*Lisbon*, 1521]. With an introduction and English translation by H. Thomas and a transcription into modern Portuguese by Armando Cortesão. 1938.

There is a MS. Catalogue (980.h.32), of *c.* 1778, of the Banks Icelandic gift.

Catalogue of the Books printed in Iceland. (By T. W. Lidderdale.) 1885. There are three supplements to this, Nos. 1, 4, 5, of W. Fiske's *Bibliographical Notices*, 1886, etc.

Catalogue of editions of the Edda . . . and of works commenting upon Edda Literature. (By T. W. Lidderdale.) 1884. In MS. (1878, f. 24.)

16. AMERICANA

Something is said above (p. 103) of the American collection and of the part played in gathering it by Henry Stevens of Vermont from

THE LIBRARY OF THE BRITISH MUSEUM

his first chance call in 1845 till his death. In 1858 he was able to claim that the collection built up in the last thirteen years, amounting to 30,000 volumes, was more than double the size of any then existing in the United States. When he died in 1869 this figure had been increased to probably 100,000. But in more recent times the activity of American libraries and private collectors has naturally made it impossible to continue securing rare Americana except occasionally. Great numbers of modern American publications come in by copyright as bearing alternative London imprints; and a large selection of others is purchased in the same way as other foreign books.

Americana have figured little in the chief bequests and gifts; but from Grenville came the series of illustrations by John White, made on the spot in 1585 and used to illustrate Hariot's *Virginia*. These are now in the Print Room. In recent years proposals were put out for their publication, but the public response was inadequate.

Stevens himself compiled the following catalogues:

    American Books, 1856;
    American Maps, 1859;
    Canadian Books, 1859;
    Mexican and other Spanish-American Books, 1866.

The set was issued in one volume in 1866.

17. NEWSPAPERS

Nearly all the British newspapers of the earliest period, from 1619 to 1641, which are preserved in the Museum, are to be found in the Burney Collection. This was bought in 1818 with Dr. Charles Burney's MS. and printed classics, and was, it seems, not prized as it is today, being described in the report of the Select Committee of the Commons which led to the purchase as simply a "collection of early newspapers, filling 700 volumes, more ample than any in existence."

Apart from some isolated news-quartos dating from 1603, which Burney wrongly treated and bound up as newspapers, the Collection begins with the *News from Holland* of 1619, and there are several

THE PRINTED BOOKS

of the following years. For the Civil War and Commonwealth Burney is overshadowed by Thomason, there being many duplicate sets; but he is richer for the next generation, and for the eighteenth century very rich indeed. The Burney newspapers include Irish papers from 1691, Scotch from 1708, English provincial from 1712, and a considerable number of American eighteenth-century files of importance, notably Nos. 1–111 of the *New England Courant* on which Benjamin Franklin worked.

Burney bound the sheets, not in separate files, but as a chronological series, so that those of any one week may be found together, a plan of great service to historical students. The index in use (which this system of binding makes peculiarly necessary) is Burney's own, in two MS. volumes.

There were some newspapers among Sloane's books, but otherwise the first acquired by the Museum were those in the Thomason Tracts. Thomason secured only four numbers in his first fourteen months of collecting, but from 1642 to 1660 inclusive his collection is exceedingly rich, the numbers reaching over 2,000 in 1642 and 1648. In 1661–63 he added a few, but had ceased methodical collecting. Royston's celebrated forgery, *The English Mercurie*, "1588," is in his friend Birch's collection (No. 4106).

Newspapers were not delivered direct under the Copyright Acts till 1869. From 1823 till that time they were handed over to the Museum at intervals of three years by the Stamp Office, where they were delivered and held for police purposes under the Stamp Acts. In 1832 the Provincial papers were added.

When in 1902 statutory authority was obtained to store some part of the Library in a subsidiary repository, the British provincial newspapers from 1801 were selected for sending out of the main building; and the opportunity was taken to catalogue them and also the London newspapers of the same period. This catalogue was printed in 1906, the year of their removal to Hendon—now Colindale; it formed a second supplement to the General Catalogue, the supplementary volumes of which had just been completed.

The London newspapers of the nineteenth and twentieth centuries were sent to Colindale in 1932, when the Repository was enlarged

THE LIBRARY OF THE BRITISH MUSEUM

as the Newspaper Library. A duplicate file of *The Times* was then bought for use in the General Library.

A list of newspapers received by copyright was issued in 1884. The Provincial newspapers were catalogued in 1879, when many were found embedded in albums.

All newspapers of dates earlier than 1801 are entered in the General Catalogue under the heading Periodical Publications. The list of those of the nineteenth century was issued in 1906, as noted above.

A special catalogue of the Burney Newspapers is in preparation by Mr. L. W. Hanson, of the Printed Books.

18. Music

A. The General Music Library

There has never been in the Museum a combined Department of Music, as there was for a time of Maps. The printed collection began haphazard; in the early years of the nineteenth century Bean had charge of what there was. But in 1835 H. S. Peacock complained[21] that there was none, and in 1837, as Cowtan tells us, there was no list. Four years later a special appointment was made for the cataloguing of both manuscript and printed music, Thomas Oliphant, Secretary to the Madrigal Society, being brought in and working till 1850, when he retired.

The printed music was assembled in the westernmost of the two Reading Rooms of 1838–56, which afterwards bore the name of the Music Room; but this space proved very inadequate as copyright became more effective. It was moved in 1922 to its present quarters in the King Edward VII Wing, where, though it occupies a mile and a half of shelving, there is still fair space for expansion.

Of the sources of the collection copyright has been mentioned. Though productive of much of value, and of still greater bulk, it has not been so exhaustive as for books and periodicals, since there exists no current trade-list of music, comparable with the *Publishers' Circular*, which could be used for tracing and claiming undelivered pieces, with the result that a considerable amount of English nine-

THE PRINTED BOOKS

teenth-century music has undoubtedly been missed and remains to be retrospectively gathered by gift or purchase.

The nucleus is to be found in the Old Royal Library, to which the first substantial accessions were the libraries formed by the two leading English musical scholars of the late eighteenth century, Sir John Hawkins's collection of treatises, presented by him in 1778, and Dr. Charles Burney the elder's books on music, purchased in 1814. No other considerable addition was made for a generation; the King's Library did not contain the Royal collection of music, of which some account is given below, and though it contained a few volumes of music, these were mostly MSS. In 1846 came the bequest by Domenico Dragonetti of his collection of scores of classical operas and other works, which, though largely in manuscript, contained a number of printed editions, and in 1863 a long series, mainly of old German and Italian madrigals, was purchased from the Royal Library of Berlin, from which they were sold as duplicates. In 1886 a considerable number of works printed by the ancient firm of Phalèse at Louvain and Antwerp, which had been exhibited at the Brussels Exhibition, were purchased from M. Kockx of Antwerp. And a few years later advantage was taken of two sales which gave exceptional opportunities for strengthening comparatively weak sections and filling gaps. At the sale of the Borghese Library the Museum was a large purchaser, sharing the bulk with the Accademia di Santa Cecilia at Rome and the Conservatoire at Paris. And the second Hérédia sale (1892), at which were bought many early books needed in the Library, yielded also a number of very rare old Spanish musical scores and treatises.

Barclay Squire (of whom more below) was specially interested in the madrigals and motets of the English school of the sixteenth and seventeenth centuries and secured at different times in the next forty years a great number of rare examples, thus making the Library remarkably rich in this important class. In the last few years the troubles of Austria have given the Museum opportunities to strengthen very greatly another class, by buying many very rare first editions of works by Mozart, Haydn and Beethoven, and others have come in by gift. This School had before been rather weakly represented,

THE LIBRARY OF THE BRITISH MUSEUM

though an advance had been made on the position in 1843, when it was found that the names of Handel, Mozart, Beethoven and Rossini were not in the catalogue. Panizzi had made purchases on Oliphant's recommendation in the following years, but many gaps remained.

After Oliphant's retirement in 1850 the work of cataloguing and arranging the music was entrusted by the Keeper in succession to Edmund von Bach, to Eugene Roy, who later returned to work on the General Catalogue, to Campbell Clarke, on Clarke's retirement on account of health in 1870 to Charles Evans, in 1883 to William Barclay Squire, who joined the staff in that year and had charge of the Music till his retirement in 1920, and from then till now to Mr. William C. Smith.

On his appointment Barclay Squire was faced with an enormous accumulation of sheet music and other works awaiting cataloguing. Squire could do no other than evade the problem of dealing effectively with much of the uncatalogued music. This he did by ignoring unimportant dance music, comic songs and other trifles, among which, however, social, if not also musical, historians will assuredly find their harvest.

All this material was organized by Squire's assistant since 1901 and successor, Mr. William C. Smith, the bundles and sets being broken up and arranged in decades by alphabetical order of composers' name; any piece is therefore quickly findable, and printing and other expenses are saved. This system is still carried on. All uncatalogued vocal works are being indexed; accessions up to 1929 have been so treated.

When Squire took charge the printing of the General Catalogue of Printed Books had quite recently begun, and Accession Parts or fascicules were being issued. Uniform Parts of titles of Music Accessions were initiated and incorporated by being laid down in volumes of the Music Catalogue (now numbering 377) like those of the General Catalogue, containing transcribed manuscript titles, commenced in 1841 by Oliphant. These Accession Parts at first contained as many as twelve to fifteen thousand titles, and nominally appeared annually. The more recent practice in dealing with unimportant sheet music has made it possible to reduce the number of

THE PRINTED BOOKS

these titles to about a third, and the appearance of the Annual Parts has been regular. The titles of earlier music have also been laid down in ten similar volumes from the published catalogue of old music, presently to be mentioned, thus superseding large numbers of clumsy transcribed manuscript titles in the Catalogue. Recent additions to knowledge of the history of music have also enabled much recataloguing to be carried out. The Catalogue includes some useful collective class headings, such as Hymns, Psalms and Christmas Carols, and a special catalogue of National Music is in preparation; it would seem to be desirable to prepare other similar subject catalogues and headings.

Earlier music, i.e. that printed before the nineteenth century, was left over from the Accession Parts for separate treatment, although one Accession Part, issued in 1899, contained exclusively "Recent Accessions of Old Music, printed before the year 1800." Music occurring in liturgical books is as a rule excluded, but an attempt was made to include music printed in periodicals. In 1912 a catalogue was printed, and is kept up to date by supplements:

Catalogue of Printed Music published between the years 1487 *and* 1800 *now in the British Museum.* By W. Barclay Squire. 2 vols. 1912.
[First supplement in vol. 2.]
Second Supplement by William C. Smith, 1940.

B. *The King's Music Library*

In 1911 King George V deposited on permanent loan in the Museum the Royal collection known as the King's Music Library. Barclay Squire was appointed Honorary Curator of the King's Music, and retained the office after his retirement from the Museum, indeed till his death in 1927, since when he has been followed by successive Keepers of Printed Books. This is the explanation of the curious fact that a collection which is largely manuscript is preserved in this Department. The deposit in the Museum and appointment of its officers as Honorary Curators in no way abrogates the authority of the Master of the King's Music.

THE LIBRARY OF THE BRITISH MUSEUM

After the completion of the King Edward VII Wing in 1914 the King's Music Library was to have been transferred thither; but the war intervened, and not till 1918 was it arranged in its present quarters, where it was joined four years later by the General Music Library.

The Library is of eighteenth-century origin; its formation is due to King George III and especially to Queen Charlotte, a real music lover. The most important section is the splendid series of autograph manuscripts and contemporary copies, together with many early printed editions, of works by Handel. These were Handel's own collection, and were bequeathed by him (with his large harpsichord and little house organ and also £500) in 1750 to "Mr. Christopher Smith," i.e. Johann Christopher Schmid, the composer's amanuensis. There is a doubt whether Smith lived to inherit Handel's bequest; but the collection passed either through him or possibly directly to his son, known as John Christopher Smith the younger. He was a musician in the household of the King's mother, the Dowager Princess of Wales. On her death in 1772 the King continued his pay as a pension for life, and he in gratitude presented to his Royal patron the whole of the Handel collection he had inherited. The autograph works were most unfortunately cut down for the sake of uniformity at some period before they were deposited in the Museum; since their arrival many have been rearranged and rebound. A cast of the statue by Roubiliac on Handel's monument in Westminster Abbey presides over the Library, as it has done since the time of George III.

To this original Handel collection additions were made much later from the manuscript copies of his works formerly owned by Charles Jennens (*d.* 1773), a friend and patron of the composer, who bequeathed his collection of musical MSS. to Heneage Finch, 3rd Earl of Aylesford. In 1918 Aylesford's descendants sold the MSS. by auction, and Squire secured a number of volumes, which he presented and added to those already in the collection.

The Library is thus of immense value for the study of Handel, who is also well represented in the Museum's own collections, both manuscript and printed. The autographs not only include much that

THE PRINTED BOOKS

is not in the Händel-Gesellschaft's great edition of his works; many of them show his methods of composition. In the identification of works in the collection since its arrival in the Museum much help was received from an outside scholar, Mr. Percy Robinson.

Apart from the Handel volumes, Queen Charlotte collected musical MSS., and her collection contains music of the previous two centuries. George IV also, when Prince of Wales, had a fine collection at Carlton House, which joined the rest after his death. From various sources came some famous MSS. of the Elizabethan period, notably the John Baldwin collection of motets, madrigals, and the like, formed between 1581 and 1606, the Cosyn Virginal Book (c. 1600) and the Forster Virginal Book, 1624, besides autograph works by Purcell, Alessandro Scarlatti, and J. C. Bach, an extensive collection of manuscripts of works by A. Steffani, some early pieces by Palestrina, a number by seventeenth-century English composers such as "tuneful Harry" Lawes; full scores by Mozart and others and especially by the many native and foreign musicians who composed works for the festivals of a Court, which, if it does not bear a high reputation in history for literary culture, was genuinely music-loving. It may be noted here that the musical MSS. placed by George III in his general ("the King's") Library include autographs of Handel (King's MSS. 318 and 422) and a few other contemporaries.

The printed section of the Library, while it duplicates much of the material in the Museum's own collection, ranges over a wide field, and is of considerable importance. Not only does it include a fine collection of the early editions of Handel's works and of many other eighteenth-century compositions, both instrumental and vocal; earlier centuries are well represented, and under Queen Victoria, when less manuscript music was being acquired, many printed works by nineteenth-century composers were added.

Squire lived to see through the press the first and most important, the Handel, volume of a catalogue of the Library, and to lay down the lines of that in which the printed collection is described; the other MSS. were described by an expert from outside the Museum's own staff:

THE LIBRARY OF THE BRITISH MUSEUM

Catalogue of the King's Music Library, 3 vols. 1927–39.
    Vol. I.   Handel Manuscripts. By William Barclay Squire.
    Vol II.   Miscellaneous Manuscripts. By Hilda Andrews.
    Vol. III. Printed Music and Musical Literature. [Partly by William Barclay Squire, completed by William C. Smith.][21]

19. MAPS

In the eighteenth century the Museum possessed scattered maps and charts in the various libraries which had gone to form it, but nothing that could be called a collection. In 1801, however, the Ordnance Survey began to publish, and its maps have from that date been regularly deposited, as have those of the Admiralty, commenced later. And in 1823 there came in the organized collection, amounting to some 50,000 maps and charts, formed by George III, and separate catalogues of these were published (see above, p. 193). Little further effort was made for some time, but in 1841–43, when attention was being paid to the maps in the Department of Manuscripts (see below, pp. 263–5), William Hughes, F.R.G.S., catalogued those in the Printed Books. In the next year, however, a more permanent arrangement was made; Richard Henry Major was appointed as Assistant in the Printed Books and was almost at once put in charge of maps. In this year the Catalogue of Manuscript Maps began to appear. Major was a young man of great energy, playing a leading part in the foundation in 1846 of the Hakluyt Society, of which he was Secretary from 1849 till 1858, as several of his successors in the Museum Map Room have been. He was responsible for considerable acquisitions, notable among which was the collection of charts formed by Admiral Lord Howe; and nearly 100 Japanese maps formed part of the von Siebold Library, acquired in 1868. Major's commission extended to manuscript maps, and in 1867 an independent Department of Maps was formed, with Major as its Keeper. Unfortunately he had to retire from ill-health in 1880. Major published many works on the early discoverers, notably on Prince Henry the Navigator, and earned an international reputation. His successor, R. K. Douglas, was primarily an Orientalist, and left the real care of the maps to E. D.

THE PRINTED BOOKS

Butler, his senior Assistant, and devoted himself to the Chinese work of the Department of Oriental Manuscripts, which had been formed in the same year and by the same process as that of Maps, and to which he was definitely transferred as Keeper in 1892. Had Butler had more force the maps would not have been left in such an anomalous position, but in the following decade not only were manuscript maps transferred to the Department of Manuscripts, but that Department occasionally acquired by gift and preserved engraved as well as manuscript maps.

In 1902 the Map Room, which had been a Sub-Department, with some autonomy, was brought definitely under the Printed Books, of which it has since been an important section, on the same footing as Music. Basil Soulsby was placed in charge, and in seven years there first made his mark; he was later transferred to the Natural History Museum and acquired a great reputation on account of the Linnæan collection which he developed in the Library there (see below, p. 345). In 1909 he was followed by John (afterwards Sir John) A. J. de Villiers. In 1924 Frederick Sprent, another energetic man like Soulsby, succeeded; he unfortunately died young in 1931, and was followed by the present Superintendent of the Map Room, Mr. Edward Lynam.

The Map Room still contains a considerable quantity of manuscript maps and charts, apart from those in the King's Library, and there would seem to be good reason for reverting to the organization of 1867–80, and perhaps to follow the same policy with Music also. The Print Room contains many important engraved maps, and these should certainly be transferred; it is believed that this is under consideration. It was urged by the late Lord Curzon in 1914, before the Royal Geographical Society, that the printed and MS. maps should be recombined in a single Department; but the difficulties, historical and (especially with the Egerton MSS.) legal, are obvious.

The whole collection is press-marked on a territorial system adapted from Dewey's decimal classification. When the King Edward VII Wing was completed, space was found in it for the Map Room, but the lay-out was inadequate and a reconstruction, planned in 1938, was interrupted by the outbreak of war. The need may be seen from the fact that the figures of readers have been multiplied by six in the past twenty years.

Of the wealth of the collection it is difficult to give any idea. In official publications of the British Empire the sets must be nearly complete, as they include the Surveys of all the Dominions, not only the Indian, Australian and Canadian, but smaller and lesser known Surveys such as those of Sierra Leone, Southern Rhodesia and Sarawak. Henry Stevens's activity in procuring American books extended to maps, and he published a list in 1859. Rare maps are purchased as opportunity offers, and some of these have been issued in facsimile as noticed below, while recent gifts include some 300 of the maps and charts collected by the Duke of Cumberland and preserved at Windsor Castle, which have been presented by King George VI.[22]

A few important single maps may be mentioned. Richard Lyne's plan of Cambridge, 1574; William Cuningham's plan of Norwich, 1559; Nicolaus Visscher's magnificent view of London, 1616. Illustrating the Armada there are two copies of Robert Adams's beautifully drawn manuscript plan of the defences erected along the Thames from Westminster to Leicester's Camp at Tilbury; both of these show "The Queen's Progress" when she visited the Camp. Of similar interest, a few years later, is a map of the Beacons in Kent, produced by William Lambarde, the Kentish historian, in 1596. Among the maps of the world one at least is unique. This is the map, published in 1506, probably at Florence, designed by Giovanni Matteo Contarini. Another, of which only a second copy is known, is Abraham Ortelius's map of the World of 1564, in several sheets. "The new map with the augmentation of the Indies," with which Maria compared Malvolio's smile, published in the second edition of Hakluyt's *Principal Navigations*, 1598, is well known and is a valuable possession, though not unique. Unique and rare maps of England are numerous. Only one other copy is known of Christopher Saxton's great Map of England and Wales, published in 1583, four years after his Atlas. There are no less than three copies of the Great Survey of Scotland carried out by William Roy (later Founder of the Ordnance Survey) between 1747 and 1755. These are all in manuscript and represent different stages of the development of the map.

THE PRINTED BOOKS

All the Dominions and Colonies are also extremely well represented by maps or views from very early dates. For instance, there is a plan of allotments of ground granted by the Crown in New South Wales, dated 1814; a sketch of Sydney Cove, dated 1789, and a plan, made in 1749, of Halifax, Nova Scotia, then just taken from the French; a map of the Fiji Islands of 1875, when at their own request they came under British rule; a map of the Sommer Islands of 1626; the Plan of the Siege of Louisbourg when the British took it from the French; a map of the Burman Empire of 1823, when we were at war with Burma; and a chart of the Colony of Demerara of 1795.

The collection amounted in 1870, according to Cowtan (p. 350), to about fifty thousand printed and twenty thousand manuscript maps. Those in the Map Room may now be reckoned at over half a million; and some run to as many as eight thousand sheets.

The first catalogue, apart from those of the King's Geographical Collection, 1829, and of Manuscript Maps, 1844, was one in manuscript, commenced by Major and described by Nicoll in 1866 as new. Five years after Major's retirement appeared:

Catalogue of Printed Maps, Plans and Charts—2 vols. 1885.

The accessions, like those of music, followed those of books in being printed after 1880, and amalgamated with the published catalogue; the whole now fills 100 folio guard-volumes, uniform with the General Catalogue. The Accession Parts appear yearly.

A Catalogue of Unofficial American Maps in the British Museum. By Henry Stevens. 1859.

Of recent years the following facsimiles have been published:

A Map of the World, designed by Giovanni Matteo Contarini, engraved by Francesco Rosetti, 1506. [Edited by F. P. Sprent.] 1924.
Second edition, revised, 1926.
Unique, and unknown when acquired in 1922. Possibly the earliest map to show America, preceding Waldseemüller's by one year.

Sir Francis Drake's Voyage round the World, 1577–1580; *two contemporary maps.* [Edited by F. P. Sprent.] 1927.
Second edition, revised, 1931.

THE LIBRARY OF THE BRITISH MUSEUM

Six Early Maps, selected from those exhibited at the British Museum on the occasion of the International Geographical Congress, 1928. 1928.

An Atlas of England and Wales. The Maps of Christopher Saxton, engraved 1574–1579. Edited by Edward Lynam. 1936.

In colour. The maps of the counties and frontispiece portrait of Queen Elizabeth were issued separately.

Map of Ireland, about 1600, by Baptista Boazio. [1938.]

In colour.

20. ENGLISH BOOK-SALE CATALOGUES

Apart from those of the twentieth century to date, which are naturally fairly complete, the Museum Library possesses a collection of some 8,000 English auction sale catalogues of books, beginning with that of the library of Dr. Lazarus Seaman, formerly Master of Peterhouse, Cambridge, which was sold in London on 31st October, 1676. This was the first auction to be held in England, though the method of sale had been practised in the Low Countries and elsewhere for at least three-quarters of a century. Its introduction was in fact due to the suggestion of a Presbyterian minister, Dr. Joseph Hill, who had spent some years in Holland. By 1710 it was thoroughly established; Mr. Spectator, it will be remembered (No. 46), dropped his paper of notes one day at Lloyd's Coffee house, "where the auctions are usually kept."

The completeness of the Museum's set of the earliest book-auction catalogues is proved by the fact that out of seventy-four auctions recorded in 1686 by William Cooper, the bookseller who had held Seaman's, only five are wanting. Sales at fixed prices, as distinguished from ordinary dealers' lists on the one hand and from auctions on the other, also multiplied at the same period, and are included in the collection.

The sources are very diverse, and no attempt has been made to fill gaps. The largest single source is undoubtedly the purchase in 1838 from Thorpe for fifty guineas of Richard Heber's large collection. But there are several long and very important series of which the Museum has the auctioneers' own sets, marked with the prices obtained; such

THE PRINTED BOOKS

are the firm now entitled Sotheby & Co. (1744 to date), Evans (1825–68), Lewis (1825–52), Wheatley (1825–37) and Puttick (1846–88). These sets are kept together for easy reference; but the rest are not. There are two large series of early lists, in the Old Library (in press 821) and in the King's Library.

The Library also contains a very large collection of dealers' catalogues, but they are not treated as part of this collection.

The published List is arranged chronologically, with index of owners, and has an introduction by Dr. A. W. Pollard. Until its publication lists had to be sought in the very difficult heading "Catalogues" and elsewhere in the General Catalogue.

List of Catalogues of English Book Sales, 1676–1900, now in the British Museum. Edited by A. W. Pollard. 1915.

21. BINDINGS

It will be convenient to combine here notes on the collections of bindings in the two Western Departments.

From about 1834, when regular purchase grants began, bindings began to be purchased as such, and many of the earliest examples among the manuscripts are Additionals. As is observed below (p. 246), the Cotton and Royal Libraries are very poor in medieval bindings, possibly as a result of the fire, but it is to be remembered that an Order in Council at the time of the Dissolution directed that all gold and silver found in Popish books of devotion should be stripped off and paid into the King's Treasury; while the great collectors of the eighteenth and early nineteenth centuries had little regard for the history of a volume and rebound any that were not in notable bindings.

In armorial bindings of English sovereigns both the Printed Books and the Manuscripts are naturally very rich, and only in the Museum can these be fully studied. Not that many examples are not to be found elsewhere, for instance (as noted before) at Worcester College, Oxford, but it does not follow that a royal binding found elsewhere was made for the Royal Library; kings made gifts of books, and royal foundations sometimes used the royal arms.

THE LIBRARY OF THE BRITISH MUSEUM

Apart from the heraldic book-stamps of sovereigns and others, the successive styles of English binding are well shown in the Royal, Harleian, King's, Cracherode and Grenville libraries, for whose collectors some of the most famous binders worked, as for example, Mearne's binder for Charles II, Eliot and Chapman for Harley, giving his name to the style, Roger Payne for Cracherode (though many of Cracherode's best are not certainly attributed to Payne), Lewis for Grenville, and Bedford for Huth. And these later collectors brought in fine specimens of earlier styles made for kings and others, and once part of the Royal Library—to take a single example, a handsome calf and deerskin binding made in John Day's workshop for presentation by Archbishop Parker to Queen Elizabeth, which came with Cracherode's books.

The Tudor sovereigns, and also James I, not infrequently had books bound abroad, and some good foreign examples have thus reached the Museum. Such is a copy of *Il Fiore della retorica*, Venice, 1560, bound in the Venetian-Oriental style for Queen Elizabeth. And Cracherode and Grenville acquired bindings made for Grolier and other great Continental patrons of the art, while good specimens of the bindings made for de Thou the historian and still more of the less ornate French work of the eighteenth century abound. From various sources the Museum's series of books bound for Grolier is one of the longest and most important to be seen anywhere. The only Corvinian binding in the Library is Lansdowne MS. 836.

To these sources, and especially for foreign schools, was added in 1868 a bequest of a large number of bindings (and especially good French eighteenth-century specimens from the ateliers of the Monniers and Deromes, in which the Museum was relatively weak) made by Felix Slade.

As with prints and drawings, for fear of the power of the clique, and also of passing fashion, the work of contemporary craftsmen is not bought; but a representative though small selection has been acquired by gift of recent years, showing most of the best binders from Cobden-Sanderson downward. One was made for the Museum; this is the binding in two volumes of the Codex Sinaiticus, made in 1934 by Mr. Douglas Cockerell (see below, p. 338).

THE PRINTED BOOKS

There is no comprehensive catalogue of bindings, which would be a very large work. The following illustrated catalogues of specimens selected for their beauty or historical interest have been published:

English Bookbindings in the British Museum. Illustrations of 63 examples. With introduction and descriptions by W. Y. Fletcher. 1895.

Foreign Bookbindings in the British Museum. Illustrations of 63 examples. With introduction and descriptions by W. Y. Fletcher.

These two books followed a very similar unofficial work:

Remarkable Bindings in the British Museum. By H. B. Wheatley. 1889.

One class, in which the Museum is very rich, is the subject of a comprehensive list:

Early Stamped Bookbindings in the British Museum. Descriptions of 385 blind-stamped bindings of the 11th-15th centuries in the Departments of Manuscripts and Printed Books. Mainly by the late W. H. James Weale. With 490 illustrations of the stamps used on them. Completed by Lawrence Taylor, 1922.

A small selection of 35 specimens of bindings of MSS. forms part of the Exhibition in the Grenville Library, and is described in:

Guide to the Exhibited Manuscripts, Part III. 1923.

A much larger selection of those on Printed Books occupies seven cases in the King's Library, and is described in:

A Guide to the King's Library. 1939.

A few years ago the two Departments combined in an Exhibition of English bindings of all periods, but unfortunately no Guide was printed. Recent study of the subject has made such great additions to knowledge that a full-dress catalogue covering all three Departments seems very desirable.

THE LIBRARY OF THE BRITISH MUSEUM

22. STATE PAPERS

British Parliamentary ("Command") papers are acquired by copyright; H.M. Stationery Office presents second copies of all separately published reports. Corresponding publications of foreign and Dominion governments are received by International Exchange in consequence of an enquiry initiated by the Treasury in 1876 and the report of its Committee four years later. But different governments define official publications differently, and some deliver theirs much more completely than others; that of the U.S.A. is honourably conspicuous.

In the first printed General Catalogue State Papers were sparsely entered; in its successor they are being much more methodically included.

They are placed in the Lower Ground Floor of the King Edward VII Wing, and are read in the State Paper Reading Room there.

23. POSTAGE STAMPS

In 1891 Thomas Keay Tapling, M.P., bequeathed to the Museum his vast collection of postage stamps, and the bulk was housed in specially built show-cases in the central saloon of the King's Library, certain exceptionally valuable stamps being kept in reserve and shown on request by the Clerk in charge of the room, who at one time knew well when school holidays came round because of the stream of small boys anxious to see the "blue Mauritius." Gifts and bequests of collections in special classes have since then been received, but Museum funds have not been spent to fill gaps. The Crawford Philatelic books, bequeathed by the 26th Earl of Crawford (like his son and grandson a Trustee), increased the value of the stamps themselves to students; but the Staff numbers no philatelist, such work as was needed having been done till recently by the late Sir Edward Bacon.

Index to the Collection of Postage and other Stamps bequeathed to the British Museum by Thomas Keay Tapling, M.P. 1903.

THE PRINTED BOOKS

The Tapling Collection of Stamps and Postal Stationery at the British Museum: a descriptive guide and index. By Fred J. Melville. [1905.] Unofficial.

24. EXHIBITIONS AND GUIDES

The Permanent Exhibition of Printed Books was first arranged in the Grenville Room in 1851, and a Guide, priced at 6d., was printed in that year. When the Natural History Departments were moved to South Kensington in 1880 and the following years, the King's Library was freed for much larger permanent, and also (in the Northern half) for temporary, Exhibitions. The former was devoted to the history of Printing, and various editions of the illustrated guide have been produced, the latest in 1939. The latter have been numerous; some, of special importance, have been joint productions of the Printed Books and the Manuscripts. Notable were those of the Nelson Centenary (1905), of the Tercentenary of the Authorised Version of the English Bible (1911), of Shakespeare (1923), of Greek Printing Types (1927), and of British and Foreign Printing 1919–29 (1929), of all of which Guides illustrated with facsimiles were published. The two last named Guides were produced at the cost of the Lanston Monotype Corporation; receipts from the sale of the former (priced at £1 1s.) were ear-marked for purchases for the Department. There were also important Exhibitions of Luther (1885) and of Gibbon (1894).

A Guide to the Exhibition in the King's Library illustrating the history of printing, music-printing and book-binding. Latest ed., 1939.

II

THE MANUSCRIPTS

COLLECTIONS of manuscripts cannot be formed in quite the same methodical manner as a library of printed books. Their acquisition depends to a much greater extent on chance and opportunity. In forming a vast national collection like the Museum's it may be said that the aim is to assemble, preserve and make available the written sources of the main intellectual and historical activities of the world, and especially, of course, of this country, for which the library of printed books provides the published record and the commentary.

In the pages which follow some notes are given, first of the separate collections which have come to the Museum, and then of some of the more important classes which are represented in these and in the Additional MSS., acquired throughout the Library's existence. The sources of the Bible, of the other writings of the Christian Church, of the literatures, arts and history of Greece, of Rome and of medieval and modern Europe, are all sedulously collected. If little mention of modern foreign history is made in these notes, it must not be inferred that the Museum has little material illustrating it, but merely that, except by the papers of English diplomats, it is less well represented than the history of our own country. The aim of Robert Cotton, to save the dispersed monuments of the Christian Church and of Great Britain, remains, though others have been added to it, the chief aim of the Museum in collecting manuscripts.

1. THE COTTON MANUSCRIPTS

Sir Robert Cotton took up the work, begun by Archbishop Parker, of gathering and preserving the records of English literature and history (including coins as well as MSS.) which had been dispersed by the dissolution of the monasteries half a century before (see above, pp. 26–28). Such was his success that his library has been described as perhaps the most splendid of all those of which the Museum's

THE MANUSCRIPTS

Department of Manuscripts has been built up, though it is not much more than one-eighth of the size of the magnificent Harleian Collection, numbering at its greatest under a thousand volumes. But these included such monuments of British history as the famous Lindisfarne Gospels, written and decorated about A.D. 700; Simeon's history of Durham, with the tale of the rescue from the sea of the Lindisfarne Gospels; and yet another Durham book, the *Liber Vitae* of the Monastery[1]; the unique copy of *Beowulf*, written about A.D. 1000; the tenth-century *Heliand*, almost the only waif of the Old Saxon literature that has survived; the C text of *Piers Plowman*; the unique copy of *Pearl, Sir Gawain and the Green Knight*, etc.; early copies of *the Anglo-Saxon Chronicle*, the Athelstan Gospels, mentioned above; the book of the Charter of the foundation of New Minster, Winchester, which is the earliest surviving example of the Winchester school of illumination; the St. Albans *Lives of the Offas*, with drawings believed to be by the hand of Matthew Paris; two books with maps of Great Britain designed if not drawn by the same; an abundance of charters of the first importance, including two of the four copies of Magna Charta, one of them being regarded as the most nearly original; and political papers of the sixteenth century, among which may be mentioned the private notebook or "Remembrances" of Thomas Cromwell. Cotton also acquired some important MSS. which had no bearing on English history. Of these the chief is the famous fifth-century Greek Genesis (Otho B. vi), presented by two Greek Bishops to Henry VIII, and by Elizabeth to Sir John Fortescue, and by him to Cotton; it now consists, alas, of charred fragments, which constitute one of the few surviving monuments of classical illumination as it was passing into Byzantine, perhaps executed at Alexandria; another is the Order of Coronation of the Kings and Queens of France (Tiberius B. viii), revised and written in 1365 for Charles V, whose portrait is included in the illuminations.

Cotton has been, and indeed was in his own lifetime, criticized for his methods of acquiring MSS. The notebook of Sir Nicholas Hyde (referred to by E. Umfreville in Lansdowne MS. 841, art. 73), records that the Attorney-General produced King James I's pardon to Cotton for embezzling State Papers, evidences, etc. Cotton un-

THE LIBRARY OF THE BRITISH MUSEUM

doubtedly added to his collection State Papers from public offices. But so did other collectors, and most of all the Officers of State themselves, until comparatively recent times; such archives as that at Hatfield are largely composed of public documents preserved among family papers. But he considered his library to exist for the benefit of the public, in furtherance of the idea embodied in the well-known petition intended to be put forward by himself and others for a library of national history (see below, p. 243). He not only lent his MSS. very freely, even sending the Genesis to Peiresc in France[2]; he gave a number of volumes to Bodley in 1601 for his University Library at Oxford. More serious than conveying books and papers was his practice of dismembering them in binding and so obscuring their identity and history; but the sacrosanct character of an old book's record was not understood till later.

After Cotton's death the library remained in the possession of the family, and was consulted by scholars like Brian Walton and Dugdale, while apparently less important volumes were occasionally lent out. It survived the Civil War and Commonwealth (it is said by Stukeley that this was due to the protection given it by Bromsall of Blunham, High Sheriff of Bedfordshire in 1650), and after about 1692 was for a dozen years or more in the charge of the learned Dr. Thomas Smith, who had abandoned his position as Vice-President of Magdalen, refusing to take the oath of allegiance. In 1696 Smith produced the first published catalogue of the Cottonian MSS.

During the lifetime of Cotton's grandson, Sir John (*d.* 1702), the public importance of the library was recognized, and there was a movement to unite it with the Royal Library, but the Act that resulted in 1700 (12 & 13 William III, c. 7) "for the better settling" of it merely secured the books, house and garden under trustees, the Lord Keeper (Lord Chancellor), Speaker and certain members of the family, with power to appoint a librarian. This last they did not do, but one of the family trustees, William Hanbury, lived in the house without salary, which there were in any case no funds to pay. On Sir John's death in 1702 Humphrey Wanley enquired whether the post of librarian were to be available, though it seems that Dr. Smith was still there; it is well that he did not obtain this, for his genius

THE MANUSCRIPTS

had greater and more permanently useful scope in collecting for the Harleys what Cotton had missed than in merely preserving what Cotton had collected. In 1708 a Keeper had still not been appointed.

In 1703 Wren reported on Cotton House, which he declared to be quite unfit. The room containing the books was narrow and damp and at one end ruinous, nor was there separate access to it. He proposed to adapt a room over the Ushers near the House of Lords, but nothing was done, except that twenty-seven presses were made and the joiner left unpaid. After fresh reports from Wren and also from the Surveyor-General,[3] an Act was passed in 1706 (6 Anne, c. 30), buying the house and garden for £4,500 and providing for the building of a room on or near the same spot. Again, however, nothing was done, but when the Cottons were involved in the first Jacobite attempt of 1715, Bentley, the Royal Librarian, became Keeper of the Cotton Library as well, thus in effect carrying out an idea proposed in 1706 but not embodied in the Act of the next year, by uniting the Royal and Cotton Libraries under one control. In 1722 Cotton House was abandoned and the books were moved to Essex House, Strand, which was taken on a seven years' lease. When this expired the lease was not renewed, partly on the ground that Ashburnham House, Westminster, was "much more safe from fire," and both libraries were placed in the latter.

In spite of this opinion, two years later, in the early morning of 23rd October, 1731, there broke out in Ashburnham House a fire which did at most some very minor damage to the Royal Library but completely destroyed or seriously damaged nearly a quarter of the Cotton, including some of the most valuable volumes, the most important being the Genesis, of which only fragments remained. Bentley, whose son had succeeded him in the Keepership, was on the spot, and he and the Deputy Keeper, David Casley, were active in the work of salvage; they were forced to throw volumes out of the windows.

This terrible disaster produced much less reformation than might have been expected, in spite of Speaker Onslow, who was ex-officio a Cotton trustee, as he was later of the Museum, and who worked hard with Casley on saving the damaged volumes. It was no doubt the

THE LIBRARY OF THE BRITISH MUSEUM

fire that caused Casley to spend two years in producing his catalogue of the Royal manuscripts, published in 1734, but the two collections were stored in the New Dormitory of the Westminster Scholars, and then, when that was taken into use, in the Old Dormitory, where they remained for over twenty years; in 1753 they were reported on as dusty but dry and in the care of Mrs. Casley, whose husband had grown old and feeble. The Museum's Foundation Act solved the problem in that year by transferring the Cotton Library to the new Trust. Of the 958 volumes of which the Library consisted, 861 remained after the fire, but many of these were in woeful condition, from fire or water or both. Of 105 damaged volumes Planta restored 51, but there remained 61 bundles of leaves in 62 cases, and these seemed to him to be hopeless. Madden, however, devoted much energy to the task, and the Trustees reported in their return to Parliament for 1865 that the remainder had then recently been identified and partially bound. Of the charred remains of the Genesis four leaves reappeared much later in the Baptist College, Bristol, to which they had been left by Dr. Gifford of the Museum —showing how little they were there regarded in the eighteenth century, and the College has recently deposited them in the Museum on permanent loan. Notable among the total losses was the unique copy of the *Battle of Maldon*; but Hearne had luckily transcribed and published it in his edition of John of Glastonbury.

The press-marks of the Cotton MSS. are those of the original presses, named after the twelve Caesars, with Cleopatra and Faustina, whose busts surmounted them.

There are several catalogues, some unpublished, the earliest being Harl. MS. 6018.

Dr. Smith's catalogue, published at Oxford, is still of high value as providing the only published descriptions of some of the MSS. which were destroyed in the fire of 1731, though Wanley included descriptions of the Old English MSS. in Hickes's *Thesaurus*, 1706:

Catalogus Librorum Manuscriptorum Bibliothecae Cottonianae. 1696.

The first Cotton catalogue to be published after the foundation of the Museum was unofficial. Thomas Astle, Keeper of the Records

THE MANUSCRIPTS

in the Tower and a Trustee, who had as a young man been employed to index the Harleian Catalogue, made, and "communicated" to Samuel Hooper, who published it:

A Catalogue of the Manuscripts in the Cottonian Library . . . with an appendix containing an account of the damage sustained by the fire in 1731 and also a catalogue by Richard Widmore of the Charters preserved in the same Library. 1777.

The first action of the Commissioners of Public Records in 1800 was to write to the Trustees desiring "that the catalogue of the manuscripts in the Cottonian Library, lately compiled by their Principal Librarian [Planta] may be forthwith printed," and to offer to meet the costs. There resulted:

A Catalogue of the Manuscripts in the Cottonian Library deposited in the British Museum. 1802.

Planta's catalogue, with Nares's of the Harleian MSS., was roundly denounced by Sir Harris Nicolas (*Observations*, 1830, pp. 75–77), but its chief defect is that of any catalogue of the time, that it could not incorporate the accumulated knowledge and resulting palaeographical standards of the following century. A new Cotton catalogue is in the preliminary stages of preparation.

In 1931 the tercentenary of Cotton's death (and, as was flippantly pointed out at the time, the bicentenary of the fire) was celebrated by an Exhibition of select MSS., which was described in an illustrated Guide:

A Guide to a Select Exhibition of Cottonian Manuscripts. 1931.

2. THE HARLEIAN MANUSCRIPTS

The Harleian MSS. are that portion of the great library formed by Robert and Edward Harley, first and second Earls of Oxford, in the first forty years of the eighteenth century. They were sold to Parliament in 1753 by the second Countess and her daughter and heiress, the Duchess of Portland, for the very low price of £10,000

THE LIBRARY OF THE BRITISH MUSEUM

and included in the foundation collections of the Museum. Lady Oxford had valued them, none too highly, at £20,000 at least, but when half that sum was offered she generously "would not bargain."

Robert Harley (1661-1724), the statesman, succeeded to the family property in 1700 and at once began to collect in earnest, especially in English and French history, Biblical and early Church history, and classical literature. His son Edward (1689-1741) followed him in buying largely, and spending profusely, as he did on other things than books, without much changing the scope of the collection. In English history and in early Biblical texts it seems astonishing that his predecessors, and notably Cotton, should have left so much to glean; but the Harleys were very wealthy and employed agents to search on the Continent; no English collectors had yet methodically sought for early MSS. of classical Greek and Latin authors, a field in which, however, the Italian, French and German princes of the Renaissance had been before them, and the King of France was with them.

Robert Harley made the greatest acquisition for the library in 1708, when he gave Humphrey Wanley the post of his "library-keeper," which he held till his death in 1726. Wanley is a striking case of the "anima naturaliter bibliothecaria." He was born at Coventry in 1672, the son of the Rev. Nathaniel Wanley, a well-known writer and a man of much reading. Put to a Coventry draper as an apprentice (his father having died in 1680), he devoted all his spare time to studying and collating such ancient MSS. as were within his reach. His local fame reached Bishop Lloyd of Lichfield, who sent him to Oxford; after a year at St. Edmund's Hall, he was removed to University College at the instance of the Master, Dr. Charlett, the friend of most of the antiquaries of his day. Without taking a degree he was appointed Assistant Librarian of the Bodleian in 1695, and held this post for five years, when he went to London to become assistant to the Secretary of the newly founded Society for Promoting Christian Knowledge.

He already had a high reputation as a palaeographer, having contributed to Bernard's catalogue of manuscripts in English libraries

THE MANUSCRIPTS

(1697) and done much of the preliminary work in discovering Old English MSS. for George Hickes, which was to result in his most famous work, the Catalogue which was published in 1705 as the supplement to Hickes's *Linguarum Veterum Septentrionalium Thesaurus*. It has been well said that he "carried to the metropolis the Oxford tradition of Saxon learning." Though he was disappointed of assistantships in the Cotton and Royal Libraries, Wanley's reputation grew. In 1703 he was one of the three men to draw up an official report on the Cotton Library, with which he was familiar; and in 1707 he was the moving spirit in the meetings which ten years later took permanent form as the Society of Antiquaries. He had already advised Harley on occasion before entering his service. He was indeed recognized, as he still is, as the greatest authority on old MS. hands of his own or indeed much later times. Two of his utterances may be quoted: "Every book with a date is a standard whereby to know the age of those books of the same or a like hand," and "I conceive it as part of a library-keeper's duty to know what books are extant in other libraries besides his own."

Into Harley's service Wanley threw himself with passion, as may be seen in his Diaries, which went through the hands of West and Lansdowne and so came to the Museum in 1805 (Lansdowne MSS. 771, 772), as well as in his correspondence, which abounds in the Harleian Collection itself, in the Bodleian and elsewhere. In My Lord's interest he was a hot bargainer, with a sharp eye for all vendors' tricks, such as Warburton's, who once tried to "muddle him with drink" but failed, at any rate so far that Wanley got the books at his own price; the second Earl, a careless spender, must have suffered much in pocket after the death of so careful a steward. But keen as Wanley was not to pay too much, he was determined that My Lord should have all the finest things that were to be had, and in particular to save from destruction, or the hands of Papists, the surviving unique texts of the early Christian Church.[4] In his omnivorous gatherings for Harley of pamphlets and other despised material of still recent history it is singular that he did not secure the Thomason Tracts, which were at least once brought to his notice as being for sale.

After Robert Harley's death in 1724, or at least after Wanley's two years later, the collecting was carried on with less method and judgment. Edward Harley was not a man of the calibre of his father, and while he continued to buy freely (he made a very important purchase of ancient Latin MSS. from Nathaniel Noel the bookseller in the first year of his possessing the library), he was often cheated and by this among other sorts of expenditure fell into some money difficulties. He died in 1741, and his widow sold the printed books (estimated, but hardly credibly, at 50,000 volumes, with 350,000 pamphlets, not to mention 41,000 prints) to Osborne in 1743 for £13,000. Edward Harley's carelessness extended, according to Lady Mary Wortley-Montagu, to lending valuable MSS. and forgetting that he had done so. "I remember," she adds, "I carried him once one very finely illuminated, that when I had delivered, he did not recollect he had lent it to me, though it was but a few days before."[5]

The wealth of the Harleian MSS., even after such losses as this carelessness may have caused, has perhaps never been approached by any private collector except Phillipps. Early Hebrew, Greek and Latin books were specially sought by Harley's agent in Italy, as we have seen, and there are many which Hay or other agents found North of the Alps, such as the seventh-century Greek-Latin gloss (Harl. MS. 5792), which came from Cusa (Cues on the Moselle), and the beautifully written tenth-century Lucian (Harl. MS. 5694), bought by Edward Harley at John Bridges' sale in 1725–26. Hebrew texts of the sacred writings were, as is well known, habitually destroyed when replaced, and very early copies are not found, one of the earliest known, a Pentateuch acquired later by the Museum (Or. MS. 4445) being not older than the ninth century. But the Harleys secured a number that are relatively early, one of the most remarkable being a Pentateuch (7619) written on forty brown African skins of different sizes; and the Scriptures are supported in the collection by numerous copies of the Rabbinical writings, the Cabbalas, the Talmud, the Targum and commentaries on the Old Testament, of the thirteenth to the fifteenth century. Greek Biblical texts are headed by a Gospels (5647) of the eleventh century, illuminated with pictures of the Evangelists; while Latin Biblical texts begin with a sixth-century Gospels written in uncials (1775), and three eighth-century Gospels

THE MANUSCRIPTS

2788, 2797 and 2790, the two former being "codices aurei." Many are illuminated, some being among the finest examples.

The works of the Fathers and the Councils and Canons of the Church form a natural supplement to the Bible. This is a large class; we may perhaps select a copy of the *Martyrologium* of Usuardus (3062), written in the ninth century, very near the date of composition, and an equally nearly contemporary Epistles of Alcuin (208). The Harleys were, however, the first English collectors to be interested in the Christian Churches of the East, Syriac, Samaritan, Greek and Russian, and the Harleian copies of the liturgical books of these Churches are the foundation of that part of the Museum Library, just as are the Hebrew MSS. The service books of the Western Church were a less original subject of collection, but the Harleys were, again, the first to collect them at all methodically, and apart from the palaeographical and artistic value of many they represent the development of the Latin Liturgy through a great number of local Uses; if one is to be mentioned, it may perhaps be a ninth-century Soissons Missal in two volumes (2991, 2992).

Until the Middle Ages were nearing their end, the books chosen for illumination were all books of the Church. Of splendid examples of the foreign schools of illumination there had been no English collection to compare with the Harleys, most of the finest books in the Cotton and Royal Libraries being of the English school, good specimens of which are also to be found among the Harleian MSS., such as the Winchester Psalter (2904), the eleventh-century Bury St. Edmunds Gospels (76), and a copy of the Utrecht Psalter (603) written about A.D. 1000. Exceptionally fine are the Carlovingian Codex Aureus (2788), of the Gospels, written in gold letters about A.D. 800, with pictures of the Evangelists and illuminated borders, a ninth-century Latin Bible, the whole book being represented by the part before the Psalms only (2805), justly described by Nare as "a most pompous copy," a tenth-century Latin Gospels (2821), the eleventh-century Bible of Anjou Cathedral in two volumes (2833, 2834), a late twelfth-century Psalter (2895), a part (the rest being at Oxford and Paris) of a Latin Bible History with moralized interpretations (1526, 1527), and the mid-fourteenth-century Paris Missal (2891), given half a century after its execution by the celebrated John, Duke of Berry, to the Sainte Chapelle at Bourges; while of the Books of Hours which were the favourite subject of the illuminator in the fifteenth century there are a dainty specimen, distinguished by grisaille, which was rarely used (2952), and another (2877) executed about 1500 by an artist of (or imitating) the later Tours school. One of the finest illuminated volumes in the Harley Library (6205) was, however, secular, a volume of the copy of Albert Pigghe's *Commentaires de la Guerre Gallique* made and given by him to Francis I in 1520; in the pictures in grisaille, touched with gold and colour, we see the Renaissance arriving.

The Harleys, like other book-collectors of the day, such as Sunderland, were lovers and collectors of the classics, manuscript or printed. We find naturally, therefore, that they had early copies of some of the greater Latin authors, such as the *Paradoxa* of Cicero (2622), of the eighth, a fragmentary Aeneid (2772) of the ninth, the earliest extant text of Vitruvius *de Architectura* (2767) of the late ninth, and a Livy (2672) and a Horace (2725), both of the tenth century.

English history, secular and ecclesiastical, was a predominant object of the elder Harley's collecting at least. Cotton had been before him, but he not merely filled in gaps in Cotton's collection, as he did for example by supplying the three missing years of Edward II to the Rolls of Parliament 4 Edward II–Henry VIII. He was rich in Chronicles, Lives of the Saints and Archbishops of the English Church, Chartularies, Registers, separate Charters, etc., of monasteries and guilds, Statutes of Churches and the Universities (among them—1498—the book of the indentures between Henry VII and Westminster Abbey for the endowment of masses to be said in his Chapel); the charters number over 16,000.[6] For the two centuries before the collectors' own day everything was collected, from Royal letters and the original MS. of Coke upon Littleton (6687) down, that could bear on the history and art of the government of England, as was indeed appropriate for a Prime Minister; included are records of Coronations and other lesser ceremonies and the genealogical collections of Heralds like Peter Le Neve. Nor did the elder Harley fail to place public papers of the offices he held, such as the accounts for Marlborough's wars, among his vast accumulation of State Papers of all kinds. We may be especially grateful to him for appropriating one series, the papers of the Audit Office of the years when his brother Edward was one of the Auditors of the Imprests, seeing that all not saved by him or later by Sir William Musgrave (whose collections also came to the Museum) were destroyed by order of the government.

The Harleys historical gatherings extended to France, and also to the Vatican; among the latter are many Papal Bulls, classed among the charters, and three volumes of the original registers of the Papal Chancery (1850–52), which he bought ("ingenti dato pretio," says Wanley) from Jean Aymon, the Apostolic Protonotary who is also known in library history as having broken the heart of a French Royal Librarian by his thefts, one of them being of a volume, a ninth-century Epistles and Apocalypse, which he also sold to Harley in 1707.

A gorgeous copy of the Roman de la Rose (4425) and a fine one of *Le Trésor de Maistre Jehan de Mehun* (*Meung*) (3999) may be mentioned among the medieval French texts in the collection. The series of Middle English poets is more remarkable. They include one of the best copies of the *Canterbury Tales* (1758), given by Bishop Francis Atterbury to Harley, Lydgate's dedication copy to Humphrey, Duke of Gloucester, of his chief work, *The Fall of Princes* (1766), an illuminated copy of Gower's *Confessio Amantis* (7184) and the Hoccleve *De Regimine Principum* (4866) with the famous portrait of Chaucer in one of its margins.

The Harleys' omnivorous collecting extended beyond religion, literature and history to the arts and sciences: good early copies of Ptolemy, for example, distinguish the geographical section, and there are many herbals. It is perhaps because Wanley was himself a composer that the musical section is very rich. Wanley also intended to write a history of printing with the aid of the materials, title-pages and scraps and also many complete small pieces of printing, collected by one of his agents, the celebrated John Bagford. The Bagford Fragments (Harl. MSS. 5414, 5419, 5892–5998) came to the Museum with the manuscripts, but near the end of the nineteenth century were transferred to the Department of Printed Books.[7]

Wanley commenced a catalogue of the Harleian MSS., but died when he had reached No. 2407. He also wrote an account of the collection, which was published by Bishop Nicolson in his *English Historical Library*, 1736. David Casley, the Deputy Keeper of the Royal and Cotton Libraries, then continued the work. He was extremely concise, but made an effort to date the MSS. by centuries, which unfortunately Wanley, who was far better qualified by palaeographical skill to do so, had omitted in his descriptions, since he contemplated a "greater catalogue"—his descriptions as it was were fuller and more critical than any then known. In three years' too rapid work (he subsequently catalogued the Royal MSS. in two years), Casley reached No. 5797, and after Edward Harley's death in 1741 the Harley Trustees engaged the Deputy Keeper of the Records in the Tower, William Hocker, and he reached No. 7355. When the collection reached the Museum this composite MS. catalogue came with it and was summarily completed and published by Charles Morton with assistance for the numerous Oriental MSS. (from Brown for Arabic, from Kennicott for Hebrew, and from "Mr. Gomez, a professed Jew," for Rabbinical MSS.), and with an index by Thomas Astle, afterwards Keeper of the Records in the Tower and author of a catalogue of the Cotton MSS.:

A Catalogue of the Harleian Collection of Manuscripts . . . in the British Museum. 1759.

Later in the century Ayscough made a catalogue of the Harleian Charters, but this was never printed. (There is also an old unpublished *Index of Autograph Letters* in the collection.) In 1800, however, the Commissioners for the Public Records, as their first corporate act, wrote to the Trustees requesting them to have the Harleian Catalogue revised for printing at the Commission's expense. Planta had done some work on a revision before being promoted to be Principal Librarian in 1799, and at his own expense employed Stebbing Shaw, then engaged on his History of Staffordshire, till Shaw's death in 1802, to catalogue the topographical, genealogical and heraldic sections; the task was entrusted to Nares, and on his retirement in 1807 to his successor in the Under-Librarianship of Manuscripts, Douce:

THE MANUSCRIPTS

Nares signed the preface of Vol. I, which appeared in the following year:

A Catalogue of the Harleian Manuscripts in the British Museum. 4 vols. 1808–12.

Vol. IV consists of indexes of persons and places and a subject classification; it was the first work done for the Museum by T. H. Horne, who was employed by the Commissioners.

This catalogue, like Planta's of the Cotton MSS., was not a very good piece of work, but suffers chiefly from being over a century old. A new Harleian catalogue is one of the Department's greatest desiderata, but the vastness of the task has perhaps been clearly enough indicated even by the cursory notes above to show why a new Cotton catalogue is to take precedence of it.

3. THE SLOANE MANUSCRIPTS

Part of Sir Hans Sloane's large library consisted of some 4,200 MSS. Like his printed books they are very heterogeneous. Medicine and natural history naturally bulk largely among them, and include the papers of many of the leading practitioners and scientists of his own long lifetime. But he also had early texts, and though he was no special collector of illuminations, we may notice a thirteenth-century French *Chirurgie*, by Roger of Parma, illustrated with delightful panels of miniatures showing various operations (Sloane MS. 1977). He also collected in languages (over 250 volumes are Oriental), music and history, including 168 charters of unknown provenance, which Wanley wished to secure for Harley.[8]

As mentioned above in Part I (p. 44), Samuel Ayscough was employed by the Trustees, before he joined the Museum Staff, to catalogue the Sloane, with the Birch and other Additional MSS. to that date:

A Catalogue of the Manuscripts preserved in the British Museum, hitherto undescribed. 1782.

This catalogue was arranged in classes. It is not merely, as might be expected from its date, on modern standards very inadequate, it is also frequently inaccurate as well. It is also incomplete; for it describes 4,100 MSS., but over a hundred others were afterwards identified and entered in the early Additional Catalogue (Add. MSS. 5018–27, and 5214–5308). The printing of a revised catalogue was commenced in 1837, but the proof (all that survived) only reached No. 1091; it was continued in manuscript. The Oriental MSS. have been transferred to that Department. The Charters are described in the *Index to the Charters and Rolls*, 1900–1912. An Index to the Western MSS. other than charters was drawn up by Scott, when Keeper:

Index to the Sloane Manuscripts. By E. J. Long Scott. 1904.

4. THE OLD ROYAL LIBRARY

Apart from a doubtful handful of volumes the Old Royal Library can count Edward IV for its founder. He had resided in the house of Louis de Gruthuyse at Bruges, and it is therefore natural that when he began to collect manuscript books, which he did soon after 1470, he followed the Flemish taste, and caused to be produced for him large volumes, mostly in French, of history and historical romance, splendidly illuminated in the Burgundian style. The same taste (*mutatis mutandis*), it may be observed, inspired the introduction of printing into England from the same town and in the same decade. The books were under the control of Piers Courteys, Keeper of the Great Wardrobe, as we learn from his payments to Piers Bauduyn, stationer, in 1481, for binding a number of specified volumes.[9] Early acquisitions include some of the most beautiful illuminated volumes in the Museum, for example the celebrated MS. of Charles d'Orleans' poems (Royal MS. 16 F. ii), with a picture of the Tower of London, where he wrote them during his imprisonment, Ph. de Maizière's *Songe du Vergier* (Royal MS. 19 C. iv), a copy dated 1378, bearing an autograph note of Charles V of France, and the same author's appeal to Richard II for peace with France, the page facing the opening of which bears an exquisite design of the sacred monogram, on a background of leopards and fleurs-de-lys, surmounted by a crown

THE MANUSCRIPTS

of thorns radiating light down upon the crowns of England and France (Royal MS. 20 B. vi).

To judge from the long series of gaudy printed volumes of similar texts printed by Vérard at Paris which Henry VII bought, he is not likely to have personally deserved the flattering words in which Claude de Seyssel, Bishop of Marseilles, writes in the prologue to his translation of Xenophon's *Anabasis*, addressed to the King (Royal MS. 19 C. vi), that when on embassy in England (in 1508), he had admired the Royal Library and had heard of Henry's taste for literature. But the copy of the French and English poems of Charles d'Orleans, mentioned above, was written for him, or possibly for Arthur Prince of Wales; and there are some other fine books which seem to be of his reign.

In 1492 Henry appointed the first Librarian, a Fleming from Lille named Quintin Poulet. Poulet was succeeded at Henry VIII's accession by another Fleming, Giles Duwes or Aegidius de Vadis, whose title shows that the Library was then kept at Richmond; he was also Royal teacher of French and died in 1535, being followed by William Tyldesley. At this time there was a second library at Westminster, though whether this also was under Tyldesley's charge does not appear. The books were becoming numerous enough for rough inventories to begin to be made. An anonymous French (or Flemish) visitor who saw the books at the end of Duwes's time, in 1534, records 143 works, written and printed. Some musical MSS. illustrate one of Henry VIII's tastes, and there are some of personal interest, especially a charming little volume, containing the Princess Elizabeth's autograph copy of her Latin translation of Queen Catherine Parr's *Prayer* (7 D. x) and Henry VIII's Psalter (2 A. xvi) with a miniature of the King and his jester, Will Somers.

At this time Leland made his "laboryouse journey," and in his report to the King, published in 1546, he claims to have been commissioned by him "to peruse and diligently to serche al the libraries of monasteries of this youre noble reaulne," and adds: "First I have conserved many good autors . . ., of the whiche parte remayne yn the most magnificent libraries of your royal Palaćis. Parte also remayne in my custodye." The exact extent of Leland's search and of its results on the Royal Library is somewhat uncertain. Lincolnshire he seems to have swept thoroughly, other counties much less so.[10] And the representation in the Library of the greater houses is curiously uneven, for while Rochester yielded a hundred out of a total of perhaps 600 in its library at the Suppression, there is only one from Christ Church, Canterbury, and (even more surprisingly) from the famous library of St. Augustine's, Canterbury, only some half-dozen, thus leaving opportunities for Archbishop Parker, not to speak of Cotton and Harley. But an inventory made in the Augmentation Office in 1542 under Sir Anthony Denny reveals that by that time there were in the Royal possession 910 books, of which a large number were of monastic origin, and not long after this the number had risen to 1,450. Of this increase some part must be credited to Leland. But on 25th February, 1550, the Privy Council ordered that the Library be purged by culling out "all superstitious bookes, as masse bookes, legendes, and such like, saving however the precious metals and jewells of their bindings." This work must have had the enthusiastic co-operation of the new Librarian, appointed in 1549, Bartholomew Traheron a violent Reformer who had been a Franciscan. Traheron and the two holders of the office who followed him were specifically authorized by their patents to assemble the books from the various royal libraries, i.e. at Richmond, Greenwich and Westminster, if no others.

The accession of Mary brought an end to Traheron's period of office, and he was followed by John Clyffe, who was Keeper till 1589. It may be observed that the succession of the patents disproves the old belief that Roger Ascham was ever Royal Librarian; he is, however quite likely to have an an informal commission to oversee and advise. The Librarians were men of small weight, in marked contrast to the contemporary Royal Librarians in France, who included such famous scholars as Jacques Lefèvre d'Étaples and Guillaume Budé.

The reign of Mary brought into the Library two of its very finest illuminated volumes. The Psalter named after her (Royal MS. 2 B. vii) filled with exquisite miniatures and drawings by an English artist of the beginning of the fourteenth century, belonged (as a note

THE MANUSCRIPTS

in it tells us) to an Earl of Rutland, probably Henry Manners, who fell into brief disgrace in 1553 on the charge of favouring Lady Jane Grey's claim to the throne. In that year, as another note tells us, it was (one would suppose illegally) impounded by Baldwin Smith, a London Customs officer, when it was on the point of being carried abroad, and presented by him to the Queen, for whom it was bound in the covers it still bears. Facsimiles of the illustrated pages of this book were edited by Sir George Warner and published by the Trustees in 1912. The second is no longer in its place, having disappeared in the seventeenth century, probably by pilfering during the Civil War.[11] It is now at Chantilly. This is another Psalter, that of Queen Ingeburg, a French manuscript of the highest quality, which formed part of the wedding gift of Philip II to Mary.

About 1588, three members of the Society of Antiquaries, Sir Robert Cotton, Sir John Dodderidge and James Ley (later Earl of Marlborough), drew up a petition for the formation, mainly by gift of manuscripts from the Royal collections, of a national library, as part of an Academy devoted to the study of antiquity and history; it was to be called Queen Elizabeth's Library, and to be annually inspected by the Archbishop of Canterbury and six of the chief officers of State, a curious anticipation of the Museum Trust (Cotton MS. Faustina E. v, f. 89); the printing of this petition was one of the first acts of the second Society of Antiquaries. It may never have been presented; in any case it was abortive.

Part of the books was rearranged in 1581 by one T. Kny[vett], Gentleman of the Privy Chamber. Clyffe was succeeded in 1589 as Librarian by Anthony Marten, who died in 1597. No new appointment was made until James I gave the post about 1605 to Patrick Young (Patricius Junius), the son of Peter Young, his Librarian at Holyrood; he saw out the reigns not only of his first Royal patron, but of his son also. Young was a man of more learning, so far as we know, than any of his predecessors, and raised the credit of the Library. He was the initiator of the Polyglot Bible which was completed in 1657. With the aid of Knyvett he succeeded in evading the importunities of Bodley, to whom the King had given a warrant "for the choice of any books that I shall like," said Bodley, "in any of his houses or librarys." They attained their end by "dealing very much underhand," to Bodley's disgust.

The great events of Young's time were, first in 1609, the acquisition, for the studious young Prince of Wales, so soon to die, of the collection which had successively belonged to Archbishop Cranmer as part of his library, Henry Fitzalan, last Earl of Arundel of that name, and his son-in-law Lord Lumley, the signatures of all three of whom are to be found in many of the books. Lumley is known to have given books away, and about 80 of the 308 listed in his MS. catalogue are not present. But the remainder are of high value, and include many volumes from English monastic libraries. The printed books in this collection and also Casaubon's, acquired a few years later, are mentioned above, p. 179. With Henry Prince of Wales's death the Lumley books fell into the main Royal Library. The second great acquisition of this period was, of course, the gift in 1627 by Cyril Lucar, Patriarch of Alexandria, to Charles I (through Sir Thomas Roe, Envoy to Constantinople) of the fifth-century Greek Bible since known as the Codex Alexandrinus. This acquisition added greatly to the fame of the Royal Library of this country, and it was until late in the eighteenth century (in fact until the type-facsimile editions of the New and Old Testaments were published) in dangerously constant demand, generally out of mere curiosity, which the early Principal Librarians seem not to have thought of discouraging. Young himself borrowed it, with other Biblical MSS., after his retirement, and they were only recovered in 1664 from his executors, and then after legal proceedings.

With the death of Charles I Young's office lapsed. He handed over the keys on 14th February to John Durie, by order of the Committee presided over by Bulstrode Whitelocke, but was recalled to make inventories.

These were fortunately required for the preservation and not for the sale of books. The violent Puritans, headed by Hugh Peters, were for selling, but the moderates, probably led by Whitelock himself, prevailed; we may suppose that the influence of Selden was brought to bear on the controversy. Durie was appointed Librarian in 1650, and held the office till the Restoration. He was a moderate Protestant

THE MANUSCRIPTS

divine, and a copious and learned writer, with a passion for religious unity which took him on journeys over Europe. In 1654 he left England on his last voyage, and died at Cassel in 1680. The work in the Library was performed from 1654 till 1677 by the Deputy, Richard Pearson. Durie is also remembered as the author of *The Reformed Librarie Keeper*, which he published in the year of his appointment. He took a liberal view of a librarian's functions, which he defined as "to keep the publick stock of learning, to increase it, and to propose it [i.e. make it available] to others in the waie which may be most helpful unto all."

He was followed by another Scot, Thomas Ross, who had been in Charles II's service as tutor to the young Monmouth. In the first year of his tenure of office he bought the Morice Collection (already mentioned under the Printed Books), which contained some MSS. He nominally held the post till 1677, when he was followed by the brothers Henry Frederick and James Thynne in conjunction.

There were two libraries, at Whitehall and at St. James's. The former, which was visited by Evelyn in 1680 and again in 1681, was destroyed by one (or both) of the fires which burned the Palace in 1691 and 1697–98; the latter is shown by Bernard's Catalogue of 1698 not to have suffered subsequent loss, at any rate to the MSS. A little before this, about 1678, the last considerable addition was made to the collection by the acquisition of the MSS. gathered by John Theyer (*d.* 1673), which included many volumes from the monastic libraries of the Western Counties.

With the accession of William III a new appointment was made, the post of Librarian being given to a learned French Protestant, Henri Justel, who had given up his post of Secretary to Louis XIV and arrived in England about 1681, selling his own fine library, which included some rare MSS. The reversion of the office was granted to one of his immediate predecessors, James Thynne, who however disposed of it to Richard Bentley, its most distinguished holder. On Justel's death in 1693 Bentley was appointed, being yet a young man under thirty; he took up his residence three years later in the Keeper's apartments at St. James's, and here used to meet the brilliant circle which included Wren, Locke and Newton. The

Library was under the special patronage of Queen Mary, and was commonly spoken of as "the Queen's Library."[12]

Bentley's autocratic energy, notorious during his Mastership of Trinity, to which he was appointed in 1700, showed itself in his control of the Library.[13] He rebelled against the state of the rooms, saying that they were "not fit to be seen," a criticism supported by Franz Burman, who saw it at this time and reported that the books were lying in heaps on the floor. Though, owing to the financial stringency of the years of Marlborough's wars, he did not succeed in carrying out any great scheme, he threw himself into their conception and promotion. His scheme was for the erection of a ground-floor room projecting into St. James's Park, and the establishment of the Royal Library as a truly national institution. He issued, apparently in 1697 and not, as Panizzi thought, in 1714,[14] a leaflet strongly urging the plan of a national library in a new building.

In 1700 the Cotton Library became national property, and, after a report by Wren in 1703, the Crown in 1707 bought Cotton House and its garden, and the Royal Library was transferred to that already ruinous house. Wren suggested that both Libraries might well be purged by "the drudgery of librarians" of "much useless trash," an idea which was luckily not carried out, no one, and least of all the Librarians, having an interest in providing the drudgery.[15] From Cotton House the two collections went in 1722 to Essex House, and, at the end of the seven years' lease of that house, back to Westminster, to Ashburnham House, which was unwisely reported on as safer from fire. Only two years later the great fire broke out which so grievously damaged the Cotton MSS., but the Royal Library was little injured, beyond probable damage to bindings from throwing volumes out of the windows; few medieval bindings survive in either collection. They were stored in the Dormitory of the Westminster Scholars till 1757. David Casley, Bentley's Deputy since about 1719, carried the Codex Alexandrinus out of the house himself. Bentley was not on the spot; he had in fact ceased in 1725 to be Librarian, securing his post and pay for his son, then only a boy of about seventeen, it being understood that the Deputy did the work. Twenty years later the younger Bentley sold his office to Claudius Amyand,

THE MANUSCRIPTS

a young Christ Church man with political ambitions; Casley continued to do the work till the transfer to the Museum. In 1732, no doubt stimulated by the fire and the public interest caused thereby; especially in such men as Speaker Onslow, Casley set to work on a catalogue of the Royal MSS., which was completed and published in only two years. With all the faults which such haste implies, this catalogue was a meritorious one for its time, and it was not finally superseded till after nearly two centuries had elapsed.

In February 1754 the Museum Trustees visited the Old Dormitory, and there found the Royal, Cotton and Arthur Edwards Libraries dry but smothered in dust, and cared for by Mrs. Casley, whose husband was by that time "disabled by age and infirmity, from executing the duties of the post in person." The titular Librarian, Amyand, they ignored, describing Casley as "the present Keeper."

By Letters Patent of 6th August, 1757, George II transferred the Library to the Trustees of the newly founded British Museum, and with it the reversion, after Amyand's death or avoidance, of the Librarian's pay and appointments, i.e. a salary of £200 and an additional £100 for house-room. This document speaks incorrectly of the Library as having been begun by James I, and mentions "the noble and well-chosen collections of John Lord Lumley and Henry Fitzalan Earl of Arundel and of Isaac Casaubon," as well as "the invaluable Alexandrian Manuscript of the Old and New Testament." The King is stated to make the gift as "knowing that the encouragement of all arts and the advancement of science constitute one essential part of the true wisdom and greatness of a King." It is not to be supposed that he wrote this, but, though personally uninterested in "boetry and bainting," let us hope that he believed it; he was, be it remembered, the founder of the University of Göttingen and of its famous library.

An Appendix to Casley's catalogue was made in 1882 but remained unprinted in view of the task of recataloguing the Royal Manuscripts. This was achieved in 1921, in two volumes of descriptions, preceded by an Introduction (to which the present short account is throughout

THE LIBRARY OF THE BRITISH MUSEUM

indebted) with one describing the King's Manuscripts and containing Indexes, and one of plates.

Catalogue of Western Manuscripts in the Old Royal and King's Collections, by Sir George F. Warner and Julius P. Gilson. 4 vols. 1921.

5. THE BIRCH MANUSCRIPTS

In 1765 Dr. Thomas Birch, one of the Museum's original elected Trustees (see p. 36), bequeathed to the Museum (together with a sum of £500 to improve the salaries of the Under-Librarians, for which their successors are duly grateful) his collection of MSS. bearing on British biography. They are of minor importance. They were catalogued in 1782 by Ayscough together with the Sloane MSS. (*q.v.* p. 239). A fuller catalogue was subsequently made, but remains in MS. Before 1920 a new catalogue was in preparation, but has been delayed.

6. THE LANSDOWNE MANUSCRIPTS

William Petty, first Marquess of Lansdowne, but better known in history by his earlier title of the Earl of Shelburne, played an important part in Governments in the second half of the eighteenth century, which does not now concern us, except that it was his own intimate experience of political history in the making which inspired him to gather the material for studying that already made.

Too independent to be successful in politics, he made his celebrated house in Berkeley Square a centre of literary and artistic activity. He seems to have begun collecting MSS. after his first retirement from public life in 1763. His great opportunity came four years later, at the sale of James West's library in 1773, at which the King acquired many rare printed books. At that sale Shelburne bought 122 volumes of papers, all but one (which contained copies of early charters and similar documents) consisting of the papers of William Cecil, Lord Burghley, including the minister's private memorandum book,[17] and a mass of correspondence and other papers illustrating State affairs during the reign of Elizabeth. These papers came, in the

THE MANUSCRIPTS

careless manner of the time, into the hands of Burghley's secretary, Sir Michael Hickes; they were sold by Hickes's great grandson Sir William Hickes, to Richard Chiswell, the leading bookseller, late in the seventeenth century, and by him to Strype the historian, who made some use of them; after Strype's death they were sold to West.

The Burghley papers are no doubt the most important part of the collection; but others are not far behind them in value for English history. Fifty volumes (alas, not much more than a quarter of the original series) contain the official papers of a statesman of the generation after Burghley, Sir Julius Caesar, Judge of the Court of Requests and of Admiralty, Chancellor of the Exchequer and Master of the Rolls under James I, which, like Burghley and other statesmen of the sixteenth to the eighteenth century, he retained as his property and mixed with his personal papers. These were dispersed by auction in 1744–57. Philip Carteret Webb, the antiquary, succeeded in buying and recombining single auction lots representing fifty of the one hundred and eighty-seven volumes, and after his death in 1770 these were purchased from his heirs by Shelburne.

A third large series comprises 107 volumes of the collections for English Church History, and also especially for that of his own Diocese of Peterborough, formed by Bishop White Kennet.

Apart from these three large series there are many MSS. of miscellaneous provenance. Of those which are of interest for English history the chief are perhaps the heraldic and armorial collections of several famous Heralds, such as Segar, Lee, Dugdale and Le Neve, an ancient transcript of the *Testa de Nevill*, the collections of Parliamentary history formed by William Petyt (1636–1707), Keeper of the Records in the Tower,[16] a series of letters addressed to Henry Cromwell as Lord Lieutenant of Ireland, and collections for the history of Yorkshire. A French Bible (of the version by Raoul de Presles) illuminated in the finest French fifteenth-century style, may be mentioned (No. 1175). As interesting as any Lansdowne MS. to the Museum is Wanley's Diary (Nos. 771–72) which throws abundant light on the foundation of the Harleian Library and on other collections of that time, besides being a very human document (see above, p. 233).

THE LIBRARY OF THE BRITISH MUSEUM

After Lansdowne's death in 1805, the manuscripts were to be sold, like the printed books, and a sale catalogue was issued by Sotheby in 1807. But the Trustees made application in time to Parliament not to allow the dispersal and loss of so important a collection, stored with State Papers which were properly speaking, if not legally, national possessions. The House of Commons appointed a Select Committee, and in confirming that Committee's report purchased the Lansdowne MSS. in 1807 for £4,925 and deposited them in the Museum. Except for the Hamilton Vases and Antiquities, this was the first special grant made for the Museum by Parliament since 1753.

Lansdowne's great collections of printed books, prints, maps, coins and medals were dispersed at auction in 1806 and no attempt was made to obtain them for the nation.

Three years later the Commissioners on Public Records ordered the production at their own expense of a printed catalogue of the collection. The Trustees committed the task to the Keeper, Douce, and it appeared in two parts, the first describing the Burghley Papers, the second, produced after Douce's departure from the Museum, by his successor, Ellis, describing the rest of the collection, with an index.

A Catalogue of the Lansdowne Manuscripts in the British Museum. 2 vols. 1812–19.

7. THE HARGRAVE MANUSCRIPTS

Francis Hargrave was a Parliamentary lawyer of high distinction for his learning, and formed a considerable library of legal printed books and MSS., many of the former being annotated by him. The latter, numbering 499, contain a number of early Law Reports, Customs of London and similar documents. In 1813 his widow applied to Parliament to purchase the collection. A Select Committee recommended the purchase for £8,000, which was effected and the library deposited in the Museum. Many of the printed books bear Hargrave's annotations; they are not kept separate. Of the manuscripts, which form a separate collection, a catalogue was published by the Trustees five years after their acquisition:

A Catalogue of Manuscripts, formerly in the possession of Francis Hargrave, Esq. 1818.

THE MANUSCRIPTS

8. THE BURNEY MANUSCRIPTS

Charles Burney, D.D., son of Dr. Charles Burney the historian of music, a successful schoolmaster, devoted much of his leisure to the collection and study of the classics. After his death in 1817 his family petitioned Parliament to purchase his library for public use. A Committee of the House of Commons recommended the purchase for £14,000, but this was reduced by £500 in the vote sanctioning the expenditure.

The bulk of the library was printed, though many of the classical printed books are chiefly valuable for the MS. notes by famous scholars which they contain (see above, p. 188). But it included also some 525 manuscript volumes, which form one of the Department's separate collections.

The Burney MSS. are almost entirely in Greek and Latin or bear upon those languages and literature. Over eighty are Greek; they include a series of Gospel books dating from the tenth century down, and many copies of the great classics, notably Burney's most famous volume, the thirteenth-century Townley Homer (No. 86), with glosses and scholia, and (No. 95) a copy, also of the thirteenth century, of the Attic Orators. Most of his Latin, as of his Greek, texts are Italian humanist copies of the fifteenth century. The later MSS. contain the correspondence addressed to Casaubon and Burney's own philological notes, especially those made in the process of forming his theories on Greek metres.

The catalogue, by Forshall, appeared in 1840, as Part II of Vol. I of a new Catalogue of the Museum's MSS., of which Part I (1834) described the Arundel MSS. (*q.v.* below, p. 256).

9. THE KING'S MANUSCRIPTS

Of the King's Library, formed by King George III and presented by King George IV in 1823, the 446 MSS. are only a small part, and the Library and its history are described above under the Printed Books (pp. 188-93).

Nor are they relatively important, a number consisting of con-

THE LIBRARY OF THE BRITISH MUSEUM

temporary papers of little interest. Some historical papers were bought at the sale of William Robertson, the historian, in 1786, and a few plays at that of the Duke of Roxburghe in 1812; Johnson's first draft of his *Irene* came by gift from Bennet Langton. There are many on military subjects, and some of these, like many of the King's maps and plans, came from the collection of the Duke of Cumberland. From Consul Smith's library, which was the foundation of the collection, came some thirty-five MSS., mostly (as might be expected), in Italian literature and history or of Italian origin; these include a *Rime* of Petrarch, written about 1400 (No. 321), and some fifteenth-century Italian humanist copies of Latin classical texts, notably No. 24, a pretty Virgil. There are a few Horae and other medieval MSS., but the only one of high merit for its illuminations is No. 5, a Biblia Pauperum of about 1400, fully and finely illustrated by Flemish, or perhaps by Rhenish artists, in which it is peculiar and to be compared with the block-book editions; its provenance is unknown.[17] One MS. (No. 446) was added to the collection after its transfer to the Museum. This MS., presented in 1831 by Granville Penn, is a fifteenth-century copy of the report made for King Henry V by Guillebert de Lannoy of his travels in Egypt and Syria. There are a few Oriental MSS. in the collection; they have been transferred to that Department. The King's MSS. were very imperfectly described in Barnard's catalogue, but were more fully catalogued (with the omission of the Geographical Section) in 1832–33 by Sir Frederic Madden, with revision in 1841. All other than Oriental MSS. are fully described in Vol. III of:

Catalogue of Western Manuscripts in the Old Royal and King's Collections, by Sir George Warner and Julius P. Gilson. 1921. 4 vols.

10. THE EGERTON MANUSCRIPTS

Francis Henry Egerton, late in his life 8th Earl of Bridgewater, who died on 11th February, 1829, at Paris, originally intended, and published the intention, to found and endow a public library, to hold his collection of MSS., in the family home at Ashridge. But his elder

THE MANUSCRIPTS

brother, who occupied and intended to continue occupying the house, not unnaturally protested against such an inconvenience; Egerton was fortunately dissuaded and by his will of 1825, a will of vast length with numerous codicils, diverted the bequest to the Museum. By this he left his "dear and favourite collection of manuscripts" to be there preserved. That collection contained about 67 volumes, one in Hebrew, but chiefly consisting of the correspondence of French and Italian writers, scientists and statesmen of the sixteenth to the eighteenth century with a little under a hundred charters. There were also a few Oriental MSS. When a centenary exhibition of Egerton MSS. was held in 1929 only three out of the 202 exhibits —an autograph volume of Essays by Vauvenargues, a letter of Galileo, and a sixteenth-century Irish deed—were drawn from Egerton's own collection.

The remaining 199 were selected from among those acquired later from the Bridgewater and Farnborough Funds, and in the former and indirectly in the latter also of these is the Museum's great cause of gratitude to Egerton. For with the bequest of MSS. he made two of money: (a) one of £7,000, the income from which was to be applied to increasing the stipend of the officer who should have charge of his collection;[18] this has been until very lately of no value to the Museum, for, as recorded in Part I (p. 65 and n.) the amount was merely deducted by the Treasury; it is now added to (b) a bequest of £5,000, the income from which was to be used in purchasing additions to the collection. In 1838 Egerton's cousin, Charles Long, Baron Farnborough, a Trustee of the Museum, followed this example with a similar bequest of £2,872 for further augmentation of the Egerton collection. These Funds, the Bridgewater (so named from the testator's title, while the collection bears his family name) and the Farnborough, judiciously spent, have even in the period of high prices, and especially during that of wars and rumours of wars and consequent reduction or suspension of purchase grants, converted a small and only moderately valuable collection, however "dear and favourite" in the eyes of its creator, into one of the most noteworthy in the Museum. The MSS. have been multiplied from the original 67 or so to well over three thousand, and the charters from 96 to

THE LIBRARY OF THE BRITISH MUSEUM

over two thousand. Moreover the scope of the additions has been immensely wider than that of the original collection, most of the chief classes being well represented among them. Also it has been a constant principle to keep the standard of Egerton MSS. high.

Since 1836 the MSS. and charters bought from the two Funds and given Egerton numbers have been catalogued in the same volumes as and indexed together with the Additional MSS. acquired in the same years. For the Centenary Exhibition a Guide was published:

A Guide to some part of the Egerton Collection of Manuscripts in the British Museum. 1929.

11. THE ARUNDEL MANUSCRIPTS

Thomas Howard, 2nd Earl of Arundel (1586–1646), a great-grandson of the Earl of Arundel who founded the collection which passed through Lord Lumley's hands into the Old Royal Library, was a contemporary and friend of the great group of English antiquaries headed by Camden, Cotton, Spelman and Selden, and like Cotton fell under James I's and Charles I's displeasure. In common with them he studied and collected English historical and literary MSS. His collection abounds in early copies of the chief medieval British Chroniclers, Geoffrey of Monmouth, Higden, Hovenden, William of Malmesbury, Trivet and others, among which may be considered an important Froissart, and in monastic cartularies, notably those of St. Albans, Bury St. Edmunds, and registers, among them those of Glastonbury and of Christ Church, Canterbury; also the Rules and Constitutions of the Nuns of Sion; while the Divorce of Henry VIII is represented by a collection of correspondence and other contemporary papers. Middle English literature is also present in the shape of many important MSS. of Lydgate, Wycliffe, and others. Notable are No. 57, the autograph (and only surviving) copy of the Ayenbite of Inwit, by Michael of Northgate, who doubtless gave it, as he gave other books, to St. Augustine's, Canterbury, whence it came at the Dissolution; and No. 140, a volume containing *Ypotys, Guy of Warwick* and *The Seven Wise Masters*. Old English is represented by some MSS., of which the most important is No. 155,

THE MANUSCRIPTS

a Psalter with Anglo-Saxon glosses. The famous Arundel Psalter (No. 60 is also English; it is of the late eleventh or early twelfth century, and its illuminations are in the finest style of English art; while No. 83 is one of the earliest works of the East Anglian school.

But Howard's interests were by no means confined to the history and literature of his own country. As a young man, although his patrimony had been much reduced by the attainder and confiscations suffered by his grandfather and father, he was enriched by his marriage with Alethea Talbot, daughter of the Earl of Shrewsbury, and so commenced a series of travels abroad and especially in Italy, involving periods of residence long enough to establish intimacy with the scholars of that country, which he used to form a splendid collection of works of art, manuscripts and printed books. He also went on diplomatic missions to Holland and to the Palatinate, and it was at Nuremberg in 1636 that he made the purchase which earned the greatest renown for his library. This was that part of the collection of the Renaissance humanist Bilibaldus Pirckheimer (1470–1530) which had not been acquired by the city of Nuremberg. It is said that some of Pirckheimer's MSS. came from the collection of Matthias Corvinus, King of Hungary, but none is identifiable as such. Classical texts are richly represented, as might be expected from the sources of his library. Among Greek MSS. an Evangeliary in uncials (No. 547), and early copies of the Greek Fathers strengthened the Museum where, thanks especially to the Harleys, it was already rich; a more out-of-the-way volume is No. 518, a Cypriote history of Cyprus, 1456–74. The range and originality of Arundel's collecting is exemplified in his Latin and French as well as in his Greek MSS. Not only did he collect medieval Civil and Canon Law and French poetry and romances of the twelfth to the fifteenth century, but his knowledge of Italian Art caused him to secure an autograph MS. of Leonardo da Vinci (No. 263, and more remarkable still, he acquired volumes of medieval Latin hymns, a class of literature which until our own day, at least outside the world of Catholic antiquaries, was but little regarded.

Arundel also enlisted the services of Sir Thomas Roe, Ambassador to the Porte in 1626–28, through whom the gift of the Codex Alex-

THE LIBRARY OF THE BRITISH MUSEUM

andrinus was made to Charles I, and by his means obtained a number of Hebrew and other Oriental MSS.

These artistic and literary collections made Arundel House the chief centre of cultivation in London, which then and till long after depended, to a surprising degree for a capital city, on the chances of public-spirited private collectors. Selden's *Marmora Arundeliana*, 1628, contributed to the fame of the house. At Arundel's death there was apparently some dispersal of books, and his grandson Henry Howard (at the end of his life sixth Duke of Norfolk), who succeeded to the property, cared little for books or works of art, and allowed considerable depredations. At the end of 1666, however, he was persuaded by Evelyn, who had known Arundel, to present the printed books and half the MSS. to the newly founded Royal Society, of which both were Fellows, and the other half of the MSS. to the College of Arms, and in the following year the celebrated Greek marbles to the University of Oxford.

In its first inception and throughout its early period the Royal Society's Fellowship represented a wide field of humanist learning and research. A man of industry and active mind might then still at least aspire, if hardly attain, to be a doctor universalis. But the accumulation of knowledge, especially in the natural sciences, made this less and less possible; and the refoundation of the Society of Antiquaries drew away those whose interests lay outside the natural sciences. In 1830 therefore the Society made an arrangement, by which the Museum received its half of the Arundel MSS., with the exception of the Orientalia and of a chartulary of Howard lands, which was restored to the family. The Society received a payment of £3,559, with 2,072 duplicate scientific printed books, made so by the reception of King's copies.[19]

The catalogue was at once made by Madden:

Catalogue of Manuscripts in the British Museum. New Series, Vol. I. Part I. *Arundel*, 1834.

Part II described the Burney MSS., and contained facsimiles illustrating both parts. Part III, 1840, is a combined index to both collections.[20]

THE MANUSCRIPTS

12. THE STOWE MANUSCRIPTS

The story of the Stowe MSS. is that of a marvellous opportunity lost for the Museum by hesitation and parsimony in the mid-nineteenth century and only partly recovered a generation later.

They were collected at the beginning of the century by the Marquess (later the first Duke) of Buckingham at Stowe House in Buckinghamshire; there they remained till 1849, when the second Duke, who, like his father, only more so, had dissipated a vast estate, was forced to sell the rest of the family collections. (The first Duke had sold his large collection of rare prints in 1834.) He printed an auction catalogue of the MSS. but gave the Museum the first refusal of the MSS., and after Madden had valued them at £8,300 the Trustees were authorized by the Treasury to treat with their owner. But there must have been either an attempt to secure them for less than their value or else some dilatoriness, for they were sold to the Earl of Ashburnham for £8,000.

Three years before this the Trustees had applied to the Treasury for leave to buy the 1923 valuable early French and Italian MSS., including several important Dante volumes, with very early copies of Latin classics, papers of Napoleon and others and autographs collected by Guglielmo Libri; and then, finding the Treasury unwilling, they reduced this to £6,000 by omitting the Napoleonic papers, but Lord Ashburnham stepped in and bought the whole, again for £8,000.

In 1848 the Trustees had the offer of the 702 MSS. collected by Joseph Barrois. These were rich in French poetry and romances, in the history of the Low Countries, in illuminations and in a rarer class than any of these, early medieval bindings, seven of them being ivories. Madden valued the collection at £6,000, but the Trustees made no application to the Treasury, and they were soon afterwards offered and sold to Lord Ashburnham.

Ashburnham continued to collect, and his miscellaneous acquisitions, numbering about 250, distinguished from the Libri, Barrois and Stowe MSS. by the name of the Appendix, were of great value, including very important texts and bindings of the early medieval period, such as a Carlovingian Evangeliary with a worked metal and jewelled binding, and texts of Chaucer, Langland and Lydgate; they were bought entire in 1897 by Henry Yates Thompson, who kept the chief and sold the rest; some are now in the Morgan Library at New York.

In 1879 Ashburnham died. His successors offered his whole collection to the Museum for £160,000. This was a sum which there was no hope of obtaining, though it was not exorbitant, as not only had an offer of that amount been received from another quarter, but Maunde Thompson, who was sent down to Sussex to inspect and value, reckoned £140,000 to be a fair price. There was also a rumour that the French Government might buy, being naturally interested in the Libri and Barrois MSS., but this came to nothing. Then the Duke of Hamilton's fine MSS. came into the market and were bought entire by the Government of Prussia for £82,000. The Hamilton MSS. were mostly of classes in which the Museum was already strong, and only a few were wanted; but the appearance of this new rival (America had not yet appeared in force) was a shock, for the whole 3,800 volumes of the Ashburnham Collection were ardently desired. A serious problem might have arisen had the whole been acquired, since the Libri and Barrois sections contained no fewer than 167 MSS., valued at fr.600,000, which were found by Delisle, of the Bibliothèque Nationale, to have been stolen by those two ill-famed collectors from French public libraries; and of these stolen MSS. the return was claimed.

Finally, in 1883, the Government bought for £50,000 the 996 Stowe MSS. alone, in view of their high importance for the history of Great Britain and Ireland, which will presently appear. The MSS. of Irish interest, which included the collection of early texts in the Irish language formed by Charles O'Connor of Belanagare (grandfather of Dr. Charles O'Connor, Buckingham's librarian, who compiled the privately printed Stowe catalogue), some other early Irish MSS., an ancient Irish missal in a metal case, and the papers of the 1st Earl of Essex, Lord Lieutenant for Charles II, were deposited not in the Museum but in the library of the Royal Irish Academy at Dublin.

The rest came to the Museum. They were a notable addition to

THE MANUSCRIPTS

its wealth in English history. There are among them 646 charters (42 Anglo-Saxon), the eleventh-century Register of Hyde Abbey, with its famous drawings, other texts and chartularies of the same century, notably Sir Henry Spelman's Psalter with Anglo-Saxon glosses, the earliest copy of the Durham register known as "the Boldon Buke," a Wardrobe Book of Edward II, accounts of the robes and jewels of Elizabeth, an original rough Privy Council minute-book of 1660-70, and the letters of the Duke and Duchess of Marlborough to James Craggs the elder. Although many of the holograph letters are more essentially important to history than to literature, one at least is peculiarly illuminating for both, and may be singled out for mention. This is that written by Claverhouse in the evening after the skirmish with the Covenanters at Drumclog in 1679. What a man of imagination can make of his material is to be seen where Scott in *Old Mortality* describes this affair as seen from the other side of what Claverhouse (whose spelling is wild, perhaps the more so because he was "wearied and sleapy") called "moses and lotkes" [lochs].

Many of the Stowe historical papers, including the early charters, with a great heraldic collection, had belonged to John Anstis, Garter King-of-Arms, to whom some at least had come from the antiquary Sir Roger Twysden, and were afterwards in the possession of Thomas Astle, Keeper of the Records in the Tower; Astle directed by his will that the collection was to be offered to Buckingham for £500, or failing him to the Museum, of which he was a Trustee; Buckingham bought them in 1804, and employed Soane to fit up the Gothic library at Stowe to hold them. They form the great bulk of the whole.

As soon as the Stowe MSS. were received in the Museum a selection was exhibited; the catalogue of this was issued with or without the fifteen facsimiles:

Catalogue of a selection from the Stowe Manuscripts, Exhibited in the King's Library in the British Museum, 1883.

The full catalogue of the collection with index appeared twelve years later:

Catalogue of the Stowe Manuscripts—2 vols.; 1895-96.

THE LIBRARY OF THE BRITISH MUSEUM

13. THE ASHLEY MANUSCRIPTS

The MSS. forming part of the Ashley Library will be kept with the printed books (*q.v.*, pp. 199–201).

14. THE YATES THOMPSON MANUSCRIPTS

In 1941, too late for more than bare mention here, Henry Yates Thompson's widow's executors presented at her desire 34 of the 36 illuminated MSS. remaining after the sales of 1919–21 from his celebrated hundred, with 13 acquired later. It is intended to join with these five already given or bought.

15. THE ADDITIONAL MANUSCRIPTS

The Additional Manuscripts are all, outside the separate collections described above, which have reached the Museum by gift, bequest or purchase—or in a few cases, by having simply been left there unclaimed and without owner's name for a generation. They are, therefore, of every class and degree and by now greatly outnumber any of the collections, their numbers, which begin with 4101, following the Sloane numbers and including the Birch, having now (on 30 Nov., 1941) reached 45,877.

Ayscough's Sloane Catalogue, 1782, described the Additionals to that date (i.e. to No. 5017). For a period after that there are only manuscript descriptions; but the Museum's Annual Reports include descriptions of new acquisitions for some years up to 1835. In 1831–37 a list of Additionals since Ayscough and up to No. 7062 was made in MS. in 23 volumes. A new Additional Catalogue to this date is one of the first of the Department's projects. From 1836 descriptions of Additionals and Egerton MSS. figure in the series:

Catalogue of Additional Manuscripts.
> 1836–1840 (1843); 1841–1845; 1846–1847 (1850, 1804); 1848–1853 (1868); 1854–1875 (2 vols., and Index, 1875–80); 1876–1881; 1882–1887; and thereafter quinquennially to 1920, the volume 1921–25 being in preparation. There is also an Index to the years 1783–1835, published in 1849.

THE MANUSCRIPTS

16. CHARTERS AND ROLLS

Of the Museum's great store of British charters and rolls, which in 1805 was reported by Nares to number over 16,000 and which now reaches some 90,000, the foundation is to be found in the Cotton, Harleian, Sloane and Royal Collections. The Cotton MSS. include very many charters and rolls, especially those (originally bound up in a volume) numbered Augustus I. From Cotton also came both the Museum's two copies of Magna Carta, one of which is moreover (though damaged) the most important of the four known; the Barons' Articles for Magna Carta were also early acquired, having been presented by Earl Stanhope in 1769. But the Harleian series is also very rich, though the figures of 13,285 charters and 948 rolls are swollen by the inclusion of great numbers of foreign and especially of Papal documents. From the Harleys comes perhaps the most interesting of all, the Guthlac Roll (Harley Roll Y.6), made probably at Crowland, and consisting of a series of roundel cartoons, perhaps for stained glass, which are the high watermark of English twelfth-century drawing. The Stowe MSS. acquired in 1883, which added over six hundred, forty-two of them of pre-Conquest date, starting from the seventh century, have been the most precious single addition to these collections.

The first half of the nineteenth century saw the acquisition of many of these, such as the series, mostly relating to Beverley, which came with the Lansdowne MSS. in 1807, the 530 charters and 23 rolls presented by Lord Frederic Campbell in 1814, the charters bequeathed in 1827 with his collections for a history of Derbyshire by Adam Wolley, and the 310 Pipe Rolls, transferred to the Museum in 1833–34 by the Commissioners of the Public Records, but very properly re-transferred about 1860 to the Public Record Office; while one of the Museum's few early purchases was in this class, namely the 56 monastic charters bought at the sale in 1804 of the library of John Topham, F.R.S.

In the eighteenth century the Harleian charters and rolls were ill kept in an attic named the Charter Room; and here it was that Madden soon after his joining the Museum staff found the neglected

THE LIBRARY OF THE BRITISH MUSEUM

fragments of the Cotton MSS. which had been damaged in the fire of 1731. The other charters were stored in presses under the windows in the rooms devoted to the collections to which they belonged. The whole were catalogued by Ayscough late in the eighteenth century. His catalogue has remained in manuscript. There is also in the Department an old MS. catalogue of the Campbell, Wolley, Topham and Egerton Charters, commenced by Sir Henry Ellis. Charters acquired later were entered in the catalogues of the various collections, and notably in those of the Additional and of the Stowe MSS. A collective index was long badly needed, but was not provided till forty years ago:

Index to the Charters and Rolls. By Henry J. Ellis and Francis B. Bickley. 2 vols., 1900–12.

Vol. I of this is the Index Locorum (British only). In Vol. II the Stowe Charters and acquisitions since 1900 are indexed.

Autotype Facsimiles of Ancient Charters. 4 pt. 1873–78.
Facsimiles of Royal and Other Charters. Vol. I. William I–Richard I. 1903.
Magna Charta, collotype facsimile with Latin transcript and English translation.
Articles of Magna Charta: collotype facsimile with Latin transcript.

A selection of charters is described, with an introduction, in:

Guide to the Exhibited Manuscripts, Part II (Sect. vii), 1923.

A facsimile edition of the *Guthlac Roll* was produced by Sir George Warner in 1928 as his gift to the Roxburghe Club.

17. SEALS

The Museum's collection of Seals consists of (*a*) those attached to charters and other legal documents; (*b*) the "Detached Series," i.e. those once so attached but now separated; and (*c*) modern impressions from moulds or matrices. It includes a complete series of the Great Seals of the Kings and Queens of England.

THE MANUSCRIPTS

Original matrices are preserved not in the Department of Manuscripts but in that of British and Medieval Antiquities.

Catalogue of Seals in the Department of Manuscripts in the British Museum.
   By Walter de Gray Birch.   6 vols.   1887–1900.

There is also a mid-nineteenth-century MS. Index of Seals in two folio volumes. A selection is described in:

Guide to the Exhibited Manuscripts, Part II (Section viii), 1923.

18. Maps, Charts, Plans and Topographical Drawings

Maps, Charts, Plans and Topographical Drawings occur in many of the collections. There were, for example, some in the Royal Library by the time of Charles II; a special list (Royal MS. App. 86) then drawn up, includes printed and engraved as well as a few manuscript maps, and it is natural that a royal collection should preserve many maps made for military and other purposes of State. Some medieval maps of great importance are found in manuscripts, and pride of place in this country must be given to the three maps of Great Britain by Matthew Paris (two in the Cotton and one in the Royal), dating from the first half, or at least hardly later than the middle, of the thirteenth century, which have been reproduced (with a fourth among Parker's MSS. at Corpus), but earlier than these is a tenth-century diagram (in Royal MS. 15 B. XIX, f. 198 b) of the habitable and uninhabitable zones of the world.

Maps have been acquired from time to time, and among those purchased from the Bridgewater and Farnborough Funds are a number of beautifully executed as well as interesting Portolani of late fifteenth- and sixteenth-century date, showing the advance of knowledge of the coasts of the Eastern and Western hemispheres then being surveyed by explorers and charted for mariners. The Museum's maps of this period are representative of the work of Italian, Spanish and Portuguese cartographers, notably Graziano Benincasa, Diego Homem and Fernão Vaz Dourado. A fine French example is the map of the world drawn for Henri II in 1550 by Pierre Descaliers of Arques-en-Provence. There is also a native Mexican map of the sixteenth century, bought in 1911 (Egerton MS. 2897 (1)).

THE LIBRARY OF THE BRITISH MUSEUM

Topographical drawings have formed part of many of the collections of local history which have reached the Museum. Notable among early acquisitions are the Sussex MSS. of Sir William Burrell, with drawings by S. H. Grimm, William Cole's, Thomas Kerrich's and James Essex's Cambridgeshire, and Adam Wolley's Derbyshire MSS. There were many in the foundation collections, especially in the Cotton and Harleian MSS.; for example, among the Cotton is a series of charts and plans of English ports, made for Henry VIII in pursuance of his policy of founding a British navy. One of the most beautiful pieces of cartography is a finely drawn and coloured map of the Honour of Windsor in 1607, by the celebrated map-maker John Norden.

The Museum's map-collections have not been consistently administered. For thirteen years, from 1867 till 1880, there was an independent Department; but after that it lapsed into the Department of Printed Books, retaining however many manuscript maps acquired during those years, as well as the great collection in the King's Library (see above, p. 192). It is obvious that maps occurring in volumes not purely geographical, whether manuscript or printed, cannot be segregated from the collections of which they form part; nor, for historical reasons, can the collections be broken up. But at the present day manuscript maps may in exceptional cases be consulted in the Map Room in the Department of Printed Books, since Keepers are no longer at war with each other as they were a century ago.

About 1840 the newly founded Geographical Society obtained the Trustees' order for a special catalogue of all the maps in the various collections of the Department of Manuscripts. Madden was indignant, and not without reason, for, as he said, there was nothing to prevent any other body from persuading the Board to make a similar order; and it is obvious that the Board had in fact given no thought at all to the state of the Department's normal work or the size of its staff. However a list was compiled in 1841 by John Holmes, and was continued and published:

Catalogue of the Manuscript Maps, Charts and Plans and of the Topographical Drawings in the British Museum. 3 vols. 1844–61.[21]

THE MANUSCRIPTS

The Department of Manuscripts has joined that of Printed Books in publishing facsimiles of maps by issuing the four early maps of Great Britain mentioned above, in celebration of the International Geographical Congress:

Four Maps of Great Britain, designed by Matthew Paris about A.D.1250, *reproduced from three manuscripts in the British Museum and one at Corpus Christi College, Cambridge.* 1928.

19. MUSIC

Henry VIII's love of music is well known, and a series of volumes of motets and songs written for him and his Queens and Court, preserved in the Old Royal Library, may be regarded as the foundation of the Museum's collection of manuscript music. Not, of course, that the medieval parts of all the foundation collections, and not least of the Royal, are not rich in Church music, Tropers, Sequences, Offertories, etc., covering four or more centuries, the earlier volumes containing fine examples of notation by neums; but these were not primarily collected for their musical contents. There is, however, among the Harleian MSS. a large collection of music of various periods, with accounts of composers. It includes a comprehensive collection of services and anthems down to the time of Queen Anne, including works by Blow, Purcell, Orlando Gibbons, and indeed all the great men, collected between 1715 and 1720, by Dr. Tudway, organist of the Chapel Royal.

The Museum's first considerable musical accessions were printed books, the collections formed by Sir John Hawkins and Dr. Charles Burney the elder; but the King's Library brought some additions to the manuscript music.

In the middle of the nineteenth century three large gifts greatly increased the collection. In 1843 the Marquess of Northampton gave a series of 149 volumes formed by Gasparo Selvaggi, of Naples; in 1846 Domenico Dragonetti, a famous violoncellist, bequeathed 182 volumes, and in 1849 Vincent Novello gave 44 volumes. The last-mentioned two benefactors also gave printed collections.

Beside these gifts, a very rich collection has been built up from

THE LIBRARY OF THE BRITISH MUSEUM

various collections and other sources. English music is naturally stronger than foreign, and that of the sixteenth century, relatively to its rarity and importance, perhaps stronger even than later periods. A monument of this school is "Thomas Mulliner's Book," consisting of airs, chants for the virginal and similar pieces by Tallis and his contemporaries. A large autograph folio volume by. Purcell may be compared with that in the King's Music Library. An attractive autograph of Purcell is "The Yorkshire Feast," of 1690. Vincent Novello gave in 1849 his collection of works by English composers; Sir Henry Bishop is well represented; a series of operas by Balfe was presented in 1873 by his widow; in 1896 Miss Eliza Wesley bequeathed autographs of Samuel Wesley. Handel is well represented here, as well as in the King's Music (see above, pp. 214–16). The Granville collection of seven volumes of transcripts by Handel's amanuensis John Christopher Smith, and his *Acis and Galatea* with a few autograph passages were both acquired from the Egerton Fund (Egerton MSS. 2910–46 and 2953).

In foreign music mention should be made of the Italian schools, such masters as Palestrina and the Scarlattis being fairly well shown. While the collection of the great Austrian and German composers is not to be compared with those in Germany or Vienna, it contains representative specimens of most of them. There are, for example, original scores by Mozart (including his chorus, "God is our refuge," written by him at the age of seven and given by his father in 1765 with the volume of Sonatas to which it is attached), and volumes of drafts by Beethoven, interesting as showing his method of composition. A notable purchase made from the Egerton Fund is Egerton 274, a thirteenth-century MS. (with later additions) containing sacred and secular songs by Philippe de Grève and other chansonniers of the twelfth and thirteenth centuries.

In the last half-century many gifts have been made of autograph works of the Austrian and German composers, among which may be mentioned those of Miss H. C. Plowden, 1908 (Mozart and Beethoven), and J. E. Perabo, 1902 (Schubert), while the Egerton Fund has secured several important pieces. Many composers' hands and lives are also illustrated by autograph letters.

THE MANUSCRIPTS

The Musical MSS. are reckoned at over 3,000 volumes. They were catalogued first, apart from the collections of which they form part, in 1842 by Thomas Oliphant, Secretary of the Madrigal Society. This was superseded half a century later by Augustus Hughes-Hughes's catalogue, which unfortunately has no introduction. There are contemporary lists in MS. of the Selvaggi and Dragonetti Collections.[22]

Catalogue of Manuscript Music in the British Museum. By T. Oliphant. 1842.
Catalogue of Manuscript Music in the British Museum. By Augustus Hughes-Hughes. 3 vols. 1906–1909.
    Vol. I. Sacred and Vocal.
    Vol. II. Secular.
    Vol. III. Instrumental: Treatises: Supplement of Accessions.

The King's Music Library Manuscripts

The fine collection of manuscript and printed music by Handel and other composers in The King's Music Library, deposited on permanent loan in the Museum, is preserved in the Department of Printed Books, and is described above, pp. 213–16.

The Royal Philharmonic Society's Music Library

In 1914 the Royal Philharmonic Society deposited its collection in the Museum on permanent loan. The Library dates from the foundation of the Society in 1813. It includes autographs of Haydn, Beethoven, Mendelssohn and other composers.

A small catalogue was published by the Trustees of the Museum:

The Musical Manuscripts deposited on loan by the Royal Philharmonic Society. 1914.

20. PAPYRI

The collection of papyri in the Department now consists of Greek and Latin documents, the Egyptian having been transferred to the Antiquities (much to Madden's annoyance) in 1840, and the Coptic to the Oriental Printed Books and Manuscripts after the formation of that Department.

THE LIBRARY OF THE BRITISH MUSEUM

Papyri were hardly known in Europe before the excavation of Herculaneum in 1752. Actually the earliest papyrus to be acquired by the Museum was one of the comparatively rare Latin examples; it is a fine and exceedingly large document, measuring 8½ feet by 1 foot, and came from the Pinelli Library in 1789. Egypt did not begin to yield papyri till well into the nineteenth century and in quantity not till the century's last quarter. Among the earliest finds was the large collection of documents of the second century B.C. from the Serapeum at Memphis, excavated in 1820, of which the Museum's share, some forty in all (the rest being divided between Paris, Leyden and the Vatican), relate to a very complicated but not very important affair of two twin sisters in the Temple service, who were unable to obtain regular provision of their stipulated allowance of bread and oil. These form the bulk of Forshall's catalogue.

In 1865 Queen Victoria gave some of the charred rolls excavated at Herculaneum, and in 1906 King Edward VII added two more from the same set, which had been given by the Government of Naples to King George IV when Prince of Wales. Some of these contained parts of the *De Natura* of Epicurus and other works by him and his followers; they perhaps had formed part of the library of a Roman Epicurean. In the eighteen-seventies and eighties the Museum secured some of the few important and already well-known papyrus texts of Greek classics found in Egypt up to that period. These included "the Harris Homer" (most of *Iliad* XVIII, first–second century), nine sheets from a third-century codex containing *Iliad* II–IV, both found by A. C. Harris in the "Crocodile Pit" at Ma'abdeh, "the Bankes Homer" (*Iliad* XXIV, second century), and several orations of Hyperides, which before their arrival in the Museum had been edited by Harris and by Churchill Babington between 1848 and 1858.

Systematic excavation began in the last quarter of the century to produce great masses of Greek books, mostly fragments, and still more of official and business documents. The latter for the first time threw light on the government and social life of Ptolemaic, Roman and Byzantine Egypt, as indeed does one large class of the literary fragments, those of books of magic. From the great find of documents

THE MANUSCRIPTS

made at Arsinoë in the Fayūm, most of which went to the Archduke Rainer at Vienna, and from the later find made in the same district in 1892 (more valuable, since the documents are earlier), most of which are now at Berlin, the Museum obtained large selections. Many specimens of both classes were found by Professor Flinders Petrie; they were pasted together to form the cartonnage of mummy-cases in the necropolis of Gurob, also in the Fayūm. This find yielded the Museum many as early as the third century B.C., including parts of the lost *Antiope* of Euripides, and of Plato's *Phaedo*, at that time (though now no longer) the earliest classical texts known.

Then came in quick succession the imperfect but only known copy of the Oration against Philippides by Hyperides (who appears to have enjoyed a great popularity, seeing how many of his orations have been found), the *Mimes* of Herodas, and the even more important four rolls containing Aristotle on the Constitution of Athens, a famous work which had since the early centuries of our era only been known from quotations; all these came from finds of 1889, and seven years later came another lost book, large parts of twenty Odes of Bacchylides. The last three were edited by Mr. (now Sir) F. G. Kenyon, then a young Assistant in the Department, and officially published. Latin papyri are far rarer than Greek, and mostly later; those of the 6th–11th centuries come rather from Italy and Spain. The prevalence of Greek texts in Egypt, though the country was under Roman government for a large part of the period, is due to the fact that its culture was in Ptolemaic and Roman times purely Hellenic. The Greek classical texts discovered do not much affect the text of the great books, but they show them centuries earlier than they were previously known. Most of the new books found have been minor; but to the *Constitution of Athens*, the *Antiope*, Herodas and Bacchylides, must be added as exceptions a number of scattered poems of Sappho.

About this time began the fertile excavations at Oxyrhyncus (Behnesa) and elsewhere by B. P. Grenfell, A. S. Hunt, D. G. Hogarth and others for the Graeco-Roman branch of the Egypt Exploration Fund (now Society), and the Museum has benefited largely by the periodical distributions of finds. The most famous of these is

THE LIBRARY OF THE BRITISH MUSEUM

neither a Greek classic nor a document, but a relic of early Christianity in Egypt, the third-century *Logia* or *Sayings of Christ*, found by Grenfell and Hunt at Oxyrhyncus in 1897; a second similar fragment was found in 1903. Perhaps as important are two imperfect leaves and a small fragment from a Codex,[23] apparently of the mid-second century, containing part of an unknown Gospel. These last were acquired with other pieces, and were not at once recognized for what they are: the Museum therefore did not have to pay high for them in the market. They are earlier than the more numerous and very important Biblical papyri acquired about the same time by Mr. Chester Beatty.

Catalogues, facsimiles, etc., are:

Greek Papyri in the British Museum. By J. Forshall. 1839.
   Plain texts of 44 documents.
Greek Papyri in the British Museum: Catalogue, with texts.
   Edited by F. G. Kenyon (and H. I. Bell; Appendix of Coptic Papyri in Vol. IV by W. E. Crum). 5 vols. 1893–1917.
   This omitted literary papyri, some of which were published in the *Catalogue of Ancient Manuscripts* and in *Classical Texts from Papyri*, and in view of the following, already contemplated:

Catalogue of the Literary Papyri in the British Museum. Edited by H. J. M. Milne. 1927.
Autotype Facsimiles of Greek Papyri. 3 vols. 1893–1907.

Classical Texts from Papyri in the British Museum, with the newly discovered poems of Herodas. Edited by F. G. Kenyon. 1891.

[Text and autotype facsimile of each of the following separately:]

Herodas. Text, 1891. Facs. 1892.
Aristotle on the Constitution of Athens. Text, 1891, 3rd ed., 1892. Facs.
The Poems of Bacchylides. Text, 1897. Facs. 1898.
Jews and Christians in Egypt: the Jewish troubles in Alexandria and the Athanasian Controversy, illustrated from Greek Papyri. Edited by H. Idris Bell. With three Coptic texts, edited by W. E. Crum. 1924.
Fragments of an Unknown Gospel and other Early Christian Papyri. Edited by H. I. Bell and T. C. Skeat. 1935.
The New Gospel Fragments. [Pamphlet.] 1935.

THE MANUSCRIPTS

In 1922 an Exhibition of Greek and Latin papyri excavated by the Egypt Exploration Society and presented to the Museum was arranged, to celebrate the twenty-fifth year of the Society's Graeco-Roman Branch:

Guide to a Special Exhibition of Greek and Latin Papyri presented to the British Museum by the Egypt Exploration Fund, 1900–14. 1922. Published by the Society.

A selection of papyri forms part of the *Guide to Exhibited Manuscripts*, Pt. II. Some Latin specimens are reproduced in *Facsimiles of Ancient Charters*.

21. BIBLICAL AND OTHER ANCIENT GREEK AND LATIN MANUSCRIPTS, OTHER THAN PAPYRI

Very early texts of Greek classics are found in the Museum almost only in the form of papyri, which are dealt with above. Two leaves of a second(?) century copy of the *De Falsa Legatione* of Demosthenes (Add. MS. 34473 (1)), found, like the papyri, in Egypt, is one of the oldest vellum MSS. extant; but the Townley Iliad (Burney MS. 86), with a date read as A.D. 1059, and a thirteenth-century copy (the best) of the minor Attic Orators, also due to Burney (Burney MS. 95), are the next really important texts. In the work of the humanist scribes in Italy in the fifteenth century, however, the Museum is rich from many sources, Harley, Cracherode and others, besides Burney.

Very early Latin codices are not to be found in the Museum. The earliest are in the Vatican and a few Italian and other Continental libraries. The English collectors of such treasures came too late into the field. It is only when we come to the Renaissance under Charlemagne that we find the Museum strong. The classics were one of Harley's interests, and from them came ninth- or tenth-century texts, most of them in caroline minuscules, of Horace (Harl. MS. 2725), of Vitruvius (Harl. MS. 2767), this being the oldest extant text of his *Architectura*, of Cicero's *De Oratore* (Harl. MS. 2736),

THE LIBRARY OF THE BRITISH MUSEUM

and *Aratea* (Harl. MS. 647), while a Juvenal of the same period and style of script (Add. MS. 15600) was bought in the first half of the nineteenth century. And of beautiful Latin as of Greek texts written by humanists in Italy in the fifteenth century there is a profusion; some of these are perhaps the loveliest books ever made, especially when simply decorated only with the capitals illuminated on white "vine-tendril" work which flourished about 1470, though for beauty of illustration no classic can compare with the *Commentaires de la Guerre Gallique* by Albert Pigghe (1520) with gold and colour-touched grisaille pictures by one Godefredus "pictor Batavus," of which the Museum has Vol. I (Harl. MS. 6205), Vols. II and III being respectively at Paris and Chantilly.

With the great primary documents of the Christian Church the case is very different, for here the Museum stands, though it is a high boast to make, almost above the Apostolic Library itself. Since the foundation it has possessed the third in age—the second then known—of the capital texts of the Greek Bible, the fifth-century Codex Alexandrinus ("A") which was presented to Charles I in 1627 and came with the Old Royal Library in 1757. To it was added in 1934 with much agitation and even public controversy the Codex Sinaiticus (א), which is a century older and coeval with, or possibly a little later than, the Vaticanus ("B"). Those who asked why money should be spent on the Sinaiticus when a facsimile was in existence were shortly answered by the publication of a study embodying the fruits of a study of the original.

These two books alone would make the Museum a place of pilgrimage to Biblical scholars; but one of the arguments for buying the Codex Sinaiticus from the Soviet Government was that in the Museum it could be studied in conjunction with a mass of other related documents. These are too numerous to mention, but they include some of the oldest Hebrew texts of the Old Testament which survive (much more modern than the Greek, owing to the Jewish habit of destroying the sacred books when replaced), while among the MSS. brought from the Nitrian Convent of S. Mary Deipara were several very early Syriac texts, both of the fifth century Peshitto version and of that which it superseded, and below one of them

THE MANUSCRIPTS

(written over it as a palimpsest) the Nitrian Codex of St. Luke in Greek, of the sixth century (Add. MS. 17211). And the earliest versions in Egyptian dialects (Coptic, Bohairic and Sahidic), like those in Syriac, throw light on the lost Greek MS. from which they were translated; these too are well represented.

On Greek books, theological, liturgical or (more rarely) secular, of the Byzantine period there is no space to dwell. Many came from the Harleys, and some, the most recently acquired, in the bequest (1917) by Darea, the last Baroness Zouche, of the MSS. illustrating the history of writing collected at Parham in Sussex in the first half of the last century by Robert Curzon, whose visit to the Convent of S. Mary Deipara, so entertainingly described in his *Visits to Monasteries in the Levant*, played a part in obtaining for the Museum the Convent's splendid collection of Syriac MSS. (see above, pp. 108–10).[24]

For the oldest documents of Latin Christianity it is again necessary to go to the Vatican; but the interest taken in the early Church by the elder Harley (perhaps influenced by Wanley) led to the acquisition of a great number of Biblical, patristic and liturgical volumes, headed by the Vulgate Gospel-book in uncial script (Harl. MS. 1775), which may be as old as the sixth century; while not only Harley, but before him Cotton and the collectors of the Old Royal Library (like Bodley and Parker for Oxford and Cambridge) had assembled all that could be found from the dispersal at the Dissolution of the monasteries of the Church books of early medieval England; and both from them and from later purchases and gifts have come in a rich representation of the ecclesiastical (as of the classical) works copied in the scriptoria established in the ninth century under Charlemagne. But there is no class, country or period of Western Church books in which the Museum is not abundantly rich; they may be said to be, with English history and literature and, with early Greek Christian documents, one of the four corner-stones of the Museum's historical collections.

Ancient Manuscripts, with autotype facsimiles. Part I, Greek, 1881. Part II, Latin. 1884.

THE LIBRARY OF THE BRITISH MUSEUM

Fragment of the Iliad of Homer from a Syriac Palimpsest. Edited by William Cureton. 1851.

One of the few secular Nitrian MSS. Printed in the types cut for the facsimile of the Codex Alexandrinus.

Facsimiles of Biblical Manuscripts. With descriptive text by F. G. Kenyon. 1900.

Codex Alexandrinus; printed in facsimile type. Edited by H. H. Baber, 1816–21.
—— Autotype facsimile. [full size.] 4 vols. 1879–83. Vol. IV (N.T.), appeared in 1879.
—— Reduced collotype facsimile, N.T. and Clementine Epistle, 1909 O.T. 4 vols. 1915.
—— Photographic Facsimiles of the Epistles of Clement of Rome. [Contained in the Codex Alexandrinus.] (Edited by W. Cureton.) 1856.

[*Codex Sinaiticus.*] The Mount Sinai Manuscript of the Bible. [Pamphlet.] 1934, 4th ed. 1935.

This is superseded by:

The Codex Sinaiticus and the *Codex Alexandrinus.* 1938.
—— *Scribes and Correctors of the Codex Sinaiticus.* By H. J. M. Milne and T. C. Skeat and including contributions by Douglas Cockerell.

Guide to Manuscripts and Printed Books Exhibited in Celebration of the Authorised Version of the English Bible. 1911, repr. 1927.

22. MEDIEVAL AND MODERN LANGUAGES

The following catalogues have been published:

WELSH. Historical Manuscripts Commission: *Report on Manuscripts in the Welsh Language.* Vol. II, Pt. IV. *The British Museum.* 1910.

Up to 1650 only, and omits pedigrees. A summary account of the Museum's MSS. in Welsh was contributed to the Cymmrodorion Society's *Transactions* for 1936 by Dr. H. Idris Bell.

A Catalogue of the Manuscripts relating to Wales in the British Museum. By Edward Owen. 4 vols. 1900–22. Unofficial.

THE MANUSCRIPTS

Historical MSS. relating to Wales were collected by Cotton and the Harleys as forming part of British history (the earliest authority on Howel the Good, for example, is the Harleian tenth-century MS. of the *Annales Cambriae*), and the Museum is incomparably rich in early copies of the Laws in the Venedotian, Dimetian and Gwentian Codes, while the Harleys, whose home was in the Marches, were interested in Welsh lands and genealogies; Robert Harley bought, for example, of the collection formed by the four Randle Holmes, heralds of Chester. Though the Museum has not one of the four Ancient Books of Wales, it has great collections of the poetry, mostly in copies made by antiquaries, such as the Book of Sir Thomas Wiliems (MS. Add. 31055), and the collections made and copied in the eighteenth century by the three Morris brothers of Anglesey and the enthusiastic Welsh antiquary Owen Jones (1741–1814). The Morrisian collection (Add. MSS. 14962–15089) went to the Cymmrodorion Society, and the Jones or Myvyrian (Add. MSS. 14866–14961) to the Governors of the Welsh School in London; both were transferred to the Museum in 1844. Among the very few surviving monuments of the lost Cornish tongue are a mystery play (Harl. MS. 1867) and a Latin-Cornish glossary (Cotton MS. Vesp. A.xiv).

IRISH: An important part of the Irish collection came by the purchase in 1852 of the collection formed by the historian James Hardiman. But such early monuments as the copy made in 1517 of the sixteenth century recantation of the Tale of Deirdre (Egerton MS. 1782) have been acquired singly. Of the founders the Harleys contributed most; the Gospels written at Armagh (Harl. MS. 1802) may be mentioned.

A MS. catalogue was compiled in 1849 by Eugene Curry. The published catalogue came much later:

Catalogue of Irish Manuscripts. Vols. I–II. 1926.

Vol. I, by Standish H. O'Grady, was commenced in 1886 and nearly all printed in 1889–92, but the scale grew and O'Grady died in 1915. Vol. II is by Dr. R. Flower, and the work is to be completed by a third volume, to contain introduction and index. O'Grady, who was not a member of the Museum Staff, is described by Dr. Flower as "by early initiation and eager study an unrivalled master of Irish manuscript lore ... from boyhood in touch with the rich traditions of pre-famine Ireland."

DUTCH.—Beschryving van Middelnederlandsche en andre Handschriften in Engeland. [By] Karel de Flou and Edw. Gaillard. 3 pt. Gent, 1895–97. Unofficial. Reference may also be made to H. Bougman's *Verslagen*, 1895. Unofficial.

FRENCH.—Documents manuscrits de l'ancienne littérature de la France, conservés dans les bibliothèques de la Grande Bretagne: rapports à M. le Ministre de l'Instruction Publique. Par Paul Meyer. (Extrait des Archives des Missions Scientifiques et Littéraires, ser. 2. tom. iv–v.) 1871, etc.

Part I covers the Museum. This is not a catalogue but a detailed description of a few then little known but very important medieval French MSS.

GERMAN.—Deutsche Handschriften in England.—Von Robert Priebsch. 1896–   Vol. II, 1901, British Museum. Unofficial.

Deutsche Handschriften aus dem Britischen Museum. Im Auszugen herausgegeber von Dr. Jacob Baechtold. Schaffhausen, 1873. Unofficial; not a catalogue but a description of some select German MSS.

ITALIAN.—Catalogo di Manoscritti Italiani esistenti nel Museo Britannico di Londra. [By] Alessandro Palme di Cesnola. Torino, 1890. Unofficial; only professing to be complete for illuminated MSS.

POLISH.—Mitteilungen aus der Handschriften-sammlung des Britischen Museums zu London, vornehmlich zur Polnischen Geschichte. Von A. Warschauer. Leipzig, 1909. Unofficial.

PORTUGUESE.—Catalogo dos Manuscriptos Portuguezes [and of Portuguese interest] *existentes no Museu Britannico.* Por Frederico Francisco de la Figanière. Lisboa, 1850. Unofficial.

Catálogo dos Manuscritos Portugueses ou relativos a Portugal existentes no Müseu Britanico. [By the] Conde de Tovar. Lisboa, 1932. The preface is dated 1917. Tovar says that the Museum Portuguese collection had doubled since 1850, when La Figanière left off. Unofficial.

SPANISH.—Catalogue of the Manuscripts in the Spanish Language. By Don Pascual de Gayangos. 4 vols. 1875–93.

THE MANUSCRIPTS

We may enter here, as largely in modern languages:

Catalogue of Romances in the Department of Manuscripts in the British Museum.
Vols. 1-3. 1883-1910. Vols. 1-2 by H. L. D. Ward; Vol. 3 by J. A. Herbert. The romances are gathered into cycles. A fourth volume was projected, to deal with the Canterbury Tales and its sources.

23. ILLUMINATED MANUSCRIPTS

The Museum contains no true classical illumination, the few surviving specimens of which must be sought in Italy; and of the period when the Byzantine School had not quite passed out of the Classical it has only two fragments of books, the chief being what remains of the Cotton Genesis, of the fifth or sixth century. But in the work of all the later schools, down to the decay of the art upon the rise of printing, the Museum is abundantly rich not only by grace of the foundation collections, but by gifts, bequests and purchases throughout its history; it will be noticed how large a proportion of the exhibited specimens are Additional or Egerton MSS. Among the most valuable gifts and bequests are the Sforza Hours, a superb example of the Milanese school, presented by John Malcolm of Poltalloch in 1893 (see below, p. 281); the fourteen French, Flemish and Italian MSS. bequeathed by Baron Ferdinand Rothschild, M.P., in 1899 (Add. MSS. 35310, etc.); the thirteen MSS. bequeathed by Alfred Henry Huth in 1911 (see pp. 153, 198, 280), the ninth-century Lothair Psalter, with a portrait of Lothair, bequeathed by Sir Thomas Brooke, Bart., in 1908 (Add. MSS. 37768); the St. Omer Psalter, begun about 1330 by an East Anglian artist and completed in the next century, perhaps for Humphrey Duke of Gloucester, presented on his eightieth birthday by Henry Yates Thompson (Add. MS. 39810) and *La Sainte Abbaye* (Add. MS. 39843) executed in France about A.D. 1300, purchased at the Yates Thompson sale, 1919, in order that it might rejoin a copy (Add. MS. 28162) of *Le Somme Le Roy*—the original French from which the *Ayenbite of Inwit* was translated—with which it had once formed a single volume. (For the Yates Thompson MSS., see pp. 260, 278.) Among the nineteenth-century

THE LIBRARY OF THE BRITISH MUSEUM

purchases it may be enough to mention the Bedford Hours (Add. MS. 18850) once in the Harleian Library, bought in 1852; two MSS. rescued in 1862 from the sale of the public library founded by Archbishop Tenison, namely a Prudentius, *De Pugna Vitiorum et Virtutum* (Add. MS. 24199) written in England at the beginning of the 11th century, with outline drawings, and a Venantius Fortunatus, *Carmina*, of the 9th century (Add. MS. 24193); and lastly, a worthy addition to the Museum's series of books written and illuminated in New Minster (afterwards Hyde Abbey) at Winchester, where flourished the greatest English school of the art; this was the Gospels of Grimbald (Add. MS. 34890), which is one of the first examples of the school, dating from the early eleventh century. But there were very many others of the highest quality.

The splendid Yates Thompson MSS. came too late for more than bare mention here (see p. 260).

A summary account of the art as represented by the Museum's collections is given in the Guide to Exhibited Manuscripts, Part I, and there is no need to reproduce this here. Before setting out the titles of publications in this field it may be worth while to note some very fine examples of the English School recently acquired:

The Apocalypse of the Abbey of Abingdon (Add. MS. 42555), thirteenth century, belonging to the type with half the page devoted to picture and half to text which is associated by the famous example at Lambeth with Canterbury; as in one other copy the commentary as well as the text is illustrated. Bought in 1931. (*British Museum Quarterly*, vi. 71–3.)

The Psalter of the Abbey of Evesham (Add. MS. 44874), written for, and perhaps in, Evesham Abbey about A.D. 1250. It fills a gap in the series of mid-thirteenth-century English Psalters in the Museum. Bought and presented by the National Art Collections Fund in 1936. (*British Museum Quarterly*, xi. 22–3.)

The M. R. James Psalter (Add. MS. 44949), written in the fourteenth century for use in the Diocese of Durham. Apart from its own beauty its certainly English origin settles that of another Psalter from the same scriptorium and perhaps by the same hand

THE MANUSCRIPTS

(Egerton MS. 1894), which the late Dr. James edited for the Roxburghe Club and, while thinking it might be English, was forced to leave as of doubtful origin. After his death a group of his friends therefore subscribed and presented this book to the Museum in 1937. (*British Museum Quarterly*, xi. 175.)

The Luttrell Psalter (Add. MS. 42130), written for Sir Geoffrey Louterell about 1340, and showing not only the East Anglican school of illumination in its decadence just before it was broken short by the Black Death, with a wealth of remarkable if inartistic marginal monstrosities, but also filled with realistic scenes of domestic life and agriculture, which are the foundation of much of our knowledge of the life of the period. It was acquired in 1929 in conjunction with:

The Bedford Hours and Psalter (Add MS. 42131), executed about 1415 for Henry I's brother John, Duke of Bedford, from whose more famous Hours (Add. MS. 18850), of French workmanship, it should be distinguished. This book is by an English artist; it is one of the finest examples of the school which arose and flourished for a time after the Black Death and was the end of English illumination; it is moreover unique in containing over three hundred exquisite miniature heads, which may be portraits; they are certainly individualized.

These two manuscripts appeared in the market in 1929 from the Lulworth Castle Library. Mr. John Pierpont Morgan wrote generously proposing that the Museum should "go ahead and buy the Luttrell Psalter" at the expected auction, in which case he would lend the money free of interest for a year; and hearing a fortnight later that the Bedford book also was to be sold he extended his offer to cover both manuscripts. The owner, Mrs. Alfred Noyes, withdrew the Luttrell Psalter from the sale, and sold it to the Museum privately for £31,500. The Bedford book went through the auction room and the Museum secured it for £33,000. A subscription, backed by the Trustees, the Government and the National Art Collections Fund, raised the money to repay the loan within the stipulated year. The extraordinary generosity of Mr. Morgan will be understood when it is realized that he was the Museum's chief natural competitor and would have bought the two manuscripts for the Morgan Library, which contains some of the world's most famous and beautifully illuminated books. Both were described in *British Museum Quarterly* of 1929 (iv. 63); the Luttrell Psalter was fully published (see below) and was rightly dedicated to Mr. Morgan.

The illuminated MSS. are shown in the Grenville Room. Care has lately been taken to protect the colours of exhibited pages from fading. This has unfortunately necessitated covering the cases with green baize, and the visitor's eye is no longer delighted on entering the room by a blaze of burnished gold and lapis-lazuli blue.

Museum publications of illuminated manuscripts are:

Illuminated Manuscripts: miniatures, borders and initials, reproduced in gold and colours, with descriptive text by G. F. Warner. 4 ser. 1900–03;

Reproductions from Illuminated Manuscripts. 4 ser. 1907–28. Series I–III, 1907–08, went into a 3rd edition in 1923–25.

Schools of Illumination: reproductions from manuscripts. 6 pt. Hiberno-Saxon, English and French only. 1914–30.

Guide to the Exhibited Manuscripts, Part III. Latest ed. 1923.

A number of examples down to the twelfth century are reproduced and compared with other arts of the period in an official Guide:

Early Medieval Art in the British Museum. By Ernst Kitzinger (of the Department of British and Medieval Antiquities). 1940.

In 1932, a special Exhibition of French illumination was shown in the Grenville Library in place of the permanent selection from all schools. Unfortunately no official guide was published and it is only in large libraries that references can be made to the full illustrated catalogue:

Souvenir de l'Exposition de manuscrits français illuminés organisée à la Grenville Library (British Museum) en janvier-mars 1932. Etude concernant les 65 manuscrits exposés. Par E. G. Millar. (Paris, Société française de reproductions de manuscrits à peintures.)

Catalogue of the Fifty manuscripts and Printed Books bequeathed by Alfred H. Huth. 1912.

Guide to an Exhibition of Flemish Miniatures of the Fifteenth and Sixteenth Centuries. 1927.

THE MANUSCRIPTS

Notes on the Exhibition of Franciscan Manuscripts: Septingentenary of St. Francis. By A. G. Little. 1926.
Guide to an Exhibition of English Art. 1934.

The Museum's examples bulk so largely in the history of medieval art in this country that reference may be made to other unofficial books, in which many of them are described:

English Illuminated Manuscripts. By E. G. Millar.
    from the xth to the xiiith century. 1926.
    xivth and xvth centuries. 1928.
Early Drawings and Illuminations . . . with a dictionary of subjects in the British Museum. By Walter de Gray Birch and Henry Jenner. 1879.

The following facsimiles of celebrated single volumes have been officially published:

Autotype Facsimiles of Miniatures and Borders from the Sforza Book of Hours. 1894.

This book (Add. MS. 34294) was executed at Milan about 1490 for Bona of Savoy, widow of Galeazzo Maria Sforza, Duke of Milan. It contains besides decorations 48 splendid Milanese miniatures; in quite early days a number of leaves were abstracted and 16 Flemish miniatures of the finest style substituted.

Queen Mary's Psalter: Miniatures and drawings by an English artist of the 19th century, reproduced from Royal MS. 2. B. VII. With introduction by Sir George Warner. 1912. (See above, p. 152.)
The Lindisfarne Gospels . . . Cotton MS. Nero D. IV. With introduction by E. G. Millar. 1923. (See above, p. 227.)
An Exultet Roll, illuminated in the xith century at the Abbey of Monte Cassino: reproduced from Add. MS. 30377. [With introduction by J. P. Gilson.] 1929.

The chant "Exultet iam turba angelica coelorum," which forms part of the Blessing of the Candle on Easter Eve, was in Italy in the tenth to the thirteenth century habitually written (in Beneventan script) in roll form, with illuminations placed upside down so that they might be understood by the congregation as the roll was passed by the deacon over the back of the ambo or lectern. Monte Cassino specialized in making them. This example, executed about 1075, was purchased in 1877. The facsimile was published in celebration, of the fourteenth centenary of the foundation of Monte Cassino by St. Benedict.

The Luttrell Psalter . . . With introduction by E. G. Millar. 1932. (See above, p. 279.)

Two Museum MSS., unofficially reproduced for subscribers, nevertheless have a close and pleasant connection with the Department's history:

Miniatures and Borders from a Flemish Horae (British Museum Add. MS. 24098), *early sixteenth century.* Reproduced in honour of Sir George Warner. 1911.
"The Golf Book" (so called since the game appears in the border of one of the Calendar pages), made at Bruges by or under Simon Bening; only 30 leaves survive, but they include the exquisite Calendar. Bought in 1861.
Miniatures from a French Horae (British Museum Add. MS. 16997), *fifteenth centenary. Reproduced in honour of John Alexander Herbert.* 1927.

Of the Use of Paris, probably made, like the Bedford Hours, for an English patron during the occupation of Paris, St. George and St. Denis appearing in gold in the Calendar. Bought from the Edward Harman sale, 1847.

Postcards, monochrome and coloured, and larger reproductions of single miniatures have also been published in considerable numbers; lists are printed and published.

24. ENGLISH HISTORY

For the medieval and especially for the pre-Conquest period records other than legal documents are scarce, though the Museum has a series of royal and other public letters. For public history, though among the Cotton MSS. is an eleventh-century copy of the Laws of Canute and other pre-Conquest Kings (Cotton MS. Nero A. I),

THE MANUSCRIPTS

it is to chronicles that we have to turn, and here the Museum, thanks chiefly to Cotton, the Royal Library and Stowe, is exceedingly strong. Though Cotton's tenth-century copy of Gildas was burned, the Museum has two of the oldest of Bede, several of the Anglo-Saxon Chronicle, and good copies of practically every monastic chronicle down to those produced by the wave of patriotic interest in national antiquities which began in the fifteenth century. The unique thirteenth-century copy of the *Chronica* of Jocelyn of Brakelonde, made famous by Carlyle's *Past and Present*, is less concerned than the rest with political affairs; but in one of the first examples of genuine history, as distinguished from bare annals, the *Lesser History* of Matthew Paris, is to be found perhaps the chief monument of the historiographers of St. Albans, in whose works the Museum is peculiarly rich.

Local economic, social and family history rests on charters, court rolls and chartularies; and of all these the Museum has acquired large collections both from the foundation collectors and among the Additionals. Harley, for example, had no fewer than 200 of the known Heralds' Visitations, while one or two are found among the Cotton and Lansdowne MSS. and perhaps a dozen have been bought or received by gift singly. For most countries large accumulations made by antiquaries have come in. Gough's went to the Bodleian, as recorded above (p. 71), but such collections of MSS. and drawings as the Burrell for Sussex, the Cole for Cambridgeshire, the Wolley for Derbyshire, the Jermyn and the Davy for Suffolk, have come in ever since the eighteenth century. The latest large collection of the kind to come is the Buckler, of 10,000 topographical drawings, general in scope, acquired in 1898–99; but small additions are made almost yearly.[25]

One great series of family papers of the fifteenth century, of much more than local significance, has after a chequered history reached its final haven in the Museum. These papers are the famous Paston Letters. They were edited by Sir John Fenn and his nephew John Frere in five volumes in 1787–1823. Fenn presented the originals representing the first two volumes to King George III, after which they disappeared. Much later Frere's son discovered those printed in

THE LIBRARY OF THE BRITISH MUSEUM

Vol. V, and later again those printed in Vols. III and IV, and sold them to the Museum. But it was not till 1931 that those Fenn had given to the King reappeared in the hands of the Pretyman family, of Orwell Park, whose ancestor, Bishop Tomline, had been a royal tutor at about Fenn's time, and had no doubt been given the letters. They were secured in 1935 by the generosity of the Friends of the National Libraries.

For the post-medieval centuries the Museum's abundance of papers is so great that little can be said of it. The possession of State Papers was one of Cotton's nominal offences against the Crown; he did little more by collecting them than every statesman did in retaining them after leaving office; but he had held no office. Archives of the families of public men have gone into the accumulations of the Harleys, of Lansdowne (notably the papers of Burghley and of Julius Caesar) and of the Duke of Buckingham at Stowe. For the late seventeenth century we have the Lauderdale Papers, mostly, of course, on Scottish affairs, containing a long series of letters of James II. Similar archives of statesmen of the eighteenth to the twentieth century have been given in the last sixty years, beginning with the Newcastle Papers in 1886–89. There are, of course, large gaps; but the Newcastle Papers (given by the 4th Earl of Chichester in 1886 and following years) are the collections of the Duke of Newcastle and of the first and second Earls of Chichester, 1683–1826—they run to 537 volumes with 3,500 charters; the Hardwicke Papers in 930 volumes, forming a sort of counterpart to the Newcastle, being the papers of the first three Earls (1690–1834), bought from their descendant in 1899; also 94 volumes of the papers of William Windham, bought in 1909. The Regency period is represented by those of George Canning and the 2nd Earl of Liverpool, 1770–1828, both given by the Hon. Henry Berkeley Portman in 1911; the mid-nineteenth century by those of the Marquess of Aberdeen, 1784–1860, given by the 4th Marquess in 1925, and by Sir Robert Peel's, 1788–1850, given by the Peel Trustees in 1917, and Sir Henry Layard's; the latter part of the century by the voluminous Gladstone Papers, which were presented by the family in 1929–35, and are in process of arrangement by the Gladstone

THE MANUSCRIPTS

Librarian, Mr. A. Tilney Bassett; while Sir Henry Campbell Bannerman's, 1850–1923, given in 1925 by Lord Pentland, are the advanced guard of the papers of the statesmen of the twentieth-century. These archives of political papers are so large that the mere storing, not to speak of the arranging, binding and cataloguing of them imposes a very considerable burden upon the Trustees; but of their value (though the more modern are personal and not official and include many trivial papers) no one can be in doubt.

Similar collections of British diplomats, governors and generals abound. In 1896 General Rowland Hill's papers were bought from a special grant by Parliament; they include many autograph despatches and letters of Wellington written during the Peninsular War; and in 1895–97, also by special Parliamentary grant, 103 volumes of Nelson's papers were bought from Lord Bridport (for the Trafalgar Memorandum and the Log of the *Victory* see below). Those of General Gordon, bequeathed by Miss M. A. Gordon in 1893, may be mentioned; while the Museum shares with the India Office Library the custody of most of the extant records of British rule in India, possessing for example large collections of the papers of Wellesley and Ripon, and, above all both in quantity and in importance, of Warren Hastings.[26]

A collection formed by a humbler individual, which nevertheless is of high value, is that of Francis Place, 1771–1854, tailor and reformer, whose papers (many being printed cuttings) illustrate the passing of the Reform Bill and indeed the whole radical movement of the period; they were presented by F. C. Miers in 1897.

Single documents and smaller groups have of course come in great quantities, apart from these collections. Among them may be mentioned the signed original proclamation of 1st August, 1745, offering £30,000 for the capture of the Young Pretender; and two famous Nelson documents which have been published, his memorandum to his Captains of the tactics to be employed at Trafalgar, the official Log of the *Victory* for the eventful period, 19th September, 1805–15th January, 1806, and the original of the same, written by Nelson with his left hand; these (Add. MSS. 37953, 39862 and 43504) were all gifts, the first from Benjamin Minors Woollan, in

1909, the second from James Buchanan, afterwards Lord Woolavington, in 1919, and the third from Lord Wakefield in 1933. Among the most vivid of the many Nelson papers is (Egerton, MS. 614, f. 125) his unfinished letter to Lady Hamilton written just before Trafalgar. The foundation of the National Maritime Museum at Greenwich may now tend to divert documents in British naval history; but the Museum's pre-eminence in this field over all libraries except the Admiralty can now never be challenged.

British India has been briefly mentioned. Many documents relate to other parts of the Empire, since papers in English history necessarily include the records of discovery, colonization and government; among such papers is the original deed of purchase from native chiefs for blankets, tomahawks, knives, scissors, looking glasses, and the like, of the land on which the city of Melbourne now stands (this is, however, counted as a Charter—Add. Ch. 37766), and large series of papers relating to American history, notably (Add. MSS. 21661–21892) the papers of General Haldimand, commander-in-chief in Canada, 1778–85, though of later years the American collectors and libraries have allowed little to escape them.

Selections of Chronicles and of historical documents are described in Parts II and I respectively of the *Guide to the Exhibited Manuscripts*. The Nelson Memorandum was also described in a Guide pamphlet.

For other publications see the next section.

An Index to the Contents of the Cole Manuscripts, by George J. Gray, was unofficially published at Cambridge in 1912.

25. ENGLISH LITERATURE

Foreign literature is represented in the Museum by early copies of medieval works and by autographs of later writers, but, as with foreign history, these are necessarily inferior to the collections to be found in their native countries. For English Literature of all periods, on the other hand, the original or early copies of famous works and

THE MANUSCRIPTS

the autograph letters of authors are by far the richest to be found anywhere.

We may begin with the original *Beowulf*, damaged, alas, in the fire of 1731. From Cotton came not only this, but the best copies of the *Ancren Riwle* and the *Brut*, the volume containing *Pearl* and *Sir Gawain and the Green Knight*, the final or C-text of *Piers Plowman* and the so-called *Coventry Plays*. The equally unique fifteenth-century MS. of the 49 plays acted on Corpus Christi Day by the Crafts at York (Add. MS. 35290) was purchased in 1899. Among our debts to the Harleys in this field of Middle-English literature perhaps most of us would place highest the copy of that dull work Hoccleve's *De regimine Principum* (Harl. MS. 4866), which contains the famous marginal portrait of Chaucer; but from Arundel comes the doubly unique *Ayenbite of Inwit* (Arundel MS. 57) which is the only important medieval MS. of which the autograph copy exists, being Dan Michael of Northgate's own manuscript.

One medieval MS., a volume of Middle-English verse, while perhaps less remarkable than these, has, besides its own importance, a very pleasant place in the collection. It is called "the American Testimonial MS.," as it was presented in 1920 a sa token of national sympathy by Teachers of English in American Universities and Colleges.

Complete autograph works of poets of the sixteenth and seventeenth centuries are but few. The Museum has Sir Thomas Wyat's partly autograph poems (Egerton 2711; bought in 1889), and also the second most important MS. containing them (the Devonshire MS., Add. 17492) bought at Dr. G. F. Nott's sale in 1848. But the most debated literary MS. of that century is certainly the play of *Sir Thomas More*, which contains a passage considered by good judges (including Sir Edward Maunde Thompson, who published a study of it) to be not only by Shakespeare but in his hand. Shakespeare's life is also represented by one of the known signatures, that to the Blackfriars mortgage of 1612–13; while plays by Massinger and masques (notably *The Masque of Queens*) in Ben Jonson's beautiful scholar's hand illustrate the later stages of the Old Drama.

THE LIBRARY OF THE BRITISH MUSEUM

Milton's Bible, with the births, marriages, etc., of members of his family inscribed in it, is also in the Museum (Add. MS. 32310, bought in 1884), and so are the poet's commonplace book, from Netherby (Add. MS. 36354, purchased in 1900), and his agreement with the publishers of *Paradise Lost*, presented in 1852 by Samuel Rogers. With this last may well be compared Dryden's well-known letter of 1682 to Hyde Earl of Rochester (also here), in which he appeals for payment of arrears of his pension as Poet Laureate: "'Tis enough for one age to have neglected Mr. Cowley and sterved Mr. Butler." Had Milton not been an obstinate Parliament man Dryden might have added his name.

One of the earliest long series of letters in the Museum, and one of the most beautiful, is that of the love letters written by Dorothy Osborne to Sir William Temple in 1652–54; they were acquired from the Lodge family in 1891, after the publication of Judge Parry's edition.

From this period on there is hardly a great name in the procession of English letters which is not represented by autographs of more or less importance. The draft of Pope's Iliad, written on the blank sides of envelopes by the translator, was one of the earliest Additional MSS., and so were the surviving originals of Swift's *Letters to Stella*. The Vanessa letters joined them later. The purchase in 1853 of the Caryll papers showed up Pope's methods in publishing correspondence. Fanny Burney's Early Diary is here, and so are the Autobiographies of Burns and Gibbon, the last in all its six forms. Of Gibbon's MSS. the Museum has many, which were acquired by Lord Sheffield's gift in 1896, after the Centenary Exhibition of 1894—a good example of the value of such exhibitions considered as magnets. Percy's original MS. of the ballads, from which he drew his *Reliques*, was purchased in 1868.

Later still, in 1931, a large number of the comparatively few surviving autographs of Goldsmith were brought from Percy's descendant with the help of the Friends of the National Libraries. So much for Doctor Minor; of Doctor Major the Museum has, besides a number of letters, the original draft of *Irene*, presented to King George III by Bennet Langton. The bulk of Chatterton's manu-

THE MANUSCRIPTS

scripts of his "ancient" Rowley poems, however, are an early acquisition, having been bequeathed in 1800 by Dr. Robert Glynn, who had had them by bequest from Chatterton's patron, Barrett, in 1789. In 1862 came in a series of 120 original letters of Cowper, with autograph poems, including John Gilpin. There are, naturally, more and better Scott autographs at Edinburgh, but the Museum has his *Kenilworth*; and of the Romantic poets Keats's *Hyperion* and letters. In 1893 an autograph MS. of poems by Keats was acquired (Egerton MS. 2780), and in the previous year a similar MS. of Coleridge (Add. MS. 34225). Of Jane Austen's rare MSS. it has, besides some letters, the cancelled two last chapters of *Persuasion*. Many later authors, among them George Eliot (a nearly complete set), Hardy (with *Tess of the D'Urbervilles* and *The Dynasts*), Kipling (with *Kim* and poems), and Galsworthy (a nearly complete set) have given or bequeathed specimens of their books in autograph; and a notable accession of the great Victorians came in 1933, when the surviving children of George Murray Smith, of Smith, Elder, converted into a gift outright the bequest after their lives by their mother of the autograph MSS. of *Jane Eyre, Shirley, Villette, Sonnets from the Portuguese, The Ring and the Book*, and Thackeray's *The Wolves and the Lamb*, a minor piece, but showing both its author's hands. Trollope's *Autobiography* is one of the many gifts made by the Friends of the National Libraries in the last decade. Charlotte Brontë's life and writings are also illuminated by her late-discovered love letters to M. Héger, of Brussels, presented in 1913 by his son and daughter, which were a shock to her uncritical worshippers, but to more philosophical readers of her novels and life made for the first time an intelligible sense of what before had been legend. Robert Ross's well-meant gift of autographs of Oscar Wilde, including the full *De Profundis*, will find its level and take its place; hitherto this last MS. had been but a *damnosa hæreditas*, owing to the legal and other controversy that has surrounded it.

Authors presenting their autographs and other donors of such (not very numerous) modern MSS. as are acceptable, are earnestly desired by the Trustees to transfer to them, either at once or after a stated term, the copyright therein. By what appears to have been an over-

THE LIBRARY OF THE BRITISH MUSEUM

sight in the drafting of the Copyright Act of 1911 no term is set to copyright in unpublished manuscript, which remains vested in perpetuity in the legal representatives of the writer, who is often of course impossible, but (worse still) sometimes merely difficult, to trace —the responsibility for doing which rests with those who make application to the Trustees to reproduce such MSS. by photography and, presumably, to edit them.

Facsimiles of Autographs. 5 ser. 1896–1900.
Queen Elizabeth: early hand. 1934.
„   *later hand.* 1934.
Autotype of Shakespeare Deed—1935.
    [The Blackfriars mortgage (Egerton MS. 1787)]
John Milton, 1608–1674; facsimiles of autographs and documents. 1908.
The Nelson Memorandum; text and description of the Trafalgar Memorandum. 1910.
Guide to the Exhibited Manuscripts. Part I. Autographs and documents illustrative chiefly of English history and literature. Latest ed., 1928.
Guide to the Naval Exhibition. Nelson Centenary. 1905.
Guide to an Exhibition of Stowe Manuscripts. 1883.

The following three works are unofficial:

ELLIS, Sir Henry. *Catalogue of the Heralds' Visitations in the British Museum.* 1825.
SIMS, Richard. *Index to the Pedigrees and Arms contained in the Heralds' Visitations in the British Museum.* 1849.
ELLIS, Sir Henry. *Original Letters illustrative of English History.* 3 Ser. 1824–46. This celebrated work was drawn from originals in the Museum.

26. THE CLASS CATALOGUE

From early times the Trustees and the Museum's critics demanded a subject catalogue of the MSS., often regarding inventory catalogues by collections and numbers as of comparatively little importance, indeed a merely interim convenience. Ayscough's catalogue of the Sloane and Birch MSS. was, as we have seen, arranged by subjects, and Nares's Harleian Catalogue was completed by a classified index compiled by Horne. But those knowing most of the matter have

THE MANUSCRIPTS

naturally never subscribed to this view. Inventory and index, as exemplified in the Additional Catalogue, are the sheet-anchor of a library of MSS., to which the alphabetical author-catalogue of a library of printed books is not applicable. But of the use of a comprehensive classed guide to the contents of all the collections no one who has ever searched for the material of any one class could doubt, and as the collections and their catalogues and detailed indexes grew in number the time needed to search them grew likewise, and the need became more urgent. A general classed index had been desiderated by Nares in his Report of 1805. It was again suggested by Lord Colchester, planned by Ellis and entrusted to Millard. But Millard was, as we have seen, not a success, and the work was dropped in 1831, two years before his disappearance from the Museum. John Holmes handed in to the Committee of 1836 a specimen of a classed index which he had begun; but he very rightly believed that recataloguing was a necessary preliminary. At this time the primary duty of cataloguing the many new additions prevented the very small Staff from sparing time for anything else; and perhaps the troubles of the Department in the eighteen-forties and fifties contributed to the delay. An invaluable "stop-gap," but of course elementary in relation to the needs of research, was provided by the scholarly Attendant, Richard Sims; in his *Handbook to the Library of the British Museum*, 1854, he analysed the manuscript collections into their main classes.

But when Bond became Keeper he soon set to work on what is now one of the most valuable aids to study the Department, or indeed the Museum, possesses. The Class Catalogue was inaugurated in 1868 by cutting up and arranging under heads the entries in the existing catalogues and their indexes, and this has been kept up till the present day. But that was the easiest part of the work. Increasing knowledge, historical and palaeographical, has imposed an increase of accuracy and also of detail on cataloguers,[27] and until the old catalogues have all been rewritten, in conformity with modern standards, as has that of the Royal, no published Class Catalogue, or collective Summary Catalogue like Madan's of the Western MSS. in the Bodleian, can be contemplated. Both remain ultimate aims

THE LIBRARY OF THE BRITISH MUSEUM

which only financial constriction should prevent being realized in the next half-century. Towards them the Royal and King's MSS. have been recatalogued, and preliminary work is being done on the Cotton. The most urgent sections after these are the Early Additional and Egerton MSS., for which there is nothing more accessible or better than Ayscough and the Annual Reports, and also an additional volume of the Index Locorum of charters, which is under consideration. The Printed Books, it should be remembered, had no unified Catalogue until 1905, when the balance of the Grenville titles was incorporated in the Supplement to the General Catalogue; and in the mid-nineteenth century there were three, those of the main Library, of the King's and of the Grenville. The present state of the Catalogues of Manuscripts may appear to the next century as no less primitive. What could be and was done in the Manuscripts was to correct, enlarge and add entries from the Department's annotated copies of the old catalogues, and to incorporate the fruit of the researches of all members of the Department. Great headings, of course, required fundamental editorial brainwork as well as knowledge and industry in detail—large numbers of the MSS. were so ill-described in the old catalogues that they had to be re-examined for the purpose; and some of the largest and most difficult were constructed by Bond's chief lieutenant and later his successor as Keeper, Maunde Thompson; such were those of history and illuminations. Contributions in almost every field are perhaps the best memorial to the learning of J. P. Gilson, but many members of the Department's staff have shared in the work.

The Class Catalogue, accordingly, exists only in the copy in the Department, composed of a number of volumes filled with entries, partly printed, cut from their sources and pasted in, and partly manuscript. Microfilms of it are now being made for the Museum and for the Library of Congress.

27. Exhibitions and Guides

The permanent exhibitions began with one of autographs in the Grenville Room in 1851. It is now divided into three classes, as

THE MANUSCRIPTS

shown in the three published guide books, first published in this form in 1912:

Guide to the Exhibited Manuscripts.
> Part I. *Autographs and Documents, illustrative chiefly of English history and literature, exhibited in the Manuscript Saloon.* Latest ed., 1928.
> Part II. Manuscripts (palaeographical and Biblical series and Chronicles), Charters and Seals. Latest ed., 1923.
> Part III. Illuminated Manuscripts and Bindings of Manuscripts. Latest ed., 1923.

There is now also a small exhibition of MSS. and printed books in the Bible Room.

Special temporary exhibitions have generally been held in conjunction with the Printed Books, and some of the chief are mentioned above (p. 225). Others, confined to MSS., and also mostly mentioned in their appropriate places, have been those of Wyclif (1882), of Cotton, of Egerton, of Franciscan and of French Illuminated MSS. Official Guides (except of the last) were issued.

III

THE ORIENTAL PRINTED BOOKS AND MANUSCRIPTS

BEFORE the formation of the Department of Oriental Manuscripts in 1867 these were, with some exceptions, among the least organised of the Library's collections, the catalogues being few for want of experts on the Staff. In 1848 the Oriental MSS. numbered some 3,550, and some were covered only by a general classed inventory. Cureton was occupied till his retirement in 1850 on the Syriac and Arabic. A library covering such a range of languages could only be dealt with by being broken up into those languages, and in spite of occasional polyglot scholars such as Dr. Barnett, required more experts than the regular Staff could provide. Thus we find that as early as 1849 Dr. Duncan Forbes had been brought in to catalogue Persian MSS.; and in later generations the catalogue of Sanskrit MSS. was produced by Professor Bendall, those of various North Indian vernaculars by Dr. J. F. Blumhardt, of Sinhalese by Don Wickremasinghe of Oxford, of Armenian by Dr. F. C. Conybeare, and so forth.

Modern Indian printed books are received officially. Under the (Indian) Press and Registration of Books Act, 1867, each of the Provincial Governments produces periodical lists of current publications, and these lists are sent not only to the India Office, but also to the Museum, and there marked. The selected books are delivered without payment. No attempt is made to secure and preserve everything.

A

THE NEAR AND MIDDLE EAST

1. SYRIAC, KARSHUNI, ETC.

The Sloane and Harleian collections included each one Syriac MS. (Sloane MS. 3597 and Harl. MS. 5512). In 1825 a serious

THE ORIENTAL PRINTED BOOKS AND MANUSCRIPTS

beginning was made by the Parliamentary purchase of the collections of that remarkable linguist and character, Claudius James Rich, British Resident at Baghdad,[1] on which Professors Nicoll and Lee, among other Orientalists, gave evidence before the Committee of the House, the latter stating it to be "more valuable than any brought into England since the time of Pococke and Huntingdon." Of the 802 volumes 59 are Syriac and seven Karshuni. The Syriac, mostly found at Mosul, are particularly important in the section of the Jacobite and Nestorian recensions of the Bible; No. XIII, for example, is a Nestorian copy of the N.T., dated A.D. 768, while in Forshall's words, the Syriac MSS. "carry the received Peshitto text up to a remote antiquity." Many of these Rich rescued from the neglect of monks; at Rabban Hormuzd, he wrote: "there were formerly kept in this convent about five hundred volumes of old Stranghelo manuscripts on vellum; but they were thrown together in an old vault on the side of the hill, a part of which was carried away by a torrent; and the books being damaged, were deemed of no further value, and consequently were torn up and thrown about."

Four MSS. came in the Egerton bequest, and four in the Arundel MSS. in the next few years; but when Forshall and Rosen catalogued them in 1838, the former was still obliged in honesty to describe the Museum's collection as on the whole inferior to those of Oxford and Paris, and much so to the Vatican's. But by 1864 Madden could tell a very different story: since 1838, largely by Cureton's activity, there had been acquired 581 Syriac, Karshuni and Mandaitic MSS. Most of these, and the most valuable, had come in the successive purchases from the Convent of S. Mary Deipara in the Nitrian Desert (see above, pp. 108-10).

This marvellous collection, fragmentary as it is, and till sorted by Cureton in a state of confusion, at once placed the Museum's Syriac Library in a commanding position. The earliest assignable date is 411 (to the work of Titus, Bishop of Bostra, against the Manichaeans); many are of the sixth century, some being centuries older than any surviving Greek text of the works, and some dateable to the lifetime of the author, while hitherto lost works, such as Ephraems Syrus against Julian, abound. The collection enables us, it is said, to restore the Peshitto O.T. of the fifth–seventh centuries; the Psalter is present in a copy (No. CIX, VIII) of A.D. 600; and of the N.T. the then first discovered "Curetonian" fragments are of a version even earlier. The Apostolic Fathers and especially fourth-century patristic literature is well represented, but as the monks of S. Mary Deipara were Jacobites and therefore Monophysites, their theology was limited. Most of the books were written at Tekrit or Edessa in Mesopotamia, of which place Wright observes that "the learning of Greece migrated from Athens and Byzantium to Edessa, from Edessa to Baghdad, and from Baghdad to Cordova, Salerno and Montpellier"; it was there that Aristotle and Galen were translated into Arabic.[2]

The explanation of the appearance of these books so far from their place of origin is that the Abbot Moses of Nisibis travelled thither in A.D. 932, and not only secured many ancient codices, but caused texts to be copied for his Convent, to which he returned laden with 250 volumes.

Apart from scattered volumes acquired later, the collection was enlarged and varied by a number of volumes brought home in 1889 and 1890 by Sir E. A. Wallis Budge, afterwards Keeper of Egyptian and Assyrian Antiquities; these include not only works in classical Syriac literature, but also more modern Chaldean (Roman Catholic) literature, in which they resemble the S.P.C.K.'s collection now at Cambridge, rather than the Nitrian.

CATALOGUES.
Catalogus Codicum Manuscriptorum Orientalium: Pars. I, *Codices Syriacos et Carshunicos amplectens.* [By J. Forshall and F. Rosen.] 1838.
Catalogue of Syriac Manuscripts acquired since the year 1838. By W. Wright. 3 pt. 1870–73.
Descriptive List of the Syriac and Karshuni Manuscripts acquired since 1873 By G. Margoliouth. 1899.

2. HEBREW AND SAMARITAN

Hebrew, so vitally affecting the West through Christianity, is naturally the only Oriental language in which the Museum's foundation collections were strong. Cotton had only one Samaritan MS.

and three Anglo-Jewish charters; but Harley had not only a number of such charters but over 130 volumes, among which are an illuminated and calligraphic Mishnēh Thōrāh, the code of Maimonides, dated A.M. 5233 (A.D. 1472—Harl. MSS. 5698, 5699), a fine Bible in an Italian thirteenth-century hand (Harl. MSS. 5710, 5711). The most notable Hebrew volume in Sloane's library is (Sloane MS. 3029) a fourteenth-fifteenth century copy in a Spanish Rabbinic hand of a version of Aristotle's *Historia Animalium* and other tracts, mostly in physiology.

The *Editio princeps* of the Talmud, which came with the Old Royal Library, the only printed book in Hebrew in the Museum in 1759, was rejoined by its lost companions two years later through the gift by Solomon da Costa of three Hebrew MSS., one a Biblical codex copied in 1486 by a famous author and scribe, Abraham Farissol, and 180 printed books. All these, which bear Charles II's red Turkey morocco binding with his device, similarly to many volumes from the Old Royal Library, acquired during his reign, were left unpaid for at the binders, where Evelyn saw them in 1689. Da Costa as a young man had rescued them and he now presented them as a token of his gratitude to the British nation.[3]

The Lansdowne, King's, Egerton, Arundel and Stowe collections all made some small contribution of MSS.; King's MS. I is a very fine illuminated Bible, written by a Catalonian scribe in A.D. 1385 in a square Sefardi hand for a Tolosan rabbi; it subsequently belonged to a synagogue at Jerusalem and was brought back to France from Aleppo in 1683.

Purchases seem to have begun under Forshall in 1834, when ten Biblical codices (Add. MSS. 9398–9407) were bought from the library of Adam Clarke, the orientalist, Biblical commentator and historian. Five years later was acquired at Paris, from the Reina Library at Milan, what was described as a landmark and the Museum's "most prized Hebrew MS. of all," a Pentateuch with its Haftārōth and Targum, and with many other liturgical and poetic texts appended, written in a late thirteenth-century square French Rabbinic hand; while in 1844 the Sussex sale yielded another six important Biblical codices.

THE LIBRARY OF THE BRITISH MUSEUM

In 1840 nearly half the two hundred Hebrew MSS. in the Library were texts of the Bible. The absence of very early dates, which will have been noticed, is common to all collections of the Hebrew sacred writings; as soon as the books were damaged they were consigned to Genizas (synagogue lumber-rooms) or buried in cemeteries.

From this time, probably by the influence of Deutsch (see above, pp. 128-29) and of Zedner, who was appointed an Assistant in the Printed Books in 1845,[4] the scope of the collection, both manuscript and printed, widened. In the following twenty years about one hundred MSS. were acquired, and in 1848 the printed collection was enormously strengthened by the purchase of 4,420 volumes from the library of H. J. Michael of Hamburg, while in 1865 the Museum's agent in Germany, Asher, secured for the Museum for the very low price of £1,000 the library, MS. and printed, of Joseph Almanzi. The nucleus of this library is that acquired by Almanzi's father and collected by the traveller and scholar, Joseph David Azulai. The bulk is of Italian origin, and it is representative of many classes of literature, secular and imaginative as well as Biblical and Talmudic. In 1867 it could be claimed that the Museum's series of the Talmud was complete. The acquisition in 1882 of a Karaite collection, among many Hebrew volumes acquired from the dealer Shapira, put the Museum second only to the Firkovich collection at St. Petersburg; a special catalogue was issued.

In more recent years the chief acquisition has been the purchase in 1925 of the greater part of the collection of Dr. Moses Gaster. Gaster, who was a Rumanian Jew by birth and studied at Breslau, became Chief Rabbi of the Spanish and Portuguese Synagogue in London, and wherever he was collected Hebrew and Samaritan books and MSS. with avidity. The collection amounts to about one thousand volumes and is very representative. It is especially rich in the Bible, Midrash, Kabbālah and liturgies. Among the Biblical codices are fragments of early illuminated texts; a small but important piece among the Genizah fragments contains a few lines of the lost Hebrew text of Ecclesiasticus.

Since 1936 the Rabbinic section shares with Arabic in the income (about £150 a year) received under the will of James Mew, barrister,

THE ORIENTAL PRINTED BOOKS AND MANUSCRIPTS

a familiar figure in the Students' Room, who died in 1913 and left an eighth part of his estate, subject to life-interests, to the Trustees for the purpose.

With Hebrew is often classed YIDDISH. But this, though written and printed in Hebrew characters, is not Semitic, but European, being the dialect (Jüdisch) of the Jews in Germany. Yiddish books reaching the Museum are for convenience catalogued in the Oriental Library, but are preserved in the Printed Books and read in the Reading Room.

In 1850, at the instance of Zedner, Leopold Dukes compiled a MS. list of Hebrew MSS.; published catalogues have been:

Descriptive List of the Hebrew Manuscripts. By G. Margoliouth. 1893.

Commenced by Reinhardt Hoerning, Assistant in the Department, who had published unofficially:

British Museum Karaite MSS.: Descriptions and Collations of portions of the Hebrew Bible in Arabic Characters. 1889.

These texts, nearly all the work of Jews of the Karaite sect, are in 145 volumes (MSS. Or. 2459–2602); they are part of a collection, originating partly at Hit near Baghdad and partly at Cairo, which was acquired at Jerusalem in 1882, as noted above.

Catalogue of Hebrew and Samaritan Manuscripts. By G. Margoliouth. 4 pt. 1900–1935.

Part IV, by J. Leveen, contains Introduction, indexes, etc.

Catalogue of Hebrew Printed Books. By J. Zedner. 1867.
—— Supplement. By S. van Straalen. 1894.

This is beneath the level of its predecessor and successor.

3. COPTIC

The literature of Christian Egypt, called Coptic, is almost exclusively sacred in character, consisting chiefly of liturgical texts and lives of the African saints. Among the theological books are some of the very few surviving Gnostic texts, of which one, the Askew Codex, is in the Museum; Gnosticism was suppressed and its books destroyed, so that little is known of it except from those who wrote against it.

THE LIBRARY OF THE BRITISH MUSEUM

A large part of the interest of Coptic literature is in the light the language throws on that of pre-Christian Egypt. The three main dialects are all well represented. In that of Lower Egypt, the Bohairic, which became predominant, are written the liturgies of the Coptic Church; the books came mostly from the monasteries of the Nitrian Desert. The most ancient books are of the Middle Egyptian dialects, including three in the Ahmimic, which preceded the Sahidic. These with a wealth of documents were found in the Fayyûm, the source of so many papyri. The greatest wealth is, however, perhaps in the Sahidic, or dialect of Upper Egypt. Sahidic has long been known; Woide possessed some leaves, and he, and still more Archdeacon Tattam, published works on the language. From the latter's collection 21 MSS. were bought in 1868. Then, in 1883 a very large find was made, of which Paris secured the bulk, and the Museum a few valuable MSS.; and five years later Budge brought home to the Museum another considerable selection from a cache found at Atripe, a home of the papyrus industry. Budge edited a number of the most important of these Sahidic books, and also one in Nubian.

A few Coptic books retain their original bindings; see below, pp. 310–11.

CATALOGUE.

Catalogue of Coptic Manuscript. By W. E. Crum. 1905.
   The printing of this catalogue had been begun in 1895.

PUBLISHED TEXTS.

Texts relating to Saint Mêna of Egypt and Canons of Nicaea, in a Nubian Dialect. Edited by E. A. Wallis Budge. 1909.

Coptic Texts (in the Dialect of Upper Egypt). Edited by E. A. Wallis Budge.
    I. Homilies. From the Papyrus Codex Or. 5001. 1910.
    II. Biblical Texts. 1912.
    III. Apocrypha. 1913.
    IV. Martyrdoms, etc. 1914.
    V. Miscellaneous Texts. 1915.

THE ORIENTAL PRINTED BOOKS AND MANUSCRIPTS

4. ETHIOPIC

Of Ethiopic or Geez, the literary language of Abyssinia, the literature is for the most part comparatively late, being mostly of the seventeenth–nineteenth centuries, and none earlier than 1400; the books look older than they are. Those originally written in the language are few, chronicles of Abyssinia being prominent; but of the many translations from the Syriac and Arabic some preserve texts otherwise lost or imperfect, and the Ethiopic Bible includes a number of important apocryphal books.

The Museum is said to have the largest collection in Europe. When James Bruce returned in 1775 from his travels, he offered to the Museum the MSS. he had acquired. They were not numerous nor, with exceptions, important, but Bruce characteristically valued them at £25,000, and the offer was naturally not seriously considered. Apparently eight Ethiopic MSS. were in the Library when in 1846 the Church Missionary Society presented a valuable collection numbering 74 volumes, after which the first special catalogue was produced. Twenty years later the punitive expedition led by Napier against King Theodore in 1867 provided an opportunity which the Trustees did not fail to take. They sent R. R. Holmes to accompany the expedition and to search for MSS. On the march to Magdala he found few; but on the capture of the town and the death of Theodore in 1868 a library of about 1,000 volumes was found there, and these and many more were secured, it must be confessed, as loot. A selection of 350 was made by Holmes with the assistance of Werner Münzinger, a consul at Massawa. The bulk was presented to the Museum by the Secretary of State for India, under whose authority Napier's operations were conducted, but sixteen of some artistic merit (though no Ethiopic book has very much) were sent to the Queen; she retained six, and transferred the remaining ten to the Museum.

Catalogus Codicum Manuscriptorum Orientalium. Part III. 1847. By
  C. F. August Dillmann, who also catalogued the Ethiopic MSS. in
  the Bodleian.

THE LIBRARY OF THE BRITISH MUSEUM

Catalogue of the Ethiopic Manuscripts acquired since the year 1847. By W. Wright. 1877.

5. ARABIC

Of all the Oriental literatures this is by far the most studied in the Students' Room, accounting for about half the whole number of students; and the collection is the largest in the Library, amounting to some 5,300 MS. volumes (many of them composite), and 15,000 printed books.

The works of the Arabian doctors of medicine, based on the Greeks, reached Europe by way of Moslem Spain in the Middle Ages, and through Latin translations created what may be called a pre-Renaissance. But the original tongue was but little read in the West, nor for long did Arabic books find much place in Western libraries, though in the seventeenth century Munich and Oxford must be excepted.[5] At Oxford Laud greatly enriched the Bodleian by his gifts of the Oriental and other MSS. which he had amassed; and later in the century there were acquired for that library the collections, largely Arabic, of two of the chaplains to the Turkey merchants at Aleppo, Edward Pococke (who had also collected for the Archbishop) and Robert Huntington. But the foundation collections of the Museum included very few of the books of the Moslem East. The earliest acquisition of any note was that of the books collected (with the famous antiquities) by the French in Egypt, which fell to the British Crown after the Battle of the Nile. They were brought home in 1802 by Colonel (afterwards General) Tomkyns Hilgrove Turner, and were deposited, as were the marbles,[4] in the Museum. Three years later Nares, reporting to the Trustees, found nothing lacking to his Department but some person capable of describing these MSS.

But, as Rieu observed in the preface to the Catalogue of Persian MSS., the true founder of our Oriental Library in the four sections of Syriac, Arabic, Persian and Turkish was Claudius Rich; and of the 800 volumes in his collection nearly half were Arabic.

Nares's desideratum was supplied in the persons of Forshall and

THE ORIENTAL PRINTED BOOKS AND MANUSCRIPTS

Cureton, with the result that not only was the existing collection catalogued, but (a common consequence) more acquisitions were made. A list of the chief sources is as follows:

(1) 1845, Major William Yule, of the East India Company's service; presented by his sons;
(2) 1851, the missionary and traveller, Dr. Sternschuss;
(3) 1852, Col. Robert Taylor, British Resident at Baghdad; bought from his son-in-law.
(4) 1853, Consul Barker.

With Cureton's retirement in 1850 there is a gap of nearly twenty years; but soon after Rieu's accession in 1867 to the Keepership of the new Department of Oriental Manuscripts the series begins afresh:

(5) 1872, Alexander Jaba, Russian Consul at Erzerum;
(6) 1875, Sir Charles Murray, Consul-General in Egypt from 1844;
(7) 1877, Sir Henry Rawlinson, the famous archaeologist, who succeeded Taylor as Resident at Baghdad; the holders of that office, Rich, Taylor and Rawlinson, served the Museum in the nineteenth century as the Chaplains at Aleppo served the Bodleian in the seventeenth;
(8) 1886, Alfred Freiherr von Kremer, a scholar who lived in Damascus and Cairo and collected books illustrating the early period of Islam;
(9) 1889, Dr. Eduard Glaser, who had travelled in Yemen and collected the Zaidi literature of the country, in which his MSS. are rich;
(10) 1889 and 1891, Wallis Budge, while on official archaeological expeditions, secured at Mosul a number of MSS., notable being the illustrated Dioscorides mentioned below;
(11) 1883, a few important volumes came with the Stowe MSS. (see pp. 257–9).
(12) 1891 and 1893, E. W. Lane, the Arabic lexicographer; his MSS. include the materials gathered by him for his *Lexicon* and *Manners and Customs of the Egyptians*, the latter consisting mainly of popular tales;
(13) 1918, Darea Baroness Zouche bequeathed the MSS. Eastern and Western, collected in the eighteen-thirties by Robert Curzon as specimens of writing (see pp. 108–9, 362);
(14) 1920, the so-called Sultan's Library from Constantinople, an assemblage which contained a very few volumes from that library;

THE LIBRARY OF THE BRITISH MUSEUM

(15) 1926–1934, the late R. S. Greenshields made anonymously a long series of gifts of beautiful illuminated or calligraphic MSS., some Persian, but mostly Arabic;

(16) 1936 onwards, the Arabic collection shares with Rabbinic Hebrew (see above, pp. 298–9) in the income from the James Mew bequest.

Though inferior to the Royal Library at Cairo in copies of the Koran, the Museum has in Or. MS. 2165, containing about two-thirds of the text written in large Kufi characters, probably in the second century of the Hegira, what is perhaps the most ancient Koran ever brought to Europe; while some here are as fine as any at Cairo, such as the great seven-volume illuminated copy (Or. MS. 22406–22412), executed in A.D. 1304, for the Sultan Rukn al-Dīn Baibars, the lovely copy (Or. MS. 1270) written in a minute Maghribi script on delicate vellum about the middle of the thirteenth century A.D., probably in Andalusia, then under Moslem rule, or that of Section 25 alone executed in huge gold characters for the Sultan Uljaitu at Mosul in A.D. 1310 (710 A.H.).

Theological and secular literature are both fully represented. Greek science is present in some very rare illustrated texts, notably (Or. MS. 3366) a copy of Dioscorides on materia medica, transcribed in 735 A.H. For history might be selected Or. MS. 1617, a complete copy of the rare Kitāb al-Maghāzī, by al-Wākidī, on the campaigns of Muhammad, copied in 564 A.H., or the equally rare account of the Prophet's times, al-Muhabbar, by Muhammad b. Habīb (Or. MS. 2807). Arab scholars paid great attention to lexicography. Or. MS. 5811, Ibn Duraid's lexicon, dates in part from the tenth century A.D., almost in the author's lifetime. Another acquired only some ten years ago, al Kitāb al-Bāri‘ (Or. MS. 9811), has been published in facsimile by the Trustees; this volume is not indeed a complete copy of what must have been a vast compilation, but apart from this and a smaller fragment at Paris the work is unknown.

Printing reached Asia late, and there is no early printed Koran to be a counterpart to the Gutenberg Bible. But since the later part of the nineteenth century Arabic printed books have been multiplied in all the chief cities of the Moslem world in such quantities that the Museum has to be content with buying a selection of the best.

THE ORIENTAL PRINTED BOOKS AND MANUSCRIPTS

Of the older literature it is claimed that there is no classical work not represented by a manuscript and, where one exists, by a printed copy.

Catalogus Codicum Manuscriptorum Orientalium. Pars Secunda, Codicum Arabicorum partem complectens. [By W. Cureton.] 1847.
—— Continuatio. [Also by Cureton.] 1852.
—— Supplement. [By C. Rieu.] 1871.
—— Supplement. [By C. Rieu.] 1894.
Descriptive List of Arabic Manuscripts acquired since 1894. By A. G. Ellis and E. Edwards. 1912.
A Facsimile of the Manuscript of al-Kitāb al-Bāri (Or. 9811). Edited with an introduction by A. S. Fulton. 1933.
    See above.
Catalogue of Arabic Books.
    Vols. I, II. By A. G. Ellis. 1894, 1901.
    Supplement. By A. S. Fulton and A. G. Ellis. 1926.
    Vol. III. Index. By A. S. Fulton. 1935.

6. Persian

By the beginning of the nineteenth century the Museum was little if at all richer in Persian than in Arabic literature, possessing hardly 150 out of the 3,000 and more volumes of which the MS. collection now consists. Bentley, it is true, had acquired for the Royal Library the Persian and Zend MSS. of Parsi literature collected by Thomas Hyde, Bodley's Librarian (*d.* 1703), for his *Historia religionis veterum Persarum*; while in 1794 and 1796 were acquired the collections of two East Indian officials, Captain Charles Hamilton and Nathaniel Brassey Halhed, the translator of the Gentoo Laws,[6] and in 1825 the Rev. John Fowler Hull bequeathed that formed forty years before by James Grant, another distinguished servant of the Company in the period of the inspiration and patronage of Warren Hastings and Sir William Jones, which have thus enriched the Museum as well as the library of East India House, now the India Office, in Persian as well as in Indo-Persian, since from the one to the other is a natural and indeed inevitable step.

But in Persian, as well as in Arabic, Syriac and Turkish, Rich's collection, received in the year following Hull's bequest, placed the

THE LIBRARY OF THE BRITISH MUSEUM

Museum collection on a new footing, for its quantity, of over 300 volumes, was matched by its quality; it covered a wide range and provided a large number of very early copies of classics and also of works by hitherto unknown authors.7

The chief acquisitions later than these are the collections formed by the following:

(1) 1847 and 1850, Major William Yule, who formed his collection (267 MSS., 232 of them Persian) while Assistant Resident at Lucknow and at Delhi; chiefly history and poetry: presented in two sections by his sons;

(2) 1862, 1865, Major-General Sir John Malcolm (1764–1839), the author of *A History of Persia*, 1815, and *Sketches of Persia*, 1827, who twice went on political missions from Calcutta to Teheran, and was a great lover of Persian poetry; the MSS. collected by him included finely written and illuminated (as well as textually valuable) copies of such classics as the Shahnamah and the Bustān of Sa'di; 47 volumes of a value out of proportion to their number;

(3) 1864, William Cureton; 156 MSS., 106 Persian; bought after his death; this is the only considerable Persian acquisition since Hyde's which was collected in England, where the opportunities were naturally far less abundant than in the East;

(4) 1865, William Erskine (1773–1852), Rich's son-in-law, author of *The History of India under the first two sovereigns of the House of Timur, Baber and Humayam*, 1854; 436 volumes of his English papers, with those of John Leyden, Scott's protégé, were presented in the same year by Claude Erskine.

(5) 1868, Colonel George William Hamilton (1807–68), of whose collection of 1,000 MSS. very many were rescued by him from destruction during the Indian Mutiny, especially at Lucknow, several bearing the vermilion stamp of the library of the Kings of Oudh; a selection of 352 volumes, 253 of them Persian and Parsi, was made for the Museum;

(6) 1877, Sir Henry Rawlinson's collection, mentioned above under Arabic, included 104 Persian volumes.

(7) 1878, Sir Henry M. Elliot (1808–54), Foreign Secretary to the Government of India; Elliot expanded Erskine's scheme and collected for a comprehensive edition of the best native works on the whole Moslem period in India, and compiled a great survey of the literature; of his 458 MSS. 429 are Persian;

(8) 1883–95, Sidney J. A. Churchill, Persian Secretary to the British

THE ORIENTAL PRINTED BOOKS AND MANUSCRIPTS

Legation at Teheran, collected and presented 240 MSS., mostly history and poetry, being over half the Persian MSS. acquired in the period, many of them containing rare texts, while others contain firmans and autographs; also a quantity of rare printed books, mostly lithographed in very small editions.

Really ancient Persian MSS. are of extreme rarity, and the Museum has none earlier than the seventh century of the Hegira (the thirteenth A.D.); from this century dates our oldest copy of the Shāhnāmah, which came in 1851 with Dr. Sternschuss's (chiefly Arabic) MSS. But in all branches of the literature the collection is now very rich, and especially in its two most important classes, history and poetry. These two classes naturally afforded the best opportunities for illumination; and here the Museum's wealth can only be matched in the West, or perhaps in the East either, by the Bibliothèque Nationale, though the Bodleian and the India Office in this country and in New York the Morgan Library and the Metropolitan Museum of Art possess many splendid specimens, while the private collection of Mr. Chester Beatty ranks very high. It is indeed remarkable that so many books of high quality survive the tragedies of Asiatic history. And while calligraphy was esteemed as the queen of the arts, and the calligrapher's calling as one of honour, the strict Moslem, in fear of idolatry and of blasphemously imitating the creative act of God, obeyed the Prophet's prohibition of pictures, and most of all of pictures of the human form. Hence perhaps the frequent mutilation of the faces in illuminated books, which were often kept in the women's quarters. A. von le Cocq tells how, about 1897, a peasant in Turfan, having found a number of Manichean MSS., decorated with pictures in gold and colours, and thus important for the early history of Persian art, threw five cartloads of them into a river as unholy things.[8]

But, though abhorred by the general public, painting was always patronized in princely courts, and it was there that the finest examples were made. The ancient romance of Kalīlah wa-Dimnah, Nizāmī's Khamsah and the Gulistān and the Bustān of Sa'dī were repeatedly illuminated—the great national epic the Shāhnāmah much less so, strange as it may seem. Of the Museum's finest volumes in this class only a few can be mentioned:

THE LIBRARY OF THE BRITISH MUSEUM

Or. MS. 2265, the Khamsah of Niẓāmī, on the copying of which the celebrated calligrapher Shāh Maḥmūd was occupied for four years (1539–43); its decorations, which were made by the Court painters of Shāh Ṭahmāsp, include an equestrian portrait of that prince in the character of Bahrām Gūr hunting the wild ass—known to English readers by the lines in Fitzgerald's Omar Khayyám:

> Or Bahram, that great hunter, the wild ass
> Stamps o'er his head, but cannot break his sleep;

Add. MS. 18579, a copy of the Anwār-i-Suhailī, from the great library made for the Emperor Akbar, which occupied his Court calligrapher and painters even longer, being finished in A.D. 1016, after at least six years' labour.

Or. MSS. 6810, Niẓāmī's epic Sikandar, decorated by Bihzad, who rivals Mani as the most famous Islamic painter.

Add. MS. 6613, a late copy of the Khamsah, but of peculiar interest as containing an illustration of the beautiful legend (if it be a legend) of Jesus and the dead dog, in which the Apostles are dressed as contemporary Portuguese.

A few MSS. from Akbar's Library, and bearing the vermilion stamp of that of the kings of Oudh, are decorated and signed by Hindu artists. Separate specimens of the Hindu schools are to be found outside the Library, among Oriental Prints and Drawings.

In 1849 the Trustees engaged Dr. Duncan Forbes, professor of Oriental languages at King's College, London, to catalogue the collection, then amounting to about 1,000 volumes. But his work underwent complete revision, as well as the large additions due to acquisitions, after his abandonment of the work in 1855. A. G. Ellis, who joined the staff in 1883, was at first engaged on the Persian collection, but was very soon diverted to Arabic.

Catalogue of Persian Manuscripts. By Charles Rieu. 3 vols. 1879–83.
—— Supplement. 1895.
Catalogue of Persian Printed Books. By Edward Edwards. 1922.
Dīwān i zu'l-Fakār: a facsimile of the MS. (Or. 9777). Edited with an introduction by Edward Edwards. 1934.

THE ORIENTAL PRINTED BOOKS AND MANUSCRIPTS

7. Turkish

The Harleian Library contained thirty-four Turkish MSS., including old copies of early poetry, and also an illuminated volume (Harl. MS. 5500) containing a translation of an otherwise unknown Persian "Mirabilia mundi." Here also in 1826 the Rich collection first gave the Museum's collection real importance, adding 124 carefully selected volumes. After this 49 MSS. came in 1872 from M. Jaba, and a few volumes came with most of the Persian collections acquired, naturally enough, since Persian was the model for both the pre-classical and classical Turkish literature, i.e. the whole which preceded the Europeanizing movement of the mid-nineteenth century; like Greece, Persia "took captive her fierce conquerors." By 1888, when Rieu produced the catalogue, the collection consisted of 483 volumes. Of these the great majority are by Osmanli or Western Turkish authors; among them are perhaps a dozen illuminated volumes of the fifteenth, sixteenth and seventeenth centuries A.D.; such specimens are rare, since rigid Mohammedan iconoclasts defaced them. Eastern Turkish literature is very much less abundant, and early specimens are very rare. The collection contains, however, some archaic texts, dating from the ninth century of the Hegira (the fourteenth A.D.) and over fifty from the next. They include some rare Divans and the Senglakh, or Turki-Persian dictionary compiled by a secretary of Nadīr Shāh, which was previously unknown in the West except in an abridgment. Eastern Turkish illumination does not differ in style from Persian; it is well represented.

The collection of modern Turkish printed books, like that of Persian, owes much to the gifts by Sidney Churchill.

Catalogue of Turkish Manuscripts. By Charles Rieu. 1888.

8. Armenian and Georgian

A few Armenian MSS. are found in the Sloane, Harleian and Lansdowne collections, and two came from Rich. Others have been added casually, but not in any large number at one time. In 1836

THE LIBRARY OF THE BRITISH MUSEUM

Panizzi instigated the Trustees to secure a Parliamentary grant for the purchase of all the publications issued by the press of the Mechitarist monks of the Island of San Lazzaro near Venice, whence had just appeared the great dictionary of the language.

Georgian, a more secular literature than Armenian, which is very largely religious, is represented by six MSS., two of which were in the Sloane Library.

In 1870 Dr. Baronian commenced a catalogue of the MSS. in both languages, but left it incomplete.

Catalogue of Armenian Manuscripts. By F. C. Conybeare. To which is appended a Catalogue of Georgian Manuscripts by J. O. Wardrop. 1913.

9. NEAR EASTERN BINDINGS

Fine Eastern bindings are not so numerous as Western, in spite of the high repute which binders, like other book-artists, enjoyed throughout the Moslem world under the patronage of Caliphs and Emperors. The history of Near and Middle Asia is full of the unhappy records of the sack of rich and cultivated cities by ignorant or fanatical soldieries, whether Mongols, who destroyed the library of the Abbasids at Baghdad, or Crusaders, who burned that of Tripolis. The great library of the Moghuls, which is said, hardly credibly, to have contained in the seventeenth century 24,000 richly bound volumes, was dispersed and spoiled. The most beautiful examples which survive from the great centuries of the art of the leather-workers of Islam are now scattered in many libraries, and it can only be claimed that the Museum has a fair representation, especially of those richly worked wallet-like covers from Persia.

Its most valuable Oriental bindings are not Islamic but are earlier and from Egypt; they cover ancient Coptic books. Many such, preserved whole or more often in fragments, are to be seen in the Rainer collection at Vienna, in the Morgan Library at New York, at Berlin and elsewhere; the most ancient known is a sixth-century codex (containing two treatises of Philo) at Paris. From the next

THE ORIENTAL PRINTED BOOKS AND MANUSCRIPTS

century dates the Museum's Papyrus IV (the original contents giving the indication of date), which is in a cover of appliqué and incised leathers over papyrus millboards. One of the very few complete ancient Coptic bindings is that on Or. MS. 5000; specially important are also Papyrus V and Or. MS. 5001, the latter containing a collection of homilies which was edited for the Trustees by Wallis Budge. The geometrical figures and tools, representing rosettes and grotesque animals (sometimes also to be found in the Bestiaries) used on these and similar bindings had, by channels now unknown, an influence on the Western binders of the twelfth century.[9]

B

INDIA, WITH CEYLON AND BURMA

1. SANSKRIT AND PALI

In original works in these ancient tongues, Sanskrit, that of the sacred Vedic books and of the classical literature which followed them, and Pali, which succeeded it as the lingua franca of the learned by the fourth century before our era, the Museum is relatively less rich than in other important literatures. Sloane had six Sanskrit MSS., and in 1796 Nathaniel Halhed's collection added, with his more numerous Persian MSS., fourteen more. Under the enlightened rule of the great Warren Hastings that Indians should be governed by Indian law, it was necessary for English lawyers in the country to study the codes, which in the eighteenth century they had to do with the aid of native pandits, Sanskrit not being understood.[10] Some in fact were found to express the opinion that the Sanskrit tongue was not ancient at all, but was a modern invention of the priests, designed to support their impostures, a theory characteristic of the age of the *philosophes*. But the work of Sir William Jones was bearing fruit, and in 1798 the East India Company instituted a library of its own, directing its officers in the East to supply it with native literatures as opportunity offered. This library, now that of the India

THE LIBRARY OF THE BRITISH MUSEUM

Office, has received the bulk of the important MS. collections from India, as well as many from neighbouring countries, that have reached this country since that date; and its Sanskrit collections are especially important.[10] Oxford also became a second rival magnet with the foundation in 1827 by Colonel Joseph Boden of his Sanskrit Professorship, and the appointment to it five years later of Horace Hayman Wilson.[11]

The Museum has thus been somewhat overshadowed in this field. But a few collections missed East India House and Whitehall and came to Bloomsbury. Fourteen MSS., of interest as collected in South India, came in 1829 from the collector, T. H. Bates; and in recent times has been acquired the splendid series of 143 MSS. formed in Rajputana by Dr. H. Jacobi and for the most part bearing on Jainism. But beyond these it is significant that the Museum is chiefly indebted for its MS. Sanskrit library to three men connected with it, the omnivorous collector and great benefactor, Sir A. W. Franks, Keeper of Antiquities, William Wright and Bendall.

The MSS. described in 1902 cover, beside the Vedic literature, that of the classical period, both Brahmanic and Buddhist, and also general works by Jain authors, for among the Jain community after the earliest period Sanskrit succeeded their own dialect; works in this latter, the Jaina Prakit, Bendall reserved for another volume.

If the manuscript collection is not of the first importance, that of printed books is probably the richest in the world. The Pali printed books are most notably rich in Burmese and Ceylonese publications.

The first member of the Printed Books Staff recorded as having charge of Sanskrit books was Charles Bruce, who retired in 1866 and was succeeded by Dr. Ernst Hass. Until this time Oriental titles were forced into the Procrustes bed of the Ninety-One Rules, to which they are quite unsuited. In the Manuscripts there had been an Indian scholar near the beginning of the nineteenth century in the person of Maurice; and in the eighteen-thirties a much more distinguished scholar and a Sanskritist, Friedrich August Rosen, had been employed, though mostly, it would seem, on Part I of the General Catalogue of Oriental Manuscripts, till his premature death in 1837. In recent times the Museum's chief Sanskritists have been

THE ORIENTAL PRINTED BOOKS AND MANUSCRIPTS

Cecil Bendall and Dr. L. D. Barnett, and two provided by the Department of Coins and Medals: the late Professor E. J. Rapson and Mr. John Allan.

Catalogue of Sanskrit Manuscripts. By Cecil Bendall. 1902.
Catalogue of Sanskrit and Pali Books. By Ernst Haas. 1876.
—— *Supplementary Catalogue.* By Cecil Bendall. 1893.
—— *Supplementary Catalogue.* By L. D. Barnett. 1908.
—— *Supplementary Catalogue.* 1928.

2. HINDI, PANJABI, HINDUSTANI, SINDHI AND PUSHTU

The Hindi tongue evolved through the Northern Prakrit dialects, which in their turn were the offspring of the Sanskrit, very much as the Romance languages of Southern Europe were the offspring of Latin when it spread and declined; and its literature bears a close affinity in subject and in other ways to the classical mother-tongue. In the scarce works of the early period (the twelfth-sixteenth centuries), the Museum has not many MSS.; but the case is very different with the middle period (sixteenth-eighteenth centuries).

Hindustani, commonly called Urdu, was in its turn the offspring of Hindi. From the twelfth century, under the Muhammedan rulers of Delhi and the Deccan, it acquired an admixture of Arabic and Persian words, and in this composite form was employed by men of letters, as Chaucer and Gower employed the mixed English and French of the Angevin kings and their court of Norman-descended nobility.

Panjabi, widely used in the Panjab, is akin to Hindi. Sindhi, derived from a Western secondary Prakrit, has no large literature; while Pushtu, the Iranian dialect of Afghanistan and the North-West Frontier of India, has still less.

From William Erskine came works in Jain literature, Hindi and Panjabi religious poems, and historical texts; from Sir Henry M. Elliot MSS. in Hindustani on history and topography and on the North-West Provinces in general; from Colonel George W. Hamilton poetry, and from the Rev. A. Fisher religious treatises written in Gurumukhi characters.

All the catalogues in this group were compiled by Professor J. F.

THE LIBRARY OF THE BRITISH MUSEUM

Blumhardt, formerly of the Indian Provincial Civil Service; he was attached to the Department of Printed Books before the printed Orientalia were transferred.

Catalogue of the Hindi, Panjabi, and Hindostani Manuscripts, 1899.
Catalogues of Hindi, Panjabi, Sindhi and Pushtu Printed Books. 1893.
    For Pushtu MSS. see the next section.
A Supplementary Catalogue of Hindi Books. 1913.
Catalogue of Hindustani Printed Books. 1889.
A Supplementary Catalogue of Hindustani Books. 1909.

3. Marathi, Gujarati, Bengali, Oriya, Assamese, etc.

MSS. here are not very numerous. The group includes Marathi (formerly known as Mahratta) and Gujarati MSS. from the varied collection formed by Erskine and others; other tongues are Bengali, Oriya, Assamese, including two interesting MSS. one historical and the other poetical, written on leaves of bark, Sindhi, and Pushtu; among the last are two important and previously unknown histories of the Afghans. For Pushtu printed books see the preceding section. The Bengali is a rich literature, which flourished from the fifteenth to the eighteenth century, but was then much spoiled by a fashion of dependence on Sanskrit and a large admixture of Sanskrit words. The Museum's collection of printed texts in these tongues, but especially in Bengali, is abundantly rich.

The following catalogues, like those in the preceding section, were compiled by Blumhardt:

Catalogue of the Marathi, Gujarati, Bengali, Assamese, Oriya, Pushtu and Sindhi Manuscripts. 1905.
Catalogue of Marathi and Gujarati Printed Books. 1892.
—— *A Supplementary Catalogue.* 1915.
Catalogue of Bengali Books. 1886.
—— *Supplementary Catalogue.* 1910.
—— *Second Supplementary Catalogue* (1911–1934). By J. F. Blumhardt and J. V. S. Wilkinson. 1939.

THE ORIENTAL PRINTED BOOKS AND MANUSCRIPTS

4. Kannada, Badaga, Kurg

The Kannada, also called Canarese, the language of the Carnatic, possesses a very ancient and abundant literature, of which the oldest surviving specimen dates from the middle of the eighth century, and the classical period, extending from then to the twelfth century, is chiefly Jain. The Museum collection is important.

In Badaga, an archaic dialect of Kannada, and Kurg, or Coorg, very little literature is extant.

A Catalogue of Kannada, Badaga and Kurg Books. . . . Compiled by L. D. Barnett. 1910.

5. Burmese

The chief interest of Burmese literature lies in its preservation of early Buddhism, which its missionaries introduced into Burma, and through Burma into the Further East by means of their Pali books. There are in the collection some books printed by Christian missionaries in about 1770–80.

A Catalogue of the Burmese Books. . . . By L. D. Barnett. 1913.

6. Tamil

The Tamil collection is of special consequence, since that literature is the oldest and most varied in India with the single exception of the Sanskrit; and in one point of historical interest it even surpasses the Sanskrit, in that (with Telugu and Kannada) it is a survival of the ancient Dravidian culture which was overlaid by the Aryan conquest of the peninsula. As in Burma, so in South India eighteenth-century Christian missionaries set up a press, and the Museum has a number of their productions.

Catalogue of the Tamil Books. . . . By L. D. Barnett and G. U. Pope. 1909.

Dr. Upham Pope had commenced this catalogue some twenty years earlier; it was left to be completed by Dr. Barnett.

—— Supplement. By L. D. Barnett. 1921.

THE LIBRARY OF THE BRITISH MUSEUM

7. TELUGU

Telugu, otherwise known as Andhra, is, like Tamil, a Dravidian language. Though it is the tongue spoken by twenty million people in South India and Ceylon, and though its literature is old and rich, falling into two periods, that of poetry lasting from the eleventh to the fifteenth century, and a mature or Augustan age, following it and lasting till the eighteenth, literary Andhra later fell so low as very nearly to die out altogether in the last century. It has, however, been revived.

A Catalogue of the Telugu Books. . . . By L. D. Barnett. 1912.

8. SINHALESE

Sinhalese (or Ceylonese) is the vernacular tongue of a large majority of the people of Ceylon. It is closely allied to Pali, which was the literary language, especially of the Buddhist scholars, in Ceylon as well as in Burma, and is still kept up. Much Sinhalese literature is translated from Pali, but some is original. Sloane had five MSS. and there are two in the Old Royal Library, doubtless brought home by English traders in the East Indies. In 1737–55 Dutch missionaries printed some works in Sinhalese.

The catalogues recorded below were the first of this literature to be published, with the exception, much earlier indeed but also much smaller, of Westergaard's work at Copenhagen in 1846. Both the Museum catalogues were the work of Don Martino de Zilva Wickremasinghe, Librarian of the Indian Institute of the University of Oxford.

Catalogue of the Sinhalese Manuscripts. 1900.
Catalogue of the Sinhalese Printed Books. 1901.

THE ORIENTAL PRINTED BOOKS AND MANUSCRIPTS

C

CENTRAL AND EASTERN ASIA

1. CHINESE

As early as 1606 the Bodleian had purchased a handful of Chinese books, and more were received in Laud's benefaction.[11] A few had a place in the Sloane, Harleian, Old Royal and Lansdowne collections; in 1761 attention was called in *The General Contents of the British Museum* to those in the second Sloane Room. One of these, a New Testament harmony, provided Robert Morrison with the first material for his study of the language, between 1805 and 1807. But the earliest considerable acquisition came in 1825 as part of the bequest of Fowler Hull. In 1834 the East India Company's monopoly in China ceased, and most of the collections which reached England in the following decades came not to the Company's library but to the Museum. The first of these comprised a number of volumes taken in the course of the war in South China, 1840–42; they were sent to the Queen and transferred by her. Their preservation was undoubtedly due to John Robert Morrison, Robert's son and successor, as official Chinese Secretary, who was with the forces. His father's large Chinese library had been offered to the Museum in 1834 for £2,000, but the Trustees' small funds were curtailed at that time by the purchase for £750 of the "Alcuin" Bible, and the books went to the University of London, now University College; the books had been used by the younger Morrison after his return to England in 1834 for the education of candidates for the Chinese mission field. He followed his father's example in forming a great Chinese library, and this was bought by Government and presented in 1847. It consisted of 11,509 volumes, and included over thirty collections of the drama, practically a new element in the Museum, as well as law, geography, local history and Buddhist literature. In the year before this a large collection of MSS. and maps was deposited by the order of the foreign minister, the Earl of Aberdeen.

In Douglas's time the chief single acquisition was the purchase

THE LIBRARY OF THE BRITISH MUSEUM

of the large collection formed by Sir Ernest Satow, which consisted mainly of Japanese literature (see below, p. 320), but also included many valuable printed classical, literary and Buddhist works in Chinese from early presses in Korea and Japan. The remaining great accessions have come in since his day. These are the Backhouse and Stein collections.

The former, acquired in 1908, is distinguished by a number of fine Ming editions, a large thesaurus entitled *Yu Hai*, or the *Sea of Jade*, a complete set of the twenty-four dynastic histories, among many rare and valuable books.

The latter is part of the result of the three celebrated expeditions led by Sir Aurel Stein to the deserts of Eastern Turkestan in 1900–01, 1906–08 and 1913–16, and described by him in his great works, *Ancient Khotan* (1907), *Serindia* (1921) and *Innermost Asia*, 1928. They are doubtless the last great finds that will leave China, as native scholars are now using political pressure to withhold such facilities as Stein, and before him Bower, enjoyed. Stein's expeditions were based on a systematic scheme for exploration of these areas proposed by him to the Government of India in 1898 in consequence of Bower's and later finds made and reported by Indian officials; his expeditions were sent by that Government with contributions from the Treasury; and consequently his collections have been divided between the India Office Library and the Museum, a part of the Museum's share being the whole of the Chinese documents found, apart from some which went to Peking and Paris.

These explorations produced Chinese written and printed documents far more ancient than any previously possessed by the Library, or indeed than had been known in the West. The Gobi Desert in Eastern Turkestan is so rainless and so utterly unvisited that on his second journey Stein, travelling over the same route, found his own footsteps of several years before, a sight at least as ghostly as Friday's were to Robinson Crusoe. Its sands are therefore as perfect a preservative of paper as those of Egypt are of papyrus. As a result the 7,000 rolls (including fragments) brought to London have suffered no damage from damp, in spite of their age. The great find was made in an inner chamber of a shrine, one of the Temples of the

THE ORIENTAL PRINTED BOOKS AND MANUSCRIPTS

Thousand Buddhas, at Tun-huang, on the desert's edge, where they had lain, bricked up and forgotten, for nine hundred years. Among the MSS. are some 380 pieces, which bear dates ranging from A.D. 406 to 995, and also tablets and block-prints, several dated, the earliest being the Diamond Sutra of A.D. 868, the oldest dated piece of print in the world. The collection also contains the oldest known examples on paper.[12]

After the Four Years' War the Chinese collection grew steadily under the care of Dr. Lionel Giles.[13] The extensive series of new editions of the classics of all periods which native scholars produce, and also encyclopaedias, which are a speciality, if not the invention, of their race, have been methodically acquired. Of the great old encyclopaedias (or rather classified collections of writings), the vastest and one of the most ancient, the *Yung Lo ta tien*, made for the Ming Emperor Yung Lo early in the fifteenth century A.D., is represented, not indeed by a complete set, which is nowhere known, but by a great number of its volumes; and in recent years photostats of others have been added by exchange with the National Library of Peiping.

Before Douglas's time Chinese books were catalogued by Louis Augustin Prévost, a native of Troyes, who came to England in 1823. He was on the staff from 1843 to his death in 1858.[14]

Catalogue of Chinese Printed Books, Manuscripts and Drawings in the Library of the British Museum. By Robert Kennaway Douglas. 1877.

This was believed to be "the first catalogue ever published in Europe of an extensive Chinese library"; it described over 20,000 volumes. Chinese types had to be imported from Shanghai for its production.

—— *Supplementary Catalogue.* By R. K. Douglas. 1903.
Catalogue of the Backhouse Chinese Library. By Lionel Giles. 1908. Unofficial.
[*Catalogue of the Stein Collection.*] Completed by Dr. Giles before his retirement in 1940, but not yet published. Dr. Giles has described the dated MSS. in a series of articles published in the *Bulletin of the School of Oriental Studies*, 1935–43.
Guide to an Exhibition of the Stein Collection. 1914.

THE LIBRARY OF THE BRITISH MUSEUM

2. JAPANESE

That many Japanese books reached Europe between 1542, when the country was discovered, and the final exclusion of foreigners in 1637, may be doubted. Certainly, of any which may have been brought home either by Dutch traders or by St. Francis Xavier's missionaries, few reached England; books in the language entirely escaped Laud's broadcast net, and we find only a handful in the libraries of Cotton (where it is rather surprising to find any), the Harley's and Sloane. Banks's travels in the Pacific and widespread interest resulted in some coming with his library; but it was not till the last third of the nineteenth century that the Museum's collection assumed a representative character. In 1868 and 1884 were purchased the large collections formed by the traveller, Philipp Franz von Siebold, and by Ernest, afterwards Sir Ernest, Satow, who had played a very important part in the diplomatic opening of the country, and who had used his opportunities to seek out especially the productions of the early presses of Japan and Korea.

What must be a very important section of any Japanese library, that of works on the native arts, was first made adequate by the purchase in 1882 of the collection of William Anderson; this was increased by the acquisition in 1894 of a further similar collection from the same, and in 1900, from his executors, of yet a third. This last collection was rich in representative albums of drawings. Anderson's writings on Japanese art contributed to the knowledge of the popular and by the Japanese little-regarded, but exquisite colour-printed wood engravings of the great period (A.D. 1700–1840), and also, it is to be feared,[15] to the further degradation of the art, already fallen from its prime, by creating a large European demand only to be supplied by the mass production of poor and mechanical work. The main collection of Japanese colour-prints, separate or as published in albums, is to be seen in the Print Room.

At the end of the nineteenth century the Japanese library amounted to something over 5,000 volumes. Since the retirement of Douglas the Museum has had no expert in the language and literature either on the regular Staff of the Department or attached to it. The inevit-

THE ORIENTAL PRINTED BOOKS AND MANUSCRIPTS

able result is that the acquisitions of the last generation have been neither large nor important.

Catalogue of Japanese Printed Books and Manuscripts. By R. K. Douglas. 1898.
— *acquired during the years* 1889–1903. By R. K. Douglas. 1904.

3. TIBETAN, ETC.

The Museum's most important Tibetan books and pieces came from Stein's finds in Eastern Turkestan. The chief of these were described by Dr. L. D. Barnett in *The Journal of the Royal Asiatic Society*, January 1903. They are nearly all Buddhist, and many are as old as the eighth century A.D. There are also records of ancient sgraffiti.

Other Central Asian tongues are represented in the Stein collection, such as Sogdian (resembling Chinese), Khotanese, Kuchean, Turkish, both Manichaean and "Runic," and Uigur, with documents on leather and on bamboo-slips written in a very early Prakrit in the cursive Kharosthi script. Full accounts can be found in Stein's three great works.

4. SOUTHERN ASIA

There are in the Library a very few Javanese and other Southern Asiatic MSS.

APPENDICES

I

THE ELECTED TRUSTEES

(Those marked with an * are Trustees in Office, 1943)

First Election 1753	Archibald, Duke of Argyll Hugh, Earl of Northumberland (Duke of Northumberland, K.G.) Lord Charles Cavendish Hugh, Lord Willoughby of Parham Hon. Philip Yorke, M.P. (Earl of Hardwicke) Sir George Lyttelton, Bart., M.P. (Lord Lyttelton) Sir John Evelyn, Bart. William Sloane James West (afterwards P.R.S.) Nicholas Hardinge Charles Gray Colonel William Sotheby Thomas Birch, D.D. John Ward, LL.D. William Watson (afterwards Sir W. Watson, F.R.S.)	1783	Sir William Musgrave, Bart.
1761	Arthur Onslow Gustavus Brander		
1765	John, Earl of Bute, K.G. James Harris Daniel Wray		
1766	Charles Lyttelton, Bishop of Carlisle Matthew Duane		
1767	Hans Sloane		
1768	William, Earl of Bessborough		
1769	Hon. Edwin Sandys (Lord Sandys)		
1772	Richard Kaye, D.D. (Sir R. Kaye, Bart.)		
1773	Henry Cavendish		
1783	Sir William Hamilton, K.B.		

1784	Rev. Clayton Mordaunt Cracherode
1787	Thomas Tyrwhitt
1787	Heneage, Earl of Aylesford George, Earl of Leicester (Marquess Townshend) John Douglas, D.D. (Bishop of Salisbury) Thomas Astle
1791	Charles Townley George John, Earl Spencer, K.G
1793	Augustus Henry, Duke of Grafton, K.G. Frederick Montagu
1797	Lord Frederick Campbell
1799	Shute Barrington, Bishop of Durham
1800	John, Marquess of Bute
1801	Alexander, Earl of Rosslyn
1802	Philip, Earl of Hardwicke, K.G.
1804	Sir William Scott, M.P. (Lord Stowell) George Rose
1805	Alleyne, Lord St. Helens, G.C.H. George, Earl Macartney, K.B.
1806	George Granville, Marquess of Stafford, K.G. (Duke of Sutherland)
1807	William Wyndham, Lord Grenville
1810	Thomas Dampier, Bishop of Ely George, Viscount St. Asaph (Earl of Ashburnham, K.G.)
1811	Dudley, Earl of Harrowby
1812	Sylvester, Lord Glenbervie Charles Long (Lord Farnborough, G.C.B.)

THE LIBRARY OF THE BRITISH MUSEUM

1812	George, Earl of Aberdeen, K.G., K.T.	1855	Lord John Russell (Earl Russell, K.G.)
1815	John Henry, Duke of Rutland, K.G.	1856	William Ewart Gladstone, M.P.
1816	Henry Bankes, M.P.	1857	Sir George Cornewall Lewis, Bart., M.P.
1818	Charles, Lord Colchester (Speaker Abbott)		Spencer Horatio Walpole, M.P.
1823	Sir George Howland Beaumont, Bart.	1858	Charles, Viscount Eversley, G.C.B.)
1826	John Jeffrey, Marquess Camden, K.G.	1859	George Grote
		1860	Henry, Lord Taunton
1827	Henry, Marquess of Lansdowne, K.G.	1861	Algernon, Duke of Northumberland, K.G.
1829	Alexander Baring, M.P. (Lord Ashburton)		Sir Thomas Phillipps, Bart.
		1863	Benjamin Disraeli, M.P. (Earl of Beaconsfield, K.G.)
1830	Thomas Grenville		
	John, Earl of Eldon	1864	Robert Lowe (Viscount Sherbrooke, G.C.B.)
1833	Sir Robert Peel, Bart.		
1834	Alexander, Duke of Hamilton, K.G.	1865	George Douglas, Duke of Argyll, G.K., K.T.
	Edward, Earl of Derby, K.G.	1869	Samuel Wilberforce, Bishop of Oxford (Bishop of Winchester)
	Sir Robert Harry Inglis, Bart. M.P.	1871	William, Duke of Devonshire, K.G.
	William Vesey, Lord Fitzgerald and Vesey		John Dalberg, Lord Acton, K.C.V.O.
1837	Henry Hallam	1872	John Evelyn, Viscount Ossington.
1838	George, Earl of Carlisle, K.G.		Sir William Stirling-Maxwell, Bart., K.T.
	William Richard Hamilton		
1841	George Granville, Duke of Sutherland, K.G.	1874	Charles, Earl Somers.
		1876	Thomas, Lord Walsingham
1843	Sir John Frederick William Herschel, Bart., K.H.	1878	Major-General Sir Henry Creswicke Rawlinson, K.C.B. (Bart., G.C.B.)
1847	Thomas Babington Macaulay (Lord Macaulay)		Sir John Lubbock, Bart., M.P. (Lord Avebury)
	William Buckland, Dean of Westminster	1879	Alexander James Beresford Beresford-Hope, M.P.
1849	Henry Goulburn		
	Sir David Dundas, M.P.	1881	His Royal Highness Albert Edward, Prince of Wales, K.G. (His Majesty King Edward VII)
	Spencer Joshua Alwyne, Marquess of Northampton		
1851	Sir Philip de Malpas Grey Egerton, Bart., M.P.		Richard Monckton, Lord Houghton
	Edward Adolphus, Lord Seymour (Duke of Somerset, K.G.)	1881	Henry George Liddell, Dean of Christ Church
1852	Sir Roderick Impey Murchison, Bart., K.C.B.	1883	Archibald Philip, Earl of Rosebery, K.G., K.T.
1853	Henry Hart Milman (Dean of St. Paul's)	1883	John Alexander, Marquess of Bath

324

APPENDICES

1885 (Sir) George Otto Trevelyan (Bart.), M.P.
James Ludovic, Earl of Crawford and Balcarres, K.T.
1888 Thomas Henry Huxley
1889 Charles Drury Edward Fortnum
1891 John Evans (Sir John Evans, K.C.B.)
1893 Sir Charles Synge Christopher Bowen (Lord Bowen)
1894 John Morley (Viscount Morley of Blackburn, O.M.)
1895 Sir William George Granville Venables Vernon Harcourt, M.P.
1896 Baron Ferdinand James Rothschild, M.P.
Frederick Du Cane Godman
1898 Arthur Wellesley, Viscount Peel
1899 Hon. Lionel Walter Rothschild, M.P. (Lord Rothschild)
Sir Henry Hoyle Howorth, K.C.I.E., M.P.
1900 Henry George, Duke of Northumberland, K.G.
1901 His Royal Highness George Frederick, Duke of Cornwall and York (His Majesty King George V)
1903 Sir Richard Claverhouse Jebb, O.M., M.P.
1905 Harold Arthur Lee, Viscount Dillon, C.H.
1906 Herbrand Arthur, Duke of Bedford, K.G.
1908 Richard Henn, Lord Collins
Samuel Henry Butcher, M.P.
1911 Sir Edward Grey, Bart., M.P. (Viscount Grey of Fallodon, K.G.)
1911 Sir Alfred Comyn Lyall, G.C.I.E.
Sir William Reynell Anson, Bart., M.P.
Arthur, Lord Kilbracken, G.C.B.
1913 Lewis Harcourt, M.P. (Viscount Harcourt)
Sir Archibald Geikie, O.M., K.C.B.

*1914 George Gilbert Aimé Murray
1915 Herbert Albert Laurens Fisher, M.P.
1919 H.R.H. Edward, Prince of Wales, K.G., K.T. (H.M. King Edward VIII).
1920 George Nathaniel, Marquess Curzon of Kedleston, K.G., G.C.S.I., G.C.I.E.
Edwin Samuel Montagu, M.P.
1922 James William, Viscount Ullswater, G.C.B.
William Bateson, F.R.S.
1923 David Alexander Edward, Earl of Crawford and Balcarres, K.T., LL.D., F.R.S.
1924 Robert, Lord Chalmers, G.C.B., LL.D., F.B.A.
James Ramsay MacDonald, M.P., F.R.S., LL.D.
Lt.-Col. Sir David Prain, C.M.G., C.I.E., LL.D., F.R.S.
1925 Montague Rhodes James, O.M., Litt.D., D.Litt., LL.D.
1926 Sir Henry Alexander Miers, D.Sc., LL.D., F.R.S.
*1927 Stanley Baldwin, M.P., D.C.L., LL.D., F.R.S.
1928 Randall Thomas, Archbishop Lord Davidson of Lambeth
*1930 George Macaulay Trevelyan, O.M., C.B.E., D.C.L., Litt.D., LL.D., F.B.A.
*1931 Giles Stephen Holland, Earl of Ilchester, O.B.E.
* John Stanley Gardiner, F.R.S.
*1933 Sir Charles Reed Peers, C.B.E., P.S.A., F.B.A., F.R.I.B.A.
* Hugh Pattison, Lord Macmillan, G.C.V.O., LL.D.
1936 H.R.H. Albert, Duke of York (H.M. King George VI).
*1936 Charles Harry St. John Hornby
*1937 William George Ormsby-Gore (Lord Harlech), G.C.M.G., D.C.L.
* Sir Henry Thomas Tizard, K.C.B., A.F.C., F.R.S.

325

THE LIBRARY OF THE BRITISH MUSEUM

*1938 Sir Albert Charles Seward, Sc.D., LL.D., F.R.S.
*1940 David Alexander Robert, Earl of Crawford
*1941 Arthur Hinsley, Cardinal Archbishop of Westminster
*1941 Sir William Bragg, O.M., K.B.E., F.R.S.
*1942 Cosmo Gordon, Archbishop Lord Lang of Lambeth, D.D.
*1942 Sir Charles Scott Sherrington, O.M., C.B.E., F.R.S.

THE PRINCIPAL LIBRARIANS

(From 1898 Director and Principal Librarian)

1756 Gowin Knight, M.D.
1772 Matthew Maty, M.D.
1776 Charles Morton, M.D.
1799 Joseph Planta
1827 Henry Ellis (Sir H. Ellis, K.H.)
1856 Antonio Panizzi (Sir Anthony Panizzi, K.C.B.)
1866 John Winter Jones
1878 Edward Augustus Bond (Sir E. A. Bond, K.C.B.)
1888 Edward Maunde Thompson (Sir E. M. Thompson, G.C.B., I.S.O.)
1909 Frederic George Kenyon (Sir F.G. Kenyon, G.B.E., K.C.B.)
1931 George Francis Hill, C.B. (Sir George Hill, K.C.B.)
1934 Edgar John Forsdyke (Sir John Forsdyke, K.C.B.)

THE SECRETARIES

1787 Edward Whitaker Gray, M.D.
1806 Edward Bray
1814 Henry Ellis
1828 Rev. Josiah Forshall
1926 Arundell James Kennedy Esdaile
1940 John Humphrey Witney

APPENDICES

2

THE KEEPERS AND DEPUTY KEEPERS

PRINTED BOOKS

Keeper

1756	Matthew Maty, M.D.	1869	William Brenchley Rye
1765	Rev. Samuel Harper	1875	George Bullen (C.B.)
1803	Rev. William Beloe	1890	Richard Garnett (C.B.)
1806	Henry Ellis (Sir H. Ellis, K.H.)	1899	George Knottesford Fortescue
1812	Rev. Henry Hervey Baber	1912	Arthur William Kaye Miller
1837	Antonio Panizzi (Sir Anthony Panizzi, K.C.B.)	1914	George Frederick Barwick
		1919	Alfred William Pollard (C.B.)
1856	John Winter Jones	1924	Robert Farquharson Sharp
1866	Thomas Watts	1930	Wilfred Alexander Marsden

1943   Henry Thomas

Assistant Keeper, afterwards Deputy Keeper

1756	Samuel Harper	1880	Robert Kennaway Douglas (Sir R. K. Douglas)
1765	Rev. Andrew Joseph Planta		
1773	Joseph Planta	1884	Russell Martineau
1776	Rev. Paul Henry Maty	1888	William Younger Fletcher
1782	Rev. Charles Godfrey Woide	1890	George Knottesford Fortescue
1787	Rev. Samuel Ayscough	1895	Robert Edmund Graves
1805	Henry Ellis (Sir H. Ellis, K.H.)	1896	Arthur William Kaye Miller
		1899	William Robert Wilson (I.S.O.)
1807	Rev. Henry Hervey Baber	1900	George Frederick Barwick
1812	Rev. James Bean	1909	Alfred William Pollard (C.B.)
1826	Rev. Henry Francis Cary	1912	William Barclay Squire
1838	Rev. Richard Garnett	1914	Robert Farquharson Sharp
1850	John Winter Jones	1919	Francis Danvers Sladen
1856	Thomas Watts	1920	John Abraham Jacob de Villiers (Sir John de Villiers)
1857	William Brenchley Rye.		
1866	George Bullen (C.B.)	1924	Wilfred Alexander Marsden
1870	George William Porter	——	Henry Thomas
1871	Eugene Armand Roy.	1929	Arthur Isaac Ellis
1875	Richard Garnett (C.B.)	1930	Julius Victor Scholderer

1943   Cecil Bernard Oldman

MAPS, CHARTS, PLANS AND TOPOGRAPHICAL DRAWINGS

Keeper

1867–80   Richard Henry Major

THE LIBRARY OF THE BRITISH MUSEUM

MANUSCRIPTS

Keeper

1756	Charles Morton, M.D.	1878	Edward Maunde Thompson (Sir E. M. Thompson, G.C.B., I.S.O.)
1776	Joseph Planta		
1799	Rev. Robert Nares		
1807	Francis Douce	1888	Edward John Long Scott
1812	Henry Ellis (Sir H. Ellis, K.H.)	1904	George Frederic Warner (Sir G. F. Warner)
1827	Rev. Josiah Forshall		
1837	Frederic Madden (Sir F. Madden, K.H.)	1911	Julius Parnell Gilson
		1929	Harold Idris Bell, O.B.E. (C.B.)
1866	Edward Augustus Bond (Sir E. A. Bond, K.C.B.)		

Assistant Keeper, afterwards Deputy Keeper

1756	Rev. Andrew Gifford, D.D.	1879	Edward John Long Scott
1784	Rev. Richard Southgate	1888	George Frederick Warner (Sir G. F. Warner)
1795	Rev. Robert Nares		
1799	Rev. Thomas Maurice	1898	Frederic George Kenyon (Sir F. G. Kenyon, G.B.E., K.C.B.)
1824	Rev. Josiah Forshall		
1828	Frederic Madden (Sir F. Madden, K.H.).		
		1904	Francis Bridges Bickley
1837	Rev. William Cureton.	1906	Isaac Herbert Jeayes
1850	John Holmes	1909	Julius Parnell Gilson
1854	Edward Augustus Bond (Sir E. A. Bond, K.C.B.)	1912	John Alexander Herbert
		1927	Harold Idris Bell, O.B.E. (C.B.)
1869	William Wright	1929	Robin Ernest William Flower
1871	Edward Maunde Thompson (Sir E. M. Thompson, G.C.B., I.S.O.)	1932	Eric George Millar

ORIENTAL MANUSCRIPTS, afterwards ORIENTAL PRINTED BOOKS AND MANUSCRIPTS

Keeper

1867–91	Charles Rieu	1908	Lionel David Barnett
1892	Robert Kennaway Douglas (Sir R. K. Douglas)	1929	Lionel Giles
		1940	Alexander Strathern Fulton

Deputy Keeper

1925	Lionel Giles	1929	Alexander Strathern Fulton

APPENDICES

3

THE FIRST READING ROOM REGULATIONS

(1757, as enlarged in 1758).

THE manner of admitting persons, who desire to make use of the MUSEUM for Study; or shall have occasion to consult the same for Evidence, or Information.

1. THAT no one be admitted to make use of the Museum for Study, but by leave of the Trustees, in a General Meeting, or the Standing Committee: and that the said leave be not granted for a longer term than half a year, without a fresh application.

2. THAT a Book be kept in the reading room, under the custody of the Officer of the said room; who is to enter therein the names of the several persons who have leave of admission, together with the respective dates of the orders of the Trustees for that purpose, and the duration of the same.

3. THAT a particular room be allotted for the persons so admitted, in which they may sit, and read or write, without interruption, during the time the Museum is kept open: that a proper Officer do constantly attend in the said room, so long as any such person, or persons, shall be there: and for the greater ease and convenience of the said persons, as well as security of the Collection, it is expected; that notice be given in writing the day before, by each person, to the said Officer, what Book or Manuscript he will be desirous of perusing the following day; which Book or Manuscript on such request, will be lodged in some convenient place in the said room, and will from thence be delivered to him by the Officer of the said room: excepting however some Books and Manuscripts of great value, or very liable to be damaged, and on that account judged by the Trustees not fit to be removed out of the library to which they belong; without particular leave obtained, of the Trustees, in a General Meeting, or the Standing Committee, for that purpose; a Catalogue whereof will be kept by the Officer of the reading room.

4. THAT such persons be allowed to take one or more Extracts from any printed Book, or Manuscript; and that either of the Officers of the department to which such printed Book or Manuscript belongs, be at liberty to do it for them, upon such terms, as shall be agreed on between them.

5. THAT the transcriber do not lay the paper, on which he writes, upon any part of the Book, or Manuscript, he is using.

THE LIBRARY OF THE BRITISH MUSEUM

6. THAT no whole Manuscript, nor the greater part of any, be transcribed, without leave from the Trustees, in a General Meeting, or the Standing Committee.

7. THAT every person so intrusted with the use of any book, or Manuscript, return the same to the Officer attending, before he leaves the room.

8. THAT if any person engaged in a work of learning, have occasion to make a drawing of any thing contained in the department of Natural and Artificial productions, or to examine it more carefully than can be done in the common way of viewing the Museum; he is to apply to the Trustees in a General Meeting, or the Standing Committee, for particular leave for that purpose; it not being thought proper, unless in particular cases, to have them removed from their places, and out of the sight of the Officer who has the care of them.

9. THAT whensoever, and as often as any person shall have occasion to consult or inspect any Book, Charter, Deed, or other Manuscript for Evidence or Information,[1] other than for studying, which is herein before provided for; he is to apply for leave so to do, to the Trustees in a General Meeting or the Standing Committee. But if the case should require such dispatch as that time cannot be allowed for making such application, the person is to apply for such leave to the Principal Librarian; or, in case of his death or absence, such of the Under Librarians as shall officiate as Secretary for the time being: which leave the Principal Librarian, or the Under Librarian officiating as Secretary for the time being, as aforesaid, is hereby impowered to grant. Provided always, that no such person shall be permitted to consult or inspect any such Book, Charter, Deed, or other Manuscript; except in the presence of the Principal Librarian, or of one of the Officers of that department to which such Book, Deed, Charter, or other Manuscript shall belong.

10. THAT no part of the Collection or Collections belonging to this Museum, be at any time carried out of the General Repository; except such Books, Charters, Deeds or other Manuscripts as may be wanted to be made use of in Evidence. And that when any such Book, Charter, Deed, or other Manuscript shall be wanted to be made use of in Evidence, application shall be made in writing for that purpose, to the Trustees in a General Meeting, or the Standing Committee: and if the case should require such dispatch, as not to admit of an application to the Trustees in a General Meeting, or the Standing Committee then to the Principal Librarian; or in case of his death or absence, then to such of the Under Librarians as shall officiate as Secretary for the time being: and thereupon by their or his direction, the

same shall and may be carried out of the General Repository, to be made use of in evidence as aforesaid, by the Under Librarian or Assistant of the department to which such Book, Charter, Deed, or other Manuscript shall belong. And in case the said Under Librarian, or Assistant of the said department be disabled, or cannot attend; then by such other of the Under Librarians, or Assistants, as shall be appointed by the Trustees, in a General Meeting, or the Standing Committee, or by the Chief Librarian, or by such of the Under Librarians as shall officiate as Secretary for the time being aforesaid. And the person who shall be appointed to carry out the same, shall attend the whole time, and bring it back with him again; for which extraordinary trouble and attendance it is expected that a proper satisfaction be made to him.

THE LIBRARY OF THE BRITISH MUSEUM

4

ALIENATION, LENDING AND REMOVAL

The powers of the Trustees to alienate objects from the Collections is governed by three Acts of Parliament. The first, that of 1767 (7 Geo. III, c.18) allows "duplicates of Printed Books, Medals, Coins, or other Curiosities, to be exchanged for others, or sold, and the money spent in the purchase of others." In pursuance of this Act sales of duplicates were held in 1769, 1788, 1818, 1830 and 1831. The second Act, of 1807 (47 Geo. III, c.36), allows the similar sale for purchase, or exchange, of articles which may be found to be "unfit to be preserved" in the Museum. This power, which has its dangers from changes of fashion as well as its obvious advantages, has been not infrequently used in the Departments of Antiquities, but perhaps never for MSS., and certainly never for Printed Books, since there is no such thing as a book which is unfit to be preserved in the Museum.[1] The third Act (41 & 42 Vict. c.55), to which we shall return, legalizes the giving away of objects which were not given or bequeathed.

Since the early nineteenth century it has been a consistent principle that nothing given or bequeathed should be sold. The Act of 1767 made no such distinction. The Sloane books were considered as purchased, and therefore as late as 1818 were not excluded from the sales of duplicates; and Harper sold duplicates from the Old Royal Library, it is said, lest the Crown should repent the gift and reclaim it;[2] the sale of 1805 was the end of this practice, according to Baber's evidence before the Committee of 1836. Before the same Committee Cochran, the bookseller, stated that within the last eight or ten years the Museum had been more careful, and he specified gross examples from the earlier sales.[3] His strictures were well justified. Unique books can be found in the sale catalogues, and more than one has been bought back by later generations of Keepers. But Harper was not alone. Before the Committee of the House of Commons, on the purchase of the Lansdowne MSS. in 1807 Planta included among other things which in his opinion were "not suited to such a collection," "books deposited in conformity to [sic] an Act of Parliament by the Stationers' Company." Before the Commission of 1835–36 the subject of duplicates was much discussed. Edwards, it is true, was for giving them to other public libraries in London, such as Archbishop Tenison's. But Panizzi spoke strongly against their alienation; he would have had a lending collection formed out of them. He returned to

APPENDICES

this scheme in his Report of 1845 to the Trustees on the state of the Library. But he was all against selling: "Never sell a duplicate," he said to the Committee in 1836 (No. 4793); "that has been a misfortune; a very great misfortune." And Ellis spoke against the practice of selling them, declaring that they were needed.

Though there has been no sale of British Museum duplicates since 1831 single purchased copies have been fairly often exchanged, generally with the trade, and to good advantage, and the practice yields valuable additional funds now that grants are reduced.

In selling what had been given or bequeathed the Trustees had offended against the duty, now generally recognized by Librarians and Curators, and at any time obvious enough, of encouraging possible benefactors. When, in 1816, Lord Fitzwilliam gave his museum to the University of Cambridge, there was a report abroad, stated Sir Henry Ellis to the Commission of 1835–36 (as noted in Pt. I, ch. iii), that he had intended to give it to the British Museum, but had been deterred by knowing its practice in this matter; Ellis added that it was in consequence of this that the determination was come to that nothing but what had been bought should be sold or parted with. So, when twelve thousand King's Library duplicates (a figure much reduced by excluding large or fine paper copies), had arrived in the Museum, the last sales to be held—those of 1830 and 1831—disposed not of them but of those so created in the old Library, this condition having been made by Parliament in 1823.

In 1847, when Grenville's books came in, there was no attempt to sell the duplicates so created, which were many and valuable. His books, being fine copies, were held in reserve, and those of which other copies were to be found in the Library were not issued to readers without special application. And by the Act 41 & 42 Victoria, c. 55, which (chiefly contemplating Natural History specimens) allowed the gift of duplicates, those in the King's, Cracherode, Grenville and Banks Libraries were specifically excluded, a provision which, it may be observed, tacitly permits the gift or sale of those presented or bequeathed by anyone else—a freedom which is unused.

Much later, when the Trustees were harassed by the congestion which resulted in the Act of Parliament of 1902 permitting them to remove newspapers and other little-used material and store it elsewhere, they yielded to pressure by the Treasury, which naturally desired to find a cheaper solution than buying land and building, and they applied to Parliament for power to weed out unimportant printed matter. The Bill passed the Lords, but provoked such opposition from the more experienced and thoughtful part of the public that the proposal was dropped. But from time to time it is revived as if it were a new idea; in the summer of 1940 a letter to a newspaper suggested that the paper would be useful for pulping, in view of the scarcity due to war. Perhaps it is hardly necessary here to dwell on the folly of such proposals. Unless the books to be destroyed could be selected in broad classes (and there are none that are suitable), the labour of selection would cost more in time and high skill than that of cataloguing and storing. And no selector, however skilful, could avoid making irreparable mistakes. The fact is that we do not know what present-day books will be of value in half a century; we only know that among them will certainly be many that seem waste-paper now. School books will be wanted by historians of education, children's books by the same and also by historians of literature, art, and social life. The least valuable of all will be our "best books," the substance of which will have been subsumed by later writers, though a few may live as pure literature. Broadly we may say with truth that "the dust of today is the gold of tomorrow."

Duplicates are indeed necessary, and almost the only scheme of Panizzi's which never bore fruit was that mentioned above, to form a lending library from them. For the largest part, and the part that could best be spared for the purpose, there would be hardly any demand. Books of reference shelved in the Reading Room, and other books in frequent demand, must of course be available in more than one copy. But of rare books too duplicates will be required. Quite apart from the important variations between copies which many early, and even some later, books show, which the late Falconer Madan described as "the duplicity of duplicates," the copies deposited by copyright —or in the case of foreign books purchased on publication—of books destined to become classics go through two periods before that apotheosis. First, if they are their authors' first or early publications, they stand on the shelves neglected. So far no harm is done. That comes in the next period, when they begin to be recognized as important. They are then daily in the Reading Room, and are soon worn and have to be serviceably indeed but not beautifully rebound, and in a condition remote from that known and prized as "mint." And their authors will presently achieve centenaries and centenary exhibitions, which would be sorry affairs were there no better copies in reserve. More important than centenary exhibitions is the Museum's duty to preserve the record of the country's literature in the form of the copyright books, and the value which can often attach to study of books in their pristine state of issue. See some remarks on the Ashley duplicates, above, p. 201.

APPENDICES

Lending was much advocated by the less experienced witnesses in 1835–36. Mr. R. Hannay, for example, cited the practice of Continental and some British libraries in freely lending, and added that "the Germans think they do enough to provide books, without providing mansions to read in." Some years before Carlyle had transmitted to the Trustees, but without avail, a proposal from the Royal Library of Munich for an exchange of duplicates. The removal of newspapers to Hendon after 1902 required, it has been seen, a special Act of Parliament, and so would a lending library of British Museum duplicates have done, had it come to anything. By the Foundation Act the collections are to be preserved together in the repository to be provided; and this has always been taken to forbid the lending or other sending out of any object once incorporated. An Act of 1924 (14 & 15 Geo. V, c.23) allows lending for exhibition in institutions under public or university authority; the regulations made under this Act limit loans to duplicates and objects which can be temporarily spared without injury to students or the public, which might cover duplicate books, though strictly only for exhibition, but no printed book has yet been lent under these powers. The Act was in truth passed to sanction a practice which had grown up of lending duplicate engravings, and the power to lend watercolours to other London Galleries is obviously valuable.

The ideal is certainly twofold: first, that there should be one library where any seeker may expect to find almost any book of quality in any language and practically any book, whether of quality or of none, in our own, and to find it moreover on the spot and not to be told that it is out on loan and only recoverable after some time; and, second, that there should be, parallel to and in co-operation with it, an organization linking the libraries which do lend and provided with the necessary union catalogues and other tools.

The Royal Commissioners of 1927–29 (following the Departmental Committee on Public Libraries, 1927), recommended that the Central Library for Students, founded in 1914 by Dr. Albert Mansbridge in conjunction with the Workers' Education Association and Toynbee Hall, should reconstitute itself, in close association with the Museum and with State recognition and aid, but not as a State institution, "for the supply of bibliographical information, the promotion of the system of outlier libraries, and the preparation of union catalogues." As is recorded above (p. 165), it had been proposed that the Central Library for Students should become a Department of the Museum; but the Trustees found difficulties and were averse from undertaking the new responsibility; and the Commissioners agreed with them. The Central Library for Students became the National Central

THE LIBRARY OF THE BRITISH MUSEUM

Library, and the Museum is strongly represented both on its Board of Trustees and its Executive Committee.

Now that the National Central Library has been established and has undertaken the duty of organizing loans of books between libraries, there is little need for the Museum to enter into any such scheme as Panizzi's, which has many times been proposed, generally by inexperienced persons. The practice of lending books from great libraries, common abroad, and initiated and brought to its highest pitch of organization in Germany, has its drawbacks. It is at least something to know that, when one has found a book's title in a library's catalogue, one will find the book itself in that library when one goes there. The ideal would seem to be to support the chief stationary library by a lending organization, and little towards this ideal is needed but more liberal public support for the National Central Library.

Exceptions to the Museum's rule are cases where a book, or more often a newspaper and more rarely a MS., is subpœnaed by a Court of Law. It is then accompanied by a member of the Museum Staff. Apparently the first occasion when a Museum document was produced in a Court was when MS. Cotton Faustina B.i, containing a chartulary of the Abbey of St. Mary, Barlings, Lincs., was called for to be produced at the Lincoln Assizes.[4] During the two World Wars books and maps were required and borrowed by the War Office and other Government Departments. All binding has accordingly been done on the premises. (See the following Section.)

APPENDICES

5

BINDING

FROM the beginning the provision of the Foundation Act that the collections should not be moved out of the repository has been taken (as observed in the preceding section) to mean that all binding must be done within the gates; and though this has entailed trouble and expense, it is a salutary rule, since there have been many lamentable fires in binders' shops, where inflammable materials abound, and in the Museum precincts it has been possible to impose strict rules for fire-prevention. In 1862 the Trustees were driven by excess of books to be bound to send some to a shop on the other side of Great Russell Street, but they did so very unwillingly.

The earliest bindery was probably in the basement of old Montagu House.5 When the House was condemned a new bindery was established in an outhouse on ground by Montagu Street, subsequently occupied by the White Wing; and when the White Wing was erected in 1885, the present shops were built in the yard space to the North of the Supplementary and Arch Rooms.

The succession of binders is as follows: 1760–73, — Cook; 1773–1813, C. Elliot; 1813–25, B. Pipping; 1825–65, Charles Tuckett, senior; 1865–75, Charles Tuckett, junior; 1875–81, Darby and Would; 1881–1927, Eyre and Spottiswoode; and, from 1927, H.M. Stationery Office. It is probable that all of them till 1927 contracted to do the work, instead of being Trustees' servants, as their names do not appear in the House Lists; certainly Darby and Would and Eyre and Spottiswoode did so, the contract having on each occasion been put out to tender. H.M. Stationery Office control all similar work for Government Departments, and had long wished to undertake the Museum's, which is by far the most important financed by public money; but the Directors could and did reply that while no doubt an ordinary Government Department entering into an independent contract would pay more and be worse served than would a central organization, that was not true of the Museum, which had special needs, and whose staff were the Government's real experts. The Trustees, finally overborne, obviated the drawbacks by retaining Eyre and Spottiswoode's staff. In the Department of Printed Books there is always an Assistant Keeper who acts as Superintendent of Binding and also a technically trained Examiner of Bindings.

THE LIBRARY OF THE BRITISH MUSEUM

A number of hands employed by the binders are engaged, not in ordinary binding, but in the "Incorporation," i.e. in cutting and laying the titles from the accession parts of the General, Music and Map Catalogues as indicated by a senior member of the staff called the Incorporator.

One unusually important piece of work was done in the Department of Manuscripts, the binding of the Codex Sinaiticus by Mr. Douglas Cockerell.[6] Apart from any other argument, there would not have been room in the Bindery for the extraordinarily delicate work of flattening the leaves of this large book and doing all the repairs to the ancient vellum, without interference by—and with—ordinary work going on beside it. Repairs to MSS. and the mounting of papyri are also carried out in the Department.

A bindery was established in the Newspaper Library at Colindale when it was enlarged and opened in 1932.

The grant to the Stationery Office for the Museum's binding was increased in 1935 and 1937, when it stood at £26,500.

Calf was the material used for the mass of books till about fifty years ago, morocco being reserved for valuable and much-used volumes, manuscript or printed. The old morocco is of good quality; but the calf was too often pared and perhaps also badly tanned, and has cracked at the joints in the way that has unjustly brought all English binding into contempt abroad. The worst period seems to have been the middle of the nineteenth century, as it was for the craft in general in this country. Of late, with an increased grant for binding, the shelves of the Old Library have been examined and great quantities of volumes in broken calf, tied up with string, have been re-backed. Moreover, there has been devised in the Museum's Laboratory a mixture for refreshing and preserving the leather when it becomes dried and, as the French say, "fatigued."[7]

Modern morocco, as is well known, has given much trouble in libraries, being peculiarly liable, though perhaps not so much as russia, to a red rot. The Society of Arts' Special Committee of 1897 attributed this to acids in tanning, since old moroccos have not perished, but the leather tanned to their specification has not proved sound, and later investigations carried out in the United States seem to show that the evil comes from acids infiltrating from the atmosphere; certainly leather bindings in the great Scandinavian libraries, where the air is remarkably pure, have suffered much less than those in London and other industrial cities. Practice at the Museum, as elsewhere, has been affected by this problem. Morocco, tanned in the best way, continues to be used, cloth or (more recently) buckram being used for the sides and for the complete binding of ordinary books that will not be heavily used.

APPENDICES

But much "Cape goat" has been used in place of normal morocco, and is standing the trial well, while in the last few years very heavy volumes, including the Reading Room set of the new General Catalogue, have been bound in that strongest and most permanent of all leathers, pigskin. Heavy guard-books are now bound in sail-cloth.

Between 1932 and 1936 various trade Associations combined to form a Bookbinding Leather Committee, on which among the four librarian members was Mr. H. A. Stanley Kelham, the Museum's Superintendent of Binding. Two interim reports have been issued, and about three hundred books have been bound at the Museum for the Committee's purposes in selected leathers and are periodically examined.

There are, of course, some documents which defy ordinary binding. Rolls are simply kept in boxes, while papyri are laid between sheets of glass, which are bound at the edges, generally with leather.

Fragile leaves are made strong by laying them between sheets of transparent rice paper or, still more effective, silk mesh; specimens can be seen in some much-used old books of reference, such as *The Gentleman's Magazine*, in the Reading Room.

The practice of binding a number of pamphlets—or even stout books, in a single "tract-volume," which was the usual economy—has of late been greatly reduced. Pamphlets are now cased in plain linen-backed paper boards, which are made up in quantity. An improvement, though at an increased cost in labour and space, would perhaps be to have the backs square, so that the title can be lettered by hand in white paint, as is done in some libraries. The cloth and buckram are used in the old-established range of colours following the Library's classification, e.g. green for Geography and red for History.

The crown stamp was substituted for "B.M." in 1838.

Dusting is still done by hand in the main Library; but a vacuum cleaner, especially intended for books, is in use in the Oriental Library.

THE LIBRARY OF THE BRITISH MUSEUM

6

CLASSIFICATION OF PRINTED BOOKS

THE Printed Books, at first shelved in the separate component collections, were classified on the shelves on a "synthetical arrangement" drawn up by Ayscough about 1790, all the collections, except the Cracherode, the King's Pamphlets and Sir William Musgrave's biographical collection, being amalgamated. A table of the rooms and the classes contained in them was printed on pp. 2–3 of the *Synopsis*, first edition, 1808: and a full "Analytical Syllabus" was issued with it. The main heads, which differ in arrangement from those Ayscough had adopted five years before in his catalogue of the Sloane and Birch MSS., more widely indeed than the difference of the material alone could account for, are as follows:—

Rooms:
   I. Philology, Memoirs of Academics, Classics, Descriptions of Museums.
   II. The Cracherodean Library.
   III. Poetry, Novels, Letters, Polygraphy.
   IV. Ancient and modern History, Geography, Voyages and Travels.
   V. Modern History and Geography continued.
   VI. Modern History, continued; Biography, Diplomacy, Heraldry, Archaeology, Numismatics, Bibliography.
   VII. Medicine, Surgery, Trade and Commerce, Arts, Mathematics, Astronomy.
   VIII. Medicine continued; Natural History.
   IX. Politics, Philosophy (Moral and Natural), Chemistry, Natural History.
   X. (the Reading Room): Ecclesiastical History, Jurisprudence, Divinity.
   XI. Divinity.
   XII. Sermons, Political Tracts, the King's Pamphlets.
      Besides these twelve rooms, there are two more in other parts of the House, containing printed books, viz:
   XIII. The Acta Sanctorum, Sir William Musgrave's Biographical Collections, Reviews, Music.
   XIV. Parliamentary Records, Gazettes, Newspapers.

This arrangement was not the basis of Horne's abortive classed catalogue of the eighteen-twenties, for which he drew up the new scheme which the Trustees published.

APPENDICES

The arrangement of the Iron Library is different again, but it is still on modern standards broad. This classification, which was devised by Watts when the books were moved from the old house to the new in 1838, owes something to Horne's scheme, but more to that of "the Paris booksellers," later elaborated by J. C. Brunet, which was probably the most widely known system then existing. The main divisions are as follows:—

I. Theology.
II. Jurisprudence.
III. Natural History and Medicine.
IV. Archaeology and Arts.
V. Philosophy.
VI. History.
VII. Geography.
VIII. Biography.
IX. Belles Lettres.
X. Philology.

They are set out, with the subdivisions, in *Library Administration* (1898, pp. 153–61) by John Macfarlane, a valuable member of the Staff of whom no mention falls to be made elsewhere in this book; he retired early to become Imperial Librarian at Calcutta. Garnett also described the system (*Essays in Librarianship*, pp. 210–24).

Many times proposals have been made by members of the library profession outside for the reclassification of the whole British Museum Library on one of the modern exact systems, such as Dewey's, Brown's or the Library of Congress, but they have been resisted by the authorities. The advantages of such systems seem to be confined to libraries in which readers have free access to the shelves. Free or open access can hardly be practised in so large a library as this. As it was once put, the danger would be not merely of losing the books, but also of losing readers. And facilities are sometimes given to readers engaged in large bibliographical researches, for going through the "fourth copies," i.e. the set of titles which serves as a shelf-catalogue. And for books later than 1880 the Subject Index covers the ground after a fashion, though it is not in classified order. The disadvantages are mainly two. First, there would be the enormous cost of the work of reclassification; if the Museum could get the money it would disable it for years from getting money for more urgent needs. And, secondly, there would be the waste of space. It is bad enough, but inevitable, to have to leave space for future volumes of every one of thousands of periodicals.[8] To have to leave a gap at the end of every minutest subdivision of the books as well would mean a great expansion of the building and probably a move of part into the country, or else the separation of Library from Antiquities. When the original Iron Library was full and swinging presses were introduced, a by-product was that it continued for another half-century to be possible to

THE LIBRARY OF THE BRITISH MUSEUM

place accessions close to the books in the same classes. The Placer's problems grew more and more arduous in the years before the reconstruction of the Ironwork began; books were uncomfortably stored in basements both of the old building and of King Edward VII's Building.

It was Winter Jones who observed that the "elastic system" of shelving involved making all the presses of exactly the same measurements; he also first suggested labelling the books with their press-marks outside. Marking shelves by duplicated and even sometimes triplicated letters originated when the Hebrew books, which had been housed in presses of a single storey, were moved to the Iron Library, where they were in two—the basement then having a separate press-numeration. The duplication is so arranged that the top storey always ends at "d" or its multiple.

The marking of each book with a number or "third mark," showing its position on the shelf, began in 1875 and was not quite complete at the end of the century. The "fourth mark," showing the position of a pamphlet in a tract-volume, was affixed earlier, with maddening results where, as often occurred, a number of such volumes stood together. The press-mark in the main General Catalogue of 1880 is therefore often imperfect. The full press-mark of a pamphlet would be, say, 4175.g.20.(4).

APPENDICES

7

PHOTOGRAPHY

PHOTOGRAPHY was early used in the Museum, certainly before 1875, when regulations were issued. The studio, provided in that year, was replaced in 1914 by a roomier once, since in its turn enlarged, at the top of the King Edward VII Wing. But till 1927 there was no photographer on the Staff, photographers from outside being allowed to use the Studio under official supervision, at first having to deposit two prints from each negative made, and after 1906 paying a small charge per negative or per hour. The addition to the establishment of an official Photographic Staff filled a need to which Garnett had strongly called attention thirty years before.9

Photostat, originally in its primitive form of rotography, was introduced in 1905. It was earlier in use (by the Clarendon Press) in the Bodleian, and, as with microfilm, American use preceded English. The Carnegie United Kingdom Trustees in 1922 placed a photostat camera of their own in the Studio for the purposes of the publication sponsored by them and edited by Dr. E. Fellowes and others of Tudor Church Music. They allowed it to be used also for the Museum's purposes, and at the conclusion of the work in 1925 handed it over. Another and later type was similarly acquired in 1932 when a grant from the Rockefeller Foundation enabled the Library of Congress to make photostats of documents in many of the chief European libraries and archives bearing on American history. On the acquisition of this second machine, which had been operated in a basement room of the Department of Manuscripts, the earlier model was sent to the Newspaper Library at Colindale, thus getting rid of the very tiresome necessity of bringing large volumes up to Bloomsbury. No separate photographic staff for Colindale has been found necessary.

Microfilm photography of MSS. and rare books—and also of articles from periodicals—began to be demanded soon after 1930, and it was some time before the Museum made official provision for it; students were, and are, sometimes allowed to make their own films with their Leica cameras in a comparatively secluded corner of the Manuscript Students' Room. The method appears to have originally been the answer to a peculiarly American demand, that for complete, cheap and not bulky reproductions of whole files of newspapers. For some reason, possibly the use of mechanical wood paper, complicated

THE LIBRARY OF THE BRITISH MUSEUM

by extreme lack of moisture in the air, the paper on which American local newspapers of half a century and more ago, which are of course of high value to the history of the younger States and townships, were printed, has suffered far worse deterioration than that of English newspapers of the same or earlier periods. From this limited application the method was rapidly extended in libraries possessing projectors, or "reading machines," i.e. improved and specialized magic lanterns in which the film can be magnified and read.

Stimulated by a special demand from the firm which acts as agent for American University libraries needing microfilms, and in particular for a great co-operative linguistic undertaking involving examination of all English books printed before 1600, the Museum in 1935 made an arrangement by which this firm established a camera in the Museum Studio and a projector in the MSS. Students' Room. Very large quantities of microfilms have been made, though the number of European libraries equipped with projectors is still not large.

A word should be added as to the system of "scheduling" negatives. Many MSS. and books are too fragile or precious for repeated handling to be allowed if avoidable; and some of these are just those celebrated documents which are in frequent demand. Where an official negative exists, it is "scheduled," and must be used; where not, the negative made must be suitable to be scheduled for future general use, and is retained by the Museum, a duplicate being supplied if required (which it rarely is) at half-price. Casts of seals now or formerly attached to MSS. are also supplied.

Apparatus (a Harovia-Muir Analytic Lamp) for making faded MS. legible by ultra-violet or infra-red rays is in use in the Department of Manuscripts. The first apparatus of this kind was presented by a much-loved and regretted reader and friend of the Museum Library, the late Professor John M. Manly.

The Museum is well equipped with scientific appliances, which its Research Laboratory keeps improving. Perhaps only the Henry E. Huntington Library in California and the Vatican have developed these aids to the work of a library to so high a pitch.

APPENDICES

8

THE NATURAL HISTORY MUSEUM LIBRARY

WHEN the Natural History collections were transferred to South Kensington, it was naturally thought and hoped by many whose interests were narrowly scientific that the books and manuscripts in botany, zoology, entomology and mineralogy, and especially those in the Sloane and Banks collections, would accompany them. The Trustees, however, decided that to allow this would destroy the encyclopædic character of the Museum Library.

It therefore became necessary to form a fresh library, in addition to those of the Departments themselves, to which the objection to the move did not apply. The Trustees obtained an additional grant from the Treasury for the purpose, and have followed it up with regular annual allocations. B. B. Woodward was placed in charge of it. As a result, a very large General Library has been built up at South Kensington, consisting of printed books and periodicals, manuscripts, maps and drawings. The special strength of the Library is undoubtedly in the works and literature relating to Linnaeus, whose favourite pupil, Solander, had been one of the Museum's first Natural History Assistants; and in this field it owes much to the present Librarian's immediate predecessor, Basil Soulsby, previously in charge of the Map Room in the Printed Books at Bloomsbury.

Catalogue of the Books, Manuscripts, Maps and Drawings in the British Museum (Natural History). By B. B. Woodward, B. H. Soulsby and A. C. Townsend. 5 vols. + Suppl. 3 vols., 1903-40.

In anticipation of the then impending bicentenary of the birth of Linnaeus the Natural History Museum issued in advance of its normal appearance the section of the General Catalogue comprising that heading. Titles of books at Bloomsbury but not at South Kensington were supplied (by W. R. Wilson) and incorporated.

A Catalogue of the Works of Linnaeus, and publications more immediately relating thereto, preserved in the Libraries of the British Museum, Bloomsbury, and the British Museum (Natural History), South Kensington. 1907.

The value of Soulsby's work may be seen by comparing the 27 pages of this with the 246 of the second edition, whose appearance he just did not live to see:

A Catalogue. . . . Second edition. 1933.

THE LIBRARY OF THE BRITISH MUSEUM

9

THE STAFF: A NOTE

MUCH has been said in the text of this book about the higher ranks of the Staff, and it need not be repeated here. It may, however, be worth while to explain the system of recruitment.

Until some sixty years ago "nominations" were made outright by the Principal Trustees, subject, after the incorporation of the Establishment into the Civil Service, to qualifying and medical examination. This system had the disadvantages which are obvious, but it enabled men of high attainments but without high academic record to be recruited. Such were Watts, Holmes, Richard Garnett, Deutsch and Fortescue. Nor can it be said that the system of examination, even when competitive, as it became and remained until well into the twentieth century, protected the Museum from occasional misfits.

Of recent years the Civil Service Commission, seeing that the candidates had all taken high degrees, very sensibly waived the practice, while retaining the right, of examining. The Director sifts the candidates, who have to obtain nomination from a Principal Trustee as before, and a selection is interviewed by a Board of the Commission, with which he and the appropriate Keeper sit. Practically all candidates are expected to have taken high degrees in classics and to have reached a similar standard in modern foreign languages; for certain vacancies only are special qualifications expected.

Women have been eligible since about 1920; there are now a number on the Staff.

In the changes of 1921 the salary of Keepers was fixed at only £100 above that of Deputy-Keepers. This was deliberately adopted with the intention of freeing the latter from financial temptation to abandon scholarship for administration.

In 1930 the removal of the Natural History Museum from the Bloomsbury Director's responsibility and the retirement of Sir Frederic Kenyon gave an opportunity, which was taken, of extinguishing the obligation of incoming Directors to furnish a large bond for good conduct. That incumbent on Keepers had disappeared earlier.

The lower ranks, like the higher, were recruited till modern times by nomination by the Principal Trustees; the nominees have now to pass a qualifying examination by the Civil Service Commission. Under the old system

APPENDICES

the men had often been personal servants of Trustees, and had courteous manners and a respect and loyalty for the Museum. Some proved to have ability above the average; such was Cater, the Superintendent of the Reading Room in the eighteen-thirties. Very occasional promotions have been made to the senior Staff, as also from a short-lived middle grade of Second Division Clerks; but there is a good reason why such promotion should be rarer in the Museum than in other offices staffed by Civil Servants. This is that the work of the Senior Staff is largely research, implying advanced academic training which it is almost impossible to supply in later years. But there is some work, once done by Assistants, for example in the Copyright Office and in the registration of purchases, which is well suited to intelligent men who are not possessed of high scholarship. The regulated age limits allow much freedom, but in practice Attendants are now appointed at from sixteen to eighteen. Of late the standard of education has risen, and recruits are all from secondary schools, and generally matriculated. The unavoidably elementary nature of the work of juniors has sometimes caused disappointment to young men who have looked on the Museum, and not without reason if they would be patient, as a University.

There was originally, apart from the Domestic Staff, only one lower grade, that of Attendant. In 1921 the name was changed to Museum Clerks, but this was even more delusive than the other, and in 1928 the grade was divided into two (with subdivisions in the upper stratum), Attendants and Library (or, in the Antiquities) Museum Assistants. This certainly corresponds more closely to the facts, the work of the juniors being in fact that of attending on the Higher Staff and on readers. That the outer world understands by the term a uniformed ex-soldier is unfortunate, but unavoidable, and for quite young men unimportant.

Among the most important members of the Lower Staff are the Hall Superintendent and the Housekeeper, posts for which, and especially for the former, high qualities of loyalty, responsibility and a power of discipline, are needed. They have generally been people of character and sometimes also "characters"; Cowtan gives a charming description of the old Housekeeper of his early days, Mrs. Bygrave, and her husband, an Attendant in the Library, "a gentleman of the bygone age," who at eighty (there was no superannuation then) could run up a library ladder and even dance a minuet. The Gate Porter in the latter days of old Montagu House was also a feature of the place; he figures in a well-known lithograph, in which he has the air of being conscious not only of serving, but also of being, a great but hospitable institution.

THE LIBRARY OF THE BRITISH MUSEUM

The general instruction to the Staff, which appeared in the earliest Statutes, and was repeated in later issues, was revised in 1932 (iv. 15) to apply to all ranks and both sexes. It now runs:—

"It is considered as a general instruction to all members of the Staff that they conduct themselves as becomes persons of honour, integrity and liberality, in the conscientious discharge of the duties of their respective stations, and as persons who have the credit and utility of the British Museum truly at heart."

10

THE REPORT AND QUARTERLY

The official annual record of the Museum's work and finance began to appear in 1912 in *Accounts, Estimates, etc.* This is now represented by the *Annual Report of Progress*. But the financial details are omitted, and appear in *Civil Estimates*, Class IV (Education). And as the *Report* is unillustrated and very summary, there was founded in 1926 a journal, largely devoted to illustrated descriptions of new acquisitions, *The British Museum Quarterly*.

NOTES

PART I, CHAPTER I

1. Supplemented a year later in certain details as to the quorum at meetings of the Principal Trustees, by 27 Geo. II, c. 16.
2. The combination of high officials and family representatives had a precedent in the Cotton Library Trustees under the Act of 1700.
3. The last Royal Librarian, Claudius Amyand, went beyond this. The younger Bentley sold him the appointment at so high a price that he could not afford to employ a substitute (surely the least of his duty) and left old David Casley to do his work for nothing.
4. One Peter Leheup, a lottery agent of bad character, bought up tickets and held them for a premium, in fact made a "corner" in them. A description of a lottery, closely resembling the procedure laid down in this Act, is to be found in Z. C. von Uffenbach's *Reysen (London in 1710)*, p. 136.
5. John, the 2nd Duke, the practical joker, had died in 1749.
6. Sloane's Will had ordered that his Museum should be offered, failing the King and Parliament, to some of these Continental Academies. The first steps towards the foundation of the Royal Society were much earlier, during the Civil War.
7. J. E. Sandys, History of Scholarship, in *A Companion to Greek Studies*, ed. L. Whibley, 1905, p. 638.
8. This accusation was possibly derived ultimately from Bale, who had pronounced it half a century earlier.
9. Cf. C. L. Kingsford, *English Historical Literature in the Fifteenth Century*.
10. *Memoirs of Libraries*, i, 363–4; MS. Cott. Cleop. E. iv, f. 13.
11. Antony à Wood, *Historia et Antiquitas Universitatis Oxoniensis*, i, 271–2.
12. M. R. James calculates that there were in 1530 some 1500 volumes in Cambridge libraries recorded in surviving catalogues, and that at the end of the century, as is shown by Thomas James in the *Ecloga Oxonio-Cantabrigiensis*, there were only two or three hundred. (*Collections of Manuscripts at Cambridge: Sandars Lectures*, unpublished, 1903.)
13. There is very little trace in the old catalogues of Continental libraries of the shiploads of books from the English monasteries which Bale says were exported as waste paper, and it is obvious that he is too violent to be a trustworthy witness except on the main issue, where there is in any case corroboration.
14. Bale, *Illustrium Majoris Britanniae Scriptorum Summarium*, 1548 and 1557.
15. M. R. James, *The Ancient Libraries of Canterbury and Dover*.
16. Uffenbach, when he saw these MSS. at Corpus in 1710, perceived the absurdity of the dating. (*Reysen*, the Cambridge visit extracted and translated by J. E. B. Mayor in *Cambridge under Queen Anne*).
17. Before his death Parker gave twenty-five MSS. to the Public Library (as it was then and long afterwards called) of the University; and some of his collecting are still at Lambeth.

18. It is significant that three famous forgers of antique manuscripts, Chatterton, Ireland and Vrain-Lucas, were all attorneys' clerks.
19. Stow's are among the Harleian MSS.
20. Like Stow, Speed was a tailor.
21. There is a good portrait of Cotton, by Cornelius Jansen, in the Board Room.
22. *Discourses*, edited by Thomas Hearne.
23. In the unofficial guidebook to the Museum by J. and A. van Rymsdyk, 1778, special notice is taken of "a portrait of Chaucer in an Aegyptian pebble," and "a horn from the forehead of a woman at Tenterden." The former is still to be seen in the Mineralogical Department, but where is the latter? That the triumph of the scientific spirit of truth is not yet complete, few have such good reason to be aware as the Staff of the British Museum, who are continually interrupted by believers in old superstitions such as astrology, and still more in new, such as Bacon-Shakespeare, Anglo-Israel, and the mystic meaning of the Pyramids.
24. William Courten, alias Charlton, in the next generation made a notable "cabinet" of natural history, which was acquired by Sloane in 1702 and so came to the British Museum. It may be noted that in the same generation as the younger Tradescant the two first art-collections in England were formed: the Arundel marbles, brought from Italy and Greece by and for the 2nd Earl of Arundel, now at Oxford; and the short-lived Royal Gallery of Pictures at Whitehall, collected by Charles I and dispersed under the Commonwealth. The idea of the formation of definite collections had by the mid-seventeenth century really reached England.
25. Ray's European Herbarium entered the Museum in 1862, by the gift of the Apothecaries' Society; but Sloane's collections included many of his manuscripts and letters.
26. The meetings of the two Societies were held at times calculated to allow members to go from one to the other. (Grosley, *Londres*, 1770.)
27. He gave the other part to the College of Arms.
28. Letter from Sloane to Dr. Charlett, April 1707, *op. cit.*; Edwards, *Lives of the Founders*, p. 196 *n*.
29. It may seem surprising that Sloane did not leave his collections to the Royal Society. But, apart from the fact that forty years earlier during Sloane's Secretaryship Uffenbach had found the Society's library in a state of dust and dirt, an explanation can perhaps be found in a visit to Chelsea Manor house paid in 1748 by the Prince and Princess of Wales; the Prince called the collection "an ornament to the nation," and added that "great honour would redound from the establishing it for public use to the latest posterity." Sloane made his codicil in the following year; so perhaps we owe the Museum to "poor Fred." Uffenbach had visited Sloane's collection, and praised his courtesy, calling him "an honest fellow of great parts," and contrasting him with "that coxcomb Dr. Woodward."
30. It was sold in 1861.
31. In the *Monthly Miscellany*, June 1708, is an article on the state of London libraries. For other references and an excellent survey, see a paper "The Facilities for Antiquarian Study in the Seventeenth Century," by John Butt, in *Essays and Studies* (The English Association); vol. xxiv, 1939, pp. 64–79.

NOTES

32. *Diary*, 15 Feb, 1684; letter to Pepys, 12 Aug. 1689.
33. Nichols, *Lit. Anecd.*, ii, 509–11. Four years later, in his *History of England*, Carte was lamenting London's want of a public library.
34. In a letter 5th March, 1718–19, to Edward Hyde, 3rd Earl of Clarendon (Stowe MS.), Thomas Astle has added a sardonic note: "This scheme would have been more convenient for the Heralds than for the public."
35. Nichols, *Lit. Anecd.* v. 285.
36. The Standing Committee was re-established in 1850 as a result of the strictures of the Royal Commission of the preceding years on the want of system prevailing. The Secretary had been in the habit of summoning to meetings such Trustees as he knew to be available at the moment. The result was lack of continuity, and the scandal of the abortive Catalogue becomes intelligible. (See Part I, Chapter IV, n. 23.)
37. Later examples of a Principal Trustee's services being retained by election on his vacating his Office are those of Speaker Abbot (Charles, 1st Lord Colchester) in 1818, and of Archbishops Davidson and Lang in 1928 and 1942.
38. He was the forger of the pretended first English newspaper, *The English Mercurie*, 1588. It was Thomas Watts of the Museum who made the easy exposure of it. See Watts's *Letter to A. Panizzi, Esq.*, 1839, and a note by Sir Henry Ellis in Add. MS. 36653, f. 2.
39. Corresponding to the Reading Room regulations. See Appendix 3, above, pp. 329–31.
40. See above, p. 331, for a note on the Museum's law and practice of alienation, lending and removal of Books and MSS.
41. See D. C. Douglas, *English Scholars*, 1939.

PART I, CHAPTER II

1. St. Giles is the foreground and St. George's Church is in the background of Hogarth's "Gin Lane," three years before Montagu House was acquired for the Museum. The curious pyramidal stepped spire of St. George's, built in 1731 (the Church being one of the fifty built in new districts of London under the Act of 1713), and surmounted by a statue of King George I (as the contemporary epigram pointed out, the head not only of the Church but of the Steeple), was based by its architect, Nicholas Hawksmoor, on the reconstruction of the Mausoleum, as indicated by Pliny's description. In 1856 the site at Halicarnassus was excavated for the Museum by Sir Charles Newton, and the surviving sculptured fragments were brought to remain within a few yards of the Mausoleum's English imitation. But it is now certain that the statues of Mausolus and Artemisia did not, as Hawksmoor and others thought, crown the apex of the Mausoleum. The statue of King George was the gift of a parishioner, William Hucks, brewer.
2. About the site of Torrington Square was the "Field of the Forty Footsteps." The tradition was that, two brothers having fought and killed each other there, the grass would never grow again on that ground. It was observed in more recent times, before the land was built over, that the spot was indeed bare of grass, but for a less romantic reason, being trodden by sightseers.
3. *Londres*, 1770, 3 vols, vol. ii.
4. Apparently in 1665; see Pepys, *Diary*.

THE LIBRARY OF THE BRITISH MUSEUM

5. Lady Montagu was sister to Rachel Lady Russell, whose husband granted his brother-in-law the lease. The land on which Montagu House was built appears as "Baber's East Field Meads" in a map of the manor made for Thomas Earl of Southampton about 1640. See G. Scott Thomson, *The Russells in Bloomsbury*, 1940.
6. There are several references to it in Hooke's Diary. Evelyn saw it on 5th November 1679: "Went to see Mr. Montagu's new palace neere Bloomsbury, built by our [i.e. the Royal Society's] curator Mr. Hooke, somewhat after the French: it was most nobly furnished, and a fine, but too much exposed garden." See Ogilby's map (with panorama) of London, 1678.
7. Walpole, *Anecdotes of Painting*, ed. Dallaway, 1888, ii, 175 and *n*. 4.
8. See *The Architecture of Robert Hooke*, by M. J. Bellen, Walpole Society, xxv (1936–7), 93 *seq*. Hooke's house had a balustrade on the roof, which his successor did not repeat. The second house is described and illustrated in Colin Campbell's *Vitruvius Britannicus*.
    Uninspired but probably faithful views of both faces are shown in J. Entick's *New and Accurate History and Survey of London*, 1766, iv, pl. f. p. 427.
9. Except the King Edward VII Wing. J. P. Malcolm (*Londinium Redivivum*, vol. ii, 1803, pp. 482–531), says that the view to the North had recently been excluded by houses.
10. Reproduced in *The Buildings of the British Museum*, 1914, pl. iii.
11. Edwards's Library, consisting of some 2,000 volumes of antiquarian character (he was a member of the Society of Antiquaries), had come to the public at his death in 1743; his endowment, which was not received till 1769, is mentioned elsewhere. His character may be judged by his desire, expressed in his will, that his books might be "placed in some By-room or corner" of the library building he wished to provide for the Cotton Library. Not many benefactors are so self-effacing; and it is a pity that Edwards's books were afterwards distributed by subject among the rest of the old library, and are not now distinguishable.
12. As might be naturally assumed; but see *A View of the British Museum* [1760?]
13. Thus the Bibliothèque Nationale still has its Département des Médailles. The British Museum's Department of Coins and Medals is now treated as allied with the Departments of Antiquities, and is ignored in the present work. Coins and medals were moved from the Manuscripts to the Antiquities in 1803, when Taylor Combe, son of the well-known numismatist, Dr. Charles Combe, and from 1807 Keeper of Antiquities, was brought in to take charge of them. The Department was separated in 1861; it contains many coins from the Cotton and Sloane collections, but none came with the Old Royal, whose coins had been largely dispersed under the Commonwealth; what were left were probably inherited by George III and came after 1823.
14. Add. MS. 39311, f. 82; *B.M. Quarterly*, x, 77–78.
15. The younger Maty, thus appointed an Assistant-Librarian in the year of his father's death, was promoted in 1782 to the Under-Librarianship of Natural History. Like his father he was Foreign Secretary and Secretary of the Royal Society, and in his *New Review*, 1782, where he criticized foreign books for English readers, he aimed at the converse of his father's *Journal Britannique*.
    Ayscough's activities, divided between MSS. and Printed Books, and the

NOTES

transfers between Departments recorded above, are characteristic of the happy times before the rise of specialism. Transfers have taken place in recent times, but only of junior Assistants.

16. Woide, like Maty, the Plantas and other early Museum officers, was a foreign Protestant, being minister of the Dutch Chapel Royal in London. His scholarship was in Egyptian languages, especially Sahidic, and in Biblical Greek. He edited a facsimile of the New Testament portion of the Codex Alexandrinus which was published by subscription by John Nichols in 1786; Harper helped him with the collation of the text. He was F.R.S., D.D. (of Copenhagen), and D.C.L. of Oxford; before coming to the Museum his reputation was European.
17. An improved Table was one of Wanley's projects; that of Mabillon was criticized as falsified in many places by bad engraving.
18. Smollett, *Humphry Clinker*.
19. *Gentleman's Magazine*, 1803, i, 94, 189.
20. *Early Diary of Fanny Burney*, ed. Annie Raine Ellis, ii, 2, 9 *n*.
21. This affair was two years old; Walpole mentions it on 11th Feb., 1773 (*Letters*, ed. Toynbee, viii, 235).
22. Told by Northcote to Hazlitt in 1830.
23. Penneck had already, in 1774, on account of his health, secured the move of the Reading Room to the floor above.
24. Gray (to James Brown, 8th August, 1759) says that when he calls the Museum peaceful "you are to understand it only of us visitors, for the Society, Trustees and all, are up in arms, like the fellows of a college. The Keepers have broke off all intercourse with one another, and only lower a silent defiance as they pass by. Dr. Knight has walled up the passage to the little house, because some of the rest were obliged to pass by one of his windows in the way to it." The Principal Librarian's love of privacy, or perhaps delicacy of mind, seems excessive. The early Minutes of the Trustees are full of these childish quarrels, and the Trustees were driven in the Statutes of 1768 to rebuke their Officers: "And it is the desire and intention of the Trustees, and they do expect, that a good understanding should, as far as possible, ever subsist among all the officers belonging to the Museum; and that as on the one hand, it is necessary that a proper subordination be preserved, and a due deference be shown (in every thing relating to the Museum) by those who bear an inferior, to those who enjoy a superior office therein; so on the other hand, each of a superior, should treat those of an inferior rank, in regard to their offices, with condescension and respect: and that all of them in general should consider themselves, and the other officers, as gentlemen living under the same roof, and equally engaged in carrying on the same noble design, and among whom, for that, as well as for other reasons, no personal pique or animosity should ever find the least place; but the most perfect harmony and a true spirit of benevolence ought always to be cultivated and prevail."
25. Garrick acquired Cartwright's collection from Dulwich College, "in exchange for some more modern publications." (Lysons, *Environs of London*, 1811, p. 83.)
26. The net amount realized by the lottery was £95,194 8s. 2d. Of this £20,000 went for the Sloane collections, £10,000 for the Harleian MSS., £10,250 for Montagu House, and £28,663 15s. for the purchase of £30,000 Reduced

THE LIBRARY OF THE BRITISH MUSEUM

3 per cent Annuities, the Reserve; the remaining £26,531 odd was barely enough to defray repairs, fitting and legal and miscellaneous initial expenses. Yet in the Statement of the Money Votes of the House of Commons in aid of the Trustees, given in evidence before the Committee of 1835-6 (Appendix 33) there appears under 1753, besides the £30,000 for general expenses, £243,000 for buildings! Governments often flattered Parliament for its supposed liberality to the Museum, but imagination rarely took so high a flight as this. The author of the *Synopsis* in 1808 (p. xv) was able to speak of "Parliament, ever ready to avail itself of every opportunity for extending the utility of this Institution"; the Townley and Lansdowne grants were then fresh.

27. About 1762 George III presented some prize lottery tickets which had come to him from George II, amounting to £1,123; this sum was invested with Edwards's fund.
28. *Journals of the House of Commons*, 1784, p. 979. In the General Finance Act of 47 Geo. III, cap. 76 (1807) it is ordered that the sum of £4,925 for the purchase of the Lansdowne MSS. be paid without any fee or deduction, which marks the end of the old disorderly way of paying the salaries of Civil Servants.
29. *Ib.*, 1777, p. 237.
30. *Ib.*, 1783, p. 981.
31. There was a fee farm rent of £5 a year to the Bedford Estate. It was extinguished about 1840.
32. Note by Sir E. Maunde Thompson, Principal Librarian, in Johnson's *Lives of the Poets*, ed. Mrs. A. Napier (Bohn), 1890, iii, 374.
33. Malcolm, vol. ii (1803), p. 500. For this section, and indeed for the history of the Reading Room throughout, I am indebted above all to G. F. Barwick, *The Reading Room of the British Museum*, 1929.
34. See above, Pt. I, ch. i, n. 38.
35. Wray's books, or many of them, were destroyed at the Charterhouse in an air-raid of 1941.
36. Gray's entertainingly sub-acid letters give us a picture of the life of the first Reading Room. On 23rd July, 1759, he wrote to Mason from Southampton Row, describing the place and some of these, his fellow-readers:—

> "The Museum will be my chief amusement. I this day passed through the jaws of a great Leviathan [obviously a whale in the first Natural History Room], that lay in my way, into the belly of Dr. Templeman, superintendent of the reading room, who congratulated himself on the sight of so much good company. We were—a man that writes for Lord Royston, a man that writes for Dr. Burton of York, a third that writes for the Emperor of Germany or Dr. Pocock [Bishop of Ossory, afterwards of Meath], for he speaks the worst English I ever heard [in another letter he has become "two Prussians"]; Dr. Stukely, who writes for himself, the very worst person he could write for; and I, who only read to know if there were anything worth writing, and that not without some difficulty."

Gray worked on MSS. (especially Harleian) in English History and copied Sir Thomas Wyatt's Defence, which Walpole printed (*Miscellanea Antiqua*, ii, 1772): and a little later was reading the papers on the Rising in the North

NOTES

of 1569 (to Wharton, Jan. 23, 1760); he also speaks (to Mason, 6th Oct., 1750) of the Museum's wealth of manuscripts of "my old Lydgate and Occleve."

37. Barwick points out that as late as the eighteen-thirties it was the practice, though under no regulation, to admit women in pairs.
38. J. and A. van Rymsdyk: *Musaeum Britannicum*, 1778.
39. As it also is by Barwick, p. 30.

PART I, CHAPTER III

1. A Cracherode family Trustee would have been added to the Board, but he left no male representative. His vacancy was therefore filled by the election of his executor, Shute Barrington, Bishop of Durham. (Ellis before 1835 Committee, No. 35.) The bequest was the occasion of an Act (39 Geo. III, c. 76), exempting from duty that and any similar future bequest to a body corporate. The Trustees used the Cracherode Room as their Board Room. (F. Madden's MS. Journal, in the Bodleian, for 31 Dec. 1850.)
2. Nares was a clerical pluralist and not dependent on his post in the Museum, being at the same time and during his time at the Museum Archdeacon of Stafford, Canon Residentiary of Lichfield, and Prebendary of St. Paul's, as well as holding a succession of country livings. The Rev. Joseph Bean also entered as Assistant in 1812, the Printed Books having an extra Assistant, which the other Departments had not. He died in 1826, and was succeeded by Cary. Extra Assistants at this time were Schlichtegroll (1816) and G. H. Noehden (1819), both probably Orientalists, and Philip Bliss (1822) who, however, returned to the Bodleian in the same year. F. A. Walter, of the King's Library, was appointed a regular Assistant in 1822.
3. Edwards, *Lives of the Founders*, p. 516.
4. Obituary notice in Nichols, *Illustr. Hist. Lit.*, vii, 677–9.
5. The Miss Planta, who taught George III's children, and was Fanny Burney's fellow-sufferer under the Schwellenberg, was probably his sister; his only son, Joseph, became a diplomat. The portrait of Planta in the Board Room, printed at about sixty, shows a broad genial countenance.
6. John Pinkerton wrote to Horace Walpole on 11th February, canvassing for the post which would thus have become vacant; another candidate, favoured by Banks, was the Swedish antiquary Grimr Thorkelin.
7. Ellis's name was sent up as the first of the two required under the Statute, but it is said that someone transposed the two names, and that Ellis only secured the appointment by an undignified pursuit of Sir William Knighton, the King's physician, when he was in his carriage. The other candidate was Henry Fynes Clinton, the learned author of the *Fasti Hellenici*. Had Fynes Clinton been appointed, there would have arisen the undesirable precedent of an appointment from outside, which is always possible, though now very improbable. Clinton was a protégé of Archbishop Manners Sutton.
8. Garnett in *D.N.B.* explains this thus: "Excellent health and the absence of any machinery for compulsory retirement kept Ellis at his post till February 1856." Directors to the present day are not subject to the normal superannua-

tion rules, their appointment being direct from the Crown; but the last three have retired just before the three-score years and ten.

9. Cowtan, *Memories of the British Museum*, 1872, p. 99.
10. See above, p. 74.
11. For Douce and his collections, see *Bodleian Quarterly Record*, 1934, vol. vii, pp. 359–82.
12. Maurice was a copious but totally uninspired versifier. His first effort in this line, a translation of the *Œdipus Rex*, written at college in 1779, had been flattered by a preface by Dr. Johnson. Specimens of his "petrifactions of a plodding brain," as Byron called his *Richmond Hill*, may be found in Thornton's great botanical picture-and-poetry-book, *The Temple of Flora*, as for example:

> To THORNTON loudly strike th'applausive string,
> 'Mid desert wastes who bids an Eden spring.
> Though o'er her head the southern whirlwind rave,
> Secure behold august STRELITZIA wave;
> While amidst barren rocks and Arctic snows
> Fair KALMIA in refulgent beauty glows. . . .
> *The Mighty Work Complete*, through EUROPE's bounds
> *Thy* name is echoed, and *thy* fame resounds;
> Exulting Science weaves the deathless bays,
> And rival Monarchs swell the note of Praise.

Maurice's colleague, Dr. George Shaw, Keeper of Natural History, also contributed a number of poems to *The Temple of Flora*, but did not reach these heights.

13. Report of Commons Committee, 25th March, 1825.
14. On 10th March, 1832, the Trustees of the Museum ordered that the income intended for this last purpose should be paid to the Librarians in charge of the MSS. (later the Keeper of the Department alone, who was called Keeper and Egerton Librarian), but that their ordinary salaries on the establishment should be reduced by the amounts thus received. It may be admitted that it would have been awkward for the Keeper of Manuscripts to be paid more than the other Keepers; but why did not the Trustees do the obvious thing and obtain the permission of Egerton's representatives to add this money to the fund for purchases instead of letting it lapse into relief of taxation? It was not till just after a century of this scandal, which had become so established as to attract no attention inside any more than outside the Museum, that the authority of the Charity Commissioners and of the Treasury was obtained to use the income in future for additional Egerton purchases. Parliament had cognizance of the arrangement, the Trustees' minute being printed in the Evidence to the Committee of 1836, thus relieving them of the moral responsibility. The Royal Commission of 1850 strongly condemned the system, but without effect.

The relevant parts of Egerton's long and rambling will are printed by Edwards, *Memoirs*, pp. 449–55. Among the sources of income devised to the Museum were "all Seats, sittings and pew rents in the Church of Whitchurch-cum-Marbury." The Act 5 Geo. IV, c. 39 had empowered the Trustees to hold estates in land. But the Egerton lands were sold and the produce funded.

NOTES

15. By a rather confusing distinction the MSS. are named the "Egerton," the Fund the "Bridgewater." The later-acquired MSS. are given numbers running on from those of the bequest; they are catalogued in the volumes describing the Additional MSS.
16. Such a record could be constructed. As was stated by Baber before the Committee of 1836 (No. 4710) all books so received up to 1814 were stamped on their backs with a rose and crown in gold as being received by virtue of the King's privilege.
17. *Synopsis*, 1st ed., 1808, p. x and *n*.
18. Christian, Professor of the Law of England in the University of Cambridge, was held in small esteem as a lawyer, and at his death in 1823 was said to have "died in the full vigour of his incapacity" (see *D.N.B.*). But his combative and determined character, which he shared with his brother Fletcher, the leader of the mutineers of the Bounty, well served the cause of scholarship.
19. Until the Copyright Act of 1842, which first gave it automatic delivery, the Museum, like the other libraries, was obliged to employ a collector. The Cowtans *père et fils*, were Copyright Collectors for the Museum.
20. Barwick, *Reading Room*, p. 58. For the history of Copyright and the Museum, see R. C. B. Partridge, *The History of the Legal Deposit of Books throughout the British Empire*, 1938.
21. Committee, 1835–36, *Report and Evidence*.
22. *Ib.*
23. Nichols (*Ill. Hist. Lit.*, vol. v, pp. 574–76) gives correspondence with Beloe dealing with this episode. If Gough was right the fault was probably at the door of E. W. Gray, Keeper of Natural History and the Museum's first Secretary, 1787–1806, or of his successor, Edward Bray. Forshall denied that Gough had left his books to Oxford because of his not being elected a Trustee. Douce, he said, did not do so for a quarrel, "the quarrel, such as it was, was much older"; he saw Malone's books at Oxford and thought that his added to them would make a perfect Shakespeare library. (Committee, 1835, answers 1467 ff.)
24. Committee, 1835–36, *Report*, etc.
25. Printed as a Parliamentary Paper.
26. From now on the Staff could be required to work on three of the other days in the week, besides the two regular work-days. For these days they were paid extra. A regular whole-time week was only introduced in 1837.
27. In 1801 the Trustees raised the pay of the Senior Staff in view of the cost of living due to the war; the Principal Librarian's salary was raised from £212 to £320 (he remained Expenditor as well), the Under-Librarians', afterwards called Keepers, from £108 to £200, and the Assistant Librarians' from £69 6s. 8d. to £120; days worked above two in the week were still paid for extra.

    In 1802 three Attendants were appointed to relieve the Officers as guides to the Exhibitions and so free them for cataloguing and arranging the collections. The Attendants at this time had often been noblemen's couriers, and were nominated as knowing foreign tongues.

    At this time the Under-Librarians were first required (by the Statutes of 1805) to report annually on the progress of their Departments. This had been suggested in 1801.
28. It is only necessary to read his *Sexagenarian*.

29. A contemporary squib entitled *Fragment of a Tragedy lately acted at the British Museum* (and endorsed *The Tears of Cracherode, or News from Below*), states that "the Trust would gladly prosecute, but can't convict."
30. Edwards, *Lives of the Founders*, pp. 572–73.
31. According to Edwards (*loc. cit.*) Planta also worked on the Catalogue.
32. The scheme of classification, or "Synthetical arrangement," of the Printed Books, was issued as an Appendix to the *Synopsis*, and also separately, see above, p. 340. The Class Catalogue was largely discussed before the Commission of 1835–36, and again before that of 1847–49. Both Ellis and Panizzi (to be followed much later by Fortescue) declared that no one had used a classified catalogue if he could use an alphabetical subject-index; Panizzi had "never heard of two men agreeing on the plan of a Classed Catalogue," and thought even Dryander's Banks Catalogue usable only by a very clever botanist, mineralogist, or zoologist. But to a scientific witness of 1836, J. Scott Bowerbank, all was easy; he could, he declared, classify a thousand books a day.
33. Horne's *Introduction to Bibliography*, 1814, and *Introduction to the Critical Study and Knowledge of Holy Scriptures, with maps and facsimiles of Biblical Manuscripts*, 3 vols, 1821, were however works of value in his day, and probably contributed to recommend him to the Museum.
34. Forshall, however, could be genial with his intimates, and a pleasant side of his character is revealed by the moving words of regret at the early death of Rosen, with which at the end of 1838 he concluded the preface to Part I of the Catalogue of Oriental MSS. (See also below, Pt. I, ch. iv, n. 23.)
35. In this year, for the Jubilee of George III, the Museum Gate was illuminated with "G.R. vota publica quinquagies suscepta," a proceeding which brought on the Trustees some obloquy in Opposition newspapers, but on grounds of politics and not of danger to the buildings.
36. This room is described by J. P. Malcolm, *Londinium Redivivum*, vol. ii (1803), p. 500.
37. It was only two years after his appointment that Cater earned the praise of Lamb, quoted on p. 85. But for all his personal qualities the plan was a mistake, which was rectified at the opening of the new Reading Room.

    On 31st December, 1850, the old Attendant Bromley told Madden that when he joined the Staff in 1810 the Reading Room was in No. II (he had forgotten No. III) upstairs, between the Sandwich Islands Room and the Lansdowne Room. The Printed Books, he said, had fifteen rooms, not sixteen, as in the *Synopsis*; twelve were on the ground floor and three in the basement, of which two held periodicals and one the Hargrave law books. Madden adds that when he first visited the Museum in 1823, the Reading Room (No. V) held the Harleian MSS. (Madden's MS. Journal in the Bodleian).

    The new Reading Rooms of 1829 were of awkward access, building being in progress; H. S. Peacock said in 1835 "that they were approached by a labyrinth leading along a gutter and over two drains" (*Remarks on the Present State of the British Museum*).
38. Barwick, *Reading Room*, pp. 59–60.
39. If the Speaker took a worthy view of the Museum, it would appear that the Archbishop (Manners Sutton) did not. Replying to a canvasser for J. T. Smith's candidature in 1816 for the Assistant Keepership in charge of Prints

NOTES

and Drawings, he wrote: "With such interest as Mr. J. T. Smith possesses, I am astonished that he should think it worth while to waste his strength in pursuit of such a trifling office as that which is now vacant in the Museum." This letter Smith, who obtained the office (not trifling in his eyes), printed in his *Book for a Rainy Day* (ed. Whitten, 1905, p. 224).

40. Sentries were placed at the Gate, and were only discontinued in 1863.
41. These were the novels press-marked N., now a most useful chronological series, but when new an obvious nuisance if not withheld from readers. The MS. Catalogue, compiled in 1837, was still in use in the Reading Room in the sixties. Its compilation when many of the books were new seems very unnecessary.

Baber reported the number of books (not volumes, which would total 40,000) sent into the Reading Room during 1st March–31st May, 1855 (Committee, 1836, App. 22 (3).)

Theology	1,190	
Classics	763	
Science	2,713	
Art	624	
History	2,167	
Antiquities	481	
Law	945	
Biography	707	
Genealogy (including Peerages, Heraldry, Chivalry, Knighthood, etc.)	153	
Topography	1,286	
Voyages and Travels	797	
Encyclopaedias, Dictionaries, Grammars, etc.		421
Poetry and the Drama		1,187
Romances, Novels and Annuals		495
Reviews, Magazines and Modern Periodical Literature		870
Miscellaneous		1,725
		16,524
Deduct Classics		763
		15,761

These figures dispose pretty completely of the complaints about Virgils and novels. Similar legends have been familiar in recent times.

42. Quoted by Barwick, *op. cit.*, p. 61.
43. Committee, 1835–36, No. 5133.
44. Harris Nicolas had the sense to defend the change at the time, but later he forgot and attacked it, denouncing his own words, which Panizzi in answering him wickedly quoted without inverted commas; he then described Nicolas as "a man of so flexible a judgement and so treacherous a memory" that he need be no further answered.
45. Barwick, *op. cit.*, pp. 52–4.
46. *Letters of Charles and Mary Lamb*, ed. Lucas, iii, 62. Lamb ceased to be a regular reader in October 1827, when he moved to Enfield; he had exhausted the plays (*ib*. iii, 140).
47. Which, considering what the Trustees had spent on repairs, suggests that the rebuilding of Hooke's house had been cheaply done.
48. Probably with some such extension already in view. In 1804, when the Townley Building was planned, Smirke was still a student; it was the work of George Saunders. Bromley (see *n*. 37 above) told Madden that in 1803 (meaning 1810?) there was in the Cracherode Room (then the Trustees' Room) a large volume of plans of the Museum and its garden by Saunders. This has not been identified.

Smirke was told that there were then about thirty readers at a time in the Reading Room, but that they might be expected to increase to eighty or a hundred. Ellis, with even greater modesty, told him that some space would be needed for additional MSS., but that there were not likely to be many. Smirke retired in 1846, and was followed by his brother Sydney.

49. These new Reading Rooms had open shelves, holding some 8,400 books of reference, a great improvement. The Gallery (now the Ethnographical Gallery) above the King's Library was intended to house the national picture gallery. The Angerstein bequest, however, made a separate Gallery necessary; the Trustees of the British Museum for some time controlled the National Gallery also. The upper gallery of the new wing was then given to Natural History.
50. See above, p. 83. There were now open shelves for 10,000 books of reference.
51. Committee, 1836, ans. 4955.
52. For the buildings erected between 1823 and 1835, see Smirke's evidence before the Commission, 1836, Nos. 5271 *sqq.*; and for the whole story of the buildings to 1914, see the summary account by Sir Frederic Kenyon prefixed to the portfolio of plates, *The Buildings of the British Museum*, 1914. The Pediment is the work of Westmacott, and represents, very inartistically, the Progress of Civilization.

PART I, CHAPTER IV

1. For this, the heroic age of the Museum, there is abundant material in Fagan's *Life of Panizzi*, in Cowtan's *Memories of the British Museum*, and in Edwards's *Lives of the Founders of the British Museum* and *Memoirs of Libraries*.
2. *Observations*, pp. 12–13.
3. *Report from the Select Committee appointed to enquire into the condition, management, and affairs of the British Museum.—Report from the Select Committee appointed in the following Session to consider the same.* The evidence included (as an Appendix) elaborate accounts, with statistics, of the size, government, hours, finance, etc., of twenty-seven of the chief Continental Libraries. This document, one of great value to the historian of libraries, was chiefly due to Panizzi, who by "holding up" his leave had visited most of them for the purpose.
4. *Select Committee's Report*, 1836, Nos. 4918, 4929, etc. Panizzi had had bitter experience when employed to prepare a Classed Catalogue of the Library of the Royal Society.
5. April 5 and 23, 1836, quoting the example of C. G. Heyne's Göttingen Catalogue; this writer also dwelt on the inferiority of English libraries to that of Paris, and adopted Harris's demand for literary men rather than men of rank as Trustees.
6. Millard addressed a petition to the House of Commons on 28th July, 1836, regretting that he notices this omission in the Report, and asking the House to direct the Trustees to complete and print the Classed Catalogue in place of the Alphabetical. Millard was fighting not only for himself but for Horne, who was apparently a relative by marriage. The two men had as long before this as 1811 collaborated in a catalogue of the library of the Surrey Institution. Millard's petition was printed in *The Mechanics' Magazine* (6th August, 1836), the journal which printed Watts's early articles on the Museum Library.

NOTES

Millard also printed in the same year two editions of *A Letter to the Right Hon. T. Spring-Rice, M.P., Chancellor of the Exchequer, containing a plan for the better management of the British Museum*. But neither the Chancellor of the Exchequer nor the Trustees took any notice of him.

7. Banks's continuation grants had been estimated for in these years. Perhaps they had been diverted to other subheads, as was then possible.
8. There is today, however, at least one well-known Museum, not in this country, where the Secretary performs this function, thereby creating one more card-catalogue to no purpose.
9. Madden (1801–73) was a brilliant palaeographer, and a scholar of infinite industry, among much other work editing *Havelok the Dane* (1828), Layamon's *Brut* (1847), Matthew Paris's *Historia Anglorum* (1866–69), and above all Wiclif's Bible, 1850, in which last he collaborated with Forshall, the pair collating no fewer than sixty-five MSS. for their text. His MS. journals, covering the long period 1819–72, bequeathed by him to the Bodleian, to be opened in 1920 (MSS. Eng. hist. 140–82), abound in information. They make it clear that from need of money, especially after he was in 1832 made, like Ellis, a Knight of the Guelphic Order, he seriously overworked himself; and this may be part of the reason for the asperity which kept his Department in bad condition during his Keepership, and especially for his furious jealousy of Panizzi, with whom as Principal Librarian after 1856 he would only communicate through the Assistant Keeper, Bond.
10. Cureton resigned his post in 1849 on being appointed Canon of Westminster and Rector of St. Margaret's. He was later Royal Trustee of the Museum. While at the Museum he was distinguished in a period of jealousies for his gentleness of disposition. The Oriental Library has a bust of him.
11. It used to be an article of faith in the Library that his grandfather, Giles Jones, and not Goldsmith, was the author of *Goody Twoshoes*. He certainly wrote for Newbery.
12. Edwards, *Memoirs of Libraries*, vol. i, pp. 552–53.
13. *A Letter*, 1836; 2nd ed., 1839, entitled, *Remarks*, etc.
14. He was a member of the family which owned the open-air swimming pool in Islington, Peerless (originally Perilous) Pool. My father, who as a boy frequented the place in the fifties, was told that Watts had been used to sit and take the bathers' money, and so found time for study.
15. Bullen, Parry and Nicolas Simons were appointed temporary Assistants together specially for this work. But Parry was soon diverted to the Catalogue and its Rules. Simons remained on the staff till 1870; he wrote on the Junius mystery.
16. The condition of the Printed Books was in fact relatively what it had been when Grosley wrote in 1770: "Les livrés imprimés sont la partie la plus faible de cet immense assemblage; mais quelque étendu que soit le bâtiment du *Musaeum*, il ne pourroit, sans faire tort aux autres parties qu'il réunit, contenir une bibliothèque telle que l'Angleterre peut et doit la former pour l'ornement de sa capitale" (*Londres*, vol. ii, pp. 266–67).
17. The tale was told, and very well told, by Cureton in the *Quarterly Review* for December 1845, vol. cliii, pp. 39 ff. Even more entertaining is Robert Curzon's account of his experiences in the Nitrian convents in his *Visits to the*

THE LIBRARY OF THE BRITISH MUSEUM

Monasteries of the Levant, 1849 (ed. D. G. Hogarth, 1916, with introduction). Archdeacon Tattam's step-daughter, Miss Platt, who accompanied him, kept a diary of their travels, which was published.

18. A list of some of the MSS. Curzon brought home was produced by him in 1849 as *A Catalogue of Materials for Writing*. These, the Zouche MSS. (Curzon inherited the title of Lord Zouche) were later deposited in the Museum and were bequeathed to it in 1918; they are in Greek, Latin, Slavonic, Flemish, Dutch, French, English, Irish, Italian, Mexican and various Oriental tongues. The Zouche Mexican Codex was transferred about 1925 to the Department of Ethnography, with all but one of the other ancient Mexican documents and a volume of papers, including the "Codex Tepetlaotzoc" and tracings, formed by Lord Kingsborough for his *Antiquities of Mexico*, in which he essayed to prove that the Aztecs were the lost Ten Tribes. In the Kingsborough volume is also a tracing of one of the three surviving Maya codices, the Dresden. The Museum, though rich in Maya remains, possesses the original of none of the three.

19. "Folioing," an ugly word conventionally used in place of "foliating," is numbering the leaves. Most old MSS. bear several foliations made by previous owners, and wrong references result. The Museum's, which should always be used, is in the top right-hand corner of the rectos only, and is in *pencil*.

20. *Report and Evidence*, 1850. This vast document is even fuller than its predecessor of 1835-36, and much fuller of trivialities. All the quarrels are exposed (Ellis, good easy man, stated in evidence that he was "not aware of any private disputes" between colleagues, and thought "the Museum's business conducted as harmoniously as he could desire!"), all the memoranda, reports and even notes that passed are printed at length in Appendices, the most ample public washing of small dirty linen that could be conceived. The Commission only met three times in 1847, and is commonly spoken of as that of 1848-49. The controversy over the Catalogue is very well summarised by A. Predeek in *Festschrift Georg Leyh*, 1937, and translated, abridged, in *The Library Association Record*, Oct.-Dec. 1937—the centenary of Panizzi's Keepership. N. H. Nicolas contributed in 1846 a pamphlet, *The Supply of Printed Books to the Reading Room of the British Museum*. Accounts of the Commission are to be found in Fagan's *Life of Panizzi*, vol. i, and in Cowtan's *Memories*. The episode is so well known that it is but lightly sketched here.

21. *A Letter on the Management of the Library of Printed Books in the British Museum.—A Second Letter*, 1848.

22. *Letter to Lord Ellesmere*, 1848.

23. Forshall was placed on a pension, the first instance of this in the Museum Staff. He had been absent for a couple of years, and was not fit to appear before the Commission. He printed a protest against the Report, in which he suggested that it was a forgery.

Forshall seems to have begun very early in his career the mishandling of the Museum's internal affairs which was to be so disastrous. No one else can be meant by the kindly Baber's emphatic answer "certainly not" to the question asked him by a member of the 1835 Committee whether there was that general consultation and cordial intercourse which was satisfactory to him as the head of his Department. And in 1834, when Baber had reported on Panizzi's ability

NOTES

and energy (he did more work in a day than any two of his colleagues, worthy men of the old world) and recommended him for some mark of favour, though the Printed Books Sub-Committee proposed that his salary should be raised from £160 to £200, that of the regular Assistants, the General Meeting refused to make an exception, and according to Grenville (who left the room indignant and to his further indignation had the minute specially sent to him afterwards) this meeting was packed by Forshall and Lord Farnborough, who moved the rejection. Grenville was devoted to Panizzi, and may be thought a prejudiced witness; but there is nothing improbable in the story, except that Farnborough is more likely to have been a tool.

Probably the seeds of Forshall's insanity, which declared itself in 1850, had been slowly ripening for many years. He and Ellis disliked and feared the popularizing of the Museum and its chief prophet Panizzi. Manuscripts can never be widely used like printed books, and Forshall was a Manuscripts man. As to Forshall's disease, it is worth noticing that Gray told the Royal Commission that the conditions of life in the Museum were unhealthy and the low salaries trying to the mind. He said that in his time six men had left or died under mental disease, i.e. more than from any other cause. Whatever his conduct to his equals, Forshall treated his subordinates with great kindness, as is shown by Cowtan. (See also above, Pt. I, ch. iii, p. 36.)

The Secretaryship became too great a burden for Principal Librarians as time went on and the Museum grew larger, and in 1926 the two offices were again separated, the present writer being appointed Secretary; he was followed in 1940 by the present Secretary, Mr. J. H. Witney.

PART I, CHAPTER V

1. Watts's article, signed P.P.C.R. (="Peerless Pool, City Road," as he told Garnett), is well worth study. Of the quadrangle he writes, "The space thus unfortunately wasted would have provided accommodation for the whole library, much superior to what is now proposed to afford it. A reading room of ample dimensions might have stood in the centre, and been surrounded on all four sides by galleries for the books, communicating with each other and lighted from the top." He also suggests "some simple mechanical contrivance, such as an endless book-cradle reaching from the further end of the library to the reading room . . . to save the endless running to and fro."

   Fergusson, *Observations on the British Museum, National Gallery, and Public Record Office*, 1852.

   Copy of all Communications made by the Architect and Officers of the British Museum to the Trustees, respecting the enlargement of the building, and all correspondence between the Trustees and the Treasury, 30th June, 1852.

   Quarterly Review, June 1852, by Croker, who had been a valuable witness before the Commission.

2. The Reading Room is so well known and has so often been described that no full account need be given here. The chief facts are as follows. The quadrangle is 313 × 235 feet; the Iron Library 258 × 184 feet (leaving a clear roadway), the Reading Room enclosed in it 140 feet in diameter. Seats were provided

THE LIBRARY OF THE BRITISH MUSEUM

at first for 302 readers, but by the insertion of small tables between the main rows this number was afterwards increased to 394, and then to 458. The shelving on the walls of the Room held about 60,000 books, but the Catalogue desks and free standing BB (Bibliography) cases inserted in recent years, allow for many more. Public access is from the Entrance Hall only, service access from the North, though in Panizzi's rough first sketch of 18th April, 1852, access from other quarters is indicated. The Superintendent's table in the centre is somewhat raised, so that he can see between the radii of readers' seats. A word of praise should be given to the book-rests at each reader's seat; they can be fixed at any angle whatever, so as to get the light preferred. Electric lighting was installed in 1879, but not in the Iron Library till the next century, till when the service of books to readers from the general library necessarily ceased at dusk. The Museum has been very lucky in escaping the perils of the gas age. In 1861, the Trustees took the opinion of Captain Braidwood, the Chief Superintendent of the London Fire Engine Establishment, as to the safety of gas lighting. His reply was strongly discouraging, dwelling on the effect of gas in desiccating and discolouring; privately he is even said to have threatened to resign if gas were introduced into the Museum. The Trustees decided not to open the Museum at an hour when artificial light would be needed.

3. Smirke's model, with Alfred Stevens's scheme of frescoes and statuettes, is in the Victoria and Albert Museum.
4. *List of the Books of Reference in the Reading Room of the British Museum*, [By W. B. Rye] 1859. Winter Jones's introduction, reprinted in later editions (4th and latest, 1910) is the best source for the development of this period.

   A Guide to the Reading Room, desiderated by Lord Seymour before the Commission, was also published.

   The general approval of the new Reading Room had exceptions. *The Athenaeum*, which had for twenty years displayed the most violent animus against the conduct of the Library and especially against Panizzi, on 2nd October, 1851, protested against so large a room: "No man can *write* well at the Museum, and not one in ten can *read* to any good purpose. What would it be if there were five hundred persons coughing, scribbling, rocking, stamping, walking, talking, laughing, sneezing, snoring, fumbling, grumbling, mumbling —all in one miscellaneous chorus?" With rather more sense the author (Dilke?) suggested that Library and Museum be separated.
5. The contractors, Messrs. Baker and Fielder, should be named *honoris causa*.
6. Garnett in *D.N.B.*
7. Madden (with the assistance of his wives, as appeard in his Journals) made a large and valuable collection of cuttings, views, portraits, etc., for the history of the Museum in four volumes, now in the Library (C. 55. i, 1).
8. He was not knighted till he had been three years retired; but he had refused a knighthood in 1861. He died on 8th April, 1879.
9. Gosse's experience was not happy. So long afterwards as 1906 (in the *Daily Graphic*, Oct. 11th) he made this statement, qualifying it indeed by the remark that Panizzi was "a reformer and innovator of the first class." Other seniors roused his bile still more: "The tyranny of Sir Anthony Panizzi was repeated by a number of persons who had neither his character nor talents. The junior

NOTES

assistants were put underground . . . in ill-lighted rooms with a smell of dry-rot. . . . As far as possible the officials did nothing whatever." Gosse tells how he brought up a number of corrections of errors he had found in Scandinavian titles, only to receive the answer, "Can't you mind your own business?" But he revealed that not all his seniors were tyrants. The Keeper, finding some juniors playing cricket outside the door of his room, complained: "I wish to goodness you and your companions would play cricket when you *know* I am out at lunch."

In the manuscripts, too, the Keeper's lunch-hour had its uses. Sir George Warner recalled that when he was a new recruit he sometimes (as if still at school) "kept cavé" while a colleague used the conveniently large table in the Keeper's Room for designing cartoons for stained-glass windows.

In years long after Gosse's disappearance into the Board of Trade stupid martinets were still found. One Assistant, tired of seeing one of them walk through the Catalogue Room rattling his keys and looking fiercely about him, cured him of the practice by collecting and submitting to him daily the most unanswerable cataloguing conundrums he and his young colleagues could produce. "Oh, by the way, Sir," he would say, "I've got a little query here that no doubt you can settle?" And Mr. R. F. Sharp tells how once in his early days a group of Assistants was discussing something quite unofficial when a senior came into view, upon which one, with more presence of mind than the rest, raised his voice and said in a tone of finality, "We agree, then, that in this case a cross reference may be made from the name of Our Blessed Redeemer."

Those human-hearted Keepers, Garnett and Fortescue, broke this bad tradition, treating their juniors like colleagues and friends.

10. William Ralston Shedden, afterwards Shedden-Ralston (1828–89), did not take up Russian till after joining the Printed Books staff, but he became a most notable expert in the language, literature, folklore and history of the country, as is shown by his *Songs of the Russian People* (1872), *Russian Folk Tales* (1873), and *Early Russian History* (1874); his great descriptive work on Russia remained unpublished at his death. He was also a brilliant raconteur, but sensitive and liable to melancholy. His admirable work in succession to Watts in building the Museum's collection of Slavonic books was cut short by ill-health in 1875. Ever since his time something of a special activity in the Library, this has been continued since his retirement, chiefly by G. W. Porter, George Calderon, R. Nisbet Bain, Lawrence Taylor, and Mr. L. C. Wharton in succession.

PART I, CHAPTER VI

1. Patmore raised in 1859 a company of Volunteers in the Museum, which he claimed was the earliest in the Civil Service.

PART I, CHAPTER VII

1. Of many sources for the history of the printed Catalogue the best is Garnett's *Essays in Librarianship and Bibliography*. Edward Edwards gives in *Memoirs*

THE LIBRARY OF THE BRITISH MUSEUM

of Libraries (ii. 851–68) an excellent summary of the argument: his own verdict was for printing.

2. This device of moveable slips, still used, was simultaneously suggested in 1849 by Eugene Roy, of the Library, and by Wilson Croker. Watts had (in a letter to Panizzi of 28th May, 1855, quoted by John Macfarlane in *Library Administration*, p. 139) expressed the view that the catalogue should be printed instead of transcribed; but this was not to oppose Panizzi's chief contention, which was against publishing. The "4th copy" slips were at first called the "carbonic hand-catalogue." The slips were transcribed by "manifold writers" and laid down in the volumes. Watts suggested that these carbonic copies of titles could be used for special catalogues, and also for a shelf-catalogue; the latter use was adopted but not the former. This anticipated the modern use of cards: It is to be remembered that the General Catalogue did not contain the King's, Grenville, Thomason, or Croker collections. There is an excellent article on the Catalogue in *Edinburgh Review*, Jan. 1859.
3. In a notice of Vol. I of the new Catalogue, Bibliographical Society, *Transactions*, 4th ser. vol. ii, 1931, pp. 113–15. The revised Rules were printed in 1895. The greatest single simplification was the main-title-cross-reference, which, by introducing the titles of the books, gave meaning to the long series of plain cross-references to editors of series and the like; Miller introduced his in about 1890. Pollard quotes Russell Martineau as lamenting that the Rules were not revised before printing was undertaken. *An Explanation of the System of the Catalogue* was issued in 1888.

   It is often stated that the Museum Catalogue is in volume form, and it is (favourably or unfavourably) contrasted with card-catalogues. But it is really in sheaf, every leaf, column, and slip being movable. Experienced readers look both at "column" on the left of the left-hand page, and at "accessions" on the rest of the two open pages, and sometimes on additional inserted leaves.
4. *Daily Graphic*, 11th October, 1906. See above, Part I, ch. v, n. 9.
5. Jenner had been transferred to the Printed Books from the Manuscripts. He was a considerable ecclesiologist, and especially liturgiologist, and an expert in the Cornish language, of which he published a grammar. A scholar with a fund of instructive and amusing anecdote, he is remembered by his juniors as Gilbert Walmesley was by Johnson, for "the copiousness of his communication."
6. Garnett, "The Sliding-Press at the British Museum," in *Essays in Librarianship and Bibliography*. Special gratuities were made to Jenner and Sparrow for the saving in public expenditure they had made possible.
7. Garnett, *Essays in Librarianship and Bibliography*, p. 338.

PART I, CHAPTER VIII

1. The Royal Commission on Copyright, 1875–78, recommended that copyright should be made contingent on deposit at and registration by the Museum. This was opposed by the Trustees on the ground that it would involve great increase of staff and accommodation. The Bill of 1878, based on the Commission's Report, was dropped.

NOTES

2. Newspapers were originally deposited at the Stamp Office under the Stamp Act, and in 1822 the Trustees applied for them to be transferred to the Museum, which was effected by a Treasury Order in 1823. English provincial papers were added in 1832, and Scotch and Irish in 1848. Watts was in favour of purchase, but Winter Jones demurred on the ground that the Museum had a right to them, and that the legal character of its copies would be lost were they not legally deposited.
3. The purchase of what is known as "the Improvement Property" was made for £200,000, a price which reflects great credit on the Duke, seeing that so far back as 1859 the property had been valued at £240,000. The loan by the Government to the Trustees is being gradually paid off, and will be clear by 1949. But the difficulty in using the site will be the loss of the rents. The land and houses in the South-East corner of the island site had been purchased in 1839 under the Act 2 Vict., c. 10, in order "to complete the general design and make a suitable front and access."
4. Suggested by Sir Flinders Petrie, *Times* of 5th June, 1900.
5. Charles Pierre Henri Rieu is ignored by the *Dictionary of National Biography*, but a long obituary notice of him by Professor E. G. Browne appeared in the *Journal of the Royal Asiatic Society* for July 1902. I am also indebted to his son, Mr. E. V. Rieu, for some facts. Born in 1820 of Swiss family, Charles Rieu studied Semitic literature at Bonn, Leyden, St. Petersburg, Vienna and Paris, and made a considerable reputation. Appointed in 1847 to the Museum as a Supernumerary Assistant in the Department of Manuscripts, he was in 1867 transferred, as noted above, to be Keeper of the new Department of Oriental Manuscripts. The great catalogues of Persian MSS. (3 vols., 1879–83 and Supplement, 1895) and of Turkish MSS. (1888) stand to his credit. Rieu left behind him not only his well-deserved reputation as a scholar, but a character for good relations with his colleagues.
6. Hebrew books, important since the foundation, and greatly swollen and made more important by the Michael library, bought in 1847, were described in the excellent catalogue by J. Zedner in 1867, and its supplement by S. van Straalen in 1894.
7. Sir F. G. Kenyon quotes from Dr. Pollard a characteristic example of Proctor's independence, not to say waywardness. "When, during an epidemic of smallpox, Proctor refused to obey the order to be vaccinated (because it was an order), Thompson put it to him that he must submit, not for his own sake, but lest he should infect others. Proctor succumbed, and ever afterwards spoke of him affectionately as 'Tommy.'"
8. For sketches of Garnett see *The Library*, 1906, new ser., vol. vii, pp. 225–56. One anecdote of Garnett may be worth giving; it has the merit of including his native provincialism, of pronouncing the ŭ in such words as "put" short, as in "cut." On being consulted by a shy young Assistant as to how he should propose to his beloved—for Garnett was consulted on many very unbibliographical matters—he replied: "When I proposed to Mrs. Garnett we were sitting over the fire, with her cat on the hearthrug between us. And I said: 'Pŭss, does your mistress love me?' And she said, 'Pŭss, she does.'"
9. Fortescue died on the point of retirement on 26th October, 1912. He owed his appointment to the old system of nomination, being a cousin of Archbishop

THE LIBRARY OF THE BRITISH MUSEUM

Tait, thus showing that nepotism has its uses. Unacademic (he had been a sailor in youth) but very quick-witted and original, he was also, like Garnett, extremely human. Apart from the activities mentioned in the text, it may be observed that as Placer he had sensibly reversed an absurd act of Rye by replacing the "third-marks" or volume numbers on the shelves, without which they (and still more pamphlets in tract volumes) wasted time in the finding. There is a good account of Fortescue by his old friend Henry Jenner in *The Library*, 3rd ser., vol. iv (1913), p. 1.

10. Sir Frederic Kenyon, *Proceedings of the British Academy*, 1939.
11. Related by Mr. E. G. Millar in *English Illuminated Manuscripts*. Another illuminated Harleian MS. completed by a recent acquisition is Harl. MS. 616, a Bible in French, the second volume of which was presented in 1929 by the late Mrs. Henry Yates Thompson in memory of her husband, the collector.
12. The best notice of Thompson is that by Sir Frederic Kenyon in the *Proceedings of the British Academy*, vol. xv, to which, as well as to personal memory, this section is much indebted.

PART I, CHAPTER IX

1. Partridge, *History of the Legal Deposit of Books throughout the British Empire*, 1938, pp. 107-12, 152-56.
   A further Act of 1932 (22 & 23 Geo. V, c. 34) relieved the Museum from certain classes of copyright matter. One curious class of literature is received, but is now withheld from the public at the instance of the publishers. This consists of books of betting systems, of which copies are only sold at high prices, and public access to which would clearly be an injury to the owners of the copyright. Though these persons may not be universally regarded as very deserving, they have a good case; moreover the Reading Room is not intended for this sort of purpose, and the legitimate use of such books in a national library is only to record them; in due time their mathematical or social study will be possible.
2. Sir F. G. Kenyon, *The British Museum in War-Time*, being the 4th lecture on the David Murray Foundation in the University of Glasgow, 1934, from which most of the facts in this section are drawn.
3. The Assistant Secretary is always an officer of very great importance, growing more important with the growth of the Museum and its Staff. The holders of the Office have been: James Edward Fitzgerald, 1848-49 (the years of the Royal Commission); Thomas Butler, 1857-78; John Thomas Taylor, 1878-1903; Francis Ellis Tucker, 1903-08; Alfred Robert Dryhurst, 1908-24; John Fred Isaac, 1924-28; John Humphrey Witney, 1926-40.
4. Discussions of evacuation from Museums and Galleries were initiated by the Government in 1934; readers who remember the sequence of political events will draw the necessary inferences.
5. Sir John Sandys reprinted a summary of the controversy in a pamphlet, *A Nine Days' Wonder*.
6. Royal Commission on National Museums and Galleries: *Interim Report*,

NOTES

1928; *Oral Evidence, Memoranda and Appendices to the Interim Report*, 1928; *Final Report*, 2 pt., 1929-30.
7. The district of Hendon in which the building stands is now known as Colindale.
8. Gilson entered the Museum in 1894, and became Assistant Keeper in 1909 and Keeper in 1911. Some account of him, and an excellent portrait, are prefixed to *Legal and Manorial Formularies, edited from originals at the British Museum* [Add. MS. 41, 201] *and the Public Record Office, in memory of Julius Parnell Gilson*, 1933.

The medieval manor, on which he contemplated a work, was very far from his only special study. His few publications, which include not only the parts issued from 1903 onwards of the New Palaeographical Society's *Facsimiles of Ancient Manuscripts*, but *the Mozarabic Psalter*, which he edited (edited for the Henry Bradshaw Society) and *Gulliver* and *The Correspondence of Burke and William Windham* (Roxburghe Club), exhibit the range of his scholarship, but not the body of his work, which is to be found in the works of others and in the Department itself, where, as the editor of the memorial volume says: "Everywhere... are to be found, for record of his tireless activity, the entries which, in his compressed and sometimes none too legible hand, record his discoveries, correct errors, add details, identify the authors of anonymous tracts and introduce order and system into what was before chaos."

9. The N.T. is complete in the Sinaiticus, but imperfect in the Vaticanus.
10. G. F. Barwick, *The Reading Room of the British Museum*, 1933, frequently referred to in earlier chapters. A fanciful book, giving a picturesque and misleading description of the Room and its occupants is J. Penn, *For Readers Only*, 1936. There are a *Handbook for Readers*, 1866, by T. Nichols, and a modern work of the same sort by R. A. Peddie, 1912.

Evening opening has long been a subject of controversy, and the closing hour has been changed, ranging between 8 p.m. (till 1905), 7 p.m. (1905-14), 5 p.m. (1915-18), 6 p.m. (1918-39). Probably no useful purpose is served except by a regular six-nights-a-week closing at 10 p.m., which would require a new staff.

From 1879 till 1890 green life-tickets were issued; they remained valid after that date, and at least one, Dr. Robert Steele's, is still in force. The age-limit was raised in 1862 to 21 from a very nominal 18; T. H. Huxley was admitted, in 1840, at 14.

11. A great scholar and constant reader, Dom Henri Leclercq, in the article 'Londres' in the *Dictionnaire des Antiquités Chrétiennes*, a charmingly written and generally very appreciative article, almost wholly devoted to the Museum, accuses the place of a liability to fancy, an accusation which seems unintelligible.

PART II, CHAPTER I

1. For a note on the Natural History Library, see above, p. 345.
2. By Mr. J. S. Finch (*Trans. Bibl. Soc.*, N.S. vol. xxxii, No. 1, June, 1941, pp. 67-72).
3. C. H. Wilkinson, in *Oxf. Bibl. Soc. Proceedings*, vol. i, pt. iv, p. 300.

THE LIBRARY OF THE BRITISH MUSEUM

4. *Report*, 1850, p. 271.
5. The Library has acquired several hundred of these in late years.
6. Nichols, *Illustr. Hist. Lit.*, vi, p. 774.
7. *Trans. Bibl. Soc.*, viii, 67–9. ix, 8–10.
8. The Museum possesses many large collections of sheets and small pieces, such as ballads, playbills, the Catholic Apostolic Church, etc. G. F. Barwick entered a number in *The Aslib Directory*, 1928, and others can be found in the General Catalogue under *Collections*.
9. As was generally presumed, and the presumption is borne out by the portrait which hangs in the King's Library. If so, it is at least curious that he should have been given for a second Christian name that of his father's wife.
10. *Walpoliana*, No. CV.
11. For example, by Birkbeck Hill in *Johnson's Letters*, i, 142–47; the text is corrected and expanded from the original by Eric Millar in *Trans. Bibl. Soc.*, 4th ser., ii, 269–71. The three letters are now Add. MS. 39, 303. That Johnson was shown books offered for purchase appears from his words: "You will remember how near we both were to purchasing a mutilated missal at a high price." It is less well known that on 4th September, 1784, he wrote to Barnard congratulating the King's Library on acquiring a copy on special paper of Brian Walton's Polyglot Bible (Facsimile in *Catalogue of the R. B. Adam Library relating to Dr. Samuel Johnson*, vol. i, p. 188.)
12. And not 120,000 volumes, as estimated in the King's letter of gift.
13. Barnard's letter of thanks of 3rd October, 1786, is in the R. B. Adam collection, now in the Rochester University Library, N.Y., and is printed in Adam's Catalogue, III, 51.
14. *The Library*, ser. iii, vol. iii, p. 422. Nicolas Carlisle's copy is preserved at 11912.6.55.
15. A manuscript catalogue made in 1792 came (surreptitiously, as he stated, though why so does not appear) into the hands of the bibliographer, F. X. Laire, whose note of the fact, though not the catalogue itself, is in the Public Library of Besançon (*Cat. Gén. des MSS. des Bibl. Publ. de la France*, vol. xlv, Besançon, p. 355, No. 1737, fol. 83).
16. Thirteen only came to the Museum, as Grenville exchanged one with Sir Francis Freeling. That one, Christine de Pisan's *Moral Proverbs* [1478], is unluckily very rare, and the Museum has acquired no other copy. Grenville's was afterwards in the Britwell Library; the John Rylands and Pierpont Morgan Libraries also have copies (S. de Ricci, *A Census of Caxtons*, 1907).
17. This provision was applied in selecting a fine copy of Caxton's *Dictes and Sayings of the Philosophers*, and giving up a bad copy for it.
18. That of the whole Huth Library, compiled by F. S. Ellis and W. C. Hazlitt, was published in 1880 in five volumes; this was followed in the Sale Catalogues.
19. These reprints professed to be what they were. But some fifty small pieces, professing to be unknown first editions, each dated a little earlier than the accepted first edition, appeared on the market in the eighties and nineties. These were shown with great detective ability by Messrs. John Carter and Graham Pollard, in *An Enquiry into the nature of certain XIXth Century Pamphlets*, 1934, to be inconsistent in paper, type and other details with their ostensible dates, and in fact to be forgeries. Copies of all had passed through Wise's

NOTES

hands, and had been represented by him as authentic. Some additional relevant facts are to be found, little as either the title or the style and temper of the writing would suggest any such hope, in a recent biography of Wise, W. Partington, *Forging Ahead*, N.Y., 1941.

But the authenticity and value of the bulk of Wise's collection is unaffected by these discoveries.

20. The second part of Proctor's *Index* covers books of 1500–20, the closing date being chosen to exclude Lutheran pamphlets and the degeneracy of printing. Proctor, who had collected titles of books from all countries up to 1520, himself produced the German section in 1903; the work has been taken up again by the aid of the Proctor Memorial Fund and the Bibliographical Society, and has been completed by Col. Frank Isaac.
21. Information about the Museum's Musical collections is to be found in Grove's *Dictionary of Music and Musicians*, 3rd edition, art. "Libraries," and also in L. R. McColvin and H. Reeves, *Music Libraries*.
22. Some of these were duplicates, and by the King's permission were distributed to other libraries.

PART II, CHAPTER II

1. It is curious that Durham, the only English monastic library to survive in bulk after the Reformation, should have lost these noble volumes. Cotton bought the Lindisfarne Gospels early in the seventeenth century from Robert Bowyer, Clerk of the Parliament.
2. The Utrecht Psalter was once Cotton's, but whether he lent it is not known. He certainly lent MSS. to Ben Jonson for his *Henry V*, which was burned (luckily not with the MSS), in his study. See Jonson's poem on that event.
3. *Treasury Papers*, 1703–06. For these reports and accompanying plans see also Wren Society, vol. xi, pp. 51 *sqq.* and plates. In the Soane Museum there is a volume of drawings for a new Cotton Library. Some time between about 1720 and 1730 Kent included in his scheme for new Houses of Parliament a grandiose elevation of the Cotton Library, with colonnade and central dome (*ib.* pl. xli, xlii).
4. In this attitude towards the Papists he resembled Thomas James. See the entertaining extracts from the Diaries printed by Nichols (*Lit. Anecd.* i, 86–94), and also his letter to Thomas Harley, Envoy at the Court of Hanover, advising him how to avoid giving the owner of a MS. of Origen any impression of its true value (*ib.* i, 536–40); and another, to Andrew Hay, Harley's agent, as to the purchase of ancient Greek and Latin MSS. from the Augustinians of S. Giovanni di Carbonaria at Naples, printed by Morton and Planta in their Harley Catalogues. "This must be bought," "buy of these what you can," are Wanley's injunctions. The Diaries are being edited by Dr. Cyril Wright, of the Department of Manuscripts, for the Bibliographical Society; but completion and publication of his edition have been delayed by the war.
5. To Mr. Wortley-Montagu, 8th June, 1745 (*Letters*, ed. W. Moy Thomas, 1898, ii, 148).

6. They were estimated at 40,000 in the *Synopsis* of 1808.
7. The Bagford Fragments have never been minutely catalogued. They were broadly analysed and described by Dr. A. W. Pollard in The Bibliographical Society's *Transactions*, ser. 1, vol. vii (1904), pp. 143-49. Wanley, writing to Sloane on 6th May, 1707, called Bagford's collection, still in the latter's hands, "a noble treasure of English history and antiquities." Bagford has been widely accused of being a "biblioclast," but most of his leaves and sheets came from binder's waste and involved no outrage on books.
8. Nichols, *Lit. Anecd.*, i, 541.
9. Harleian MS. 4780; printed by J. P. Malcolm, *Londinium Redivivum*, ii (1703), 363.
10. Leland's list of libraries visited in Lincolnshire, with Henry VIII's notes, survives as Royal MS., App. 69.
11. It had disappeared in 1649, when Young recorded in his inventory, made after the execution of Charles I, the loss of "St. Lewis King of France his Psalter."
12. To be distinguished from the later and quite separate Queen's Library of Caroline of Anspach, consisting of several thousand volumes of modern, mostly foreign, literature, of which Stephen Duck was librarian. The subsequent history of the latter library seems to be unknown.
13. Also in his reception of his first appointment, made out as *durante beneplacito*, which he declined on the very justifiable ground that "while he was minding his studies some idle Courtier would beg the place over his head." He obtained an outright warrant in the following year. His controversy over the *Letters of Phalaris* also showed him as a bad man to attack without cause; the sarcastic phrase *pro solita humanitate sua* was remembered.
14. In his Report on the Printed Books, 1845.
15. "Refuse" from the Old Royal Library included a memorandum book of William Cecil, which came to the Museum in the King's Library, and was, with other strays, restored to the Royal MSS. by Madden.
16. To be distinguished from Petyt's main collection, which went to the Inner Temple Library.
17. It was fully described by Sir Edward Maunde Thompson in *Bibliographica*, vol. iii (1897), pp. 385-406.
18. For this reason the few Oriental MSS. in the Egerton Collection, unlike those in the other Collections, have not been transferred to the Oriental Library, though catalogued there, but remain in the custody of the Keeper of Manuscripts as Egerton Librarian.
19. Nearly a century later the process had gone much farther, and the Society sold Arundel's printed books at auction; the Museum was able to buy a few volumes, but was not offered a first refusal. The Fellows rested their right to disperse the books on the terms of Howard's gift, which allowed them to "dispose" the library as might be convenient. But even in the twentieth century "dispose" does not mean "dispose of," and in the seventeenth it merely meant "arrange" or "place." A striking instance of the modern divorce between physical and linguistic science.
20. The College of Arms produced in 1829 a catalogue of its portion of the MSS., compiled by Sir Charles George Young, Garter King-of-Arms.
21. Of Vol. 3, produced after Holmes's death, practically the entire stock was

NOTES

destroyed in a fire at the binders' in 1865, and it now only survives in a single copy kept in the Department.

22. Grove, *Dictionary of Music and Musicians*, 3rd edition, art. "Libraries," and L. R. McColvin and H. Reeves, *Music Libraries*, have some information on the collection.
23. For some reason which has not yet been explained, whereas pagan literature does not appear in codex form till the 2nd century at earliest, and then very rarely, the roll being preferred, Christians used the codex almost from the first.
24. Quality is of more account than quantity, but it may be worth while to give other figures of Greek MSS. in the Museum, as analysed by Henri Omont in 1894 (*Bibliothèque de l'Ecole des Chartes*, tom. xlv):—Old Royal 53, Cotton 3, Harleian 248, King's 2, Burney 80, Arundel 36, Egerton 4, Sloane and Additional (to that date) 329, totalling 755.
25. The Crace London collection is in the Department of Prints and Drawings.
26. The tercentenary of Hastings's birth was celebrated in 1932 by an Exhibition, organised in co-operation with the India Office. The Museum's contribution included a selection from the mass of Hastings's personal papers, running to over three hundred volumes (Add. MSS. 28973–29236, 30871–31994, 39871–39704, 41606–41611), and minor collections, such as Sir Elijah Impey's, illustrating them. The Philip Francis papers are in the India Office, as of course are Hastings's own official reports and papers.
27. There is said to exist in one of the old Catalogues of MSS., but the present writer cannot give a reference, the following modest palaeographical note: *ni fallor, saeculo duodecimo, tertiodecimo vel quartodecimo, scriptum.*

PART II, CHAPTER III

1. For Rich see *A Narrative of a Residence in Koordistan*, edited by his widow, which illustrates his wonderful talent and noble character; he died, aged 33, from his devotion to his people in a plague of cholera at Baghdad. The Report of the House of Commons Committee is dated 25th March, 1825.
2. For the Nitrian Syriac MSS. see an article by Cureton in *Quarterly Review*, Dec., 1845, vol. cliii, p. 39.
3. Evelyn's letter to Pepys, 12th August, 1689. Da Costa's charming letter to the Trustees, offering the books "as a small token of my esteem, love, reverence and gratitude, to this magnanimous nation, and as a thanksgiving offering, in part, for the generous protection and numberless blessings, which I have enjoyed under it," is printed by Edwards, *Memoirs of Libraries*, 1859, vol. i, pp. 453–4, from the *Gentleman's Magazine* of 1859. It was originally written in Hebrew and is in the Oriental Library (Add. MS. 4710, ff. 1, 2). See also *The Jewish Encyclopaedia* and *Encyclopaedia Judaica*. The particular cause of da Costa's gratitude was no doubt the naturalization of the Jews enacted in 1753 in the teeth of popular clamour; the Bishop of Norwich, who voted for it in the House of Lords, was followed by street boys calling upon him to circumcise them.
4. For many years, according to Cowtan, Hebrew and Arabic books were catalogued by Isaac Pinto, who died in 1870.

5. François I sent agents to the East to collect MSS. for his Royal Libraries at Blois and Fontainebleau; and in 1558 Albert V of Bavaria founded the Hofbibliothek of Munich by the purchase of the library of the celebrated Orientalist, Johann Albrecht Widmannstetter. But, in general, interest in Oriental literatures other than Hebrew did not spread in the West till well into the next century.
6. Halhed studied Sanskrit through Persian translations, the original tongue not being yet understood by English scholars. Of his 93 MSS., 59 are Persian.
7. Four Persian MSS. (Or. MSS. 2194–2697), acquired by Rich at the end of his life, were retained by his widow and were acquired in 1879 from his son-in-law Charles Erskine.
8. Sir T. W. Arnold, *Painting in Islam*, 1928, p. 40. Under Islam calligraphy thus took the place of the arts of decorative representation; hence the great beauty of inscriptions in Arabic script.
9. *Op. cit.*, pp. 30–42, pl. 17c, 19b; B.M. *Catalogue of Coptic Manuscripts* and *Catalogue of Greek Papyri*; Morgan Library, *Codices Coptici*; Douglas Cockerell, "The Development of Bookbinding Methods—Coptic Influence," in *Bibl. Soc. Trans.*, 4th ser. xiii (1932), pp. 1–9; H. I. Bell, "Early Codices from Egypt," in *Library*, 2nd ser., vol. x (1909), pp. 303–13.
10. Elsewhere in England Oriental studies suffered a set-back in consequence of Macaulay's celebrated judgement of 1834 in favour of English instead of native education for Indians. "I never found one among them" [Orientalists], he wrote, "who could deny that a single shelf of a good European library was worth the whole native literature of India and Arabia." Even if true this would be irrelevant; the native literature was the literature of the people to be educated, and the European was foreign. The effect of Macaulay's words may possibly be seen in the number of foreign-born Orientalists who worked in England in the middle and later nineteenth century. See A. J. Arberry, *The Library of the India Office*, 1938, for my debt to which this general acknowledgement must suffice.
11. W. D. Macray, *Annals of the Bodleian*, 1868, pp. 28, 63.
12. Professor Paul Pelliot reached Tun-huang just after Stein, and removed a quantity to Paris. The great bulk of the collection was left behind and was eventually removed to Peking. See the vivid account of the Tun-huang find in Stein's *Serindia*, chapters xxi, xxii; also "The Discovery of the Tun-huang Library and its effect on Chinese studies," by Dr. Cheuk-woon Taam, in *The Library Quarterly*, xii. 3 (July, 1942), pp. 686–705. The Diamond Sutra is a long roll, 17¼ feet long, printed on paper of very moderate quality.
13. Dr. Giles's Chinese scholarship is hereditary; he is the son of the late Professor H. A. Giles, of Cambridge. From Professor Giles, it may be remembered, came as a gift one of the Museum's set of the *Yung Lo ta tien*.
14. Cowtan, pp. 358–62.

APPENDICES

1. The term "unfit" may have covered some leaves stolen by Jean Aymon, from MSS. in the Bibliothèque Royale in 1707, and in the Museum since 1753; they were returned on Delisle's application in 1879. More recently a deed,

NOTES

given under a misunderstanding, was returned under the same clause. There is, however, an opinion given by the Law Officers of the Crown, that defect in a vendor's or donor's title does not constitute "unfitness" under the Act.

2. *Quarterly Review*, Dec., 1850, p. 158, on what authority I do not know; but the statement is probable enough.
3. He specified the copy of Henry VIII's *Assertio septem Sacramentorum*, given by the King himself to Archbishop Cranmer, and bearing notes by the latter, also Luther's own copy of his German Bible, with notes in the hands of several leading Reformers!
4. Barwick, *op. cit.*, p. 41.
5. This is one of the many points which investigation of the Trustees' archives, now inaccessible, might clear up.
6. This beautiful binding, in two volumes, with tooled morocco backs and wooden boards, and the work of preparing the delicate vellum sheets, are described and illustrated by Mr. Cockerell in *British Museum Quarterly*, x, 180–82.
7. Other similar mixtures exist and are serviceable; but this is believed to be the best. It is not to be bought ready made up; but any chemist can make it up from the formula, which, with the method of application, is described in an official leaflet; see an account of it by its inventor, Dr. H. J. Plenderleith, Deputy Keeper in charge of the Research Laboratory, in *B.M.Q.*, 1927, ii, 3; see also *The Library Association Record*, 1927, new ser. v, 327.
8. This waste of space is avoided by arranging all but the most important newspapers chronologically, all of any one year being placed in a single series. Readers much more often need a number of papers of one year than volumes of a single paper of several years; but if they do need the latter it is easy to produce them.
9. *Essays in Librarianship*, pp. 234–52.

INDEX

Abbot, C., Lord Colchester, 82
Abyssinian MSS., 301
Accessions. *See* Registration
Additional MSS., 260
Ainsworth, W. Harrison, 85
Akbar, the Emperor, 308, 310
Alienation, 331–5
Allan, J., 313
Almanzi, Hebrew Books, 298
American Testimonial MS., 287
Americana, 103, 207–8, 286
Amyand, C., 50, 246
Anderson, W., 320
Andhra lit. *See* Telugu lit.
Andrews, Hilda, 216
Arabic lit., 302–5, 373
Architecture. *See* Buildings; Essex, J.; Iron Library; Reading Room; Saunders, G., Smirke, Sir R.
Argyll, A., 3rd Duke of, 36
Armenian lit., 309–10
Armstrong, W., 76
Arundel MSS., 31, 65–6, 254–6; printed books, sale of, 372
Ashbee, H. S., bequest, 150
Ashburnham Library, 107, 257–8
Ashley Library, 169–70, 199–201, 370–1
Asiatic lit., Southern, 321
Assamese lit., 314
Astle, T., 230–1, 259
Autographs, modern, gifts of, 289–90
Ayscough, S., 44, 48, 56, 238–9, 262, 353

Baber, H. H., 56, 58–9, 75, 97
Bach, E. von, 106–212
Backhouse Chinese Collection, 318
Badaga lit., 315
Baechtold, J., 276
Bagford Fragments, 237, 372
Bain, R. N., 365
Bale, Bp. J., 349
Bankes, H., 70

Banks, Sir J., gives Icelandic books, 49; library, 62, 187
Banks, Lady, 62
Banks, Sarah S., 62
Barham, R. H., 84
Barker, Consul, 303
Barnard, Sir F. A., 76, 189–93, 370
Barnett, L. D., 145, 294, 299, 313, 315, 321
Baronian, Dr., 310
Barrois, J., 107, 257–8
Barwick, G. F., 149, 171, 353
Bates, T. H., 312
Bean, J., 355
Beauclerk, T., 38, 53
Bedford Hours, 107
Bedford Hours and Psalter, 279
Bedford, H. W., 56
Bell, H. I., 168, 270–1, 274
Beloe, W., 56, 59
Bendall, C., 294, 312–13
Bengal lit., 314
Bentley, R., Royal Librarian, 180, 229, 245–6, 372; books with his notes bought, 62
Bethnal Green Public Library, 138
Bible: C. Combe's Bibles, 62; A. Onslow's, 48–9; Harleian, 41, 234; the "Alcuin," 107; Grenville's English, 195; Greek, 271–4; Codex Alexandrinus, 75, 244, 274; Sinaiticus, 168–9, 274; Vaticanus, 169; Hebrew, 234, 297–8; Latin, 117, 273–4; Syriac, 234, 295–6 Exhibition (Tercent. of A.V.), 224–5; Exhibition Room, 166
Binding of Museum books, 51, 336–8, 375
Bindings, Western, 184, 196, 221–3, 246; Near Eastern, 310–11
Binyon, L., 161
Birch, T., a Trustee, 36; his MSS., 48, 239–40, 248; his Fund, 248
Birch, W. de G., 263, 281

376

INDEX

Blackstone, Sir W., 52
Bliss, P., 355
Bloomsbury, 38–9; St. George's Church, 351
Blumhardt, J. F., 294, 314
Bodleian Library, 38, 71, 78–9, 98, 302, 312, 317
Bond, Sir E. A., appointed, 98; Keeper of MSS., 129–30; Principal Librarian, 132–40; founded the Class Catalogue of MSS., 291
Book-Sale Catalogues, English, 220–1
Book-selection. *See* Purchase
Bréquigny, L. G. de, 53
Bridgewater Fund, 65, 253, 357
Bright, B. H., sale, 103, 107
British Empire, 286
British Museum Quarterly, The, 171, 347
Brooke, Sir T., 277
Brougham, H., Lord, 84
Browning, R., 85
Bruce, C., 312
Bryant, J., 190, 193
Buckingham, Dukes of. *See* Stowe MSS.
Buckingham House, 19
Budge, Sir E. A. W., 296, 300, 303
Buildings (1823–52), 86–9, 360; (1854–57), 117–20, 364; (1885–87), 137–9; (1900–18), 142–4, 149–50, 157–8; (1918–30), 164–7. *See* Improvement Property; Lighting, artificial; Montague House; Natural History Departments
Bullen, G., 100, 127, 204–5
Burghley, W. Cecil, Lord. *See* Cecil
Burke, E., 52
Burmese lit., 315–16
Burney, C., library, 61, 188; MSS., 251; Newspapers, 208
Burrell, Sir W., MSS., 49
Burton, John, 52
Butler, Allan, 52
Butler, E. D., 216–17

Caesar, Sir Julius, papers, 106, 249
Calderon, G., 365
Calligraphy, Islamic, 307
Camden, W., 25–6

Canadian books, 208
Canarese lit. *See* Kannada lit.
Canterbury, Archbishops of, Trustees, 34; *See* also Cranmer, T.; Herring, T.; Howley, W.; Manners-Sutton, C.; Parker, M.; Tenison, T.; MSS. from the city of, 24
Carlisle, N., 76
Carlyle, T., 84, 182, 334
Caroline (of Anspach), Queen, 372
Carr, Lady Mary, 53
Carshunic MSS. *See* Karshuni MSS.
Cary, H. F., 76–7, 85, 99.
Casaubon, I., 179
Casley, D., 229–30, 246–7
Catalogues, Rules for the. *See* below, Catalogues, etc. A (*a*)

CATALOGUES, FACSIMILES AND OTHER PUBLICATIONS:
A. Printed Books—
 (1) *General*
  (*a*) *Alphabetical*
   (1787), 48, 72
   (1813–19), 72–5
   (1841), 94, 97; printing the, 111–14
   (1881–1905), 132–4, 365–6; movable slips, 133, 366
   (1931), 167
   Rules for compiling, 100, 112, 366
   Transcribers of, 133, 135, 366
  (*b*) *Subject*
   Classed, 75–6, 94, 97, 111
   Subject Index, 135–7
 (2) *Special*
  Americana, 207–8
  Banks, 187
  Bindings, 223
  English Book Sale Catalogues, 221
  English Books, early printed, 135–6, 205
  French books, early printed, 206–7

377

THE LIBRARY OF THE BRITISH MUSEUM

CATALOGUES, FACSIMILES AND OTHER PUBLICATIONS:
A. PRINTED BOOKS—
(2) *Special—continued*
French Revolution Tracts, 149, 186
Grenville, 197–8
Huth, 199
Icelandic, 206–7
Incunabula, 204
King's Library, 193
Maps, 219–20
Music, 213, 216
Newspapers, 210
Notable Books, Three Hundred (acquired 1891–9), 146
Portuguese, early printed, 206–7
Postage Stamps, 224
Reading Room, books of ref. in, and guides to, 119, 224, 304, 362
"Short title" lists, 205
Spanish, early printed, 206–7
State Papers (Indian), 224
Thomason Tracts, 150, 183
(3) *Exhibition guides*, 225
B. MANUSCRIPTS—
(1) *General State of*
(1836–52), 110
(1866–79), 129–30;
(1879–88), 139–40
(1888–1910), 151–4
(1919–39), 170
(2) *Collections and Classes*
pamphlet describing, by J. P. Gilson, 369
Additional and Egerton, 129–30, 260
Bindings, 223
Birch. *See* below, Sloane
Burney, 251
Charters and Rolls, 262
Cotton (1777), 48; (1802), 74–5, 230–1
Egerton (with Additional), 129–30, 260; Exhibition Guide, 254
English hist. and lit., 290

CATALOGUES, FACSIMILES AND OTHER PUBLICATIONS:
B. MANUSCRIPTS—
(2) *Collections and Classes—continued*
Hargrave, 75, 250
Harleian (1759), 44, 48, 49, 51, 238–9; (1808), 74–6, 238–9
Huth, 199
Lansdowne, 75, 250
Maps, 264–5
Music, 267
Papyri, 270–1
Royal and King's, 247–8
Seals, 262–3
Sloane, Birch and Add. (1782), 48, 239–40
Stowe, 259
(3) *Subject:*
Class, 130, 290–2
Handbook by R. Sims, 291
Topography, Genealogy and Heraldry, 286
(4) *Guides to Exhibitions*
225, 231, 254, 293
C. ORIENTAL—
(1) *General*
131, 145
(2) *Special*
Arabic, 305
Armenian and Georgian, 310;
Chinese, 319
Coptic, 300
Hebrew and Samaritan, 299
Hindi, etc., 314
Japanese, 321
Kannada, etc., 315
Marathi, etc., 314
Persian, 308
Sanskrit, 313
Syriac and Karshuni, 296
Tamil, 315
Telugu, 316
Turkish, 309
D. GENERAL—
47, 93, 170, 350
Annual Report, 347
The British Museum Quarterly, 171, 278–9, 347

INDEX

CATALOGUES, FACSIMILES AND OTHER PUBLICATIONS:
D. GENERAL—*continued*
   The Buildings of the British Museum, 360
   Synopsis, 67, 72
   Reproductions, 171
Cater, J., 80–81, 358
Cecil, W., Lord Burghley, 26, 249, 372
Central Library for Students. *See* National Central Library
Cervantes, Ashbee's coll. of, 150
Cesnola, A. Palme di, 276
Ceylonese lit. *See* Sinhalese lit.
Chandler, S., 51
Charles I, King, 179, 244
Charles II, King, 179
Charlotte, Queen, 214–15
Charters and Rolls, 261–2
Chesterfield, P. D., Earl of, 43
Chinese lit., 64, 103, 129, 317
Church Missionary Society, gift of Ethiopic MSS., 301
Churchill, S. J. A., 306–7, 309
Clarke, Campbell, 212
Classed Catalogue, (*a*) of Printed Books, *see* Catalogues A (1*b*); (*b*) of MSS.; *see ib.* B
Classics. *See* Greek lit., ancient; Latin lit., ancient
Classification of printed books, 48, 72, 94, 101, 339–41, 358. *See* Catalogues, etc.: A (1*b*), The Classed Catalogue.
Clergy, beneficed, on the staff, 93; Cobbett on, 97
Clyffe, J., 242
Cobbett, W., 97
Cockerell, D., 274
Codex Alexandrinus, Sinaiticus, Vaticanus. See Bible, Greek
Coins and Medals, 41, 45–6, 73, 352
Colchester, Lord. *See* Abbot, C.
Cole, W., MSS., 49, 286
Colindale, *See* Newspaper Repository (Library)
College of Arms, 256
Collier, J. Payne, 84, 113–14

Combe, C., 62
Conybeare, F. C., 294, 310
Coorg lit. *See* Kurg lit.
Coptic bindings, 310–11
Coptic MSS., 299–300
Copyright deposit in 18th cent., 49; Act of 1814, 66–9, 357; of 1842, 105; of 1911 and 1915, 158–60, 368; of 1932, 369; Planta thought Copt. books not worth keeping, 331; in MSS., 289–90; in music, 210–11; in newspapers and colonial books, 141–2
Corpus Christi College, Cambridge, Parker's MSS. at, 24
Costa, S. da. *See* da Costa
Cotton, Sir R., 17, 25–7; Library Acts, 17; MSS., 226–31; the Genesis, 45, 227, 230; damaged, restored, 230
County History, 61, 283
Cowtan, R., sen., 76
Cowtan, R., jun., 81, 347, 363
Coxe, H. O., 78–9
Cracherode, C. M., library, 56, 183–5, 355
Cranmer, Abp. T., 179, 244
Crawford, 26th Earl of, 224
Croker, J. W., 63, 185–6, 204, 366
Crum, W. E., 270–1, 300
Cumberland, R., 62
Cureton, W., 98, 109–10, 274, 295, 305–6, 361
Curry, E., 275
Curzon, R., 108–9, 361–2
Cymmrodorion Society, 275

Da Costa, S., 48, 180, 297, 373
Davenport, C. J., 135
De Morgan, A., 84, 114
Departments, the original, 41; reorganizations of, 73, 93, 131, 144–4; co-operation between, 75, 224
Deutsch, E., 128–9
de Villiers, Sir J. A. J., 217
Dilke, C. W., 85
Dillmann, C. F. A., 301
Diplomatic papers, 285

379

Directors, *see* Principal Librarians
D'Israeli, I., 54, 84
Douce, F., 52, 59–60, 71, 250
Douglas, Sir R. K., 129, 145, 216, 319, 321
Dragonetti, D., music, 211, 265, 267
Dryander, J., his Banks Catalogue, 62, 94, 187
Dukes, L., 299
Duplicates, 51, 192, 198, 331–4
Durham Minster Library, 227, 371
Durie, J., 179, 244–5
Dutch MSS., 276
Duveen, Joseph, Lord, 167
Duwes, G., 241
Dyer, G., 84

East India House. *See* India Office Library
Edward IV, King, 240
Edwards, A., bequest, 17; fund, 50, 62, 70; library, 41, 352
Edwards, E., author of *Lives of the Founders*, 92, 95, 100–1, 331
Edwards, E., of the Dept. of Or. P. B. and MSS., 308
Egerton Bequest and MSS., 65, 252–4; Librarian, 356
Egypt, papyri found in, 267–71
Egypt Exploration Society, 153, 269–270
"Elastic" system of placing books, 102
Elizabeth, Queen, 178, 241, 243
Elliot, Sir H. M., 306, 313
Ellis, A. G., 145, 305, 308
Ellis, A. I., 171
Ellis, Sir H., enters, 57; Keeper of Pr. Bks., 56, 58; works on General Cat., 75, 111–12; criticized by Panizzi for his part in, 58; Keeper of MSS. and Secretary, 58; Principal Librarian, 58, 355; relations with Forshall, 97; attacked by Nicolas over the Joursanvault MSS., 106–7; publications, 290; views on accession-catalogues, 111; on duplicates, 332; retirement, 120, 355; character, 58, 97, 120, 355

Empson, J., 42–3
English history, 226, 282–6; in Cotton MSS., 26, 227–8; Harleian, 236–7; Lansdowne, 248–50; Royal 240–2; Stowe, 258–9; catalogues, etc., bearing on, 286, 290
English lit., 199–200; early printed, 204–5; MSS. in, 286–90
Erskine, W., 306, 313–14
Essex, James, drawings, 65
Ethiopic MSS., 301
Eumorfopoulos, G., 169
Evacuation in war, 161–2, 170
Evans, Sir A., 163
Evans, C., 212
Evelyn, Sir John, 36
Exhibitions and Guides thereto, of MSS., 166, 225, 231, 254, 293; of Printed Books, 225; Galleries closed in wartime, 163

Facsimiles. *See* Catalogues, etc.; Harris, J.
Farnborough, Lord, 363; his Fund, 65, 253
Fees, Staff forbidden to take, 37; proposal for charging, for use of Reading Room, 162
FINANCE—
 (a) General, 49–51, 69–70, 94, 347, 353–4
 (b) Purchase grants—
  (1) Annual
   Pr.Bks., 102–3, 163, 169–71
   MSS., 106
  (2) Special:
   Sculptures, 60–1
   Lansdowne MSS., 61
   Hargreave MSS., 61
   Burney Library, 61–2
   Ginguené library, 62–3
   Rich Or. MSS., 64
   British books, 69
   Stowe MSS., 258
   Codex Sinaiticus, 169
  The printing grant used to supplement, 75
See Buildings; Staff

INDEX

Fisher, A., 313
FitzGerald, E., 85
Fitzwilliam, Lord, bequest diverted, 71, 332
Fletcher, W. Y., 146
Flou, K. de, 276
Flower, R., 275-6
Forbes, D., 294, 308
Foreign books, purchase of, 103, 126-7, 175
Forgeries, 350-1, 370-1
Forsdyke, Sir J., 168-9
Forshall, J., enters, 60; catalogues Burney MSS., 251; Rich MSS., 110; papyri, 268; Keeper of MSS. and Secretary, 77-8; whole-time Secretary, 97; conduct as such, 97-8, 112, 358, 362-3; retires, 116, 362; character, 358, 362-3
Fortescue, G. K., Supt. of Reading Room, 136; founds Subject Index, 136-7; catalogues French Revolution Tracts, 149, 186; Thomason Tracts, 150, 183; Keeper of Pr. Bks., 149-50; death and character, 367-8
Foundation, the, 17-19, 33-7; origins of, 19-33
Franks, Sir A. W., 312
Frederick, Prince of Wales, 350, 370
French lit., Ginguené coll. of, 63; vol. of sotties, 104; Ashbee's, 150; cat. of early printed, 206-7; MSS. in, 235-6, 277; Arundel, 255; Egerton, 65, 253; Harleian, 235-6; Royal, 240-1; catalogues of, 276-7
French Revolution Tracts, 63, 77, 149, 185-6
Friends of the National Libraries, 171, 288
Fulton, A. S., 305

Garnett, R., sen., 99
Garnett, R., jun., enters, 99; Placer, 137; Supt. of Reading Room, 137; promotes sliding presses, 137-8; and printing of Gen. Cat., 134-5; edits it, 135; urges addition of photographer to Staff, 342; Keeper of Pr. Bks., 146; retires, 148; character, 148-9, 367
Garrick, D., plays, 48, 84-5, 353
Gaster, M., 298
Gate Porter, 346
Gayangos, P. de, 276
Genealogy and heraldry, 98, 259, 286, 290. *See also* County history
Geography, studied in 16th and 17th cent., 29-30; Banks Coll. of, 187; King's, 192. *See also* Maps
George II, King, 33, 177, 247
George III, King, presents Thomason Tracts, 48, 181; and money, 352; collects King's Library, 63, 188-9, 251-2; and the King's Music, 214
George IV, King, presents King's Library, 63, 191-2, 215, 251-2; adds to King's Music, 215
George V, King, deposits King's Music, 213
Georgian MSS., 309-10
German MSS., 276
Gibbon, E., 43
Gifford, A., 42, 45-6
Giles, L., 145, 319, 374
Gill, Eric, 161
Gilson, J. P., enters, Assistant Keeper of MSS., 369; Keeper, 152, 369; publications, 248, 369; work on Class Cat., 292; death, 168; career and character, 369
Ginguené, P. L., library, 62-3
Glaser, E., 303
Glover, J. H., 76
Godwin, W., 84
Gosse, Sir E., 123, 175, 364-5
Gough, R., 71, 357
Grabham, J., 81
Grants, Parliamentary. *See* Finance
Gray, E. W., 43
Gray, J. E., 113
Gray, J. G., 286
Gray, T., a reader, 52; on the Reading Room, 53, 354; on the Museum's finances, 49-50; on its feuds, 353

381

Greek lit., ancient, 20–21, 62, 188, 234, 251, 271; *see also* Papyri; modern, 103
Greenshields, R. S., 304
Grenville, T., his library, 104, 193–8; and Panizzi, 98, 104, 123, 195, 197, 363
Grote, G., 84
Guide-Lecturers, 171
Gujarati lit., 314

Haas, E., 312–13
Halhed, N. B., his Indian MSS., 64–5, 305, 311
Hallam, H., 84
Hamilton, C., 305
Hamilton, G. W., 306, 313
Handel, G. F., 214–16, 266
Hardwicke, P. Yorke, 1st Earl of, 36; P. Yorke, 2nd Earl of, 36, 51
Hargrave, F., a reader, 52, his library, 61; MSS., 250
Harleian Library, 17–18; MSS., 27, 41, 107, 231–9; catalogues of: (1759), 44, 48–9, 51, 238–9; (1808), 74–6, 238–9; printed books, 33–4
Harley, Robert and Edward, 1st and 2nd Earls of Oxford, 17–18, 27
Harper, S., 43–4, 56, 75
Harris, J., 76–7
Hastings, Warren, papers of, 139, 311, 373
Hawes, Sir B., 92
Heber, Richard, sales, 66
Heberden, W., Dr., 52
Hebrew lit., 48, 128–9, 180, 234, 296–9, 373
Hendon. *See* Newspaper Repository, (Library)
Henry VII, King, 178, 241
Henry VIII, King, 241, 265
Henry, Prince of Wales, 178, 244
Heraldry. *See* Genealogy and Heraldry
Heralds' College, *See* College of Arms
Herbert, J. A., 151, 282
Herring, Abp. T., 36
Hill, Sir G. F., 168
Hindi lit., 313–14

Hindu paintings, 308
Hindustani lit., 313–14
Hoare, Sir R. Colt, 63–4
Hoerning, R., 299
Holman, J., 78, 98, 264, 291
Holmes, Sir R. R., 78, 301
Hooke, R., 39
Horne, T. H., 76, 239, 358
Housekeeper, 346
Howard, Henry, and Thomas, Earl of Arundel. *See* Arundel MSS.
Howley, Abp. W., 98
Hughes, W., 106, 216
Hughes-Hughes, A., 267
Hull, J. Fowler, 64, 305, 317
Huth Bequest, 153, 198–9, 277
Hyde, T., 305

Icelandic books, 49, 187, 205
Illuminations. *See* Manuscripts, Illuminated
Improvement Property, 143, 367
Incunabula, 146–7, 184–5, 190, 194, 199, 202–4
India, MSS. relating to, 106. *See also* Hastings, Warren
India Office Library, 311–12, 317
Indian lit., 60, 64–5, 214, 311–16, 374
Indo-Persian lit. *See* Persian lit.
Irish books, 160; MSS. 258, 275–6
Iron library, 119–20; 164, 166; the sliding presses in, 137–8
Islamic calligraphy, 307; illumination, 304, 307–9; lit., *see* Arabic lit.; Persian lit.; Turkish lit.
Italian lit., 62–4, 195–6; MSS., 180, 276

Jaba, A., 303, 309
Jacobi, H., 312
Jainism, 312, 315
James I, King, 178, 243
Japanese lit., 129, 320
Javanese lit., 321
Jennens, C., 214
Jenner, H., 138, 204, 281, 366

INDEX

Johnson, Samuel, and libraries, 31–2; and Maty, 43; admitted to read, 52; and the King's Library, 189–91, 370
Jones, J. Winter, 99–100, 114, 125–6, 341
Jones, Sir W., 311
Joursanvault, Baron de, 106–7
Justel, H., 245

Kannada lit., 315
Karaite MSS., 299
Karshuni MSS., 294
Keay-Tapling, T., 224
Keepers and Deputy Keepers, 326–8
Kenyon, Sir F. G., enters, 154; publishes Greek texts, 154, 269–70, 274; Director, 157–68
Kerrich, T., drawings, 65
King Edward VII Wing. *See* Buildings, (1900–18), (1918–30)
King's Library, the, formed, 188–90; acquired, 63, 191–2; staff absorbed, 76; the building, 86–7; pr. bks., 188–93; books reserved from, 193; MSS., 251–2.
Kitzinger, E., 280
Knight, G., 42
Kremer, A. Frhr. von, 303
Kurg lit., 315

La Figanière, F. F. de, 276
Lamb, C., 84–5
Lambarde, W., 25
Lane, E. W., 303
Langton, E., 51
Lansdowne MSS., 61, 248–50
Latin lit., ancient, 20–21, 184, 190, 194, 236, 271–2; papyri, 267, 269
Law, 25, 61, 190, 250
Lean, V. Stuckey, bequest, 142–3
Leland, J., 23, 241–2
Lending, 37, 331–5
Leveen, J., 299
Lever, C., 85
Leyden, J., 306

Libraries, Renaissance foundations of, 20; the chief Continental reported on (1835–6), 360; public, 95, 100–1; paucity of in 18th cent. London, 31–2, 350; now relieve Reading Room, 171. *See* Bethnal Green Public Library; Bodleian Library, Tenison, Abp. T.
Libri, G., 103, 107, 257–8
Licensing Acts, 179
Lighting, artificial, 132, 364
Linnaeus, C., 45, 345
Little Gidding, 179
Little, A. G., 281
Lockhart, J. G., 85
London, Crace coll., 373; paucity of public libraries in 18th cent., 31–2; now relieve B.M., 171
Lottery, for foundation, the, 18, 33, 349
Lowth, Bp. R., 51
Lumley, J., Lord, 178–9, 244
Luther coll., 103
Luttrell Psalter, 279
Lyttelton, George, 1st Lord, 36

Macaulay, Catherine, 53
Macaulay, T. B., Lord, 84, 374
Macclesfield, George, 2nd Earl, 36
Macfarlane, J., 340
Madden, Sir F., enters Dept. of Pr. Bks., 76; transferred to MSS., 78; Keeper, 98; claims Grenville MSS. for Dept., 104; wishes to buy Stowe MSS., 107; finds Cotton fragments 262; restores, them, 230; retires, 121–2; relations with Panizzi, 104, 361; character, 121–2, 361; collection of cuttings on B.M., 364
Magna Carta, 49, 261
Major, R. H., 106, 131, 216–19
Malcolm, J., of Poltalloch, 277
Malcolm, Sir J., 306
Mallet, Lucy, 49
Manly, J. M., 343
Manners-Sutton, Abp. C., 358–9
Manuscripts, history and growth of the Dept., Part I, *passim*; the

Collections and Catalogues, 226–92; Students' Room, 138; Reading Room, previously used for, 119; Exhibitions, 225, 231, 259, 292; Keepers and Deputy-Keepers, 328; and *see* names there set out. *See also* Binding; Copyright; Lending

Manuscripts, illuminated, Western, 151–3, 171, 198, 235–6, 276–82; Oriental, *see* Oriental Library

Maps, printed, Winter Jones develops the coll., 100; first catalogued, 106; 216–20; the Map Room, 164; Dept. of, 131, 139–40; American, 208; Chinese, 317; MS., 217, 263–5. *See also* Geography

Marathi lit., 314
Margoliouth, G., 145, 299
Marsden, W. A., 168
Marten, A., 243
Martineau, R., 146
Mary I, Queen, 242–3
Mary II, Queen, 246
Maty, M., 42–3
Maty, P. H., 44, 352
Maurice, T., 60, 80, 312, 356
Mayhew, H. M., 135
Mearne, S., 179–80
Medieval and Modern Languages, 274–7
Medievalist learning, 37
Mew, J., bequest, 298
Mexican codices, 362
Meyer, P., 276
Michael, H. J., Hebrew library, 298
Millar, E., 151, 280–1
Millard, J., 91–2, 291, 360–1
Miller, A. W. K., 135, 150
Milne, H. J. M., 270, 274
Mogul Emperors' library, 308, 310
Moll, Baron von, library and nat. hist. coll., 62
Monasteries, Suppression of the, 21–4, 26
Monboddo, Lord, 52
Monson, Lady Ann, 53

Montagu House, 18–19, 39–41, 86–7, 351–2
Morgan, J. Pierpont, jun., 279–80
Morrison, J. R., Chinese books, 129, 317; Robert, 317
Morton, C., 42, 44–5, 56
Murray, Sir C., 303
Musgrave, S., 52
Musgrave, Sir W., bequest, 49, 56
Music, printed, 106, 164, 210–13; MS., 265–7; the King's, 213–16

Nares, R., 56, 291, 355
National Art-Collections Fund, 171
National Central Library, 165, 334–5
National Library of Wales, 162
Natural History, books, 176, 187; Depts. of, removal of, 121, 139; library of, 344; *see* Banks, Sir J.; Moll, Baron von
Naval papers, 285, 290
Nelson, H., Lord, 285–6
Newcastle Papers, 139, 284
Newspapers, 141–4, 208–10, 367; Burney coll. of, 62, 188; copyright, 141–2, Repository (Library) of, 143–4, 166, 209–10
Newton, Sir C., 132, 134
Nicolas, Sir N. Harris, 90–1, 106–7, 359
Nitrian MSS., 110
Noehden, G. H., 355
Northampton, Marquess of, 265
Northumberland, Hugh, Duke of, 36
Novello, V., 265
Novels, 164, 359
Nowell, Dean L., 25

O'Grady, S. H., 275–6
Old Royal Library, 27–8, 50–1, 177–80, 240–8
Oliphant, T., 106, 267
Onslow, A., Speaker, 33, 36, 48–9, 249
Oriental Library: MSS., 21, 59–60, 64–5; Dept. of, proposed, 115; formed, 131; pr. bks., added to, 144–5; Printed Books and MSS., the combined Dept. formed, 144–5;

INDEX

the collections, 294–321; Keepers and Deputy-Keepers, 328, and *see* names there set out; Student's Room, 166
Oriental studies, 374
Oriya lit., 314
Oudh, Royal library of, 306, 308
Owen, E., 274

Painting, strict Moslem fear of, 307
Pali lit., 311–13
Panizzi, Sir A., reader, 85; joins staff, 77; evidence before Parl. Committee, 95–7; visits Continental libraries, 360; Keeper of Pr. Bks., 99; and the Gen. Cat., 111–12; survey of and report on collections, 102–3; secures Grenville Library, 104, 197; enforces Copyright Act, 105; before the Royal Commission, 113–15; plans Reading Room and Iron Library, 117–20; Principal Librarian, 120–1; retires, 121; relations with Baber, 59; with Ellis, 58; with Forshall, 98; with Grenville, 104, 123, 195–7; with Madden, 104, 361; with Nicolas, 359; on classification, 94; on duplicates, 331–3; on scientific men, 93, 123; achievement and character, 115, 121–4, 364
Panjabi lit., 313–14
Papyri, 153–4, 267–71
Parker, Abp. M., 24–6, 349
Parliament, Committee of, on B.M., 90–6, 360; Rolls of, deposited, 19
Parry, J. H., 100
Paston Letters, 183–4
Patmore, Coventry, 128, 365
Peacock, T. L., 85
Peel, Sir R., 115–16
Pelham Papers. *See* Newcastle Papers
Penneck, R., 46–7, 54
Periodicals, 176. *See also* Newspapers
Perrins, C. W. Dyson, 162
Persian lit., 305–7, 309
Photography, 158, 342–3
Pinto, I., 373

Pirckheimer, B., 65, 255
"Placing." *See* Classification
Planta, A., 44, 56–7
Planta, J., 44, 56–7, 231, 355
Political papers, 284–5
Pollard, A. W., 146–8, 164, 204
Pope, A., 49
Pope, G. Upham, 315
Porson, R., 83
Porter, G. W., 146, 365
Portuguese lit., 62, 206–7
Postage stamps, 224
Poulet, Q., 241
Pratt, J. Tidd, 76
Prévost, A., 319
Priebsch, R., 276
Principal Librarians and Directors, 326, and *see* names there set out
Printed Books, history and growth of the Dept. of Pt. I, ch. ii–ix, *passim*; principles of collecting, 175–6; collections and catalogues, 177–225; exhibitions, 225; Keepers and Deputy-Keepers, 327, and *see* names there set out. *See also* Binding; Catalogues, etc.; Classification; Copyright; Iron Library; Lending; Reading Room
Prints and Drawings, 73–4
Proctor, R., 146–7, 203–4, 367
Publications. *See* Catalogues, etc.
Punjabi lit. *See* Panjabi lit.
Purchase of books, 103, 126–7, 175; of books and MSS., grants for. *See* Finance
Pushtu lit., 313–14

Quaritch, Bernard, Ltd., 176

Ralston, W. R. S., 365
Rapson, E. J., 313
Rawlinson, Sir H., 303, 306
Ray, John, 30
Reading Room, the 1st (1759), 40–2, 51–4; the 2nd (1774), 54–5; the 3rd (1803), 79–80, 358; the 4th (1809), 80–1, 358; the 5th (1829), 81; the 6th (1838), 81–2, 360; the

385

7th (1857), 117–20, 363–4; closed (1907), 149–50; Lamb and Thackeray on the, 85; readers, in 18th cent., 51–5; in early 19th cent., 83–5; admission of, 54, 82, 115, 171–2, 328–30, 369; fees proposed for, 162; evening opening, 369; need for space occasions printing of Gen. Cat., 134; classes of books sent into (1835), 359; Reference Catalogue and Guides, 119, 364, 369; and *see* Catalogues: A (2); works on, 369; Superintendents of: P. Templeman, 40, 42, 46, 53; R. Penneck, 46–7, 54; T. Maurice, 80; J. Cater, 80–1; J. Grabham, 81; T. Watts, 119, 127; G. Bullen, 127; R. Garnett, jun., 137; G. K. Fortescue, 136; W. R. Wilson, 149; G. F. Barwick, 149; R. F. Sharp, 171; F. D. Sladen, 171; A. I. Ellis, 171; Fortescue's definition of the ideal, 81

Special Rooms: Manuscripts, *see* Manuscripts, Department of; Students' Room; Newspapers, 139, 144, 166; Oriental, *see* Oriental Pr. Bks. and MSS., Dept. of; Students' Room; Rare Books (Large Room and North Library), 8, 157–8, 166; State Papers, 166; Reference Books, 360; *see* Reading Room

Reformation, 21–4
Registration of accessions, 93–4, 97
Removal of objects from Museum, forbidden, 331–5; of Natural History Depts., 121, 139
Report, Annual, 347
Rich, C. J., his Near Eastern MSS., 64, 295, 302, 305–6, 373
Richards, W. U., 79
Rieu, C., 131, 305, 308–9, 367
Robertson, W., 51
Robinson, P., 214
Rockefeller Foundation, 167

Rolls and Charters, 260–2
Rosen, F. A., 312
Ross, T., 245
Rossetti, G., 85
Rothschild, Baron F., 277
Roy, E. A., 146, 148, 212, 366
Royal Commission (1847–9), 112–16, 362; (1927–29), 364–5
Royal Library. *See* King's Library, Old Royal Library
Royal Philharmonic Society, 267
Royal Society, 30–1, 65, 123, 256, 372
Rye, W. B., 100, 128, 197–8
Rymer, T., 19
Rymsdyk, J. and A. van, 53, 350

Samaritan MSS., 296–9
Sandys, Sir J., 163
Sanskrit lit., 64–5, 311–13
Satow, Sir E., 318, 320
Saunders, G., 61, 359
Schier, Dr., 99
Schlichtegroll, —, 355
Science in 16th–17th cent., 28–31; men of, desired for Trustees, 92, 113; but not by Panizzi, 93; his attitude towards, 123
Scientific books, 176–7, 187. *See* Natural History, books
Scott, E. J. L., 151, 153–4, 240
Scott, Sir W., 83–4, 259
Seals, 262–3
Secretaries, 326
Secretaries, Assistant, 368
Secretaryship, 93, 97, 116
Selvaggi, G., 265, 267
Sharp, R. F., 167–8, 171
Siebold, P. F. von, 129, 320
Simons, N., 361
Sims, R., 98, 130, 286, 290–1
Sindhi lit., 313–14
Sinhalese lit., 316
Skeat, T. C., 271, 274
Slade, F., bequest, 222
Sladen, F. D., 171
Slavonic lit., 365

INDEX

Sloane, Sir Hans, Uffenbach visits, 350; will, 17; Frederick, Prince of Wales influences, 350; collections, 19–20; library, 177; MSS., 239–40; family Trustees, 36
Smirke, Sir R., 86
Smith, Christopher, 214
Smith, J. T., 358–9
Smith, Joseph, Consul, 188
Smith, Sydney, 84
Smith, W. C., 212–13, 216
Smollett, T., 45
Solander, D., 45, 187
Sotheby, W., 36
Soulsby, B. H., 217, 344
Southey, R., 84
Southgate, R., 42, 46
Spanish history, 66; lit., 62, 150, 180, 195–6, 206–7; -American books, 207–8
Sparrow, —, locksmith, 138
Sprent, F., 217
Squire, W. Barclay, 211–13, 215–16
Staff, the earliest, 42–7; their quarrels, 42–7, 353; duties and hours of, in 18th cent., 47–8; salaries improved (1801), 357; Parl. Committee recommend full-time work and pay, 93; this done, 97; incorporated in established Civil Service, 120; salaries improved (1898), 141; with reorganization (1921), 167–8; methods of recruitment, 345; discipline, 123, 364–5; specialised scholarship of, 175; influence of the service upon, 172; general note on, 345–7. *See also* Catalogues A(1); Gate Porter; Housekeeper; Keepers and Deputy Keepers; Principal Librarians; Secretaries; Secretaries, Assistant; Transcribers
Stamps, Postage, 224
Stanhope, Earl, 49
State Papers, 224; Reading Room for, 166
Statutes (1757), 37; (1807), 73; (1850), 115–16

Stein, Sir A., Chinese collection, 318–19
Sternschuss, Dr., 303, 307
Stevens, Alfred, 6, 364
Stevens, Henry, of Vermont, 103, 207–8
Stevenson, J., 378
Stow, John, 25
Stowe MSS., 107, 139, 196–7, 257–9
Stuart, James ("Athenian"), 52
Students' Rooms. *See* Reading Room: Special Rooms
Stukely, W., 52, 53
Subject Index. *See* Catalogues, A1*b*.
Surtees, R., 84
Sussex, Duke of, sale, 103, 107
Syriac MSS., 294–6; Rich's, 64, 295; the Nitrian, 108–10, 295–6

Tamil lit., 315
Tapling, T. Keay, postage stamps, 224
Tattam, Archd. H., 108–9
Taylor, Canon John, 51
Taylor, L. H. E., 365
Taylor, R., 303
Telugu lit., 316
Templeman, P., 40, 42, 46, 53
Tenison, Abp. T., his Library, 32, 350
Thackeray, W. M., 85
Theatrical collections, C. Burney's, 61–2, 188
Theyer, J., 245
Thomas, H., 206
Thomason Tracts, 48, 100, 150, 181–3
Thompson, Sir E. Maunde, enters, 129; works on the Class Catalogue of MSS., 292; Keeper of MSS., 139–40; Director, 141–56; character, 154–6
Thompson, H. Yates. *See* Yates Thompson
Thynne, H. F. and J., 245
Tibetan lit., 321
Tomkins, C., writing master, bequest, 64
Tovar, Conde de, 276
Townsend, A. C., 344
Tradescant's Museum, 29–30
Traheron, B., 242

387

Transcribers. *See* Catalogues: A(1); Sims, R.
Trustees, constitution of the Board of, 18, 34; the first election, 34–7; list of the elected, 323–6; qualities needed for, 35; Sir N. H. Nicolas attacks aristocratic composition of, 91; the Parl. Committee on, 92–3; agitation for more scientific, 113; elections (1836–47), 96–7; and the Gen. Cat. (1841), 111–16; nominations to the Staff by the Principal, 345
Tun-huang library, 319, 374
Turkish lit., 309, 321
Turner, Col. T. Hilgrove, 302
Tyldesley, W., 241
Tyrwhitt, T., a reader, 53; a Trustee, 56; bequest, 49

Urdu lit. *See* Hindustani lit.
Utrecht Psalter, 130, 371

van Straalen, S., 299
Verard, A., 178
Visitations, Heralds'. *See* Heraldry

Walpole, Horace, 33, 36, 38, 53
Walter, F. A., 355
Wanley, H., 27, 232–3, 238, 249, 371
War-time, the Library in, 160–4, 170
Wardrop, J. O., 310
Warner, Sir G. F., enters, 129, Keeper of MSS., 151–4; publications, 151–2, 280–1; memorial to, 282; character, 152
Warschauer, A., 276
Watson, Sir W., 36–7
Watts, T., origin, 361; enters, 100; plan for a Reading Room, 117, 363; organises removal of Pr. Bks. to new building, 101; devises classification, 102; selects in all tongues, 103, 126–7; Supt. of Reading Room, 119, 127; Keeper, 126–7; achievement and character, 127
Welsh MSS., 106, 274–5
West, James, 36
Westmacott, Sir R., 360
Wharton, L. C., 365
White, Taylor, 52
White, William, bequest, the White Wing, 138–9
Wickremasinghe, M. da Z., 294, 316
Wilkes, J., 52
Wilkinson, J. V. S., 314
William IV, King, 193
Wilson, W. R., 149
Windsor Castle Library, 193
Wise, T. J. *See* Ashley Library
Woide, C. G., 44, 59, 75, 352–3
Wolley, A., MSS., 65
Women, on the higher staff, 345; readers, 53
Woodward, B. B., 344
Worcester College, Oxford, 179
Wray, D., 51
Wren, Sir C., 88–9
Wright, W., 144–5, 362, 312

Yates Thompson MSS., 170, 258, 260, 277–8, 368
Yiddish lit., 299
Yorke, Philip. *See* Hardwicke, Earl of
Young, Patrick, 178–9, 243–4
Young, Peter, 243
Yule, Col. W., 303, 306

Zedner, J., 298–9
Zend MSS., 305
Zoological books, B.M. weak in (1836), 94–5
Zouche MSS., 273, 303, 362